SPANISH COLONIAL
ADMINISTRATION 1782–1810

Spanish Colonial Administration, 1782-1810

The Intendant System in the Viceroyalty of the Río de la Plata

by

JOHN LYNCH

GREENWOOD PRESS, PUBLISHERS
NEW YORK

PRINTED IN THE UNITED STATES OF AMERICA

PREFACE

FROM THE EARLIEST DAYS of colonial expansion Spain had
tried to do two things, to govern an empire on just and Christian
principles, and to exploit the wealth of that empire in the
interests of the domestic exchequer. In the mid-eighteenth
century, however, it could hardly be said that she was accom-
plishing either objective. By this time her empire in America
showed all the signs of moral and material stagnation. Its
organization and institutions remained substantially the same
as they had been in the sixteenth century. The heroic spirit of
discovery and conquest had long since spent itself. The Christian fervour of the missionaries and the social awareness of men
like Las Casas and Quiroga were things of the distant past, and
where their tradition managed to survive, as it did in the
Jesuit reductions of Paraguay, it was regarded with official
suspicion and private distrust. Meanwhile in North America
the spectacular progress of British power cast a menacing
shadow southwards over an empire which seemed destined to
remain the prey, if not to become the victim, of vigorous commercial nations more powerful than its owner.

Spain herself seemed as unfitted to bear the burden of empire
as she was of reaping its fruits. Yet the situation drew from her
an effort which, if overdue, demonstrated once more her
colonial inventiveness and staying power. There was a spirit
of revival which breathed new life into the sleeping body. Commercial reforms were undertaken from 1765 onwards, designed
to open new routes and new ports for trade between Spain and
her colonies. Territorial readjustments were carried out, and in
1776, in the interests of defence, the vast land mass stretching
from Tierra del Fuego to Upper Perú, from the Atlantic to the
Andes, an area hitherto governed uncertainly from Lima, was
erected into an independent viceroyalty. For a brief spell the
traditional and the novel were united; the old yet exaggerated
wealth of Potosí, linked for two centuries with Lima, 'the City

of the Kings', was joined to the new and brash prosperity of Buenos Aires and its pampas, rich in livestock and inspired with the prospect of freer commerce. This newcomer to the political scene of Spanish America was given a modern administrative organization, the intendant system, of French origin and already operating in Spain itself. In 1782, following experiments in other parts of the empire, the viceroyalty of the Río de la Plata was divided into eight intendancies, to each of which was assigned an intendant with carefully defined powers in the four departments of finance, justice, war and general administration. The system was designed to provide more effective government and more conscientious administration to a region which had hitherto been neglected by the home authorities. The prospects, for South America and for Spain, looked distinctly more hopeful.

Existing studies of the intendant system in Spanish America are scanty and concentrate on policy to the exclusion of practice. It is no reflection on the pioneer work of Miss L. E. Fisher or on the incidental study of the late Professor Ravignani to say that they leave many problems unsolved. The operation and results of the system remain obscure. Did the intendants improve the royal revenue? Did they play any rôle in the economic life of the colonies? Did they provide better government for the Indians? What were their relations with existing institutions? With the viceroy, the *audiencia*, and the *cabildo*? And where did they stand with regard to the revolution for independence in which they were shortly engulfed? The present work is designed to provide some answers to these questions, and to form a contribution to the study of Spanish colonial administration at a period—the eve of the revolt of the Spanish colonies—and in a place—the newly-created viceroyalty of the Río de la Plata—which were crucial for Spain and South America. By utilizing manuscript as well as published sources, particularly the rich store of Spanish colonial documents in the Archivo General de Indias in Seville, it becomes possible to observe the intendants at work, and to estimate their significance not only in terms of official intentions but also in the light of practical results.

It is a pleasure to acknowledge the help I have received in

preparing this book. My greatest debt and my warmest thanks are due to Professor R. A. Humphreys, under whose supervision the subject was first presented as a doctoral thesis in the University of London; without his friendship, encouragement, criticisms and innumerable kindnesses, I could never have begun or finished this work, and I can think of few of its pages which have not benefited from his perception and knowledge— though needless to say the defects are mine. I am deeply grateful also to my former teacher, Professor R. Pares, whose interest and assistance have carried me over many obstacles. I wish to thank the University of Edinburgh for awarding me the George Scott Travelling Scholarship which enabled me to spend six months in Spain, and I am glad to record my appreciation of the generous services provided by the staffs of the Archivo General de Indias, Seville; the Biblioteca Nacional and the Archivo Histórico Nacional, Madrid; the Public Record Office, the British Museum, the Institute of Historical Research, and University College Library, London. Finally, I am indebted to University College, London, for a generous grant in aid of publication.

University of Liverpool   J.L.
June 1957

CONTENTS

MAPS

ABBREVIATIONS

A.C.B.A.	*Acuerdos del extinguido cabildo de Buenos Aires.*
A.C.C.R.C.	*Actas capitulares de la villa de Concepción del Río Cuarto.*
A.C.S.E.	*Actas capitulares de Santiago del Estero.*
A.G.I.	Archivo General de Indias, Seville.
A.H.N.	Archivo Histórico Nacional, Madrid.
B.I.I.H.	*Boletín del Instituto de Investigaciones Históricas*, Buenos Aires.
B.M.	British Museum, London.
B.N.	Biblioteca Nacional, Madrid.
D.G.I.E.A.	*Documentos referentes a la guerra de la independencia y emancipación política de la República Argentina.*
D.H.A.	*Documentos para la historia argentina.*
H.A.H.R.	*Hispanic American Historical Review.*
H.N.A.	*Historia de la Nación Argentina.*
Ord. Ints.	*Real Ordenanza para el establecimiento e instrucción de intendentes de exército y provincia en el virreinato de Buenos-Ayres.*
P.R.O.	Public Record Office, London.

CHAPTER I

Spanish Colonial Reorganization
under Charles III

THE political and economic bankruptcy of Spain at the end of the Habsburg régime has become proverbial. To the already overwhelming weight of the economic problem—an amalgam of chronic unemployment, huge untilled estates, a chaotic currency and absence of industry—war added the final burden. Without an army, the treasury empty, administration in chaos, and royal authority virtually unknown in the provinces, the Spain which confronted Philip V was 'hardly less defunct than its dead master'.[1] The Spanish Bourbons set themselves to redress this situation, and to apply in Spain some of the principles of government which had been fashioned by the more effective and more centralized French monarchy. Assisted by French economic advisers like Orry and Amelot, and guided by ministers like Patiño, Campillo and Ensenada, the rule of Philip V (1700–46) provided at least some sense of direction. Internal customs barriers between the constituent kingdoms were reduced, model factories were established, nascent industries were protected by duties and subsidies, and reforms in public finance were promoted.[2]

The tradition of the Bourbons was centralizing, and it was taken for granted that the best means of achieving the revival of Spain was through a powerful monarchy, removing every pocket of independence and eliminating all privileges, social,

---

[1] The phrase is that of José de Gálvez, Charles III's Visitor-General in New Spain and Minister of the Indies, in 'Informe y plan de Intendencias que conviene establecer en las provincias de este Reyno de Nueva España', Gálvez and Croix, 15 January 1768, A.G.I., Indif. General 1713.

[2] See E. J. Hamilton, 'Money and economic recovery in Spain under the first Bourbon', *Journal of Modern History*, xv (1943), pp. 193, 206.

ecclesiastical and municipal, outside the crown. The Catalan revolt of 1705 had afforded the pretext for inaugurating such a régime. Local immunities disappeared and the juridical liberties of Aragon, Catalonia and Valencia were destroyed. The 'regalism' of the jurists, embodied particularly in the Council of Castile, produced new agencies and replaced the old organs of regional autonomy, typical of the Habsburg system, by captaincies, intendancies and *audiencias*. Absolutism was intensified by the absence of any constitutional checks. The Bourbons were even less enamoured of representative institutions than the Habsburgs had been, and while the Cortes virtually disappeared from the national life, the municipalities were subject to strict supervision.

The movement of reform from above reached its apogee in the reign of Charles III (1759–88), who has become the exemplar of so-called 'enlightened despotism' in eighteenth-century Spain.[1] Yet his achievements are often exaggerated. The slogan which is sometimes applied to his rule, 'todo para el pueblo, nada por el pueblo', is misleading, for strength rather than welfare was his aim. It is instructive to remember that the greatest obstacle to agricultural progress and to the welfare of the rural masses in Spain—untilled *latifundia* and strict entail—remained untouched at his death. Moreover, his absolutism was less imposing in practice than it was in theory; as late as 1787 there were in Spain over ten thousand towns and villages subject to the seignorial jurisdiction of the nobility and thereby removed from direct royal control.[2] It is true that he gave the country a more modern political appearance and some measure of economic recovery. But his policy was not uniformly intelligent. He rashly anticipated his own strength and prospects by joining France in the Seven Years War against Britain two years after his accession. Sharing in the defeat, he lost Florida, lost prestige, and above all revealed what was already suspect, that the Spanish navy was a second-rate thing and Spanish military strength negligible. Spain was now left as the sole rival

---

[1] There is no good modern work on Charles III but useful information is to be found in M. Danvila y Collado, *El reinado de Carlos III* (6 vols., Madrid, 1890–6), and F. Rousseau, *Règne de Charles III d'Espagne* (2 vols., Paris, 1907).

[2] G. Desdevises du Dezert, *L'Espagne de l'ancien régime* (3 vols., Paris, 1897–1904), i, 130–1.

to a victorious Britain in America. Yet it was many years before Charles's commercial-colonial reforms came to fruition. At home he had his limitations. Seeking the answer to the government's financial problems, he set little example of economy in the court itself. The British minister at Madrid in the early 1760's thought that there was extravagant spending at court: large remittances sent to Naples, excessive sums spent on the king's amusements, too many pensions to high-ranking officers who had done little to earn them.[1] It is a mistake, in fact, to regard this simple and benevolent personality—faithfully portrayed by Goya—whose addiction to the chase eventually became an obsession, as another Philip II organizing an empire in detail from the Escorial.

Yet Charles III had considerable qualities. Having ruled successively as duke of Parma and, since 1735, as king of Naples, he had acquired experience of government as well as a taste for reform which was fashionable at the time in the Italian peninsula. Already before his accession to the throne of Spain he had become convinced of his mission to reform his country. And this he pursued with a sense of purpose and an obstinacy for his own opinions which make it impossible to regard him, as Menéndez Pelayo did, as a puppet of his ministers. Even the British ministers in Madrid, who generally took a supercilious view of Spanish government, were sensitive to the change. 'The Catholick King is indefatigable in his application to business; he passes many hours alone in his closet every morning before the arrival of the Ministers; as His Catholick Majesty rises constantly at Five, no matters are postponed, as formerly, from day to day, and then often left unexecuted. . . .'[2] But the essential secret of his success was a singular inspiration in choosing his advisers and ministers; these he selected not from the traditionalists nor from the aristocracy, whose political function the Bourbons were concerned to make even less than it had previously been, but from a small and enlightened group of men, whose emergence in the second half of the eighteenth century was the most promising feature of Spanish public life. Roda, Minister of Justice; Floridablanca, Procurator of the Council of Castile and

---

[1] P.R.O., S.P., Spain, 94/163, Bristol to Pitt, 15 June 1761.
[2] P.R.O., S.P., Spain, 94/161, Bristol to Pitt, 14 January 1760.

later Foreign Minister; Aranda, President of the Council of Castile; Campomanes, Procurator of the Council of Castile; Gálvez, Minister of the Indies—these men supplied the ideas and set the pace of reform in government circles. While conferring with them regularly Charles was also wise enough to give them sufficient scope for action.

The background of progressive opinion against which these ministers worked and in which they themselves had been formed—a select group of philosophers, economists, prelates and men of letters—was important in promoting the movement of economic and scientific revival.[1] Waging their own campaign against ignorance and poverty they looked to the government to remove both. Most of them were attached to institutional reforms rather than to abstract speculation, and to economic reforms above all others. The measures canvassed were various —equitable taxation, industrialization, the expansion of colonial and foreign trade, improvement of communications by the opening of canals and the building of roads, a programme of internal colonization like that undertaken by Olavide in Sierra Morena, projects for the disentailing of estates and church property, the ending of the pasture privileges of the powerful Mesta. Agencies multiplied in typical Spanish bureaucratic fashion. Numerous boards, commissions, institutes and societies sprang up to study the problems of rational economic development. Of these the quasi-official economic societies were the most important. Their aim was simply the prosperity of the country, particularly by applied science. Their methods were various—they founded libraries, sponsored schools and institutes for instruction in agriculture, natural sciences and manual arts, gave travelling scholarships to students, organized experimental workshops and farms, and submitted to the government numerous reports on current economic problems. Owing to the penetration of encyclopaedism from France the whole movement has been condemned by Spanish traditionalists as heterodox and deviationist, but the truth is that most of these reformers, in and out of the government, were, like Charles III himself, orthodox Catholics, who saw no conflict between their

[1] See J. Sarrailh, *L'Espagne éclairée de la seconde moitié du XVIIIe siècle* (Paris, 1954), and L. Sánchez Agesta, *El pensamiento político del despotismo ilustrado* (Madrid, 1953).

religion and the advancement of skill and knowledge; and for the political salvation of Spain none of them looked beyond absolute monarchy.

To many Spaniards at the time, and certainly to Charles III himself, it seemed even more urgent to strike a new direction in colonial affairs than in the peninsula itself. In her overseas possessions Spain had wealth indeed, if only that wealth could be tapped. And not only were her rivals tapping it more effectively than she was herself, but, in Spanish opinion, they were even threatening to appropriate it. It was not surprising, therefore, that colonial reform should occupy first place in the programme of Charles III. While still king of Naples he had declared that his first preoccupation, as soon as he were master in Spain, would be the security of the Spanish empire.[1] The survival of Spain as a colonial power and therefore as a power to be reckoned with in Europe was the basis of his entire policy.

To effect any reform at all Charles III needed more efficient agencies, which would combine the two principles of centralization and specialization. Habsburg government had not known the system of individual ministers to which the Bourbons were accustomed in France. Habsburg government was conciliar government, or administration by committees. The different spheres of governmental operation were assigned to their particular Council, such as the Council of Castile, the Council of Finance, the Council of the Indies, and in each were concentrated political, administrative and judicial powers. Each Council consisted of a small number of councillors and a horde of minor officials, and as their system of working was one of hearing and discussing written reports with all the formality of a court of law, the delay and inefficiency were notorious. The king, then, ruled with the help of these consultative committees. But the Bourbons, drawing on the experience of the French monarchy, began to experiment with individual ministries which gradually came to threaten the authority of the supreme Councils.[2] Immediately after the accession of the first Bourbon a general Secretariat of State was created. In 1705 this was

[1] V. Palacio Atard, *El Tercer Pacto de Familia* (Madrid, 1945), pp. 28–9.

[2] Desdevises du Dezert, *op. cit.*, ii, 60 ff., and J. M. Ots Capdequí, *Manual de historia del derecho español en las Indias y del derecho propiamente indiano* (2 vols., Buenos Aires, 1943), ii, 221–2.

divided into two secretariats, one for War and Finance and one
for remaining affairs. Further departmentalism was logical. In
1714 Philip V increased his ministries to four: State, Justice,
War, and Marine and the Indies. Finance at this point was
usually managed by a controller-general and intendant, but in
1754 it reverted to a secretariat of its own. In 1787 in recognition of the growing burden of work imposed on the Minister of
the Indies Charles III separated colonial affairs from those of
Marine and divided them between two ministers, one in charge
of appointments and judicial matters, the other in charge of
military and exchequer affairs as well as commerce and navigation. But this arrangement was short-lived and hardly surviva-
the rule of Charles III; within three years both colonial departments were suppressed and their functions shared among the
remaining five ministries.[1]

While these Bourbon ministries were potentially useful in
giving a new precision and unity of direction to Spanish
government, it was some time before this was achieved. The
older Councils survived alongside them, and for many years
after 1714 the attributes of the secretaries were not completely
clear. It was not until the reign of Charles III that from being
mere general assistants to the king they came to act as more
authentic ministers, directing affairs and exercising a measure of
personal influence on policy. And it was Charles who gave the
impulse towards a specialization of departments. This was noted
by foreign observers:

. . . the King of Spain since he has been at Madrid has never mentioned to General Wall what was out of his department of Foreign
Affairs and War, nor has asked the Marquis Squillace's advice in
what did not relate to the Finances, or consulted with Monsieur
Arriaga, except with regard to the Marine; each Minister suggests,
prepares and executes what properly belongs to his Office, by which
means all reciprocal jealousies of each other are removed.[2]

Along with the progress towards more departmentalism there
was another trend towards a proper co-ordination of departments. There began a more frequent and more systematic use
of the *Junta*, or committee, where ministers could meet and

[1] See C. H. Haring, *The Spanish Empire in America* (New York, 1947), p. 116.
[2] P.R.O., S.P., Spain, 93/161, Bristol to Pitt, 11 February 1760.

co-ordinate policy. At first the practice was to appoint *ad hoc* juntas for specific purposes. Gradually a *Junta de Estado* began to meet, though irregularly, and was found to be a useful way of resolving differences between departments and of devising a concerted policy. Floridablanca, prime minister from 1777, encouraged his ministerial colleagues to assemble more frequently and impressed on the king the need of giving a formal and permanent existence to this cabinet together with instructions for its constitution and procedure. This was done by royal decree of 8 July 1787, a measure which Floridablanca considered 'the greatest, most necessary and most useful' of all the reforms of Charles III.[1] Here was an instrument of concert, collective responsibility and continuity, which had long been needed in haphazard Spanish government.

The rise of the Ministry of the Indies and the emergence of the Junta reduced the Council of the Indies, previously the supreme authority under the crown for all colonial affairs, to the nadir of its influence. Already in 1717 its executive and legislative functions had been removed and its competence restricted to judicial affairs. Now under Charles III its functions were practically nullified and it was reduced to a purely consultative rôle with no other purpose than to furnish the crown with news and information. The reforms of 1787 confirmed its fate.

When, therefore, Charles III began to implement the reforming projects which were being prepared he had a central agency, at once efficient and manageable, which afforded far greater possibilities of control over colonial affairs than had ever been available to the Habsburgs. But the creation of more efficient agencies was only a means to an end. The end was to increase the revenue of the crown from its overseas possessions and strengthen their defences. And this demanded in the first place a break with the antiquated commercial system which had governed economic relations between the mother country and its dominions for over two centuries.

In an attempt to monopolize all the American trade for Spain

---

[1] 'Memorial presentado al Rey Carlos III,' in A. Ferrer del Río, *Obras originales del conde de Floridablanca, y escritos referentes a su persona* (*Biblioteca de autores españoles,* lix, Madrid, 1912), p. 343; see also 'Instrucción reservada', *op. cit.,* pp. 213–72. Both are key documents for an understanding of the reforming aspirations of Charles III and his government.

and to protect it against the attacks of foreign raiders, trade between Spain and the Indies had been confined to the Spanish ports of Cádiz and Seville and to the American ports of Havana, Vera Cruz, Cartagena and Porto Bello.[1] This commerce was restricted to convoyed fleets sailing at stipulated intervals over prescribed routes. According to the organization perfected in the years 1564–6, two fleets a year were to be equipped in Spain. One of these was to sail in the spring and make its way to Vera Cruz, detaching on the way ships destined for Honduras and the islands. The other was expected to sail in August and proceed to Porto Bello on the isthmus of Panamá, taking with it vessels for Cartagena for trade with the provinces on the Caribbean coast. After wintering in America, both fleets would rendezvous at Havana in the early spring and return to Spain together. New Spain and most of Central America were supplied from Vera Cruz. From Porto Bello goods were carried across the isthmus of Panamá, from there to Lima by another fleet, and from Lima distributed throughout South America, even to Buenos Aires on the far Atlantic coast. Spain naturally prohibited any share in the trade to foreigners and even proscribed the carriage of any goods of non-Spanish origin to the Indies. Moreover trade between the various colonies was severely limited, and intercolonial trade in products that competed with Spanish exports was in general forbidden. Although individual ships were occasionally licensed to sail independently of the fleets to minor ports, the above principles governed Spanish commerce with America throughout the Habsburg era. To regulate the whole system the crown had two special bodies in Seville: the *Casa de Contratación*, or board of trade (transferred in 1717 to Cádiz) which was a government agency in charge of all matters concerned with economic relations between Spain and America; and the *consulado*, a semi-official guild of merchants engaged in the colonial trade. In addition there was a substantial corps of royal treasury officials in American cities.

But while theoretically the Spanish empire was enclosed within this immense monopolistic structure, the machinery to enforce it was pitifully inadequate. The law was so perfect that

[1] See C. H. Haring, *Trade and Navigation between Spain and the Indies in the time of the Hapsburgs* (Cambridge, Mass., 1918), pp. 1–20, 123–54, 201–30.

it could not be administered. Yet the crown preferred to maintain such legislation even at the cost of inviting disobedience, even at the cost of disobeying it itself. The programme of fleet sailings could not be sustained. Although spasmodic attempts were made to enforce the laws excluding foreigners and foreign-produced goods from the Indies trade, they were not effective. Spain in fact could not satisfy the colonial market. But other European nations could. The French, British and Dutch, among others, had heavy investments in almost every fleet and consequently took a major share of the returns of the trade. Usually the foreign interest outweighed that of the native Spaniards, and it became notorious that 'Spain kept the cow and the rest of Europe drank the milk'. One method, for example, adopted by foreign merchants was to import goods from abroad into Spain or buy Spanish products and ship them through Spanish 'cover-men', who signed the documents that disguised foreign-owned shipments on the fleet and took initial delivery of any returns. And this subterfuge was so well established that the Spanish government is said sometimes to have taken action against 'cover-men' who absconded.[1] But with a foot in both camps, Spain enjoyed the benefit of neither world. The colonies suffered from excessive prices and inadequate supplies. In granting a practical monopoly to the *consulado* of Seville the crown hit not only foreign merchants but also its own commercial classes in other parts of Spain; and Spanish nationals never managed to break the monopoly of the Seville and Cádiz merchants as foreign interlopers did. Finally, the whole system was an immense invitation to contraband, in which the public revenue itself was the loser.

Already before Charles III the early Bourbons had experimented with minor adjustments to this structure, though still operating within existing canalized commerce. There was an attempt to improve communications in order to give more accurate knowledge of conditions and markets. By decree of 29 July 1718 eight dispatch boats were to be sent each year to New Spain at the expense of the trade.[2] It was hoped that the

[1] See A. Christelow, 'Great Britain and the trades from Cadiz and Lisbon to Spanish America and Brazil, 1759–1783', *H.A.H.R.*, xxvii (1947), p. 3.

[2] R. Antuñez y Acevedo, *Memorias históricas sobre la legislación y gobierno del comercio de los españoles con sus colonias en las Indias occidentales* (Madrid, 1797), p. 118.

fleet system, by now faltering badly, would be reanimated by the *Proyecto de Galeones* of 5 April 1720, which was intended to stimulate greater regularity of voyages and simplify duties.[1] But this was an illusion. Fleet sailings continued to be spasmodic. In time of peace they suffered from the competition of an efficiently organized contraband, and in time of war they were a sitting target for enemy ships. So in 1735 the government began to attack the fleet system itself. The dispatch of galleons to Tierra Firme was temporarily suspended, and while the flotas for New Spain were to continue they were now restricted to some seven or eight ships.[2] In 1740 all fleets were suspended, and single ships licensed by the crown supplied South America, as they did New Spain until 1757. Some of those which sailed to Buenos Aires had the right of *internación*, which meant in practice the passage of goods across the Andes into Chile and Perú. Moreover, after 1740 ships were permitted to sail directly to Perú via the Horn, and the Porto Bello fleet was never revived. In this way the Spanish government began to appreciate the variety of available communications between the mother country and its own colonies and to exploit routes which had been inexplicably neglected for so long. But the Cádiz monopolists did not surrender without a struggle. As contraband continued they pressed for the revival of the Vera Cruz fleet, and, from their point of view, the convenient restriction of supplies. And this they gained. In 1754 the fleets were formally re-established, and in 1757 they sailed again to New Spain, continuing fitfully until 1789, when the system was finally abolished.

Another experiment in the first half of the eighteenth century was the development of trading companies, which meant that the monopoly enjoyed by the merchant oligarchy of Cádiz and Seville was extended to other privileged groups. Organized with capital from Catalonia and the Basque provinces, these chartered companies were granted special privileges, if not a complete monopoly, in the trade of one of the more backward areas of the empire which had been by-passed by the old canalized system of commerce and where in the absence of Spanish trade

---

[1] *Documentos para la historia argentina*, Facultad de Filosofía y Letras, Universidad de Buenos Aires (Buenos Aires, 1913–), v, 21–77.

[2] *Ibid.*, v, 115–23.

the foreign interloper had pretty much his own way. The first and most important of these ventures was the Caracas Company, created in 1728 with a monopoly of trade with the coasts of Venezuela.[1] It is true that the company performed a valuable service in a limited part of the empire. When it undertook operations, Venezuela was a poverty-stricken province and a liability to Spain. Within twenty years the Caracas Company had increased the amount of cocoa production and thereby lowered prices, and exploited a new export commodity in Barinas tobacco. The royal revenues were increased and Venezuela was converted from a province dependent on an outside subsidy for administrative expenditure to one with a surplus. But there was a limit to what a single company, or even a number of companies, could accomplish, and the others were by no means as successful as the first.

It was clear, then, that neither the early trade reforms nor the monopolist companies provided the answers to Spanish colonial problems. The fundamental principle of monopoly and restriction remained untouched, revenue showed no significant rise, and contraband still flourished. This was the situation which confronted Charles III. In addition, three factors operated to persuade him to take action: the influence of economic theorists, fear of British encroachments, and pressure from France.

The principles of non-restriction and equality of opportunity were being advocated with increasing persistence by economists. They argued that it was futile to maintain laws against foreign goods as long as national producers could not satisfy the needs of the peninsula, much less those of the colonies. To combat contraband it would be best to permit free exchange among all Spanish nationals on equal terms. Thus it would be possible to lower prices to meet foreign competition, and to remove the temptation to contraband among Spanish subjects who were barred from opportunities.[2] It would be misleading to suggest that there was a 'school' of Spanish economists or any well developed body of doctrine which the leading writers professed in

[1] See R. D. Hussey, *The Caracas Company, 1728–1784* (Cambridge, Mass., 1934), pp. 86–9.
[2] M. Colmeiro, *Historia de la economía política en España* (2 vols., Madrid, 1863), ii, 365–74.

common. They were interested in practical reforms rather than in economic speculation, and the term *comercio libre* simply meant freedom for *all* Spaniards within the national monopolistic structure, and certainly not free-trade in the normal sense of the term. But given the Spanish devotion to tradition, it was an achievement to promote even this limited concept of freedom.

Already in 1743 José Campillo y Cossío, minister of war and finance under Philip V, had written his *Nuevo sistema de gobierno económico para la América*, an accurate reflection of the new spirit of Bourbon rule in Spain and an eloquent appeal not only for the liberation of commerce but for a radical reorganization of colonial government.[1] Basing his conclusions on a comparison of the experience of the rival colonial powers, he underlined the opportunities that Spain was missing in America, her failure to exploit the economic and human resources of her own possessions, and her inability to assure Spanish subjects and products an adequate share in the colonial trade. To bring more land under cultivation and at the same time improve the condition of the Indians Campillo advocated tax-free land grants to the natives, as well as their training in farming and other crafts. He pointed out that the most effective way of eliminating contraband trade, would be to make legitimate trade more attractive, that is by reducing the crippling taxation on Spanish commerce and the customs duties on foreign goods and by promoting inter-colonial trade. Finally, to open up the entire traffic between Spain and her colonies and improve communications Campillo suggested the operation of a regular maritime mail service, and the curtailment or even abolition of the Cádiz monopoly and the fleet system. Although Campillo's work remained unpublished until 1789, there are reasons to believe that it circulated in manuscript form in government circles and had some influence on opinion. At any rate many of the reforms advocated by Campillo were also recommended, as will be seen, by the royal commission which reported in February 1765. Moreover they were borrowed by Bernardo Ward, who was the most notable theorist in the mid-century. Ward, an Irishman by origin, rose through the accountancy offices to membership of

[1] M. Artola, 'Campillo y las reformas de Carlos III', *Revista de Indias*, xii (1952), pp. 685–714; Haring, *Spanish Empire* pp. 340–1.

the *Junta General de Comercio y Moneda* in 1756, and gained further recognition as an economic administrator before his death in 1762. He had been commissioned by Ferdinand VI to make a tour of investigation through Europe in order to study the colonial systems and policies of other nations and propose a plan of reform. This opportunity for a comparative study of eighteenth-century colonial policy in Europe he never exploited as he might have done, but after his return he did write a *Proyecto económico*, completed in 1762 though not published until 1779, in which he advocated a general freeing of Spanish commerce from restrictions and from the weight of taxes, freedom of export, and the opening of more Spanish ports for trade with the Indies. Although Ward's work is in many places simply a transcription—it has been called a plagiarism—of Campillo's, it does bear testimony to the circulation of ideas on freer trade.[1] It is true that the Spanish government was interested less in any theory of economic liberty than in the increase of revenue, and that the progressive application of the policy of freer trade was merely a twelfth-hour expedient, adopted when everything else had failed. Nevertheless it would be wrong to underestimate the effect which this fashionable climate of opinion had on Spanish administrators. In the first place many of the theorists were themselves administrators; Campomanes, who early entered the Council of Finance and became fiscal of the Council of Castile in 1762, was possibly a more convincing example than Ward.[2] Moreover, men like Miguel de Muzquiz, Minister of Finance during much of Charles III's reign, and José de Gálvez, the energetic Minister of the Indies, often paid lip-service to what were for Spaniards liberal economic views. It was realized, in fact, that the *comercio libre* was a better proposition than the old obscurantism.

This view was reinforced by the conviction that it was now essential for Spain to define her attitude *vis-à-vis* her greatest colonial rival. Almost since its foundation Englishmen and English governments had looked with envy on the resources and markets of the Spanish empire. Their problem was to find a way

---

[1] Artola, *op. cit.*, pp. 692–3, 711–14.

[2] On Campomanes see F. Álvarez Requejo, *El Conde de Campomanes. Su obra histórica* (Oviedo, 1954).

for British goods into the Spanish dominions and a way out for the bullion, so indispensable to Great Britain in her commercial relations with the Far East. And up to a point they were successful. By the eighteenth century British merchants had clearly become predominant in the Cádiz-Indies trade and were outstripping all the other foreign interlopers. The Spanish diagnosis of the situation was that this predominance derived from the fact that the British enjoyed advantages as a result of favourable treaties with Spain. Such treaties established conditions that enabled British merchants to land their goods in Spain and the Indies at lower cost than those of their competitors. This meant that British goods were either sold at lower prices or earned higher profits than similar goods of non-British origin. Moreover, by allowing British naval vessels free right of entry into Spanish ports while preventing any effective search of British property and merchantmen, the treaties had the effect of enabling the British to export from Spain unlicensed gold and silver coin and bullion, which was the only way the Spanish merchants could pay the adverse balance of trade, even though such exports were contrary to law. Charles III concluded that the basis of British commercial dominance lay in her treaty privileges rather than in the superiority of her capital resources and the quality of her goods. Therefore his policy was to end preferential tariffs, enforce the right of search, and prevent the unauthorized export of bullion. In this way, it was hoped, the profits of the American dominions would accrue largely to Spaniards. From 1759 to 1762 Charles III pursued a policy based on the belief that war with Britain would enable him to drop the British treaties, and thereby restore Spanish industry and recapture the colonial trade for his own subjects. When he declared war in 1761, joining France in her struggle with Britain, he was confident that victory would enable him to refuse to renew the treaties which, of course, ceased to operate when the war began. His mistake lay in overrating the prospects of the Family Compact, and defeat meant that he was in no position to refuse renewal. However, he believed that another chance would come, and meanwhile he had other cards to play. He managed to stop one gap through which bullion escaped into British hands by refusing to renew permits for British mail boats to call at La Coruña where before the war they had met the *despachos* from the Indies. Then he issued orders for the strict search of all foreign merchantmen entering Cádiz, and in 1768 he prohibited the importation into Spain of certain types of textiles. Instructions were also issued that no merchandise of foreign origin was to be shipped to the Indies and that returns consigned to known 'cover-men' were to be seized. It has been argued that the attack of Charles III upon the commercial treaties failed to appreciate the fact that the basis of British commercial strength rested less on treaty privileges than upon superior technical and financial resources.[1] There is some truth in this, but it is only fair to remember that the attack upon the treaties was only one part of a wider policy. Given a more liberal commercial régime and the stimulus of free competition for all Spanish nationals, then Spain's own resources might have a chance of improving. During the war Charles III gave serious consideration to proposals for ending the Cádiz monopoly and for opening the Indies' trade to other Spanish ports. No doubt he was not uninfluenced by the fact that the most valuable of the British fiscal privileges applied only in Cádiz. But there were other factors leading to the same conclusion—among them pressure from the French government.

The disastrous defeat of 1762 hastened the programme of reform. Pressure from France had its origin in Choiseul's attempt to convert Spain into a formidable military ally after the Peace of Paris in order to redress the balance against Britain. Such a policy responded to Charles III's own alarm over British progress in America, and to his anxiety to maintain a territorial and commercial equilibrium in the New World.[2] The enormous flank of the whole of Spanish America, virtually undefended in the absence of Spanish sea-power, was a standing temptation to any rival contemplating attack. Therefore everything was subordinated to the growth of military and naval strength. But this growth was itself dependent on an increase of royal revenue. So the Spanish empire was regarded as a source

---

[1] Christelow, *op. cit.*, pp. 2–29, on which this paragraph is based.

[2] See Palacio Atard, 'El equilibrio de América en la diplomacia del siglo XVIII', *Estudios Americanos*, i (Sevilla, 1948–9), pp. 476–7; and the document printed in the same author's *El Tercer Pacto de Familia*, pp. 295–6.

to be exploited as well as a zone to be defended. This transatlantic balance of power was a constant preoccupation of
Charles III, and now that France had completely disappeared
from North America Spain responded promptly to her prod-
dings. Choiseul used numerous agents for the advancement of
his policy.[1] Many military and naval experts were transferred
from the French services to those of Spain. A secret committee
of ministers, under Choiseul's prompting was formed in Madrid
to work out a scheme of reform. Above all, the French minister
had two important channels. On the economic side he was
served by the French agent-general of marine and commerce in
Spain, the Abbé Beliardi, a clever Italian adventurer in the
French service, who was a rich source of information on Spanish
trade and colonial matters, and through whose influence
numerous French experts found their way into the various services of Spain.[2] Further political influence was supplied by José
de Gálvez, future Visitor-General of New Spain and Minister of
the Indies, who was to some extent indebted for the advancement of his career to French interest and intervention.[3]

French interest in Spain was no secret at the time. In 1764 the
British minister in Madrid observed that 'tho' the French will
do all they can to stir up this court to prepare themselves in that
part of the world [America], from what I can at present see they
will only pursue those measures that tend to their own interests'.[4]
There was much truth in this remark, and it suggests the first of
two qualifications which must be put to the extent of French
influence on Spanish affairs. The basic idea of Franco-Spanish
co-operation had from the commercial point of view of Spain
certain serious disadvantages inherent in the nature of economic
relations between the two countries. France was arguing that the
two countries should pool their economic and colonial resources:
Spain should concentrate on the production of raw materials
such as wool and silk in Spain and minerals, dyewoods, drugs

---

[1] A. S. Aiton, 'Spanish colonial reorganisation under the Family Compact',
H.A.H.R., xii (1932), pp. 269–80.
[2] On Beliardi see R. Hilton, *Four Studies in Franco-Spanish Relations* (Toronto,
1943), pp. 51–7.
[3] See H. I. Priestley, *José de Gálvez, Visitor-General of New Spain (1765–71)* (Berkeley, Calif., 1916), pp. 35–6, 39–40; also Aiton, *op. cit.*, pp. 273–6.
[4] P.R.O., S.P., Spain, 94/166, Rochford to Halifax, 13 February 1764.

and hides in the colonies, and give French merchants special buying facilities; France, on the other hand, with her more advanced industrial economy, could supply at a low cost all manufactured goods needed within Spanish territories. Thus the merchant marine of the Bourbon powers would be increased and Britain excluded from trade.[1] Charles III was well aware, however, that apart from American products, silk and wool were the only Spanish exports which France wanted, while it was evident that France was always reluctant to grant privileges to Spaniards in her own territory. Moreover, Charles III was preoccupied with the industrial and commercial revival of Spain. When the Spanish ministers issued stricter regulations for the inspection of shipping and prohibited the import into Spain of various types of manufactured goods, such as cotton, these measures, as the British minister was informed, referred to France as well as to Britain.[2] France, in fact, procured no commercial concessions from Spain.[3] And at a political level, Choiseul's offer of French help for Spain to annex Portugal while France by some means or other acquired Brazil was no more attractive than any other French plan.[4]

Consequently, while Spain selected foreign experts and borrowed and adapted to her own use foreign ideas, the reform programme remained Spanish in conception, in leadership and in its objectives. At the end of 1763 a *Junta Interministerial* was formed, consisting of the Ministers of State, Finance, and the Indies, which had to meet every Thursday to discuss matters relating to the future security of the empire, the increase of revenue therefrom, and the reconstruction of the navy.[5] In 1764 the *Junta Técnica* was created; this consisted of five specialists, commissioned to resolve the commercial problem. The words of Revillagigedo, viceroy of New Spain, might well have been a commentary on the policy which it pursued:

[1] Christelow, 'French interest in the Spanish Empire during the ministry of the Duc de Choiseul, 1759-1771', *H.A.H.R.*, xxi (1941), pp. 524-5.

[2] P.R.O., S.P., Spain, 94/189, Grantham to Rochford, 13 February 1772.

[3] For an account of the strained commercial relations between France and Spain 1763-8 see L. Blart, *Les rapports de la France et de l'Espagne après le Pacte de Famille, jusqu'à la fin du ministère du duc de Choiseul* (Paris, 1915), pp. 45-70.

[4] O. Gil Munilla, *El Río de la Plata en la política internacional, Génesis del virreinato* (Sevilla, 1949), pp. 92-3.

[5] Aiton, *op. cit.*, p. 274.

That the Indies yield more revenue to the crown ought without doubt to be the greatest concern of our government; but improvements must not be pursued by means of new and excessive taxes and duties on American subjects, because that is a sure way to alienate and cause disaffection among the people, with disastrous results; if a suffering and submissive slave, ill-treated by his masters, sees others who would treat him better, he will soon change his master, so that he can enjoy freedom. Therefore, these improvements ought to be attained chiefly by improving commerce.[1]

Although more vigorous measures against contraband were suggested and taken and the coast-guard system was improved, the main attention of the Junta was concentrated on the commercial system which maintained the conditions under which contraband flourished. There had recently been a pertinent example of the defects of over-controlled trade. General O'Reilly, who was appointed Visitor-General in the Antilles after the war, reported that Havana, to which normally Spain sent two ships a year and from which she received import and export duties to the value of 30,000 pesos, under British occupation in 1762 was visited by numerous ships and yielded 400,000 pesos a year.[2] There was no shortage of evidence of this nature before the committee. It submitted its report in February 1765, adding the weight of its authority to opinions which were now common currency in informed circles. The Cádiz monopoly, the use of fleets, the limitations on the number of licensed ships, the cumbersome formalities of dispatching vessels, the high duties on exports and imports, the antiquated method of taxation on volume of goods without reference to value—all were condemned by the committee, and their replacement by a more liberal policy was advocated.

Up to this point reform had been primarily a liquidation of the past. Now more positive reorganization began.[3] In 1764 a maritime mail service had been established: one mail packet left La Coruña for Havana every month and this was later supplemented by a similar service every two months to Buenos Aires. A decree of 16 October 1765 ended the policy of restricted ports of clearance from Spain and of entry to the Indies. Trade

---

[1] Quoted in Gil Munilla, *op. cit.*, p. 101.
[2] Rousseau, *op. cit.*, ii, 24–5.   [3] Haring, *Spanish Empire*, pp. 341–2.

with the colonies was now open to Cádiz, Seville, Alicante, Cartagena, Málaga, Barcelona, Santander, La Coruña, and Gijón, while in the West Indies Cuba, Santo Domingo, Puerto Rico, Margarita and Trinidad were open to trade from Spain. The dispatch of vessels no longer required special licence from the crown, while many of the more irksome taxes on articles of colonial trade were revised or abolished and replaced by a simpler *ad valorem* duty of 6 or 7 per cent collected in Spain. The experiment seemed to work, and from 1765 to 1779 the government progressively extended the geographical zones to which these new principles were applied. In 1768 the recently acquired Louisiana, a frontier colony adjacent to British territory, was granted even more generous commercial concessions. In 1770 Campeche and Yucatán were included in the benefits of *comercio libre*. In 1776–7 Santa Marta and Río de la Hacha on the coast of New Granada were brought in. And by the famous decree of 12th October 1778 the new system was applied to the whole empire except New Spain and Venezuela, an exception which lasted until 1789. Meanwhile from 1772 there had been a series of decrees which reduced duties still further, and more and more articles, Spanish and colonial, became duty free. The removal of restrictions on transatlantic trade was accompanied by an equally important lessening of restrictions on trade between the colonies themselves. By 1774 Perú, New Spain, Guatemala and New Granada were allowed to trade among themselves, though this trade was restricted to colonial products. From 1776–7 Buenos Aires could trade with the provinces of the interior, including Upper Perú, and with Chile. In short, by 1789 Spain had abandoned the commercial regulations which had been held sacred for over two centuries; while still preserving the principle of protection against all foreigners, she had opened up the entire empire to a commerce in which all her subjects and all her main ports could partake.

It has already been suggested that commercial motives and innovations were closely connected with imperial defence. Spain was anxious to defend her possessions from the attacks of rivals as well as to protect her trade from foreign interlopers. Charles III feared that British commercial penetration, which his trade reforms were intended to check, was simply part of a larger plan of aggression, which he would also have to resist. His suspicions were not without foundation. During the whole of the eighteenth century it was a subject of serious discussion in commercial circles in Britain that Spanish America ought to be emancipated and a vast market of enormous possibilities thrown open, without any inhibitions, to British commerce. These notions became more persistent and at the same time as Charles III was liberalizing colonial commerce for Spanish merchants, some people in Britain were looking to the British government to appropriate it for British merchants. It was now argued that more could be gained by depriving Spain of her colonies than by attempting to penetrate a Spanish-controlled system of trade. It was clear from the instructions given to the British ministers in Madrid that Britain was examining the possibility: Sir James Gray, who left England as minister to Spain in July 1767, was instructed to procure exact information about the state of Spanish America, the existence of creole or native discontent, the strength of fortifications, the best points of attack.[1]

The fact that emancipation rather than annexation was canvassed naturally meant little to the Spanish authorities. In either case they were concerned to defend their territories from possible British expeditions, especially in time of war. Earlier in the century Spain had taken steps to tighten up the territorial and military organization of the empire. In 1717 New Granada was erected into a viceroyalty, and though this was dissolved in 1723 it was permanently re-established in 1739 when the growth of British power in the Caribbean made necessary the presence of a military leader nearer than Lima. In 1731 the provinces of Venezuela were erected into a captaincy-general which in 1777 was freed from dependence on New Granada. Cuba became a captaincy-general in 1764, and somewhat later the captaincy-general of Guatemala became more independent of the viceroyalty of New Spain. By these territorial subdivisions the principle of smaller units of administration, more manageable in terms of defence, was promoted; in particular the coasts of New Granada and Venezuela were now subject to closer surveillance. After 1761 the danger of a British landing loomed even larger.

[1] Christelow, 'Great Britain and the trades from Cadiz and Lisbon to Spanish America and Brazil, 1759–1783', op. cit., p. 24.

Colonial viceroys had orders to maintain troops in arms and to keep a sharp eye on possible points of attack. At the close of the war the crown instituted the *visitas*, or inspections, of Gálvez in New Spain and of O'Reilly in the Antilles, part of the purpose of which was to improve fortifications and militia forces. Northern New Spain, a land of arid wastes and rough mountains, presented particular difficulties. Here the Spanish population was sparse and scattered and constantly menaced by bands of cruel and rapacious Indians who plundered Spanish herds and settlements. Garrisons on the northern frontier were few, widely separated and poorly manned. But Spain could not afford to abandon her posts on this frontier, which was the gateway to New Spain and to the silver region, least of all at a time of increasing British and Russian interest in the Pacific coast of North America. To improve the security of the area against possible British penetration from the north was one of the duties which Gálvez assumed. Apart from encouraging further colonization along the Pacific Coast, he also devised an entirely new administrative plan for the northern provinces of New Spain, separating them from the rest of the viceroyalty and giving the new unit a government of its own, at the head of which was a *Comandante General*, virtually independent of the viceroy and directly responsible to the king. This was the origin of the so-called Interior Provinces of New Spain which came into existence in 1776 and which comprised Coahuila, Texas, New Mexico, Nueva Vizcaya, Sinaloa, Sonora and the Californias.[1] And this attempt to buttress the northern extremities of the empire was accompanied by an even more radical project for the southernmost parts which was to involve, as will be seen later, the creation of the viceroyalty of the Río de la Plata and a noticeable change of direction in Spanish imperial strategy.

So far two aspects of Spanish colonial reform under Charles III have been considered: the economic, which found expression in the regulations for freer commerce, and the strategic, which bore fruit in various defence measures. These reforms were reactions to specific conditions, to the perennial ache of an

[1] See Bernardo de Gálvez, *Instructions for Governing the Interior Provinces of New Spain, 1786*, trans. and ed. Donald E. Worcester (Berkeley, Calif., 1951), especially he editor's introduction, pp. 1-24.

empty exchequer and jealous awareness of foreign encroachments. There was, finally, a third element in the imperial
reorganization undertaken by Charles III: this took the form of
provision for better government in the colonies, the establishment of new agencies, the purification of administration in the
financial and the judicial sphere, an attempt to tackle the Indian
problem.

The need for better administration had been apparent for
some time. At this point it is sufficient to notice that the kind of
evidence submitted by viceroy Amat of Perú (1761–76) could
not be ignored indefinitely: in his *Memoria de gobierno* he gave
numerous examples of corruption in exchequer offices and
declared that he had been unable to find a single official of
undoubted integrity.[1] At a purely administrative level the
inadequacies of the existing system received their classical
expression in the *Noticias secretas* of the versatile Jorge Juan and
Antonio de Ulloa who used the opportunity of a scientific expedition to Perú to take stock also of the general situation there,
and who submitted their conclusions in a secret report to the
crown in 1749. Their evidence indicated that colonial government was generally ineffective and corrupt. But they focused
particular attention on that traditional representative of the
crown in local districts, the *corregidor*, the very archetype of
erring officialdom, whose repertoire included almost every
device known in the history of administrative corruption—the
farmed and unaccounted revenue, the holding of royal funds in
deposit to be used as private capital, the forced Indian labour
without pay, and above all the notorious *repartimiento*, or
forced sale of merchandise at outrageous prices to the unfortunate natives.[2] A more recent commentator has concluded that
the misgovernment and malpractices of the *corregidores* 'was one
of the fundamental causes for the administrative reforms that
were introduced in the last quarter of the eighteenth century'.[3]

One instrument of administrative reform was the *visita*, or
general inspection of the state of a given viceroyalty by a special

---

[1] V. Rodríguez Casado y F. Pérez Embid, eds., *Memoria de gobierno de virrey Amat* (1776) (Sevilla, 1947), p. 390.

[2] J. Juan y A. de Ulloa, *Noticias secretas de América* (London, 1826), pp. 229–44.

[3] C. E. Castañeda, 'The *corregidor* in Spanish colonial administration', *H.A.H.R.*, ix (1929), p. 447.

commissioner appointed by the crown. This device, it has been seen, was resuscitated by Charles III, but it was found to be unsatisfactory in its methods and impermanent in its results.[1] A more radical remedy was needed, one which would impose uniformity and discipline in colonial government, give greater scope for action to local officials and at the same time assure higher standards of bureaucratic morality. Such a remedy, the intendant system, had already been tried and approved in Spain. And it was on this device, as will be seen, that the crown pinned its hopes for the reform of colonial administration.

Released from the old commercial restrictions, secured against attack, and with the promise of better administration, the Spanish empire assumed a new look. In Spain itself the signs of economic revival which were already present in Catalonia by 1760 spread throughout all the periphery, and the littoral regions of Valencia, Málaga, La Coruña and Bilbao began to surpass those of the interior in prices and standard of living. The industries of Catalonia and Vizcaya, especially cotton and metallurgy, whose growth had been one of the influences determining the measures of freer commerce, further benefited from the expansion which that freedom afforded, while the Catalan merchant marine responded quickly to new opportunities.[2] Shipping between Spain and the empire multiplied. The whole trade with Spanish America is said to have expanded by as much as 700 per cent in the period from 1778 to 1788.[3] In New Spain there was an unmistakable increase in royal revenue.[4] It seemed the beginning of a new history for the Spanish empire, though in truth these reforms also helped to stir up profound forces of discontent among Spain's American subjects and to precipitate its collapse in the not too distant future.

[1] See below, pp. 122–3, 138–42.
[2] See A. Ruiz y Pablo, *Historia de la real junta particular de comercio de Barcelona 1758–1847*) (Barcelona, 1919), pp. 57–140. Catalan economy was already picking up before it was admitted to the American trade. See J. Vicens Vives, 'Coyuntura económica y reformismo burgués. Dos factores en la evolución de la España del antiguo régimen', *Estudios de Historia Moderna*, iv (1954), pp. 349–91.
[3] Haring, *Spanish Empire*, p. 342.
[4] From 13,268,847 pesos in 1787 to 20,600,267 pesos in 1795. A.G.I., Aud. de Lima, 1,119, Informe de la Contaduría, which includes report of Ramón de Posada, Fiscal of New Spain, 6 March 1801.

In no part of the empire, however, did the new policy have more spectacular results than it did in Spain's colony in the southern Atlantic. For the rest of the empire it meant an economic and political revival; but for the Río de la Plata it meant a new existence. It is in these provinces that the possibilities, and the limitations, of all the elements of reform can be most effectively studied.

CHAPTER II

The Provinces of the Río de la Plata

POOR in mineral wealth and remote from the commercial routes between Spain and the Indies, the provinces of the Río de la Plata at the beginning of the eighteenth century presented an unattractive spectacle to the world. With their port closed to direct commerce with Spain and their imports canalized through distant Lima, they languished on the periphery of the empire.

The colony comprised various provinces of ancient foundation —Buenos Aires, Paraguay, Tucumán and Santa Cruz de la Sierra—and was the product of more than one line of colonization. Buenos Aires, Paraguay and Santa Cruz de la Sierra were colonized directly from Spain across the Atlantic and penetrated by way of the great rivers which unite to give birth to the Plata. Tucumán, on the other hand, was conquered from Perú after cruel marches across the high plateau which is present-day Bolivia. But wherever they came from the Spaniards, like their compatriots in other parts of the empire, founded cities which gradually became the centres of extensive territorial jurisdictions. In 1536 Buenos Aires was founded for the first time and in the following year Asunción, the present capital of Paraguay. The settlers in Buenos Aires were driven out of their city by hunger, illness and native attacks, and in 1541 they joined their companions in Asunción. The population grew through mixed marriages of conquerors and Indians, and Asunción became a permanent base from which other colonies were founded. In 1547 contact was established with Perú and following this posts were established, such as Santa Cruz de la Sierra in 1561, to protect the routes. Other cities were founded including Santa Fe in 1573 and Corrientes in 1588. Buenos Aires was refounded in 1580 and by the end of the century had supplanted Asunción in wealth and importance. Meanwhile Tucumán had also become studded with townships. Santiago del Estero was founded in 1553, Mendoza in 1559, San Miguel de Tucumán in 1565, Córdoba in 1573, and Salta in 1582. Then, from 1607 the Jesuits founded missionary villages called 'doctrinas' in the territory of 'Misiones' along the rivers Paraguay, Paraná and Upper Uruguay; by 1739 there were thirty of these 'doctrinas' —the famous Jesuit reductions of Paraguay—which later declined after the expulsion of 1767. Finally, there was the Banda Oriental, or eastern shore, of the Río de la Plata, the rough equivalent of modern Uruguay. The Spaniards made little attempt to colonize this and it was not until 1726, over forty years after the Portuguese had founded the Colônia do Sacramento, that they established themselves in Montevideo in an attempt to contain the Portuguese encroachments.

The sense of frontier insecurity, however, was engendered not only by the presence of Portugal in Brazil, but also by the persistence of the Indian danger. In the eighteenth century savage and predatory tribes were still a threat to cattle and ranches and even approached to within a hundred miles of the capital. The frontier, marked by a chain of fortified outposts, followed approximately the 35° S. parallel, crossing the country from the mouth of the River Salado to the Andes, and unconquered tribes still occupied the Chaco, the savage subtropical region extending between Upper Perú, Paraguay and Brazil.

Despite their optimistic name, the provinces of the Río de la Plata possessed little mineral wealth.[1] There were a few small gold, silver, copper and quicksilver mines, but their yield was insignificant compared with that of other Spanish colonies. The conquistadores of the south were beaten to Potosí by those from the north and returned to Asunción to take up more peaceful but less lucrative occupations. This lack of precious metals was the most important single fact in the economy of the region. A colony without silver was of little use in the eyes of the Spanish government and of scant attraction to Spanish settlers. Consequently it was neglected by the mother country, avoided by emigrants, and in general had to fend for itself.

[1] On the economy of the colony see R. Levene, *Investigaciones acerca de la historia económica del virreinato del Río de la Plata* (3 vols., La Plata, 1927).

The nature of the land was the second factor determining the economic life of the country. The famous pampas of Argentina, a vast grassy plain rising smoothly from the Atlantic coast to the foothills of the Andes, interrupted only by mountains around Córdoba, and the more undulating Banda Oriental were magnificent pasture. Here the first animals left by the Spanish explorers, the cattle and the horses, reproduced themselves rapidly in a zone ideal by reason of its climate, pasture and water. Livestock came to form the richest possession of the colony, though until the eighteenth century there was little attempt to exploit this wealth.[1] Such a concentration on livestock was due not simply to physical reasons but also to the fact that the Indians here did not allow themselves to be peacefully exploited; consequently the labour *repartimientos* in this region were completely theoretical and there was not sufficient labour for agriculture. What agriculture did exist was confined to stretches of land around the towns and served a purely urban purpose.[2]

The littoral region of Buenos Aires, Santa Fe, Entre Ríos and Corrientes was, therefore, almost exclusively a cattle region, radically different in its economic and social forms from the zones of the interior. In these western provinces plants and cattle had been introduced at an early date by the Spanish colonists, and radiating from Santiago del Estero in the north the settlers had dispersed the material factors of European civilization.[3] Crops were cultivated and farmers began to look for a market. This they found in Upper Perú. As the precious metals were the greatest incentive to colonization Upper Perú had become a focal point of settlement. But the mineral deposits were situated above the altitude limits within which agriculture was possible, and consequently the densely populated mining centres of Potosí and Oruro relied for their provisions on outside producers. So these urban communities exercised a powerful economic attraction on the agricultural and cattle zones surrounding them. Neither Upper nor Lower Perú could satisfy the

[1] E. A. Coni, 'Contribución a la historia del gaucho', *B.I.I.H.*, xviii (1934-5), pp. 48-79.

[2] See Coni, *op. cit.*, p. 57, and the same author's chapter 'La agricultura, ganadería e industrias hasta el virreinato', in R. Levene, ed., *Historia de la nación argentina* (10 vols., Buenos Aires, 1936-42), IV, i, 369.

[3] *Ibid.*, IV, i, 362-5.

demands of the mining centres: owing to shortage of pastures their cattle was scarce, and although their agriculture was potentially rich it was hampered by the fact that Indian labour was being rapidly expended in the mines. In this situation the interior provinces of the Río de la Plata became the purveyors of Upper Perú and owed whatever prosperity they enjoyed to this fact. Tucumán supplied cotton, grain and meat. In Córdoba the economy was more varied. Near to the city lay the fertile valleys of the *sierra*, with sufficient streams for irrigation. Although cotton did not prosper in Córdoba, there was a fairly intense cultivation of wheat, rice, maize, olives, vine and all classes of vegetables. Some of these products were industrialized in a modest way, and by the mid-eighteenth century a water mill and various bodegas existed. Cattle ranches appeared in Córdoba in the seventeenth century and extended over the plains of the south, specializing in sheep, goats and mules. From about 1600 Córdoba began to export mules to Potosí and by the mid-eighteenth century good profits could be made: bought while still young in Buenos Aires, Córdoba and Santa Fe at a price of 3–4 pesos, they were fattened up in Salta where they were bought at 7–8 pesos and then exported to Perú where they sold for 14 and sometimes as much as 20 pesos.[1]

Throughout Spanish America industrial activity was on a small scale; but in spite of the laws against it industry increased in the seventeenth century, partly as a result of the decline of Spanish industry, in whose favour the laws had been imposed, and partly because of the restrictions of the trading system. In this period the first industries of the Río de la Plata were able to develop. Although the economic isolation imposed on the colony by Spain was a fundamental drag on its progress, nevertheless the very restrictions of this policy gave protection against overseas competition to colonial production and interprovincial commerce, permitting local industries to supply the country. Consequently the provinces of the interior were able to develop certain industries, which, in addition to supplying local needs, even produced surpluses for export to other provinces. The

[1] B.M., Add. MS 17,592, fol. 412. Description of Perú, Chile, and Buenos Aires compiled by members of an expedition fitted out in 1783–4 by the Spanish government.

Spanish crown had forbidden viticulture in America in the interests of peninsular produce, but in spite of the prohibition freedom of cultivation existed in fact. The cultivation of wine and brandy reached a high degree of development in Mendoza, San Juan, La Rioja and Catamarca. In Córdoba, Catamarca and Corrientes manufactures of various kinds were carried on, such as linens, woollen cloth and blankets. Coarse textiles were produced in considerable quantities in the Jesuit missions of Mojos and Chiquitos.[1] In San Miguel and Córdoba wagons were manufactured. And Corrientes was the manufacturing centre for tackle and spars.

But the variety of this economic life of the colony could not disguise its modest proportions. The Río de la Plata was assigned a very humble rôle in the Spanish imperial system. What wealth it had was frozen in the place of its production because it was sealed off from commercial exchange. The commercial route to South America remained imposed from the beginning and had its origin in the unequal progress of colonization. The Spanish colonization of Perú, anterior to and much more rapid and productive than that of the Río de la Plata, gave Lima a brilliant start. The merchants there immediately formed a powerful interest and pressure group. The flota system increased their wealth and their power, for Lima, with the best port on the Pacific, linked by the Inca roads to the consumer markets of the interior, became—logically it seemed —the great entrepôt for the distribution of European goods to Guayaquil, to the cities in the interior of Perú, to Chile, to the Río de la Plata itself, and above all to the wealthy mining areas of Upper Perú. The farmers of Tucumán might compete for the agricultural market, but manufactures came via Lima. And to the stringencies of the monopoly and fleet system another limitation was added to confine the colony's life within an economic straitjacket: not only was it forbidden to trade directly with Spain, but, like other colonies, it was denied commercial intercourse with the rest of the empire.

Naturally the agricultural producers of Tucumán resented the monopoly of the Seville-Lima merchants and the exorbitant

[1] R. R. Caillet-Bois, 'Un ejemplo de la industria textil colonial', *B.I.I.H.*, xx (1936), pp. 21–2. The textiles of the Mojos were apparently exported to all parts of Perú.

prices charged for commodities when eventually they reached the south. For some time in the sixteenth century they had recommended a southern approach to Perú, running through Tucumeño territory, in place of the tortuous line of communications via the isthmus of Panamá.[1] Determined to keep her trade system intact, Spain rejected these proposals. She was, however, concerned to ensure that what she had closed as a legitimate route should not be opened as a contrabandist one. Buenos Aires was a potential gap in her economic defences through which smugglers could undermine her trade monopoly and drain off the wealth of Potosí, which she and her rivals regarded as her most precious possession in America. To stop this gap it was essential to maintain Buenos Aires, fortified and populated, as a key defence point. But how could she attract settlers to this distant possession and at the same time enforce a closed-port policy which made it impossible for those settlers to survive? To solve this problem Spain tried to do two things at once: to maintain her trade system, and to relax it in the smallest possible degree in favour of Buenos Aires. From 1618 she licensed individual ships between Seville and Buenos Aires; theoretically there could be two every year, but in fact they were irregular and insufficient. And what Spain granted with one hand she took away with the other. Trade was still impeded by the provision which prohibited specie and bullion to be taken from the port of Buenos Aires. Moreover, to seal off Buenos Aires from the hinterland, an interior customs house was established at Córdoba in 1622 to cover traffic between the coast and the interior; only upon payment of 50 per cent of the regular duties were goods that had been freely introduced into Buenos Aires permitted to penetrate into the remote provinces. And after this every commercial concession in favour of the La Plata region provoked protests from the merchants of Perú, who resented the competition produced by goods introduced through Buenos Aires with the exorbitant prices of articles arriving by way of Perú. In Potosí prices were four times as high as in Lima, while in Tucumán they were eight times as high.[2]

---

[1] See Mario Rodriguez, 'The genesis of economic attitudes in the Río de la Plata', *H.A.H.R.*, xxxvi (1956), pp. 171–89.

[2] R. Levene, *La moneda colonial del Plata* (Buenos Aires, 1916), pp. 20–1.

In these conditions there was little likelihood of social progress. The population was meagre. Buenos Aires in mid-eighteenth century had hardly more than 19,000 inhabitants in the town and 6,000 in its surrounding country. Here there was no rich and influential merchant nobility as in Lima. Capital was scanty: it was estimated that in 1767 in the entire province of Buenos Aires only one person possessed property to the value of 500,000 pesos, while only four had 150,000 and three 100,000. Altogether the capital of the group of richest citizens reached not quite 2,000,000 pesos.[1] Compared with the merchants of Lima those of Buenos Aires were humble indeed; they managed to survive from trade with the interior, legal or otherwise and always impeded by local taxes; this procured them some gold and silver, with which they bought from Brazil, Spain and European contrabandists iron, textiles and negroes. With industry slight and primitive the characteristic citizen was the artisan rather than the capitalist. Except perhaps in Tucumán, the farmers, lacking the stimulus of producing for export, lived little above the poverty line. For most of the inhabitants of the eastern provinces the standard of life was low. As the pampas were almost treeless, fuel and building materials were lacking. The way of life of the 'gaucho', or white plainsman who owned little or no land and spent most of his life on horseback, was hardly less primitive than that of his enemy the Indian. His main occupation was hunting and killing the wild cattle, whose flesh and skins provided him with food and clothing; the hides he sold wherever he could find a market in order to supply himself with woollen cloth, tobacco and Paraguayan tea. The proverbial independence of the 'gaucho', whose existence alternated between complete idleness and violent exercise, was symptomatic of the sentiments of the entire settler population. Ignored by Spain and with their interests subordinated to an imperial system in which they played a servile rôle, the creoles, or colonial-born Spaniards, of the Río de la Plata were bound by only the slightest ties of sentiment to the mother country, while their aversion to the monopolists of Perú was only a degree less

[1] J. Torre Revello, 'Noticia de los vecinos mas acaudalados de Buenos Aires en la época del primer gobierno de Pedro de Cevallos, 1776', *B.I.I.H.*, iv (1927-8), pp. 498-9.

than their aversion to the Spaniards of the Peninsula. This independent temper of the creoles was intensified by the immense distances which separated community from community —Córdoba was some 500 miles from Buenos Aires, and Salta del Tucumán 1,200 miles. Dispersed in these vast spaces and clinging to the cities, the small centres of population were effectively isolated from each other. In such conditions the germs of powerful sentiments of provincial as well as of national independence were already present, and these would grow into a movement of emancipation first from Perú and finally from Spain itself.

Meanwhile, the Spanish crown, lacking adequate sanctions to enforce its commercial code, could not prevent the economic life of the colony from breaking out of these unnatural confines. The inevitable course of economic growth, supported by obvious geographical facts, acted in a direction contrary to official intentions. If Spain did not appreciate the most natural route to South America, other Europeans nations did. Drawn by the wealth of Potosí, the English, the Portuguese and the Dutch converged upon the Río de la Plata. Through Buenos Aires developed one of the most flourishing contraband trades in the whole of America. This was possible owing to two things. In 1680 Portugal founded the colony of Sacramento. Close to Buenos Aires, in an area where the Spanish authorities could provide no systematic patrols, Sacramento became a huge entrepôt for English contraband: what Jamaica was for the Caribbean, Sacramento was for the Río de la Plata. Britain was able to operate in the Lisbon-Brazil-Sacramento trade because, while trade with Portuguese colonies, like trade with Spanish colonies, was explicitly forbidden to foreigners, it had been open to Britain since Cromwell's well-known treaty of 1654, the price of English support for the House of Braganza. Consequently, as the British merchants themselves later put it,

a trade commenced between the Portuguese and the Spaniards on the Rio de la Plata . . . and was carried on and encouraged by the cheapness with which the Spaniards were supplied with English goods sent from Lisbon in the Rio de Janeiro fleets, and from thence transported by sea to Nova Colonia do Sacramento, whither the Spaniards resorted to purchase these goods which were paid for in dollars returned to Lisbon by the Rio fleet, the greatest part of which may be said to centre in England.[1]

The amount of English goods supplied to the southern colonies by these means assumed large proportions and the returns were high: in 1761, for example, the returns from Sacramento amounted to 4,000,000 cruzadas in silver.[2]

The gap through Spanish economic defences opened by Sacramento was further widened by the famous *asiento de negros*. Spain needed negro labour in her colonies, and unlike Portugal did not possess her own sources of supply in Africa. By the Treaty of Utrecht (1713), which ended the War of the Spanish Succession, not only was Sacramento recognized to belong to Portugal, but Britain was given the privilege of operating the slave traffic for thirty years in the ports of South America. To implement this treaty, Britain placed agents in most of the ports of Spanish America upon the pretext of regulating the negro traffic, and under cover of this was able to develop a thriving trade in various commodities, not least with Buenos Aires. Faced with the prospect of being commercially eliminated by Britain and anxious to promote a revival of her own manufactures, Spain had to follow in the wake of her rivals and develop more liberal economic relations with her own colonies. Cautiously she felt her way. The fleets were gradually and partially suspended by measures which have already been described, and in place of the old system the method of single registered vessels destined for a port in the colonies was made more and more general; ultimately this led to complete *comercio libre*, and the opening of Buenos Aires for continuous direct trade with Spain and the Spanish Indies. Combined with the already existing English commercial penetration, this meant that the potential wealth of the region was now capable of realization. Livestock, hitherto hardly exploited, now had a commercial value and a way out to markets abroad; and this incentive was responsible for the development of the famous *vaquerías* of the Río de la Plata, the cattle being slaughtered at

[1] 'Memorials of the British Consul and Factories at Lisbon to His Majesty's Ambassador at that Court and to His Secretaries of State of This Kingdom' (London, 1766), quoted in Christelow, 'Great Britain and the trades from Cadiz and Lisbon to Spanish America and Brazil, 1759–1783', *op. cit.*, p. 5.   [2] *Ibid.*

first only for hides, and then, with an assured market in Europe, for fats and jerked beef. Moreover, with the termination of the artificial trade routes via Panamá and Lima, the colonial consumer could now get his goods more directly and more cheaply, and consequently the emancipation of the Río de la Plata from the economic domination of Perú was begun, to the accompaniment of a continuous campaign of protests and pressure from the merchants of Lima. So the colony entered upon a period of unprecedented commerce; more European goods entered and at better prices and its wealth was stimulated by the demand for its own produce.

Yet the emergence of the Río de la Plata as a prime factor in Spanish colonial policy was due less to a realization of its economic possibilities than to its strategic importance.[1] In this period Buenos Aires acquired a strategic significance of the first order, in that it was the best base in the South Atlantic, the most effective guard over the route to the Magellan Straits and so the Pacific, and the best point of penetration into the interior of South America. From the time that she founded Montevideo in 1726 to contain the Portuguese advance, there is abundant evidence that Spain was concerned about the defence of her territories in the southern part of the continent, especially in the second half of the century when, as has already been noticed, she was uneasy about Britain's intentions in South America in general. Her experience of British encroachments in Central America, involving continual bickering over the rights of English logwood cutters in the Bay of Honduras, was likely to put her on guard against the evident British interest in the South Seas. Such suspicion was undoubtedly behind her cancellation of the negro asiento. And it was responsible for her sensitivity over the Falkland Islands question. After his world voyage Lord Anson wrote that he considered the Falkland Islands a useful place for anchorage and refreshment of ships on their way to the South Seas.[2] Spain made known her anxiety to

[1] For excellent discussions of this see G. Céspedes del Castillo, 'Lima y Buenos Aires. Repercusiones económicas y políticas de la creación del virreinato del Plata', *Anuario de Estudios Americanos*, iii (Sevilla, 1946), pp. 669–874; and O. Gil Munilla, *El Río de la Plata en la política internacional. Génesis del virreinato*.

[2] Vera Lee Brown, 'Anglo-Spanish relations in America in the closing years of the colonial era', *H.A.H.R.*, v (1925), pp. 390–2.

prevent the Falklands falling into the hands of any other power, and the British were well aware that she would view any settlement in those islands as a threat to the security of her dominions on the mainland.[1] This concern was reinforced by awakening Spanish interest in the China trade and by her appreciation of the advantages of direct trade between Spain and the west coast of South America. Of no value in themselves, the islands were of great importance as a watering station for vessels going to China and the East Indies, and for service as a depot for merchandise which could be introduced as contraband into Spanish America. Consequently Spain believed that Britain was interested in the Falklands as a British-controlled station on the sea route to China and the Far East, which would at the same time serve as a base for descents upon the Spanish settlements in time of war and for illicit trade with them in time of peace. From 1765 when Britain procured a footing in the Falklands the question caused continual tension, leading to a major crisis in 1770-1 and the establishment of a British garrison there in 1771.[2] But while the dispute was settled without recourse to war, this was largely due to the fact that Spain could not count on French assistance for hostilities at that particular time; the problem was not solved and Spain remained unsatisfied, and all the more determined to fortify her defences in southern America.

Meanwhile the behaviour of the Portuguese colonial authorities was strengthening this resolve. Portuguese pressure southwards from Brazil was a constant factor in the political and strategic situation in South America. When Portugal was able to affirm her dominion over Sacramento she could control the north side of the Plata estuary. The transfer of the vice-regal capital of Brazil from Bahia to Rio de Janeiro in 1763 was symptomatic of her forward policy in this area. From 1755 when Pedro de Cevallos became governor of the province of Buenos Aires he sent home constant reports of Portuguese infiltrations, and insisted on the necessity of preparing for war in order to bring the matter to an issue. After the Seven Years War Sacramento had to be restored to Portugal, but now there was a stricter insistence on the part of Spain that

---

[1] P.R.O., S.P., Spain, 94/175, De Visme to Shelburne, 6 October 1766.
[2] Vera Lee Brown, *op. cit.*, pp. 396 ff.

her neighbour keep within the limits established by treaty, and Cevallos was given another battalion of troops to protect Spanish rights.[1] Furthermore, Spanish reaction to the threat to her supremacy in the southern part of the continent took three specific forms. First she began to colonize and fortify the Banda Oriental, and struggled to repulse Portuguese encroachments into the *pueblos de misiones* on the Brazilián frontier.[2] Then she undertook the colonization of the Patagonian coast, the importance of which was publicized in England by the expelled Jesuit, Thomas Falkner, in his *Description of Patagonia* which he published in Hereford in 1774.[3] Above all, however, British and Portuguese pressure forced Spain to focus her attention more and more on Buenos Aires, her principal military bastion in South America, and it is in this concern over Buenos Aires that the origins of the future viceroyalty can be more directly observed.

Hitherto Buenos Aires had been regarded as a mere appendage to the viceroyalty of Perú. Its economic insignificance was reflected in its political dependence on its wealthier neighbour. But now, even before the creation of the viceroyalty of the Río de la Plata, Buenos Aires began to acquire considerable *de facto* autonomy *vis-à-vis* Perú. New powers were given to its governors. In 1763 Cevallos was authorized to procure the necessary money for military expenses directly from Potosí, instead of through the medium óf Lima. In 1766 the recently established governor of the Falkland Islands was made responsible directly to the governor of Buenos Aires instead of to the viceroy of Perú. In 1771 direct communications between Spain and Buenos Aires were increased when a packetboat began to visit the southern port every two months. In his campaign against the Portuguese, governor Vértiz, who succeeded Cevallos, was allowed considerable freedom of action. All this reflected the new strategic situation. The men appointed to the government of these provinces were precisely soldiers, like

---

[1] Gil Munilla, *op. cit.*, p. 109.

[2] Vértiz, 'Memoria de gobierno', 12 March 1784, in S. Radaelli, ed., *Memorias de los virreyes del Río de la Plata* (Buenos Aires, 1945), pp. 80 ff.

[3] T. Falkner, *Description of Patagonia and the adjoining parts of South America* (Hereford, 1774). Falkner had lived among the Patagonian Indians from 1740 to 1767.

Bucareli, Cevallos and Vértiz, all of proved ability and experience and with more military prestige than their viceroys in Lima.

To formulate a policy was one thing; to finance it was another. Buenos Aires suffered from a chronic lack of public revenue. The penury of its treasury was not surprising in view of the fact that its territory was still under-populated and under-developed: it still lacked that complete freedom of commerce which it needed to exploit its natural riches or to attract to the Río de la Plata extensive traffic with the rest of the continent. To a certain extent it was possible to increase revenue by better administrative devices. Public funds were collected and managed with more zeal. From 1767 the new Office of Accounts established in Buenos Aires organized the operation of all the subtreasuries of the provinces which until then had been ill-supervised from Lima.[1] The struggle against the contraband trade was conducted with more determination, and there was a notable increase in confiscated goods between 1769 and 1775.[2] The collection of revenue duties in the subtreasury of Buenos Aires was more than doubled between 1773 and 1776.[3] But in the final analysis none of these measures was adequate to meet government expenditure, and economic assistance was necessary. In Buenos Aires complaints were made of lack of interest in their problems on the part of the Lima authorities. But from such a distance the only useful thing the viceroy of Perú could do was to send money; and even the considerable subsidies from Perú were not sufficient for expenses. Within these terms the dilemma of Buenos Aires could not be resolved. On the one hand it was being entrusted with more autonomy and the execution of a more vigorous policy in the southern continent. On the other hand it did not have the resources adequate to the task. Was there any solution to the problem?

In 1770 Charles III requested from Álvarez de Acevedo, fiscal of the *audiencia* of Charcas, information on the possibility of organizing new reductions of Indians in the frontier territory of Tucumán, and the effect of such a project on the organization of the exchequer. Fortunately Acevedo interpreted his terms of

[1] J. M. Mariluz Urquijo, 'El Tribunal Mayor y Audiencia Real de Cuentas de Buenos Aires', *Revista del Instituto del Derecho*, iii (Buenos Aires, 1951), pp. 116–17.
[2] Céspedes, *op. cit.*, pp. 773–4.   [3] Levene, introd. to *D.H.A.*, v, liii.

reference rather widely, and his dispatch of 12 January 1771 initiated a series of reports on the project of a new viceroyalty in South America.[1] Acevedo argued that the provinces of the Río de la Plata could not be adequately governed from Lima on account of the enormous distances involved. Moreover, the new signs of prosperity and the increase in population of the provinces demanded the establishment in Buenos Aires of its own political and judicial organizations. The obvious disparity of problems and interests between Perú and the Río de la Plata led him to suggest that a new political and administrative entity should be established under the authority of a viceroy and an *audiencia*, and embracing the whole of the Río de la Plata. The Council of the Indies, however, conservative to the last, would not commit itself. But the interest of the king was aroused and he began to collect more information. In July 1775 viceroy Amat of Perú submitted his opinion to Madrid. Amat recognized a difficulty which Acevedo had missed: what the Río de la Plata lacked was precisely the economic resources to maintain itself without assistance from Perú, for administrative autonomy would be illusory without an independent economic and financial basis. In face of this problem Amat thought he found a remedy in the inclusion of Chile, whose economic potential he knew from his own experience as governor there. In making this suggestion Amat revealed a lack of appreciation of the external factors of strategy and defence which were the main preoccupation of the central government; for the resources of Chile were unrealized and speculative, while the need of Buenos Aires was urgent.[2]

This material was simply filed by the Council of the Indies as routine matter of no great consequence. There was still insufficient information about the problem in Spain, and the Council itself actually used to refer to the project as that of the *audiencia* of Tucumán, so vague was its notion of the issue.[3] The

[1] See E. Ravignani, 'El virreinato del Río de la Plata (1776–1810)', *H.N.A.*, IV, i, 88–96: and E. Ruiz Guiñazú, *La magistratura indiana* (Buenos Aires, 1916), pp. 199 ff.

[2] In proposing Santiago de Chile as capital of the projected viceroyalty viceroy Amat showed the same blindness to strategic realities as did the *cabildo* of Santiago which made a similar suggestion about the same time.

[3] Gil Munilla, *op. cit.*, p. 369.

viceroyalty of the Río de la Plata was born not out of an ideal theory or a planned proposition, but of an interplay between external and internal factors. What Buenos Aires could not procure in its economic and administrative interests it could obtain by virtue of its strategic position. None of the reports on the project of the new viceroyalty responded to the critical nature of the situation. But they did have the effect of making attractive an idea, of revealing its possibility and confirming its sanity: they ensured that the new seed would fall on fertile ground. And what really saved South American aspiration for better government from oblivion in the files of the Council of the Indies were the essentially political motives of Charles III who, for reasons really unconnected with the internal problem of administration, wanted a bastion in the South Atlantic against Britain and Portugal, and who found the projected viceroyalty the best form this could take.

Such a policy was finally implemented in 1776. The crisis over the Falkland Islands had put Spain on her guard. Now, Portuguese sorties south from Brazil were increasing all through 1775–6 when Portugal was seizing Spanish merchant vessels, attacking Spanish privateers near Sacramento and preparing an expedition against Montevideo.[1] The Spanish government decided to bring the matter to an issue by force. Conditions seemed favourable: British diplomatic opinion was sounded and Spain discovered that Britain was not averse from a Spanish expedition which was only going to defend Spanish rights and recover lost territory.[2] The British minister in Madrid was convinced that the expedition did not involve any wide issues or general war with Franco-Spanish co-operation, but would be simply concerned with boundary disputes between Brazil and the Río de la Plata.[3] Above all, however, Spain was able to act decisively in 1776 because Britain had her hands tied in North America where she was struggling with her rebellious colonies: this was an opportunity which could not be missed, for Britain was in no position to help her Portuguese ally even had she wished.

[1] Vértiz, 'Memoria de gobierno', in *Memorias de los virreyes*, pp. 85–8.
[2] Gil Munilla, *op. cit.*, pp. 305–7.
[3] P.R.O., S.P., Spain, 94/201, Grantham to Weymouth, No. 30, 8 August 1776; 94/202, Grantham to Weymouth, No. 50, 20 October 1776.

At the beginning of the preparations for the expedition to the Río de la Plata in June 1776 there was still no sign of the government's intention to found a new viceroyalty. It was left to Cevallos, whose experience as governor of Buenos Aires qualified him to speak and act with authority in this matter, to formulate the project in precise terms. He himself was now in Madrid, in touch with colonial authorities there, and a few days before receiving official appointment as leader of the expedition (but after he had been notified privately) he issued an important report which was in effect a resumé of his conception of the enterprise.[1] He argued that political authority was needed if military leadership was to be effective. At the same time, to ensure the success of the whole action in which a considerable number of troops and a large amount of equipment was to be involved he wanted all the resources of the region at his disposal. But as these were notoriously slight, he sought something more —that his command extend not only to Buenos Aires and Paraguay, but also to Tucumán, Santa Cruz de la Sierra, Potosí, and all the district of the *audiencia* of Charcas. Cevallos, in short, wanted not the potential resources of Chile which would need a long-term economic programme to make effective, but the existing, though perhaps exaggerated, wealth of Upper Perú, and especially of Potosí. And nothing was denied him. Seeking military and political authority in direct dependence on the central government, he was named a few days later commander of the expedition and viceroy of Buenos Aires, with jurisdiction over the territories of the *audiencia* of Charcas. He was granted

all the functions and rights which, in accordance with the Laws of the Indies, belong to this office, for as long as Your Excellency is involved in this expedition . . . then, when the expedition is concluded, you will leave the government and the military and political authority of the provinces of the Río de la Plata within the boundaries which have existed until now.[2]

The apparent impermanence of the arrangement is deceptive: it was merely an insurance against disaster. The expedition

---

[1] F. Arribas, *La expedición de D. Pedro de Cevallos a Buenos Aires y la fundación del virreinato del Río de la Plata, 1776–1778* (Valladolid, n.d.), p. 17.
[2] Quoted in Gil Munilla, *op. cit.*, p. 376.

itself was the largest Spain had yet sent to South America. The military campaign and the subsequent diplomatic negotiations were a success. In October 1777 Spain and Portugal signed the preliminary treaty of boundaries, and in March 1778 a general treaty of friendship was concluded. With the acquisition of Sacramento Spain at last gained undisputed dominion over the estuary of the River Plate. And what apparently began as an improvisation, with no more immediate object than to apportion economic resources to a military enterprise, continued on a permanent and stable basis. In July 1777 Cevallos urged the necessity of permanence in a message to José de Gálvez, Minister of the Indies. In October of the same year this was formally granted, and the viceroyalty of Perú was permanently dismembered. Already the economic policy of Cevallos was ensuring vigorous life to the new creation, and now that the campaign was over commercial reforms received exclusive attention and were the most convincing evidence that, whatever the reaction might be in Perú, the new viceroyalty intended to preserve its identity. In June 1777 the first petition from the merchants of Buenos Aires was delivered to Cevallos, requesting him to extend the Indian frontier, create an *audiencia* and a university, and authorize the construction of docks. The primary concern, however, was to achieve freedom of commerce to Upper Perú; now that Sacramento was in Spanish hands, the favourite argument used in Lima, that smuggling from Sacramento justified prohibition of trade from Buenos Aires to the interior, was no longer valid. But the merchants of Buenos Aires wanted more than simple justice: a month later they were taking the offensive against Lima, petitioning Cevallos to exclude Peruvian commerce from all the territories of the new viceroyalty, and expressing surprise that Chile had not been included in the new creation and that Perú had not been even further reduced in territory.

Cevallos encouraged these pretensions. On 8 July 1777 he issued his famous proclamation prohibiting the export of gold and silver bullion from the viceroyalty of the Río de la Plata with destination for Perú.[1] Such an order was more fundamental than it appeared, and given the existing circumstances it

[1] Levene, introd., *D.H.A.*, v, lxxii–lxxv.

radically altered the economies of the two viceroyalties. For Upper Perú bought its extensive imports with gold and silver from its mines. The *Casa de Moneda*, or royal mint, was the only place in the territories of Charcas where money could be coined, but it was notoriously idle and inefficient. Therefore the medium of exchange was uncoined metal, which in exchange for manufactures and agricultural products went mainly to Perú. Cevallos ordered that all the metal produced in Upper Perú should be minted in Potosí, knowing that such a task was impossible. Thus the acute shortage of money together with the embargo on bullion which had hitherto served as money sufficed to paralyse trade between Lower and Upper Perú and change the course of the flow of precious metals from Lima, their previous goal, to Buenos Aires, the new mistress of Upper Perú, and so into the overseas trade or the Spanish exchequer. Then, in November 1777 viceroy Cevallos, anticipating the consent of Madrid, authorized freedom of trade between all provinces and cities of the viceroyalty.[1] With this measure Buenos Aires was able to begin its own trade drive and secure the markets of the interior, particularly of Upper Perú, to the detriment of Lima. One more example will suffice to illustrate the economic policy now pursued by Buenos Aires: in order to control the supply of mercury for his mines without having recourse to Lima Cevallos ensured that from October 1777 supplies sent from Spain should proceed via Buenos Aires.[2] Consequently, by 1778, and including the comprehensive legislation of that year,[3] direct trade with Spain, with other colonies, and between her own provinces, had become normal and legal for the new viceroyalty.

In all this activity Cevallos had the constant support and encouragement of his superiors in Spain. By the time that its first viceroy returned to Europe in June 1778 Buenos Aires and its territory had become the prime preoccupation of the home government in colonial affairs and had gained in two years what it had been denied for two centuries. The foundations had been laid whereby Spanish power in South America might cease to

---

[1] *Ibid.*, v, liv–lxxi; see also Bando de Cevallos, in *Documentos para la historia del virreinato del Río de la Plata* (3 vols., Buenos Aires, 1912–13,) iii, 41–3.

[2] Levene, introd., *D.H.A.*, v, lxxvii; see also Cevallos, 'Memoria de gobierno', in *Memorias de los virreyes*, pp. 15–16.

[3] See above, p. 19.

revolve on Lima and find its true centre in Buenos Aires. As has been seen, the idea of permanence had been accepted. On 27 October Gálvez sent the title to the second viceroy, and six months later gave the necessary instructions concerning the new arrangement to the *audiencia* of Charcas and the viceroy of Perú.[1] These messages summarized the reasons for the continued existence of the new viceroyalty: it was justified by its results, for the region of the Río de la Plata was now much better governed than it had been from Lima; above all it was necessary for military defence in time of war. And it was precisely because military and strategic factors were still paramount that the economic and administrative elements now came to the fore. For although it was true, as Cevallos pointed out to Gálvez in November 1777, that the Río de la Plata 'is the only genuine bastion in South America, whose prosperity has to be pursued with all zeal', being 'the only point through which South America can be retained or lost',[2] nevertheless military defence depended upon a sound economy.

Consequently, the fostering of wealth in the Río de la Plata was no longer merely a local aspiration, but also an essential concern of the home government. Never was a Spanish American colony given more economic protection than the nascent viceroyalty. This policy found expression also in the administrative agencies through which it was to be effected. Manuel Ignacio Fernández, intendant-general of the army of Cevallos, was soon made superintendent-general of finances in the viceroyalty, with instructions to increase public revenue and stimulate production; and the progress of revenue and commerce in Buenos Aires was marked by the foundation of the customs house in 1778 and the chamber of commerce in 1794. There was a striking increase in the prosperity of the region as a result of the new policy. Men and money poured into the viceroyalty. The prohibition of the export of precious metals to Perú and elsewhere doubled within a few months the transmission of the silver of Upper Perú to Buenos Aires.[3] Anything

---

[1] V. M. Maúrtua, *Juicio de límites entre el Perú y Bolivia. Prueba peruana presentada al gobierno de la República Argentina* (Barcelona, 1906), iv, 35–8.
[2] Quoted in Céspedes, *op. cit.*, p. 791.
[3] *D.H.A.*, I, 71.

that could create wealth was protected and relieved of heavy duties. As early as 1777 the purchase tax on the sales of building sites was reduced by 50 per cent. The livestock industry received increased attention, and its methods began to be modernized.[1] For the complete prosperity of the industry a proper salting technique was necessary: this was encouraged from Madrid by the sending of information and by tax relief.[2] The tanning industry also began to prosper. The export of hides made spectacular progress: 1,400,000 hides were exported from Montevideo in 1783.[3] And their price rose steadily from then until the close of the Napoleonic Wars. In the interest of increasing the supply of labour in the colony commercial practices which had been sacrosanct for years were quickly jettisoned. Juan José de Vértiz, second viceroy of the Río de la Plata, authorized on his own initiative the import of negroes from Portuguese slave traders and the necessary licences were readily granted by the crown. Vértiz estimated that by 1782 5,000 negroes had been admitted from Portuguese ships in this way.[4] Complete freedom of import of negroes into the viceroyalty of the Río de la Plata was granted in 1791, four years before a similar concession was extended to Perú.[5]

The net result of this favoured treatment was to enable Buenos Aires to take from Lima the provision of the markets of Upper Perú, and even some of Lower Perú. Articles from Europe now invariably arrived by way of Buenos Aires, at a lower price than hitherto. In 1800 the import capacity of the Potosí market was assessed at 2,806,700 pesos: imports from Lower Perú accounted for 308,700 pesos, while as much as 600,000 pesos was accounted for by European merchandise arriving by way of Buenos Aires.[6] Exemptions and partial reductions of duty on commerce, besides a normal level of taxation that was lower than in any other place in South America, helped to create a novel commercial

[1] Cevallos, 'Memoria de gobierno', in *Memorias de los virreyes*, pp. 12–13.

[2] B.M., Add. MS 32,606, fol. 12, Gálvez to Cevallos, 26 April 1778 (Duplicado), enclosing a 'Disertación sobre el método, reglas y ventajas de este Comercio de Carnes de esas Provincias' (fols. 13–17); see also *D.H.A.*, VI, 154, 177–8.

[3] B.M., Add. MS 17,604, fol. 129v, 'Informe sobre la Banda Oriental', Francisco de Ortega to Sanz, 23 August 1784.

[4] 'Memoria de gobierno,' in *Memorias de los virreyes*, pp. 109–10.

[5] *D.H.A.*, VII, 4–9, 283–4.

[6] Levene, introd., *D.H.A.*, V, lxxiii note.

prosperity.[1] A report submitted to the viceroy by the merchants' deputies in Buenos Aires in 1789 gives some idea of the new conditions:

Since the establishment of free commerce until now, there has undoubtedly been experienced a vast increase in the number of merchants. A necessary consequence of this has been the distribution of wealth in many hands, more contributors to the royal and municipal revenue, the increase of towns arising out of the pressure of population, the construction of buildings, stores as well as houses. In short, the wealth which was formerly held by a few has now been made available to many . . .[2]

Such conditions, testifying as they do to profound changes in every department of public life, inevitably raised new problems of administration. The administrative agencies of the colony, inadequate even in its former humble existence, were pitifully inappropriate to its new rôle. Consequently, the third element in Spanish policy at this period—the concern for better colonial administration—was even more relevant here than it was in any other part of the empire. The economic and strategic value of the new viceroyalty depended in the ultimate analysis on its internal order and security. And whether the new life stirring within the colony could be directed and controlled by the crown depended on whether the crown had officials there who were adequate to the task. It is in this context that Charles III's decision to apply to the Río de la Plata the administrative system of intendancies with which he had already experimented in other parts of the empire has its full significance.

---

[1] For example, in 1780 the intendant of Buenos Aires considered that a temporary doubling of the *almojarifazgo* (import-export duty) could easily be borne by these provinces—see Intendant of Buenos Aires to Gálvez, 20 October 1780, in *D.H.A.*, VI, 189–90.

[2] Manuel Rodríguez de la Vega and Martín de Sarratea to viceroy Loreto, 21 July 1789, in *Documentos referentes a la guerra de la independencia y emancipación política de la República Argentina* (3 vols., Buenos Aires, 1914–26), i, 339.

CHAPTER III

The Origin of the Intendant System

OF all the reforms introduced by the Bourbons in Spain and America in the eighteenth century the one which involved most institutional change was not of pure Spanish origin. For a new agency of government which would combine effective action in local administration with complete subordination to central authority Spanish government, traditionally weak in this principle, looked to France, where the crown had at its disposal precisely such an instrument. Although they had antecedents in the sixteenth century in the form of royal commissioners in the provinces, the French intendants really made their appearance in the first half of the seventeenth century, and it was Richelieu who fashioned them into an office worthy of the French monarchy.[1] Suppressed during the Fronde, they were re-established by Mazarin, gradually applied to the whole of France, acquired a definite constitution, and showed their worth in the application of Colbert's programme of reform. Under Louis XIV the *intendants de justice, police et finances* were supreme royal agents in the thirty-four *généralités* or local districts into which France was divided for governmental purposes, and were endowed with almost illimitable powers in matters of justice, finance and general administration.

Such officials, the fruit in France of a gradual development which was tending to affirm the absolute power of the king and eliminate those interests and forces capable of opposing him, were created in Spain by simple legislative act. The circumstances,

---

[1] See G. Hanotaux, *Origine de l'institution des intendants des provinces d'après les documents inédits* (Paris, 1884), criticized in R. Doucet, *Les institutions de la France au XVIe siècle* (2 vols., Paris, 1948), i, 422–36; also C. Godard, *Les pouvoirs des intendants sous Louis XIV* (Paris, 1901). For a general comparison of the French and Spanish American intendant see A. Vieillard-Baron, 'L'intendant americain et l'intendant français', *Revista de Indias*, xii (1951), pp. 237–50.

it is true, invited drastic remedies. Spanish administration was moribund, and the most obvious symptoms of sickness were a chronic inability to balance budgets and absence of royal control in the provinces. The crown lacked the personnel competent to deal with this situation and assistance had to be sought elsewhere. Philip V naturally turned to France, and at the suggestion of Cardinal Portocarrero asked Louis XIV to send an expert to reform the administration of finances in Spain.[1] This was the occasion of the mission of Orry, an economic expert and administrator who was for many years a counsellor in the service of the Spanish crown. Orry and his assistants were the moving spirits behind the rapid introduction of the intendant system into Spain.

At first the office of intendant seems to have been conferred by title in individual cases before the introduction of the complete system in 1718. In the form of *intendentes de ejército*, several men were appointed to office, some as early as 1711, with their functions confined to the economic aspects of army administration.[2] José Patiño, for example, one of the associates of Orry and himself an administrator of marked ability, was appointed army intendant first of Extremadura then of Catalonia.[3] These intendants were created to absorb the financial and administrative functions previously reserved to the captains-general, who were the highest military authorities in the various provinces into which Spain was divided, and who, through their presidency of the main provincial courts, the *audiencias*, exercised a general supervision of administration. Consequently in this early period the intendants were occupied solely in supplying the army with arms, money and provisions and in looking after accounts. The success of the experiment encouraged the king to place an intendant at the head of each province and thus give what had hitherto been a purely functional office a completely territorial application; provincial intendants would control the administration and finance not only of the army but of the

---

[1] M. Danvila y Collado, *El poder civil en España* (6 vols., Madrid, 1885-7), iii, 506.

[2] See Desdevises du Dezert, *L'Espagne de l'ancien régime*, ii, 133-8, and the same author's 'Les institutions de l'Espagne au XVIIIᵉ siècle', *Revue Hispanique*, lxx (1927), pp. 164-8.

[3] See A. Béthencourt Massieu, *Patiño en la política internacional de Felipe V* (Valladolid, 1954), p. 14.

entire province in which they were appointed. This was the origin of the Ordinance of 4 July 1718 which established in each of the provinces of the kingdom an *intendente de provincia* with full authority in the departments of justice, administration, finance and war. But the move was premature. The new legislation produced such a strong reaction from the existing bureaucratic class, which looked upon any reform as a threat to its interests, that its operation had to be suspended by decree of 1 March 1721. Nevertheless, Ferdinand VI managed to re-establish it in October 1749 and thenceforth the system took root.

The two classes of intendant, army and provincial, gradually became assimilated to each other and, as in France, the new official assumed the main burden of government work. The competence of the intendant within his province was almost universal.[1] To him was assigned general administrative and economic control. In this capacity he was expected to maintain the peace within his province, keep an eye on the conduct of government officials, and resolve the inevitable conflicts of jurisdictions among them. In addition he was expected to promote the wealth of his province, produce maps showing the property of the crown, the church and the nobility, furnish reports on the condition and possibilities of arable and pasture land, woods, mineral resources and the like, and foster industry and agriculture. Then he had his financial duties. As representative of the superintendent-general of finances in Madrid, he had supervision over all the collectors and other officials of the treasury in his province. It is true that the financial powers of the intendants did not include management of municipal finance, which was the traditional prerogative of the *cabildos*; but the royal instruction of 30 July 1760 which granted to the Council of Castile the right to supervise and examine the annual accounts of the municipalities and created a *contaduría general*—a typical example of the extension of central control under the Bourbons—also provided for the formation of a municipal *junta de propios y arbitrios*, or finance committee, in each town. Over this the intendant had to preside, as well as supervise its administration and remittance of accounts.[2] Finally the military duties

[1] Desdevises du Dezert, *L'Espagne de l'ancien régime*, ii, 133–8.
[2] Ravignani, *H.N.A.*, IV, i, 195.

of the intendant included matters of conscription, provision and payment of troops, and the maintenance of military supplies. The task thus assigned to the intendants was an immense one. Responsible for the general administration and for the economic affairs of their provinces, for the supervision of government, for the maintenance of law and order, they had to carry an almost overwhelming burden. In July 1789 an observer voiced a scepticism which contained some truth:

The ordinance of intendants is admirable, but in the large provinces it has all the appearances of Plato's Republic or the Utopia of Thomas More. How is it possible for an intendant of a province like that of Andalucía to cope with the detail of the operations assigned to him? I would like to concede him a divine omniscience, but human nature being what it is this ordinance will always remain in the sphere of a perfect romance.[1]

And this was not the only flaw. There was always the danger that the intendant would clash with the jurisdiction of existing officials, particularly with that of the *corregidores*, who in smaller divisions of the provinces mirrored the activities of the intendants and who represented for the masses of the Spanish people the real embodiment of State authority. Moreover, as if their other duties were not sufficient, the intendants had also been assigned judicial powers in their provincial capitals and the surrounding districts. By royal *cédula* of 13 November 1766 Charles III relieved them of these in order to free them for their other duties.[2] But it is doubtful whether this edict was fully implemented, and the Spanish tradition of confounding the judicial and administrative functions was continued.

In spite of its defects, however, the system had sufficient success to encourage royal counsellors and political thinkers to advocate its extension to America, where the political and administrative problems which the intendants were expected to solve were even more urgent than those of the mother country. Already in 1743 Campillo had made the suggestion. His *Nuevo sistema de gobierno económico para la América*, which has already

[1] A. Rodríguez Villa, ed., *Cartas político-económicas escritas por el conde de Campomanes al conde de Lerena* (Madrid, 1878), p. 204. It is now agreed that these letters were wrongly ascribed to Campomanes. See Sarrailh, *L'Espagne éclairée*, p. 554, n. 3.

[2] *Novíssima recopilación de las leyes de España* (Madrid, 1805), vii, xi, 26.

been noticed in another context, advocated a complete reform of government in America which would begin with a general visitation of all the colonies and be crowned with the establishment of intendants there who would investigate the economic potential of the colonies, distribute land to the Indians, promote agriculture and industry and advance commerce.[1]

But if political speculation was making feasible an extension of the intendant system, practical conditions were making it essential. In 1762 the British captured Havana; during the ten months of British occupation the city experienced a new lease of life and a more intense activity in shipping and commerce than it had ever known. The British régime, in fact, provided such an object lesson in the political and commercial value of the island, that when it regained possession the Spanish government undertook a programme of reform which was to have far-reaching results. With a new governor in the person of the Conde de Ricla (1763–5), and a *visitador*, General O'Reilly, Spanish rule was restored, fortifications and ports were begun, the military establishment was strengthened, new taxes were imposed, public works undertaken, investigations started. O'Reilly completed his visitation and submitted his report: it contained two major recommendations, that there should be freer trade with Spain, and that administrative corruption and inefficiency, especially in finance, required urgent remedy. For once government reaction was prompt. An important decree providing for mail boats to ply between La Coruña and Havana heralded an era of freer trade, while at the same time the first experiment in the extension of the intendant system to the colonies was begun with the *Instrucción* of 31 October 1764.[2]

The new legislation explained the royal motives in clear and simple terms:

The advantages which the establishment of the intendancies in the Kingdom of Castile has brought to my royal exchequer in the better administration of its revenues, and to my army in the secure provision of supplies, have moved me to think that the application of the

[1] Artola, 'Campillo y las reformas de Carlos III', *Revista de Indias*, xii (1952), pp. 690–705.

[2] See W. W. Pierson, 'The establishment and early functioning of the Intendencia of Cuba', *James Sprunt Historical Studies*, xix (Chapel Hill, 1927), pp. 81–2 and note 16.

same system in the island of Cuba can obtain similar results. There-fore I have resolved to establish in the said island an intendant, based on Havana, who will have cognizance of the two departments of exchequer and war in the same way as the intendants in Castile.[1]

In this way the intendant in Cuba was given not full territorial jurisdiction in all departments, but simply functional authority in matters of finance and war, 'with that over the former prac-tically complete and exclusive and that over the latter limited to matters of finance'.[2] The governor of Havana continued to exist as the political chief of the island, but the intendant was given the management of civil, ecclesiastical and military revenues which had previously belonged to the captain general, and was assigned charge of matters concerning contra-band, trade, fortifications and royal lands; he also presided over the tribunal of accounts at Havana. Receiving his instructions from the king, the intendant was permitted to correspond directly with him,

The first intendant, Miguel de Altarriba, took office in March 1765. He did not have an easy passage. In Cuba com-plaints from established officials were considerable,[3] while in Spain voices were raised against the experiment in a special *Junta* which the king had appointed to review and report on the matter. But these were the voices of reaction, of an aristocratic bureaucracy disinclined to renounce its privileges. The king himself was determined to proceed further: royal decrees of 1765 and 1767 clarified the position in Cuba and defined the func-tions of the intendant more explicitly, so that within a few years the system had gained a secure foothold in America, but was confined to one small area. The second stage in its extension begins with the famous visitation of José de Gálvez to New Spain, in 1767.

Gálvez's attention was clearly directed towards a possible application of the intendant system to New Spain. Apart from the fact that he himself was given the title of intendant of army in the viceroyalty and that many of the articles of his

[1] The *Instrucción* is printed in J. M. Zamora y Coronado, *Biblioteca de legislación ultramarina* (6 vols., Madrid, 1844–6), iii, 597–606. There is a translation in Pierson, *op. cit.*, pp. 113–33.
[2] Pierson, *op. cit.*, p. 83.   [3] *Ibid.*, pp. 95, 98–9.

instructions, especially in financial affairs, were identical with the instructions for the intendant in Cuba,[1] he was explicitly ordered to

ascertain . . . whether it will be useful and conducive to the good of my service and of my vassals to establish one or more intendancies in New Spain on the same model as those of Spain, or with some limitations or amplifications.[2]

Gálvez's other tasks in New Spain were multifarious and exhausting; nevertheless his searching inquiries into the state of the colony equipped him to draw up, in conjunction with the viceroy, the Marqués de Croix, a Plan of Intendancies for New Spain which was the most substantial contribution yet made to the debate on the extension of the intendant system.[3] In this report Gálvez gave the problem its widest context and its most fundamental application:

The vast kingdoms of Spanish America in the course of two and a half centuries and with the government which they have still modelled on that which formerly prevailed in the metropolis, have reached a point of decadence which threatens them with immediate and total ruin, and which demands the application to these dominions of the salutary remedies which have already cured the ills of their head.

Now was the time to extend to Mexico the system which had contributed so much to the restoration of Spain herself, and thus draw the colonies into a closer union based on a uniform organization with the mother country. The corrupt and ignorant officialdom which dominated the colonial scene, the *corregidores* and *alcaldes mayores*, could only be reformed by being removed; their place should be taken by intendants, who would at the same time eliminate the great evil of the *repartimiento* system. In emphasizing these two defects of the existing régime, Gálvez brought into relief two of the most urgent motives which

[1] Priestley, *José de Gálvez, visitor-general of New Spain (1765–71)*, p. 20.

[2] *Instrucción Reservada*, 14 March 1765, art. XXXI, translation printed in Priestley, *op. cit.*, pp. 404–12.

[3] A.G.I., Indif. General 1713, Informe y plan de Intendencias, Gálvez and Croix, 15 January 1768. This has been summarized by Priestley, *op. cit.*, pp. 289–92, Ravignani, *op. cit.*, pp. 198–201, and L. E. Fisher, *The intendant system in Spanish America* (Berkeley, Calif., 1929), pp. 12–15.

were to promote the establishment of the intendant system in America.

The report then went on to point out that if the viceroy were to cope with the administration of such extensive territories he needed the assistance of intendants who would relieve him of the intolerable burden of administrative detail. These officials would be eleven in number, a superintendent of army and treasury in Mexico city, and ten provincial intendants. They would all be subject to the viceroy who would remain the highest official in the country and superintendent of exchequer. All these intendancies, the report continued, should be established under the same rules as prevailed in the system in Spain, except in regard to the encouragement of manufactures, which were forbidden in the colonies, and the intendants would have charge in their provinces of the four departments of justice, exchequer, war and general administration.[1] In order to improve the standard of royal service, the salaries of the intendants would be much higher than those received by former officials, and the increased expenditure would be offset by greater returns from revenue which better administration would effect. The offices of *corregidores* and *alcaldes mayores* should be abolished: in their place the intendants could appoint subdelegates in the larger towns of their district to collect the revenues, and these officials should be paid reasonable salaries as was done in Spain. Only Spaniards were to be chosen as subdelegates, even for revenue collection in Indian towns. Such was the reluctance to employ creoles that it was suggested that if there were a scarcity of Spaniards for these offices, the administrators of the tobacco monopoly might be entrusted with the duties of subdelegates. In place of the forced *repartimientos* of goods practised by the *corregidores*, the Indians would buy their supplies directly from the merchants and therefore obtain them at lower prices.

To reinforce the Plan it was submitted to the bishops of Mexico and Puebla who were asked to give their opinion. Both supported the project, emphasizing the benefit which would accrue to the Indians in freeing them from the tyranny of the

---

[1] It is notable that the Ordinance of Intendants subsequently did not forbid colonial manufactures: on the contrary, the intendants were enjoined to protect industry: see below, p. 149.

alcaldes mayores and from exploitation by forced commerce. Already, therefore, the intendant system was heralding social and economic reforms.

The Plan was then submitted for royal approval, and by royal order of 20 May 1768 it was referred to the opinion of the highest authorities in the public life of the country, the Conde de Aranda, the Duque de Alba, Jaime Masones de Lima, the Marqués de Grimaldi, the Marqués de San Juan de Piedras Albas, Ricardo Wall, Miguel de Muzquiz, and Juan Gregorio Muniain. With the exception of the Marqués de San Juan, all the statesmen consulted favoured the suggested reform. The most revolutionary opinion was that of Aranda, who eloquently pleaded for a more genuine incorporation of Americans, Indians as well as creoles, into Spanish political life in America, particularly by accepting them for offices, for which personal merit should be the sole criterion.[1] Muzquiz put his finger accurately on a point which would need some consideration. He pointed out that the intendants in Spain, while they were admirable agents for getting things efficiently and quickly done, frequently came into conflict with the *audiencias* and *corregidores* in the exercise of their functions, a conflict which was not surprising in view of the fact that the intendants were given authority in the four departments of war, exchequer, administration and justice, while at the same time the *audiencias* and *corregidores* had long-standing cognizance in matters of justice and administration. In New Spain there would be even more likelihood of conflict of jurisdiction and even more need for precise definition of the boundaries of cognizance in order to avoid conflict with viceroys, governors and *audiencias*.[2]

Grimaldi thought that the measure should be adopted without delay, and on 26 July 1769 the king expressed his agreement: a royal order of 10 August 1769 authorized viceroy Croix to establish intendancies in New Spain, with the proviso that it would be well to take sufficient time for the choice of suitable officials. Croix and Gálvez worked out the administrative details: with royal sanction they named Pedro de Corbalán

[1] Ravignani, *op. cit.*, p. 203.
[2] A.G.I. Indif. General 1713. Muzquiz to Arriaga, 7 June 1768, Dictamen sobre los Proyectos de Intendencias . . . de Nueva España.

provisional intendant of Sonora and Sinaloa, and the governor of Vera Cruz was authorized to exercise certain functions of an intendant in financial matters.[1] By October 1770 they had proposed candidates for all the projected intendancies.[2]

Yet still the system made little headway in New Spain. What it lacked was a full-scale ordinance which would give it unequivocal legislative force; at the same time a slow discussion was proceeding in Spain, which seemed to cast doubts upon the whole system, so that by the beginning of 1772 little had yet been done. But with the return of Gálvez from Mexico in May 1772 and his admission to the Council of the Indies the affair entered a new stage, for he was now able to concentrate all his energies on the court and attack the issue at the centre. On 15 February Arriaga, the Minister of the Indies, remitted all the documents referring to the establishment of intendancies to the new viceroy of Mexico, Antonio Bucareli y Ursúa.[3] Bucareli tried to kill the measure by delay. He replied two years later, on 27 March 1774, giving a minute analysis of the revenues of New Spain but of nothing else, ignoring all the other aspects of the intendant system, and strongly advising against its application.[4] On 8 November 1774 Gálvez also submitted his considered opinion, and the two reports were put before Muzquiz, the secretary of state for finance, who evaded the issue in an ambiguous answer:

> After reading the propositions, reflections and arguments of Gálvez I decided in favour of the intendancies of New Spain, but the considerations adduced by viceroy Bucareli cause me to doubt that the intendancies are useless.[5]

Muzquiz took refuge in advising further study of the problem. Accordingly in May 1775 all the documentation was presented once more to Grimaldi for his opinion. This circulation of material and interminable discussion could well go on indefinitely, providing a convenient but unrealistic alternative to

[1] Priestley, *op. cit.*, pp. 20, 275–6.

[2] Ravignani, *op. cit.*, p. 204.

[3] On Bucareli see A. Vieillard-Baron, 'L'établissement des intendants aux Indes par Charles III', *Revista de Indias*, xiii (1952), pp. 537–8.

[4] Ravignani, *op. cit.*, pp. 207–8.

[5] *Ibid.*, pp. 208–9.

action. To end the paralysis the resolution of one determined will was needed. This was now supplied by José de Gálvez himself who succeeded Arriaga as Minister of the Indies in January 1775. Yet at first he could not take action on the intendancy question, for although the time was now opportune, the government had to turn its attention to more urgent matters. The years 1775-7 were a period of intense administrative activity in which the Spanish authorities had to organize the details of the military expedition to the Río de la Plata and the creation there of the new viceroyalty. It is true that by royal *cédula* of 8 December 1776 the king created an intendancy of army and treasury for Venezuela; the new official was to reside in Caracas and hold jurisdiction in Cumaná, Guayana, Maracaibo and the islands of Margarita and Trinidad, as well as in the province of Venezuela itself.[1] But such an appointment was of the same *ad hoc* nature as those of Cuba and New Spain, and it represented no organic advance in the extension of the intendant system. It was May 1778 before Gálvez found an opportunity to form a Junta to consider the creation of a definite instrument of legislation and the establishment of a full intendant system. Out of the deliberations of this Junta came an *Instrucción* to the intendants of New Spain. The text was thus ready, but still royal promulgation was withheld: not New Spain but the viceroyalty of the Río de la Plata was to enjoy the privilege of initiating the full system.

There had already been indications of the change of direction. On 25 October 1777 Manuel Ignacio Fernández, intendant-general of the army on the Cevallos expedition to the Río de la Plata, was appointed intendant of army and exchequer for the new viceroyalty. His title was granted and his status defined by the royal *cédula* of 21 March 1778.[2] This explained the purpose of the office, which was to be separate and independent of the viceroy, as the increase in the yield and improvement in the management of the royal revenues, and the promotion of agriculture and commerce. The new official was given exclusive cognizance of exchequer affairs, as well as the economic side of

[1] W. W. Pierson, 'La Intendencia de Venezuela en el régimen colonial', *Boletín de la Academia Nacional de la Historia*, xxiv (Caracas, 1941), p. 264.
[2] R.C., 21 March 1778, printed in *D.G.I.E.A.*, i, 27.

the war department; in this capacity he was to serve as immediate subdelegate to the Minister of the Indies in Madrid.[1] But the antecedents of the intendant system were not only economic. They were also social and humanitarian. While viceroy Vértiz and superintendent Fernández were beginning their separate functions in Buenos Aires in 1778, in Upper Perú another great reform was beginning which was intimately connected with the establishment of intendants. The evils of the *repartimiento* system, clearly described for Perú in the *Noticias Secretas* of Juan and Ulloa in 1742,[2] had been even more severely analysed for Mexico in the Plan drawn up by Gálvez and Croix in 1768. Other reports from various sources contributed to a stirring of the royal conscience in this matter. In April 1776 the bishop of Arequipa denounced it in no uncertain terms, asserting that each *corregidor* was not content with the profits enjoyed by his predecessor but invariably set about improving on them, thus causing the flight of many Indians to the mountains and creating a situation which was ripe for revolution.[3] These reports moved the crown to take action, and the first step was an attempt to control the prices of goods charged to the Indians by the *corregidores*, and to insist on the condition of voluntary purchase.[4] But this policy was ineffective and it soon became evident that a more radical remedy was necessary. It was not yet obvious, however, that the alternative to the *corregidores* and their *repartimientos* was inevitably the intendant system. The plan of viceroy Guirior of Perú did not involve the abolition of the *corregidor* but only stricter supervision and regulation. Similarly viceroy Cevallos of Buenos Aires thought in terms not of abolition but of control: in answer to the royal order of 24 August 1777 requesting him to report on the matter, he condemned the abuses arising out of forced sale at high prices but regarded a just and voluntary *repartimiento* as useful in

---

[1] Fernández was allowed 1,000 pesos a year in addition to his salary for expenses of a secretary, to be paid from the treasury of Buenos Aires. See A.G.I., Aud. de Buenos Aires 354, R.O. to Fernández, 24 March 1778.

[2] See J. Juan y A. de Ulloa, *Noticias Secretas de América*, p. 260, where the authors advocate abolition of the *repartimiento* system.

[3] A.G.I., Indif. General 1713, Bishop of Arequipa to Crown, 10 April 1776.

[4] A.G.I., Indif. General 1713, R.O. 12 January 1777; Vértiz to Gálvez, 16 July 1778.

supplying the Indians with necessary goods; he used the opportunity as an excuse to make a long plea for free commerce for Buenos Aires which would lower the prices of goods in general and would provide the strongest impulse for the reform of the oppressive *repartimientos* of the *corregidores*.[1] On the other hand, Areche, visitor-general of Perú advocated the complete extinction of *repartimientos* and proposed that in place of the income from this commercial source, the *corregidores* should receive a fixed wage.[2] A royal order to Areche issued on 24 April 1781 explained that the king agreed that the *repartimientos* ought to be abolished once and for all, but that as it was proposed to establish well paid intendants in the viceroyalty of the Río de la Plata, Areche was to defer his plan and await the *Instrucción de Intendentes*, which would summarily remove all these evils.[3] A month later, however, there was a sudden reversal of this policy, and a royal order issued on 25 May authorized the viceroy of Perú and visitor Areche to abolish the *repartimientos* in Perú and to substitute salaries for the *corregidores*, explaining that the evils of the system, increasing every day, had caused the recent rebellions in Upper Perú, and that the urgency of the situation brooked no delay.[4]

By now the plan of intendants for Buenos Aires was completely prepared. Under the direction of Gálvez and the auspices of the *Junta de Ministros*, the legislative instrument was fashioned, modified and clarified. The finished product was published as the Ordinance of Intendants for Buenos Aires on 28 January 1782.[5] This formidable piece of legislation comprised 276 articles, covering 325 printed pages with an index of 57 more pages. The document begins with a preamble stating the general purposes for which it is issued; 11 articles treat of the intendant system as a whole; 41 of the department of justice; 18 of the department of general administration; 149 of the department of

---

[1] A.G.I., Indif. General 1713, Cevallos to Crown, 26 January 1778.

[2] A.G.I., Indif. General 1713, Areche to Guirior, 18 June 1779.

[3] A.G.I., Indif. General 1713, R.O. 24 April 1781.

[4] A.G.I., Indif. General 1713, R.O. 25 May 1781. This refers to the rebellion of Tupac Amaru. See below, p. 60.

[5] *Real Ordenanza para el establecimiento e instrucción de intendentes de exército y provincia en el virreinato de Buenos-Aires*, 28 January 1782 (hereafter referred to as *Ord. Ints.*), printed in *D.G.I.E.A.*, i, 21–95.

finance; and 56 of the department of war. The last article formally imposed the Ordinance on all colonial officials, and gave it the force of law; from now on this was the political code for the viceroyalty, and all other laws contrary to it were annulled. With this ordinance the intendant system advanced from the stage of partial and functional reform and became an organic institution with a complete territorial application.

In July 1782 copies of the Ordinance were sent to the viceroy and superintendent in Buenos Aires, with orders that they should communicate it to no one except the secretary of the viceroyalty, the Marqués de Sobremonte, but should examine it closely and forward their opinions, especially on its defects: it was explained also that it was the king's intention to confer the new intendancies on the existing governors in Paraguay, Santa Cruz de la Sierra, Potosí, La Plata, La Paz and Tucumán (which was to be divided into two provinces). Yet although the pace of reform was now quickening, caution was still immense: when instructions similar to those sent to the viceroy and superintendent were communicated to Flores, president of the *audiencia* of Charcas, and to Pino Manrique, governor of Potosí, they were informed that it was not intended to alter the names of their offices but simply to amplify their faculties.[1]

Similar secret orders were sent to the governors of Paraguay, Santa Cruz de la Sierra, Potosí, La Paz and Tucumán. At the same time the viceroy was informed that the king had already approved the erection of an *audiencia* in Buenos Aires. Meanwhile the actual appointment of intendants was postponed until opinions from Buenos Aires had been received and the relevant information sifted. This began to arrive in 1783. The viceroy and the superintendent sent a joint report on 15 February in which they expressed their approval and support of the plan, pointing out that its proper operation depended upon first-class appointments, and offering concrete suggestions for its improvement.[2] They thought it would be advisable to sweeten the pill of innovation by conserving something of the old and familiar nomenclature and adopting the title not of intendant but of

[1] See Ravignani, *op. cit.*, pp. 217–19.
[2] A.G.I., Aud. de Buenos Aires 354, Vértiz and Fernández to Gálvez, Carta 684, 15 February 1783.

governor-intendant. The suggestion, typical of the caution which characterized all Spanish reform, was taken up by the king and his advisers, and this became the title normally used in official documents, although the simpler one of intendant was also current. On the Indian question the viceroy and superintendent were concerned to know what would replace the *repartimiento* system, and gave the warning that not only officials but also priests must be strictly ordered to refrain from any *repartimientos*. Among the many other comments offered by the viceroy and the superintendent the most interesting was one of a social-economic nature in which it is possible to observe the influence of the American-born Vértiz. Speaking of the classification of the tribute-paying class the report made the point that it was wrong to include the *cholos* and *zambaigos*—mestizos and mulattos—with the Indians as liable for exaction of tribute; apart from the fact that Areche's attempt to do this in Perú (1778–9) had caused intense resentment and been responsible for the fact that the *cholos* joined the Indians in the rebellion of Tupac Amaru, the *cholos* regarded it as an insult to be classified with the tribute-paying classes 'for they consider it an honour to ascend to the class of the white or free Spaniards and are in fact regarded as such in their own towns'. Yet properly handled, these people could be won over as valuable support for the régime. On this point too the king decided to follow their advice.[1]

In addition to the joint report, Vértiz sent one of his own which he could not reveal to Fernández, for it contained a criticism of the proposal to strip the viceroy of his financial and economic powers and vest them in the separate office of superintendent. Although this was criticism of a fundamental point, it did not prejudice his approval of the Ordinance as a whole.[2] Gálvez replied to Vértiz reassuring him of the sanity of the proposed change, to which he was determined to adhere. To many of the other points of criticism, however, a favourable hearing was given, and from them stemmed the resolutions of

[1] Ministerial comment on the margin of Vértiz's report: 'Instruido el Rey de los inconvenientes que representan, ha determinado que no se altere por aora la practica, ni se empadronen los Cholos y demas castas.' *Ibid.*

[2] For this incident see below, Chapter V.

5 August 1783 which, to the number of fifteen, were appended as a supplementary part of the Ordinance of 1782. At the beginning of November 1783 printed copies of the Ordinance were sent to the viceroyalty and the titles of the intendants issued. The intendant system was thus finally planted in the viceroyalty of the Río de la Plata.

This Ordinance was then used as a pattern for the extension of the system elsewhere. In March 1783 Gálvez informed the second intendant of Venezuela, Francisco de Saavedra, that the instructions for Buenos Aires should serve as a norm for the intendants already established in other parts of the empire as well as for those to be established in the future.[1] In 1784 the system was exported to the Philippines, and in the same year it was introduced in Perú. In 1786–7 it was extended to Chile. In addition to the Ordinance of Buenos Aires the king approved in 1786 a more up-to-date Ordinance for New Spain, which in turn became the norm outside the viceroyalty of the Río de la Plata. Slowly the régime was extended so that by 1790 it covered almost the entire empire.

[1] Pierson, *Bol. Acad. Nac. de la Hist.*, xxiv (1941), p. 265.

CHAPTER IV

The Establishment of the Intendant System in the Viceroyalty of the Río de la Plata

I

THE Ordinance of Intendants divided the viceroyalty of the Río de la Plata into various political units over which, by means of officials with carefully defined powers, royal control could be exerted with more certainty. As far as territorial organization was concerned the establishment of the intendant system was the culmination of a policy of political and administrative integration which the Spanish government had been pursuing for some years. Struggling with the organization of a far-flung empire on which rested the envious eyes of other European powers, and where often unruly subjects did not take naturally to governmental control, the crown recognized the need for a simpler and more efficient grouping of territory and for a shortening of the distance between central organs of government and remote communities. The creation of the viceroyalty of New Granada earlier in the century, and that of the Río de la Plata in 1776 were important milestones in a process which received its most precise and minute definition in the Ordinance of Intendants.

The political divisions of the Río de la Plata before 1776 were cumbrous and inefficient. The territorial charter of the area was the royal *cédula* of 16 December 1617 which divided it into two provinces of equal category, the province of Paraguay, composed of Asunción, Villa Rica, Ciudad Real and Jerez, and the province of Río de la Plata, consisting of Buenos Aires, Santa Fe,

Corrientes and Concepción del Bermejo, that is, the area which now forms the littoral of Argentina.[1] In the interior the settlements which had been founded from the west formed the province of Tucumán; this, however, did not include Mendoza which formed part of the Chilean *corregimiento* of Cuyo. The governors of these extensive provinces had difficult tasks: instructions from the inadequately informed central government arrived late, and no effective support could be counted on from the distant authorities in Perú. The enormous distances made it impossible for the governor to supervise or even acquaint himself with the affairs of the various districts. It is true that in the middle of the eighteenth century the crown began to create new political units. Out of the vast territories in the eastern part of the province of Río de la Plata contiguous to Brazil two subordinate entities were created with governors of their own but dependent upon the higher authority of Buenos Aires: the area of Montevideo which later embraced almost the whole of the Banda Oriental, and the *Misiones* which was formed upon the expulsion of the Jesuits from the Guaraní communities. In 1766 was created the government of the Falkland Islands which was also subordinate to Buenos Aires. The pre-eminence thus acquired by Buenos Aires was formally recognized and the territorial consolidation thus begun was advanced when the creation of the viceroyalty of the Río de la Plata in 1776 made Buenos Aires the capital of the vast territories comprising the governments of the Río de la Plata, Montevideo, Misiones, Malvinas, Paraguay and Tucumán, together with the presidency of Charcas or Upper Perú, and the territories under the jurisdiction of the cities of Mendoza and San Juan del Pico which had hitherto come under the government of Chile.[2] But this miscellaneous collection of units of varying status and different traditions still needed more careful definition.

If the territorial division lacked uniformity before the reforms of 1776 and 1783, so did the status and authority of the officials who administered it. These various units of local jurisdiction were governed by officials who were sometimes

---

[1] See J. Torre Revello, 'Los gobernadores de Buenos Aires (1617–1777)', *H.N.A.*, iii, 459–65.

[2] See above, p. 40.

called governors and sometimes *corregidores*.[1] There was no evident system behind the distinction, but whereas the Río de la Plata, Paraguay and Tucumán always had governors, Cuyo and the districts of Upper Perú were governed by *corregidores*. Certain empirical distinctions between the offices can be observed. The district administered by a governor was usually of greater territorial extent than the *corregimiento*, and its territory less definitely associated with a single town.[2] The status of a governor certainly ranked higher than that of a *corregidor*, and he normally fulfilled the office of captain-general of his district, which *corregidores* rarely did. In spite of these distinctions, however, the duties of both officials were roughly similar. They had two attributes, political and judicial: they were the highest political authorities in their districts, subordinate of course to the viceroy of Perú and the president of Charcas, and they were superior judges. As political governors, they had ample faculties for making decisions and taking action, certain powers of appointment, authority to report and recommend to the viceroy or to the crown on measures necessary to the well-being of their areas, and the right to preside over the *cabildos*. The actions of these officials were controlled by the *audiencia* of Charcas to whom individuals or *cabildos* could appeal against measures which they considered prejudicial to their rights, and also by their immediate superior, the viceroy, whose orders they had to obey; this latter control, however, was more nominal than real owing to the immense distances and slowness of communications between Lima and the Río de la Plata. In the Río de la Plata the governors maintained direct communications with the authorities in Spain from whom they received instructions without intervention of the distant viceroy; and shortly before 1776 they acquired, as has been seen, other attributes of autonomy.[3]

As superior judges in their districts these officials were magistrates of considerable status who had cognizance in causes

---

[1] The following account is based on J. M. Ots Capdequí, 'Trasplante en Indias de las instituciones castellanas y organización legal de Hispano-América hasta fines del siglo XVII', in *H.N.A.*, iii, 68–74; R. Zorraquín Becú, *La organización judicial argentina en el período hispánico* (Buenos Aires, 1952), pp. 44–7; and Haring, *The Spanish Empire in America*, pp. 138–42.

[2] Haring, *op. cit.*, p. 138.   [3] See above, p. 36.

of government, in matters of military law, and in the more important civil and criminal cases. They were judges of first instance for the district of their own capital, and judges of appeal from the decisions of the municipal magistrates, while there always remained the possibility of a third appeal to the *audiencia*. Unless the governor or *corregidor* were a qualified lawyer, he called in an assessor, or legal assistant, to conduct the trial of judicial cases.

This long-established system of provincial government was modified in two ways by the Ordinance of Intendants. It was given a clarity and uniformity which it had hitherto lacked; and above all, its officials were given greater scope for action. The Ordinance divided the viceroyalty of the Río de la Plata into eight intendancies which were to take their names from their capital cities, where the intendants would reside.[1] From the province of the Río de la Plata was created the intendancy of Buenos Aires, which was designated General Intendancy of Army and Province. The remaining intendancies had the status of provincial intendancies. They were as follows: Paraguay, whose capital was Asunción and whose territory embraced the bishopric of Paraguay, Villa Rica, Curuguay, and thirteen of the thirty *pueblos de misiones*; La Plata, with the territory of all the district of the archbishopric of Charcas, except Cochabamba and Potosí; Cochabamba which included jurisdiction over Santa Cruz de la Sierra; La Paz, comprising the bishopric of La Paz and the provinces of Carabaya, Lampa and Azangaro; Potosí, consisting of Porco, Chayanta, Atacama, Lipes, Chichas and Tarija.[2] Out of the former province of Tucumán two intendancies were created, Córdoba and Salta. Until now Córdoba had formed part of the province of Tucumán and had had only a lieutenant-governor with limited powers and no initiative in administration. The division of this unwieldy province had been contemplated for some time: a royal order of 6 June 1778 explained to viceroy Vértiz the necessity of such a division on account of the large distances involved (the province measured

[1] *Ord. Ints.*, art. 1.
[2] Ravignani, *op. cit.*, pp. 223–4. In 1785 Loreto with royal approval transferred to the intendancy of La Paz the districts of Sicasica and Pacajes from the intendancy of La Plata. A.G.I., Aud. de Buenos Aires 71, Loreto to Gálvez, 21 March 1785.

370 × 190 leagues), the dispersal of its tribunals and the difficulty it presented for administration by one individual, and asked him to submit advice and information on the project. Vértiz obtained this from the actual governor of Tucumán, Andrés Mestre, who recommended a division of the province into two: Salta should be the capital of one province which would include Jujuy, San Miguel del Tucumán, Santiago del Estero and Catamarca, while the other would be headed by Córdoba, with Rioja, Mendoza, San Luis and San Juan.[1] Vértiz forwarded these proposals to Madrid with his support on 26 January 1781.[2] The recommendations were given effect by the Ordinance of Intendants and by a further order of 29 July of the same year; these, however, assigned the capitals of the two provinces to San Miguel and Mendoza, an arrangement which was changed by royal *cédula* of 5 August 1783 when Salta and Córdoba were designated capitals.[3]

There were still further territorial adjustments to be made after the publication of the Ordinance. On 30 December 1783 viceroy Vértiz and superintendent Sanz submitted a joint report in which they suggested the addition of another intendancy in what were formerly called the provinces of Collao, embracing the districts of Puno, Lampa, Chucuito, Azangaro, and Carabaya, as this territory was too extensive to be included in the one intendancy of La Paz and too heavy a burden for one intendant. The authorities in Madrid were convinced by this reasoning, and by royal order of 5 June 1784 a ninth intendancy was created with its capital in Puno. Thus from 1784 to 1796, when the intendancy of Puno was transferred to the more proximate jurisdiction of the viceroyalty of Perú, the viceroyalty of the Río de la Plata had nine intendancies. The creation of the *audiencia* of Cuzco in 1787 complicated this situation, for although most of its district lay in the viceroyalty of Perú, it was also assigned jurisdiction in the three districts of Acabaya, Lampa and Azangaro, which lay in the intendancy of Puno and in the viceroyalty of the Río de la Plata. Thus one part of the intendancy of Puno recognized the *audiencia* of Cuzco and therefore by

[1] A.G.I., Aud. de Buenos Aires 50, Mestre to Vértiz, 24 December 1780.
[2] A.G.I., Aud. de Buenos Aires 50, Vértiz to Gálvez, 26 January 1781.
[3] *Ord. Ints.*, art. 1; *D.G.I.E.A.*, i, 31, note 2.

inference the viceroy of Lima, while the other part looked to Charcas and Buenos Aires.[1] By royal *cédula* of 1 February 1796 this problem was solved by the incorporation of Puno into the viceroyalty of Perú. In 1793 intendant Viedma of Cochabamba requested that an additional intendancy should be created for Santa Cruz in order to strengthen government there and control a tyrannous and independent creole class of *alcaldes ordinarios*.[2] His suggestion, however, made no progress.

At the beginning of November 1783 the titles and appointments of the first intendants were issued. To Salta was appointed Andrés Mestre, the existing governor; the Marqués de Sobremonte, secretary of the viceroyalty, to Córdoba; governor Pedro Melo to Paraguay; Ignacio Flores to La Plata, where he would combine the office of intendant with that of president of the *audiencia*; Francisco de Viedma, the actual governor of Santa Cruz de la Sierra, to Cochabamba; Sebastián de Segurola to La Paz; Juan del Pino Manrique, the actual governor, to Potosí.[3] By appointment of 24 March 1783 Francisco de Paula Sanz replaced Fernández as superintendent of the viceroyalty. On 25 November 1783 viceroy Vértiz issued a proclamation for the whole of the viceroyalty, ordering the inhabitants to recognize as their immediate chiefs the new governors-intendant, and informing the Indians of the end of the forced *repartimientos* of merchandise.[4] He then distributed the first thirty copies of the Ordinance to arrive from Madrid to the intendants, the sub-treasuries, the *cabildo* of Buenos Aires, the governor of Montevideo and the *audiencia* of Charcas.[5]

The intendants were given charge in their provinces of the four departments of justice, general administration, finance and war, with due subordination to and dependence on the viceroy and the *audiencia* according to the distinction of duties, the nature of the cases, and the matters within their cognizance.[6] But

---

[1] A.G.I., Indif. General 1713, Machado to Nestares, Madrid, 17 April 1789.

[2] Viedma to Arrendondo, 2 March 1793, in P. de Angelis, *Colección de obras y documentos relativos a la historia antigua y moderna de las provincias del Río de la Plata* (2nd edn., 5 vols., Buenos Aires, 1910), ii, 515.

[3] For biographical details of the intendants see Appendix I.

[4] Ravignani, *op. cit.*, pp. 223–4.

[5] A.G.I., Aud. de Buenos Aires 66, Vértiz to Gálvez, 31 December 1783.

[6] *Ord. Ints.*, art. 6.

although the viceroy was the political and military superior of the intendants, in matters of finance the latter were responsible to the superintendent in Buenos Aires, who, apart from being an ordinary intendant in his own province, was also the financial chief of the viceroyalty and as such responsible directly to Madrid.[1] All the old political units of the viceroyalty, the *corregimientos* and other governments, except those of Montevideo and the thirty towns of the former Jesuit missions, were to be suppressed when they became vacant or when the existing officials had completed their five years' term of office; meanwhile these officials were to be immediately subordinate to the intendants of their district and would be regarded as his subdelegates. In the excepted regions the departments of justice and general administration remained united to the department of war, and a military governor controlled the administration of these districts.[2]

Together with Montevideo and the *pueblos de misiones*, the provinces of Mojos and Chiquitos also continued as military governments outside the intendant system and immediately subordinate to the viceroy. All four were significant exceptions to the régime because they were distant frontier regions where contiguity with Portuguese territory demanded a specialized military government. The military governors differed from the new intendants in that whereas the latter had authority in the four departments of government and exercised the ecclesiastical vice-patronage in their districts, the former had jurisdiction in matters of war, *policía* and justice only. In finance the governor of Montevideo was subject to the intendant of Buenos Aires, and the governor of the Misiones to both the intendant of Buenos Aires and the intendant of Paraguay.[3] The governors of Mojos and Chiquitos were subordinate in exchequer matters to the superintendent and in economic affairs—industry, agriculture and commerce—to the *audiencia* of Charcas.[4]

[1] *Ord. Ints.*, arts. 2–3.
[2] *Ibid.*, arts. 6–7.
[3] See below, pp. 111–13, 191–95.
[4] Viedma to Arredondo, 2 March 1793, in Angelis, *Colección*, ii, 420. See also Fisher, *Intendant system*, p. 21.

II

The successful operation of the Ordinance of Intendants depended ultimately on the quality of the intendants themselves. To obtain a high standard among its new officials the crown adopted many devices. The appointment of intendants was retained exclusively in its own hands.[1] Only in the case of sudden vacancy through death could the viceroy appoint an intendant, and then the appointment was merely a temporary one until the royal nominee arrived; in such an event the viceroy was advised to take the opinion of the *audiencia* and the superintendent before acting.[2] At the same time it was the royal intention to break completely with the tradition of ill-paid officials, and to assign to the intendants salaries commensurate with their status and duties, which would at once remove temptations and maintain them in dignity. A salary of 10,000 pesos was assigned to the superintendent and 6,000 to each of the provincial intendants, except the intendant of Potosí who, since he had other offices such as the directorship of the royal mint, was granted a salary of 10,000 pesos.[3] In addition, by article 15 of the royal *cédula* of 5 August 1783 the intendants were allowed a further 600 pesos for the expenses of a secretary. For reasons of exchequer, however, it proved impossible to maintain this standard of remuneration: a royal order of 11 May 1792 forbade any further applications for salary increases,[4] and decrees of 12 September 1792 and 7 February 1797 reduced the salaries of intendants to 4,000 pesos, although this was not to affect existing incumbents.[5]

[1] *Ord. Ints.*, art. 1.

[2] A.G.I., Aud. de Buenos Aires 44, Crown to Loreto, 9 February 1784, Instrucción de gobierno, art. 25.

[3] *Ord. Ints.*, art. 273. The salaries of the intendants of New Spain were higher still: 12,000 pesos were assigned to the superintendent, while the salaries of provincial intendants varied between 7,000 and 5,000. *Ord. Ints.* . . . . *Nueva España*, art. 303, in Fisher, *Intendant system*, p. 328.

[4] *D.G.I.E.A.*, i, 95, notes 1 and 3.

[5] A.G.I., Aud. de Buenos Aires 48, R.O. 12 September 1792 and 7 February 1797. In 1804 Domingo Reynoso, intendant elect for Buenos Aires, claimed that his proposed salary of 5,000 pesos a year was inadequate to maintain a dignified standard of living, least of all in Buenos Aires which, he argued, had the highest cost of living in South America. A.G.I., Aud. de Buenos Aires 86, Reynoso to Minister of Grace and Justice, 10 April 1804. His request was refused.

Various checks and controls were applied to assure honesty and efficiency on the part of the intendants. In view of their authority and responsibility, especially in financial matters, they were required to give bond to the amount of 10,000 pesos.[1] This provision had been severely criticized by Vértiz and Fernández in their joint report on the Ordinance.[2] They regarded the bond as an extremely heavy one which the intendant would have difficulty in raising; he would have to find a wealthy subject to stand surety for him, and experience in Perú had shown that such guarantors, usually merchants or mine owners, regarded themselves as exempt from taxation and expected privileged treatment; if the intendant did not respond to this expectation he would be subject to obstruction and calumny, all too common in this region, while if he tried to pay the bond out of his own salary he would be financially crippled.[3] These arguments made little impression at court: it was decided that as the first intendants were going to be appointed from the existing governors they would not be obliged to give surety, but that their successors, unless excepted by special royal favour, would have to comply with the Ordinance.[4]

In Spanish colonial administration the classical means of controlling the actions of distant officials was the *residencia*, or judicial review of an official's conduct at the end of his term of office by a specially designated commissioner. This device was applied to the intendants by the Ordinance,[5] though once again not without the opposition of Vértiz and Fernández, who argued that if possible another means of control should be adopted in place of the *residencia* which was often a means of inviting revenge against a governor of integrity.[6] This advice was not accepted: it was decided to retain the *residencia* system as the traditional means whereby the subject could obtain justice against dishonest or despotic officials, though with the

---

[1] *Ord. Ints.*, art. 274.

[2] See above pp. 59–60.

[3] A.G.I., Aud. de Buenos Aires 354, Vértiz and Fernández to Gálvez, Carta 684, 15 February 1783.

[4] R.C. 5 August 1783, art. 15, in *D.G.I.E.A.*, i, 95, n. 3.

[5] *Ord. Ints.*, art. 275.

[6] A.G.I., Aud. de Buenos Aires 354, Vértiz and Fernández to Gálvez, Carta 684, 15 February 1783.

proviso that the king would exempt those of good repute.[1] By inference most of the intendants of the viceroyalty of the Río de la Plata were considered of good repute: judging by the extant records of *residencias* only four intendants, Sanz, Pino Manrique, Mestre and Alós, appear to have undergone judgment, and none of them was compromised. The *residencia* on Francisco de Paula Sanz after his term of office as superintendent was taken by Martín José de Asco, governor elect of the province of Guarochiri in Perú; the procedure was uncomplicated, and after considering the evidence the judge commended Sanz's service and declared him innocent of any charge.[2]

Intendant Alós of Paraguay had to undergo *residencia* in 1797, his judge being Vicente Martínez Fontes, accountant of the tobacco revenue for Paraguay. Not only was Alós himself judged but also his secretary, clerks and servants, the *alcaldes*, *regidores* and all the other officials in Asunción who had been in office during his régime. Evidence was taken in various towns of the intendancy on whether Alós had exercised his command in accordance with the laws, whether he had made his proper visitations, whether he had devoted due attention to the *pueblos de misiones*, whether he had preserved public morality, appointed to offices impartially, engaged in commerce or wronged anyone.[3] The judge published a proclamation inviting anyone in the province with complaints against the intendant or any of the other officials to come forward within the usual sixty days.[4] Subsidiary officials, commissioned by the judge, took evidence in each town. The whole process was a routine affair, and no scandal emerged: there were a few complaints, mainly of partial appointments, and some recommendations.[5] In this case the judge pronounced no verdict but simply forwarded all the evidence to the crown.

In view of the fact that only four out of the thirty-five intendants seem to have undergone judgment, it cannot be said that the requirement of the *residencia* was rigidly enforced in the era of the intendants in the viceroyalty of the Río de la Plata. It is

[1] Ravignani, *op. cit.*, p. 240.
[2] Archivo Histórico Nacional, Madrid, Consejo de Indias, leg. 20410/4/1, fols. 261-2, 16 February 1790.
[3] A.H.N., Consejo de Indias, leg. 20413/3, fols. 1-2.
[4] *Ibid.*, fols. 5-6.   [5] *Ibid.*, fols. 27, 183-99.

true that a royal decree of 24 August 1799 demanded the *residencia* only of political officials below the rank of intendant if complaints against them had reached the *audiencia* or president,[1] but even before this the *residencia* had played no significant part in the intendant system.

The sense of responsibility induced by the payment of bond and at least the possibility of a *residencia* was reinforced by the obligation upon the intendant to report his actions in regular correspondence with the authorities in Madrid and with the viceroy. Methods of communication between the intendants and their superiors were established by trial and error. An intendant had the right to communicate directly with the king through his Minister of the Indies: this was called *por la vía reservada*. The government, however, did not wish the intendants thereby to bypass the viceroy, nor to abuse the *vía reservada* with unimportant detail which could take the normal channels. Intendant Sobremonte of Córdoba sent his first report directly to Gálvez, the Minister of the Indies. The latter confirmed the intendant's right to do so, but ordered that he should also give account to his more immediate chiefs, the viceroy and the superintendent, and should dispatch by the *vía reservada* only that which he considered important and urgent enough to reach the prompt notice of the crown.[2]

Administrative checks would mean little, however, unless men of quality were appointed to staff the new offices. The status and salary were attractive,[3] and when an intendancy was known to be vacant or about to be vacated there would be many applications for the post from soldiers, career administrators, former *corregidores*, subdelegates and others, from without as well as from within the viceroyalty. When the intendancy of La Paz, for example, became vacant on the death of intendant Segurola in 1789 there were nine applicants for the position;

[1] Haring, *op. cit.*, p. 151, n. 20.

[2] A.G.I., Aud. de Buenos Aires 50, Gálvez to Sobremonte, 5 December 1785, and R.O. 7 August 1786.

[3] Intendant Pino Manrique, however, complained that considering the high cost of living in Potosí his salary was inadequate, and that the lot of an intendant in that remote and chilly spot 'was like that of a minister exiled to Siberia, because the rigorous climate of this intemperate region differs little from the cold of that country'. Pino Manrique to Gálvez, 16 February 1783, printed in G. René-Moreno, 'El Alto-Perú en 1783', *Revista Chilena*, viii (1877), pp. 207–34.

the royal choice, however, was not restricted to applicants, and in this case none of them obtained the appointment. In spite of the notorious nepotism of José de Gálvez, Minister of the Indies, the government of Charles III had a record of making good appointments to offices. The material from which they could choose was limited. There was no trained civil service, no system of competitive examinations. A man had to attract the royal notice either by influence at court or by outstanding performance in the royal service. As the latter was most easily accomplished in the army, this was a useful opening to higher things, and in fact most of the intendants in the viceroyalty of the Río de la Plata graduated to their political posts from a military career. This did not necessarily mean that they brought to their offices purely military qualities, for as the army was one of the few careers possible for the upper and middle classes in Spain it naturally attracted men who had general ability and intelligence. There was, it is true, a good supply of trained lawyers in Spain, but these seem to have preferred appointments to *audiencias* rather than to intendancies.

As a class the intendants of the viceroyalty of the Río de la Plata were men of competence and integrity, though not of brilliance nor even of political leadership.[1] It is true that three of them, Pedro Melo de Portugal, Joaquín del Pino and the Marqués de Sobremonte, of aristocratic lineage, became viceroys of the Río de la Plata, but none was an outstanding success in this more exacting rôle: indeed Sobremonte, at the moment of crisis when an English expedition invaded the Río de la Plata (1806–7), became quite incapable of constructive action, and the difference between his remarkable record as an intendant and his failure as a viceroy is the measure of the difference between administrators, which the intendants were, and leaders, which they were not. The same judgment can be made of intendant Pizarro who had a long and worthy career as a competent administrator in various posts but failed lamentably to cope with the revolutionary situation in Chuquisaca in 1808–9.

The social composition of the intendant class in the Río de la Plata was orthodox. Intendants were recruited from the middle

[1] The following generalizations are based on the biographical material contained in Appendix I.

class and from the lower ranks of the aristocracy, the traditional source of supply for Spanish administrators. Of those on whom it is possible to fix a professional label, seventeen were army officers, most of whom had given distinguished service in Europe and America, three were naval officers, three were lawyers and three could be described as professional administrators, one of whom was from the financial service. Although it was the royal intention to break completely with the infamous *corregidor* system, two of the intendants were former *corregidores*. The administration of Joaquín de Alós as *corregidor* in the province of Chayanta in Upper Perú had come under suspicion in connection with the native discontent leading to the rising of 1780; after trial and vindication he was appointed second intendant of Paraguay where he rendered efficient service, though it must be admitted that such an appointment in the early years of the intendant system was hardly reassuring to native opinion.

To assist him in local administration an intendant had subordinate officials called subdelegates, who were put in charge of *partidos* or subdistricts within the intendancy. These subdelegates of the royal exchequer were also generally *comandantes de armas*, and combined with their revenue and administrative powers those of chiefs of the local militia. They were executors of the orders of the intendants in the three departments of general administration, exchequer and war, and also had authority to hear contentious cases in matters of exchequer and war, but only to the extent of preparing them for judicial decision, in which form they had to be submitted to the intendant of the province for judgment.[1] The subdelegates had much the same jurisdiction over municipal finance in the towns of their district as the intendants had in the capital of the province.[2] These officials were unpaid, but as remuneration for collecting the tribute tax they received 3 per cent of the amount which entered the treasury from this revenue. At first the subdelegates were appointed by their own intendant, but gradually this power of the intendant was circumscribed. By royal order of 25 October 1787 the intendants were ordered to give notice of the appointments they made to the viceroy for his countersignature and to the *audiencia* for its information.[3] In 1792

[1] *Ord. Ints.*, art. 73.   [2] *Ibid.*, art. 38.   [3] *D.G.I.E.A.*, i, 44.

power of appointing subdelegates was transferred definitely to the viceroy: the intendants proposed three names to the viceroy (*propuesta en terna*) who would choose one on the list; the king's approval was then needed.[1] In the absence of the viceroy the *audiencia* would appoint subdelegates upon presentation by the intendant; for example in the interregnum between the death of viceroy Pino and the appointment of Sobremonte the *audiencia* of Buenos Aires appointed subdelegates for Cochabamba.[2] In this way any autonomy which the intendants had in the early days of the system in the matter of appointments was diminished, and the traditional Spanish policy of administrative checks and balances was reaffirmed.

When the new régime was established in Potosí intendant Pino Manrique published for his subdelegates an *Instrucción* in which he explained to them their duties in the four departments of government in the light of the Ordinance of Intendants.[3] As this Instruction received royal approval, it gives an indication of the sort of rôle expected of the subdelegates. There had to be no delay in the administration of justice, and they were to apply the Laws of the Indies and of Castile, being particularly zealous in maintaining peace between the Spaniards and the Indians. As for public administration, they were particularly enjoined to collect and forward economic and social information, to encourage industry and agriculture, and to promote public building. In matters of exchequer they were reminded that the management of royal revenues was under the exclusive authority of the intendant whose subdelegates they were, and while they could prepare the material in exchequer cases in their districts they were to see that all such cases went to the intendant for judgment and to no other tribunal. If they had any doubt or difficulty in the exercise of their jurisdiction they were to consult their intendant.

[1] R.O. 19 January 1792, in *ibid.*, i, 33. It was also laid down that a subdelegate must serve for five years only, and could not be dismissed without cause before royal decision.
[2] A.G.I., Aud. Buenos Aires 152, Audiencia of Buenos Aires to Caballero, 28 April 1804.
[3] A.G.I., Aud. de Buenos Aires 354, Instrucción metódica para el Régimen y Gobierno de los subdelegados de esta Intendencia de Potosí, y su Provincia, 28 January 1784.

An unpaid position in remote areas populated almost entirely by Indians was an unattractive prospect, and for this reason it was difficult to find suitable candidates for the subdelegacies, least of all from among Spaniards, to whom the office was legally confined.[1] President-intendant Flores of La Plata considered the problem of the subdelegates the most critical of the whole system of intendants. He pointed out that what the government was really seeking were honorary unpaid officials of decent eduation and with some standing in their district; but even if such men existed in every area, they would not be prepared to serve in subordinate offices far from the main centres of civilization. Flores considered that subdelegates ought to be assigned a reasonable and official salary.[2] This warning was echoed from many quarters. In 1784 intendant Pino Manrique of Potosí reported that he considered it essential for subdelegates to be granted a fixed salary, otherwise worthy candidates would not be found found.[3] In the same year visitor-general Escobedo made the same criticism from Lima and prophesied the return of the practices of the *corregidores*.[4] These are only a few examples of widespread complaints, and soon subdelegates came under heavy criticism for their corruption, inefficiency and oppressive behaviour. As early as 1784, for example, the bishop of Santa Cruz was protesting about what he called the low and unsuitable character of most of the subdelegates of Cochabamba;[5] Viedma changed the appointments, but not with entire success, for he was later (1789–9) involved in a vociferous dispute with the subdelegate of Arque, Juan Álvarez de Arenales, whom he accused of usurpation of tribute revenue and exploitation of the Indians.[6] The crown tried to maintain standards by insisting that its approval must be obtained for all appointments, by demanding that proper reports on the merits and

[1] *Ord. Ints.*, art. 9. Subdelegates had to be 'precisamente españoles'.
[2] A.G.I., Aud. de Buenos Aires 354, Flores to Gálvez, 15 January 1784.
[3] B.M., Egerton MS 1815, fol. 168, Pino Manrique to Loreto, 16 October 1784 (copy).
[4] B.M., Egerton MS 1815, fol. 181, Escobedo to Loreto, 16 December 1784 (eopy). In the province of Oaxaca in New Spain it appeared that the subdelegates were still making *repartimientos* to the Indians. See A.G.I., Indif. General 1713, Consulta del Consejo, 2 December 1801.
[5] A.G.I., Aud. de Buenos Aires 140, Viedma to Gálvez, 3 November 1784.
[6] A.G.I., Aud. de Charcas 424, Consulta del Consejo, 29 April 1806.

services of candidates be submitted for its information, and by
rejecting candidates whom it considered unsuitable; at the
same time the viceroys were ordered to adhere to this procedure.[1] But at the subdelegate level what Spanish government
really suffered from was the lack of a creole administrative class
from which it could recruit minor officials; and this defect
was itself the result of an official policy which consistently
debarred creoles from political service, a policy which continued to the end of the colonial régime.

Appointments to the posts of intendant and subdelegate were
legally reserved to peninsula-born Spaniards, who now, as
always, monopolized the highest offices in Church and State,
and who were regarded as the bulwark of Spanish rule in
America. It is true that the first intendant of La Plata, Ignacio
Flores, was a native of Quito, but his case was exceptional. He
was appointed not by the king but by viceroy Vértiz, who,
faced with the task of filling the presidency of the *audiencia* of
Charcas, chose a man who had given outstanding service in the
recent native rebellions in Upper Perú and could be relied upon
to restore order and tranquillity there. Being a viceregal
appointment it was only a temporary one, was never confirmed
and, in fact, was soon terminated.[2] It is significant perhaps that
Vértiz himself was American-born:[3] certainly he showed a
partiality towards the integration of the creole classes into the
Spanish political system. But the authorities must have viewed
the application of such a policy with some misgivings. For while
Vértiz appointed a creole to an intendancy, Flores himself
appointed creoles to subdelegacies within his intendancy. This
sudden vertical intrusion into a closed bureaucracy was too
much to be tolerated: after Vértiz's departure from Buenos
Aires Flores was pursued with vindictiveness by the new viceroy, Loreto, and by the *audiencia* of Charcas. In a report to
Madrid on the quality of his subordinate Loreto declared himself unsatisfied with his intelligence and style of reporting, suspicious of his tact and diplomacy, and convinced that he was
unsuitable for the government of so remote a district 'where my

[1] A.G.I., Aud. de Charcas 430, R.O. to viceroy of Buenos Aires, 26 June 1796.
[2] See below, Chapter X.
[3] See J. Torre Revello, *Juan José de Vértiz y Salcedo, gobernador y virrey de Buenos
Aires* (Buenos Aires, 1932).

influence can hardly reach. . . .'[1] Flores' appointments to sub-delegacies were also under suspicion: in April 1785 Minister Gálvez ordered the viceroy secretly to investigate and report on the appointments made by Flores.[2] Loreto commissioned intendant Segurola of the neighbouring intendancy of La Paz to make a discreet inquiry into the situation. This Segurola did, and his report was the sort of thing Loreto was only too anxious to hear: Flores had appointed as his *teniente asesor*, or legal assistant, a mulatto, Juan Josef de Segovia, a man whom Segurola described as 'discolo, audaz, intruso, y codicioso', with a reputation for subversion, though admittedly capable in his own profession.[3] Apart from this, three of Flores' sub-delegates were creoles, and all of them men of meagre abilities.[4] This report confirmed the official prejudice against Flores; his tenure of office was made as uncomfortable as possible and he was soon relieved of it.[5]

This incident, occurring at the very beginning of the intendant system, can be regarded as a test case for the attitude of the Spanish authorities towards the employment of creoles.[6] American-born subjects were still not trusted for political appointments involving any authority or responsibility. Such an attitude, while it was due in large part to a consciousness of class and social distinctions, and a contempt for the colonial-born Spaniard, also arose out of a genuine desire to preserve standards of government, for the creole class, ill-educated and far from disinterested, had no record of administrative efficiency and still less of concern for the Indians. In 1793 intendant Viedma reported from Cochabamba:

---

[1] A.G.I., Aud. de Buenos Aires 68, Loreto to Gálvez, 8 October 1784.

[2] A.G.I., Aud. de Buenos Aires 354, R.O. 3 April 1785.

[3] A.G.I., Aud. de Buenos Aires 354, Segurola to Loreto, 5 October 1785. Segovia was soon replaced by a royal nominee.

[4] A.G.I., Aud. de Buenos Aires 354, Segurola to Loreto, 6 December 1785.

[5] See below, Chapter X.

[6] Spaniards differed in their classification of social variations. Reporting on the social composition of Potosí in 1787 intendant Pino Manrique described it as follows: 'The greater part of the neighbourhood consists of Indians and *cholos*: of these some come to serve in the *mita* and once they have completed their stint they return to their district; while others who are called creoles are settled in the town and maintain themselves by their work. Another part is of European and American Spaniards who work in commerce, mines, as engineers, storekeepers. . . .' Pino Manrique to Loreto, 6 December 1787, in Angelis, *Colección*, ii, 7.

as the government and administration of justice has devolved upon the *alcaldes ordinarios*, who are natives of the country [*hijos de la patria*] and in many cases related by marriage to each other, they become despots, oppressing the poor and unfortunate; and although the cries of the latter reach the intendant who resides in Cochabamba, his orders are not very effective on account of the distance.[1]

Quite apart from this evidence, however, Viedma had a prejudiced attitude towards creoles which deserves quoting as typical of the Spanish point of view:

For these positions [political appointments] natives of the country are not suitable, because they are extremely difficult to dissuade from the customary ways ingrained in them even in contravention of the laws; they lack that mode of thinking, at once pure, sincere and impartial, prevalent in Spain, and even Spaniards who live for some time in these parts come to acquire the same or worse customs.[2]

Nevertheless, what was not conceded in principle often had to be granted in practice, and the shortage of Spaniards willing to take humble and unpaid assignments in unattractive regions meant that an intendant had sometimes no alternative to nominating a creole for a subdelegacy. Even intendant Viedma could not avoid it: in 1797 all three of the candidates proposed by Viedma to the viceroy for the *partido* of Hayspaya were American-born.[3] There were other examples of similar procedure.[4] There was, however, always a basic assumption in favour of Spaniards, and if of three candidates one was a Spaniard he would invariably obtain the appointment, regardless of the qualifications of the other two candidates.[5]

[1] Viedma to Arredondo, 2 March 1793, in Angelis, *Colección*, ii, 515. It was in this context that Viedma advocated the creation of another intendancy based on Santa Cruz.

[2] A.G.I., Aud. de Buenos Aires 140, Viedma to Gálvez, 3 November 1784.

[3] A.G.I., Aud. de Buenos Aires 85, Viedma, Propuesto en terna, 1797.

[4] In 1797 president-intendant Pino of La Plata submitted three creole candidates for a subdelegacy. See documents reproduced in *Revista del Archivo General de Buenos Aires*, iv (1872), pp. 245–6. In 1798 president-intendant Pizarro submitted three creoles for nomination to the viceroy. See A.G.I., Aud. de Buenos Aires 83, Pizarro, Propuesta en terna, 1798.

[5] Of the three candidates nominated for the *partido* of Paria in the intendancy of La Plata in 1798, the first, a Spaniard, was chosen against the other two who were creoles. A.G.I., Aud. de Buenos Aires 83, Propuesta en terna, 1798. The same thing happened in 1796 for the subdelegacy of Cinti in the intendancy of La Plata when one of the creole candidates clearly had superior legal qualifications. *Ibid.*, Pino, Propuesta en terna, 25 December 1796.

Yet the policy of Charles III did grant some recognition, however tentative, to creole aspirations, and a small place was found for Americans within the intendant system. In offering his opinion on the Ordinance of Intendants in 1783 viceroy Vértiz directed government attention towards this problem:

From the experience we have of the country and of the character of its inhabitants, it would be extremely convenient to attract the interest of the native Spaniards [*Españoles naturales de el*] in order that this new plan may be more readily accepted, for we know how persistently they clamoured to be employed in departments of revenue and exchequer for the support of their poor yet distinguished families; we are convinced that it would be very expedient to employ those of good education and judgment in subordinate exchequer posts, some qualified lawyers of ability as legal assistants to the intendants, and other worthy subjects in other positions. . . .[1]

The suggestion was taken up by the authorities in Madrid, and given effect by royal order of 5 August 1783 as article 17 of the seventeen supplementary resolutions appended to the Ordinance; this explained the desire of His Majesty to attend to the American-born Spaniards and to choose the best among them as legal assistants to the intendants, providing they were qualified, as well as others of good education and character for subaltern positions in exchequer offices; but they would have to serve outside the provinces of their birth.[2] In practice there were many examples of such appointments, especially during the régime of viceroy Vértiz.

III

The Ordinance of Intendants introduced certain modifications in the administration of justice in the colony. Apart from the fact that the intendants were not always lawyers, they could not be expected to cope with all the legal work involved in the administration of an intendancy.[3] After the suppression of the governors and *corregidores*, 'the royal jurisdiction had to devolve

---

[1] A.G.I., Aud. de Buenos Aires 354, Vértiz and Fernández to Gálvez, Carta 684, 15 February 1783.

[2] Ravignani, *op. cit.*, p. 240.

[3] In the early days of his tenure in Buenos Aires, superintendent Fernández had had to ask for an assessor to assist him. See A.G.I., Aud. de Buenos Aires 355, Fernández to Gálvez, Carta 102, 6 August 1779.

upon the respective intendants as chief justices of their provinces, but without prejudice to the authority belonging to the *alcaldes ordinarios*.[1] This clause, however, must not be interpreted literally. As regards ordinary civil and criminal law the intendants lacked authentic juridical attributes, since they only exercised this power through the medium of the lieutenant-lawyers or assessors (*tenientes letrados o asesores*), who were created precisely to exercise for them 'jurisdiction over civil and criminal litigation in the capital of their particular territory'.[2] These lawyers were at the same time ordinary assessors in all the administrative business of the intendancy, exercising the authority of the intendant in his absence.[3] They had to be examined and approved by the *audiencias*, and were appointed by the king from three candidates presented by the Council of the Indies.[4] The provincial assessors were assigned salaries of 1,500 pesos plus perquisites,[5] and the assessors of the superintendent 2,000 plus perquisites. They were appointed for a term of five years, though the king could prolong it if he thought fit, and they could not be removed without cause.[6] Appeals from their judicial sentences went to the *audiencia*, but it was emphasized that they were never to be deprived of their cognizance in judicial matters since they received their titles from the king and were responsible for their decisions.[7] A royal *cédula* of 22 August 1793 declared that intendants (and other officials) for whom assessors had been appointed would not be held responsible for

[1] *Ord. Ints.*, art. 8.
[2] *Ibid.*, art. 12.
[3] This simply formalized existing practice, since the *asesores letrados* of the former governors were in fact the real judges in the province; their opinions were generally accepted by the governors. See R. Zorraquín Becú, *op. cit.*, p. 99, n. 76. If the intendant and his assessor both died or were incapable then the senior minister of the treasury in the province would temporarily perform the functions of intendant. In the case of death of the intendant the viceroy could appoint a temporary intendant. R.C. 5 August 1783, in *D.G.I.E.A.*, i, 34, n. 1. For subsequent changes see *ibid.*, i, 34, n. 2.
[4] But this did not prevent intendants recommending candidates to the Minister, as Rivera of Paraguay did in 1805. See A.G.I., Aud. de Buenos Aires 140, Rivera to Caballero, 19 September 1805.
[5] But 1,000 pesos of this were to be paid from municipal funds; as Escobedo pointed out this would be in some cases an unreliable source for an official's salary. A.G.I., Aud. de Lima, Voto particular de Jorge Escobedo en el Expte. de Intendencias, 23 November 1801.
[6] *Ord. Ints.*, art. 13.   [7] *Ibid.*, art. 14.

the decisions or sentences which they gave on the advice of the assessors. When intendants did not agree with their assessors they could suspend the decisions of sentence and consult the superior authority.[1]

The jurisdiction of the lieutenant-lawyers was confined to the capital of the intendancy. Consequently, as the Ordinance made no provision for the appointment of lawyers in the provincial towns and districts, the judicial powers which had previously been enjoyed by the lieutenants of the governors devolved upon the *alcaldes ordinarios*, who thus became the sole judges of first instance in their districts.[2] To replace the former lieutenants in the exercise of powers in the departments of administration, exchequer and war, subdelegates were created as has been seen. These officials, however, only had judicial attributes in matters of exchequer and war, for civil and criminal litigation was the province of the *alcaldes ordinarios*. This arrangement was not without defects. In 1792 intendant Sobremonte of Córdoba reported to the viceroy his opinion that the subdelegates ought to exercise jurisdiction in all four departments, that is in justice and general administration as well as in exchequer and war. In this way they would be able to act as veritable deputies of the intendants in their districts, and thus put more energy into local government, a thing which the *alcaldes ordinarios* by virtue of their preoccupation with their own private affairs were unable to do. Sobremonte also argued that it was extremely difficult to procure subdelegates on these terms.[3] Similar complaints were made by the intendants of Salta and Paraguay, but the Council of the Indies advised that no change be made.[4]

As heads of the department of justice the intendants had various functions to perform. They or their lieutenants presided over all municipal councils and public functions of their capitals. They were enjoined to study the laws of the Indies carefully, in order to provide good administration of justice. They were especially charged to protect the Indians and to prevent local officials tyrannizing over them as the *alcaldes mayores* had done,

[1] Fisher, *op. cit.*, pp. 34–5.
[2] See below, Chapter IX.
[3] A.G.I., Aud. de Buenos Aires 13, Consulta de Negocios Seculares, 1798.
[4] A.G.I., Aud. de Buenos Aires 80, Arredondo to Acuña, 23 May 1793.

referring them for correction to a superior tribunal if necessary. They were to ensure that the local magistrates did not delay judicial cases or exact excessive revenues.[1]

In effect, the contentious jurisdiction in exchequer matters which until then had been exercised by the exchequer officials was transferred to the exclusive cognizance of the intendants in their respective provinces, with appeal only to the *junta superior de hacienda*. The same applied to matters of the tobacco revenue, gunpowder and playing cards, and to cases of shipwrecks, contraband, vessels seeking refuge, and unclaimed property of any kind.[2] The intendants were also sole judges in litigation which occurred in the sale, composition and distribution of royal lands or private domains. In this way the intendants assumed an exclusive jurisdiction in all matters in which for reasons of exchequer or of public interest the crown had a special interest in assuring that justice was administered by its own agents, reserving to the king through the medium of the respective minister cognizance of the case in third instance. And as the decisions of the intendants were appealable in all such matters before the *junta superior de hacienda*,[3] the competence of the *audiencia* which had hitherto taken cognizance of these cases in second and third instance, was correspondingly limited. The hierarchy of officials and administrative centralization were thus firmly established by means of the new organization, which reached even to the most minute local units in that the intendants had to keep watch over the proper administration of justice with authority 'to call to attention their lieutenant-assessors, subdelegates, *alcaldes ordinarios* and other subordinate judges, in order to bring to their notice their duty and exhort them to perform it'.[4]

With the suppression of the superintendent of Buenos Aires in 1788 on account of the interference of his functions with those of the viceroy,[5] the faculties of this office passed to the viceroy, who henceforth exercised greater judicial powers than those normally falling to his charge, for he now had authority not only to decide military cases but also to judge the other matters assigned to the

---

[1] *Ord. Ints.*, arts. 15–18.   [2] *Ibid.*, arts. 76–7, 80, 212.
[3] On the *junta superior* see below, pp. 124–7.
[4] *Ord. Ints.*, art. 17.   [5] See below, pp. 104–5.

superintendent. But though the superintendency was suppressed, its lieutenant-lawyer remained in existence and continued to act as judge in cases of ordinary law within the intendancy of Buenos Aires. Later an intendant of Buenos Aires and its province was appointed with juridical attributes confined to the rural district of the city.[1]

The intendants also succeeded the former governors in jurisdiction in matters of military law. The subdelegates had to prepare the case and then remit it to the intendant who would pronounce sentence in accord with his assessor. He had similar jurisdiction, with appeal before the *junta superior*, in all cases arising out of provision of troops.[2] In military matters the intendants were given purely administrative functions: they had to look after the supply of the army, transport, food, pay and arms. The clauses in the Ordinance devoted to the department of war deal exclusively with these details, for the intendants were given no military authority and had no right of command in the field; in case of war the intendants were subordinate to the viceroy who was captain-general, and in his absence to the inspector-general of the army in the viceroyalty.

Finally, the intendants also had jurisdiction in certain matters which, though they were ecclesiastical in substance, formed part of secular law. They heard as judges of first instance all the cases arising out of the collection of alms imposed by the Bull of Crusade, with appeal to the *junta superior*, and in cases concerning *espolios* or property left by prelates, in which case the appeals went to the *audiencia* of the district.[3]

IV

In Spanish America the Church was under strict royal control.[4] In return for support given to the missionary enterprise of the early days of colonization, the papacy had granted to the crown the privilege of appointing to bishoprics and other benefices. By

---

[1] See below, pp. 108–10.

[2] *Ord. Ints.*, art. 247.

[3] *Ibid.*, arts. 148, 198.

[4] See L. Ayarragaray, *La iglesia en América y la dominación española* (Buenos Aires, 1935); J. Lloyd Mecham, *Church and State in Latin America* (Chapel Hill, 1934), pp. 1–44; Haring, *op. cit.*, pp. 179–82.

virtue of this right of patronage the Spanish crown considered itself exclusively responsible for the progress of religion in its colonies, to such an extent that the Church in America developed in direct dependence on the crown. But as the early missionary justification of this situation was forgotten or neglected, so the Church was subordinated more and more to the State, of which in practice it was regarded as a department or an instrument of policy, while its clergy were viewed as one class of royal officials among many. The Bourbon monarchs sought to consolidate their inheritance; the preservation of royal patronage in ecclesiastical affairs was always their concern.[1] It was natural, therefore, that Charles III in tightening the reins of royal government should assign the exercise of the vice-patronage to his new officials. And if the Ordinance of Intendants devoted less attention to the vice-patronage than previous legislative codes had done—only part of one article deals strictly with vice-patronage—this was not because of lack of interest but because the existing system was so well established that it could be taken for granted. The Ordinance simply stated that the ecclesiastical vice-patronage in the viceroyalty of the Río de la Plata was to be exercised by all the intendants except that of Buenos Aires where the viceroy was to hold it.[2]

Methods of presentation of clergy to ecclesiastical benefices were relatively simple. A bishop would present the names of three candidates with their merits and qualifications to the intendant. The latter would appoint an *asistente real*, a priest, who would set the necessary examinations, place the candidates, and report the result to the intendants. The intendant would then make his appointment and report his choice to the king.[3] Apart from this right of appointing to benefices the attributes of

[1] The instructions given to viceroy Loreto on his appointment in 1784 specifically enjoined him to preserve the Patronato Real; 'We charge you to take particular notice of the preservation of the Royal Patronage, ensuring that the prelates, ecclesiastical as well as monastic, do not infringe it but keep it exactly as it has been conceded to kings of Spain by the Holy Apostolic See.' A.G.I., Aud. de Buenos Aires 44, Crown to Loreto, Instrucción de Gobierno, art. 9, 9 February 1784.

[2] *Ord. Ints.*, art. 6. This clause also excepted La Plata where the president was to exercise it, but as he was also intendant of La Plata the distinction was not significant.

[3] A.G.I., Aud. de Buenos Aires 140, Viedma to Gálvez, 31 October 1785, reporting the election to a canonry in Santa Cruz.

the intendants also included authority to submit reports on the state of the clergy.[1] At the same time any ecclesiastical work which a bishop wished to perform, such as the building of a church or a college, needed royal approval. The procedure was that the bishop applied in the first instance to the intendant, seeking his support; the intendant submitted the matter to the viceroy, and the latter to the appropriate ministry in Madrid for royal approval.[2] In financial matters the Ordinance of Intendants directed that a *junta de diezmos* be appointed in the more important cities under the supervision of the intendants.[3] This *junta* was to make arrangements for the collection of the tithe within its district, generally farming it out to individuals who might not be ecclesiastics; but its faculties were purely administrative, for contentious jurisdiction was reserved to *jueces hacedores* with appeal to the *junta superior*.[4]

Difficulties soon appeared in the application of the vice-patronage within the intendant system. Intendancies did not necessarily coincide with dioceses, and this imprecision was to cause trouble. In 1785 intendant Sobremonte of Córdoba reported that he was encountering great difficulties in the exercise of the vice-patronage in Mendoza, San Juan and San Luis, which came under the ecclesiastical jurisdiction of the bishop of Chile, for it was difficult for the two authorities to work in harmony when the vice-patron resided in Córdoba and the bishop in Santiago de Chile. Another obstacle to good administration, reported Sobremonte, was the fact that the immense size of the diocese of Tucumán made proper ecclesiastical visitations almost impossible, a situation which was even worse in the district of Cuyo which belonged to the diocese of the bishop of Chile, for in addition to the 200 leagues' distance between Santiago and San Luis there was the *cordillera* of the

[1] See intendant Rivera's report on the irregular conduct of a priest in the district of Santiago, in A.G.I., Aud. de Buenos Aires 142, Rivera to Caballero, 19 January 1803, and his eulogy of bishop Videla of Paraguay, in A.G.I., Aud. de Buenos Aires 140, Rivera to Crown, 15 November 1805. See also Viedma to Arredondo 2 March 1793 in Angelis, *Colección*, ii, 493.

[2] See, e.g., the request of the bishop of Santa Cruz for permission to build a seminary, in A.G.I., Aud. de Buenos Aires 78, Arredondo to Porlier, art. 36, 25 November 1790.

[3] *Ord. Ints.*, art. 151.

[4] *Ibid.*, arts. 154–5.

Andes. Sobremonte therefore advised that the diocese of Tucumán should be divided into two, as a proper sequel to the division of the province of Tucumán into two intendancies.[1] In September 1791 the archbishop of Charcas criticized the system whereby the vice-patronage of his diocese was divided between the four governments of La Plata, Potosí, La Paz and Cochabamba, and advocated a return to former practice, whereby the president of the *audiencia* of Charcas exercised a united vice-patronage for the whole diocese. Meanwhile, antagonism between the intendants and the bishops in Perú, and to a certain extent in Mexico, raised many voices in criticism of the transfer of the functions of ecclesiastical patronage to the intendants.[2] Consequently a royal *cédula* of 9 May 1795 redefined the position: the vice-patronage was now granted to the intendants only as subdelegates of the respective proprietors, the viceroys and presidents, to whom was reserved absolute exercise in the district of the province in which they resided and the regalia of ecclesiastical presentation in all the other provinces.[3] The intendant of Potosí, resentful of this loss of regalia, interpreted the *cédula* after his own fashion, and using his assessor Cañete as spokesman, claimed that it only referred to temporary intendants, and that the vice-patronage devolved only on the viceroys and not on the presidents, who were no less subdelegates than the intendants.[4] Cañete published a paper to this effect which he circulated among the other intendants of Upper Perú and which drew from fiscal Villava of the *audiencia* of Charcas a declaration that in the matter of vice-patronage the intendants of Córdoba, Salta, and Paraguay were subdelegates of the viceroy of Buenos Aires, and the intendants of Potosí, La Paz, Cochabamba and Puno subdelegates of the president of the *audiencia* of Charcas.[5] This was a fair inference from the *cédula*, but Cañete accused Villava of interpreting the

[1] B.M. Egerton MS 1815, fols. 292–9, Sobremonte to Gálvez, 6 December 1785. (Duplicado.)
[2] Fisher, *op. cit.*, pp. 68–9, 84–6.
[3] *D.G.I.E.A.*, i, 32, n. 2r. This rule had already been established for Mexico in the Ordinance of Intendants for New Spain, 1786, art. 8, in Fisher, *op. cit.*, p. 104. It was now formulated for the whole of the empire. See A.G.I., Aud. de Charcas 589, R.C. 9 May 1795.
[4] A.G.I., Aud. de Charcas 589, Consulta del Consejo, 9 July 1796.
[5] A.G.I., Aud. de Charcas 589, Vista Fiscal, 6 October 1795.

royal message perversely and declared that the president, the fiscal, the archbishop and all the priests were united against the intendant. But this argument made no impression in Madrid, and a royal *cédula* 28 July 1796 reaffirmed the previous one of 1795.[1]

Certain institutions remained in practice outside the normal system of presentation. The University of Córdoba and the Royal College of Monserrat recognized as their vice-patron not the intendant of Córdoba, whom they refused any intervention in university affairs, but the viceroy of Buenos Aires. In spite of the representation of intendant Sobremonte to Buenos Aires and Madrid he could at first obtain no resolution on the matter. Viceroy Loreto maintained a firm opposition to his claims, pointing out that the previous governors had exercised the vice-patronage in their province but had never claimed it over the colleges.[2] In 1791, however, Sobremonte procured a declaration from viceroy Arredondo to the effect that the intendant could exercise the authority of vice-patron as commissioner of the viceroy. This jurisdiction included the right of presentation to university chairs and approval of university accounts.[3]

In Asunción del Paraguay the intendants had some difficulty in preserving intact the royal patronage. In October 1795 the *cabildo eclesiástico* invited applications for a vacant Chair of Philosophy in the Royal College of San Carlos, without stating that this was done by commission of the king; examinations were dispensed with and the appointment was given to a candidate who was not even a graduate. Intendant Alós informed the viceroy of this irregularity and the latter ordered the *cabildo* to make a new election which would clearly acknowledge royal patronage. But this made no impression on the *cabildo*, and intendant Rivera had to report that it had proceeded a second time in the same way.[4]

A notable dispute was the one between the intendant of Cochabamba and the bishop of La Paz over the appointment of

---

[1] A.G.I., Aud. de Charcas 589, R.C. 28 July 1796.

[2] A.G.I., Aud. de Buenos Aires 324, Loreto to Crown, 14 June 1787.

[3] Sobremonte, 'Memoria de Gobierno', printed in I. Garzon, *Crónica de Córdoba* (Buenos Aires, 1898), p. 382. For the ceremonial to be observed by the intendant in church see *ibid.*, p. 383.

[4] A.G.I., Aud. de Buenos Aires 48, Rivera to Crown, 23 February 1797.

a priest to a benefice.[1] In 1790 intendant Viedma appointed the second of the three candidates presented by the bishop, whereupon the latter protested to the crown against what he regarded as a slight to his dignity. Viedma argued that the vice-patron was under no obligation to choose the first-named candidate but only the most suitable one. Out of this disagreement arose a wider dispute between the bishop and intendant in which both sides indulged in general accusations about the probity of the other.[2] Then in 1801 relations between bishop and intendant collapsed amidst a dispute which disturbed government circles in Upper Perú for the next four years.[3]

But these instances of hostility between the intendants and the hierarchy were few and exceptional. Normal relations were devoid of significance, and there were even cases of positive amity, such as that of intendant Rivera and bishop Nicolás de Videla of Paraguay.[4] The intendant system, while it introduced a certain amount of confusion in the administration of the royal patronage, made no fundamental modification in the existing relations between Church and State in the viceroyalty of the Río de la Plata; these remained ones of close unity, dominated by royal control of Church affairs and characterized on the part of most churchmen by an excessive regalism This was given naïve expression in 1790 by archbishop San Alberto of La Plata who in a pastoral letter directed against subversive propaganda in his dioceses preached obedience to monarchical government in an interesting and up-to-date flight of imagery:

> If kings reign, govern, order, reward and punish on God's account and by virtue of the authority which He has granted them, within their kingdoms they are Vice-Gods, His Vicars or visible images ... You the clergy, scattered among the twelve provinces and hundred and fifty four districts of our jurisdiction, are like Ministers or Intendants of the Lord's Exchequer . . . while we are the Super-intendent-general.[5]

[1] There had already been disputes between the two authorities over the appointment to a cathedral canonry in La Paz. See A.G.I., Aud. de Charcas 726, Archbishop of La Paz to Crown, 3 December 1787.

[2] A.G.I., Aud. de Buenos Aires 140, Viedma to Llaguno, 16 January 1796.

[3] See below, Chapter X.

[4] A.G.I., Aud. de Buenos Aires 140, Rivera to Crown, 15 November 1805.

[5] A.G.I., Estado 76, Carta Pastoral del Illmo Sor. D. Fr. Josef Antonio de San Alberto, Arzobispo de la Plata, 4 March 1790.

CHAPTER V

The Intendant and the Viceroy

IN establishing the intendant system Charles III and his ministers hoped to create an administrative device which would combine two principles, division of labour and concentration of power; labour divided between central and provincial governors in the colonies, and power concentrated in the hands of the crown. But the crown already had a supreme political representative for each of its dominions, the viceroy, a figure of considerable stature and prestige in the government of the Indies. It was not easy to prophesy whether the new would merge with the old, whether the intendants would work in harmony with the viceroys.

It is true that the Ordinance of Intendants tried to define and delimit the powers of viceroy and intendant. In financial and economic affairs the superintendent-general of army and treasury was to act with absolute independence of the viceroy, while the latter was to continue to exercise all his other powers according to the Laws of the Indies.[1] This division of power limited the authority previously enjoyed by the viceroy in that it took away his supreme control over financial matters. But would he be satisfied with the point of view expressed by superintendent Sanz?

No one has recognized more than I have the superiority of the office of Your Excellency, nor knows how to respect it with more deference in all circumstances; but at the same time I believe that this practice is not incompatible with the free exercise of my own functions and faculties.[2]

The very statement of the issue implies tension, and there must be an initial presumption against harmony. The bitter opposi-

---

[1] *Ord. Ints.*, art. 2.
[2] A.G.I., Aud. de Buenos Aires 70, Sanz to Loreto, 5 June 1785.

tion of viceroy Croix of Perú to the new system seemed to confirm that a viceroy and superintendent could not work together. A later historian suggested that they could not work at all:

A government without income is no government, and quite soon it would notice the inconvenience of having two superior heads, since the viceroy could do nothing without money and the superintendent could do nothing without genuine executive powers . . .[1]

The intendant was not the first agent to relieve the viceroy of his original deposit of power. A viceroy was the direct representative of the crown for a given area, and as such he exercised supreme authority in civil and military matters in his province. He also had supervision over justice and the secular aspects of church government. But the centralization of power in the hands of the viceroys was not unlimited even before the establishment of the intendants. Their authority was modified by the fact that higher officials were appointed and removed by the king and could correspond directly with the central government in Spain; by the very minuteness of the colonial legislative code which circumscribed their action down to the smallest details; and above all by the *audiencia*. To a considerable extent the *audiencia* shared with the viceroy the political functions of government, and as a court of law it maintained an unquestioned supremacy.[2] Furthermore, appeals could be made to the *audiencia* from the viceroy's decisions.[3] Viceroys changed and their abilities varied, while the *audiencia* provided the most important element of permanence in Spanish colonial institutions. This power of the *audiencia* was not always exercised in the interests of good government. And a viceroy with an eye on his own future would be unwilling to alienate an *audiencia*, one of the judges of which would probably be his own *juez de residencia* upon completion of his term of office. 'This is the reason why the majority of government matters which the viceroy himself ought to determine with only the opinion of an *asesor*, he passes

[1] V. G. Quesada, *Virreinato del Río de la Plata 1776–1810* (Buenos Aires, 1881), p. 393.

[2] Ruiz Guiñazú, *La magistratura indiana*, pp. 18–19, 244–6. But the viceroy as captain-general of his province had exclusive competence in military cases. See Zorraquín Becú, *La organización judicial argentina en el período hispánico*, p. 90.

[3] L. E. Fisher, *Viceregal administration in the Spanish American colonies* (Berkeley, Calif., 1926), pp. 137–8.

on to the *audiencia* to be dealt with.'[1] Although the viceroy was president of the *audiencia* situated in his own capital, he was not expected to intervene directly in cases, nor did he have a vote in judicial decisions: a royal *cédula* of 14 July 1800 reassured the *audiencia* of Buenos Aires of this rule.[2] And in 1776 the establishment of the office of *regente*, a kind of chief justice, even reduced the viceroy's function as president of the *audiencia* by relieving him of the performance of many duties.[3]

Enough has been said to indicate that the problem should not be presented in terms of local governors clashing with a despot. Nor should it be suggested that the purpose of the king in handing over financial power to a superintendent was to limit the power of a too mighty authority,[4] for the power of the viceroy was already far from autocratic. The king would still use the device of the *residencia* and the viceroys of the Río de la Plata were not all as fortunate as the Marqués de Branciforte, viceroy of New Spain, who in spite of grave accusations levelled against him, was exempt *residencia* through the influence of his brother-in-law, Godoy. The administration of viceroy Loreto was subjected to the rigorous scrutiny of Victorián de Villava, fiscal of the *audiencia* of Charcas.[5] Although viceroy Vértiz was relieved of the formal *residencia*, superintendent Sanz had to publish an edict inviting complaints which could be submitted within six months.[6] A similar measure was ordered in the case of viceroy Arredondo, although here the time was reduced to forty days.[7] Viceroy Avilés was examined in full *residencia*.[8]

But while it is true that a viceroy's hand could be checked by many agencies, the new system of intendants offered a greater threat to his authority than any other. Already before the publication of the Ordinance of Intendants in 1782 there

---

[1] Juan y Ulloa, *Noticias secretas de América*, pp. 473–4.
[2] R. Levene, ed., *Cedulario de la Real Audiencia de Buenos Aires* (3 vols., La Plata, 1929–38), iii, 61.
[3] Zamora y Coronado, *Biblioteca de legislación ultramarina*, v, 297–306.
[4] See Quesada, *op. cit.*, p. 392, who uses this argument, for which no positive evidence can be adduced.
[5] R. Levene, *Vida y escritos de Victorián de Villava* (Buenos Aires, 1946), pp. 14–16.
[6] A.G.I., Aud. de Buenos Aires 44, Royal Order to Sanz, 24 September 1783.
[7] A.G.I., Aud. de Buenos Aires 39, R.C., 3 April 1795.
[8] R. Levene, *La revolución de mayo y Mariano Moreno* (2 vols. Buenos Aires, 1946), i, 126–8, discusses the limitations on the authority of the viceroys.

were premonitions of approaching tension. The ubiquitous activities of superintendent Fernández, for example, gave food for thought to the viceroys, containing, as many of them did, an implicit criticism of viceregal administration. Viceroy Cevallos had ordered that saleable offices must be auctioned in the capital of the viceroyalty, as was the practice in Lima. But Fernández abolished this provision as from 28 September 1779, on the grounds that it was inconvenient for the interested parties to travel all the way to Buenos Aires or suffer the expense of appointing an attorney. He based his action on the Laws of the Indies which ordered that saleable offices should be auctioned by ministers of the treasury in the towns to which they belonged.[1] Fernández was extending his jurisdiction in other directions and exercising judicial powers which belonged to the *contaduría mayor de cuentas* of Buenos Aires.[2]

These alarming precedents were in the mind of viceroy Vértiz when, in reply to the royal order of 29 July 1782 requesting him and the superintendent to report jointly on the recently completed Ordinance of Intendants, he returned in addition a separate and private report in which he criticized the whole basis of the division of powers devised by the new legislation.

I am of the opinion that the total independence of the intendant from the authority of the viceroy depreciates the high office which the latter represents and which is indispensable for maintaining order and utilizing his powers in the serious event of a rising or enemy invasion.[3]

He went on to argue that in such a situation discord between viceroy and intendant would mean that the viceroy would be left without the revenue to execute a policy. Conversely, in a matter like contraband the intendant could not work alone, for he needed the assistance of the viceroy to control the foreigners who were its agents. Vértiz also thought that in proportion as the viceroy's power was decreased the people and the clergy would cease to pay the respect due to him.[4]

[1] A.G.I., Aud. de Buenos Aires 18, Fernández to Gálvez, Carta 29, 5 February 1779.
[2] A.G.I., Aud. de Buenos Aires 18, Francisco de Cabrera, Contador Mayor de Cuentas de Buenos Aires, to Gálvez, 1 December 1778.
[3] A.G.I., Aud. de Buenos Aires 354, Vértiz to Gálvez, Carta 685, 15 February 1783. See above, pp. 59–60.   [4] *Ibid.*

This report received close attention in Spain. The result was a lengthy dispatch from the Minister of the Indies reassuring Vértiz that the position of the viceroy would be by no means undermined. Although the superintendent, as subdelegate of exchequer, would be immediately responsible to the Minister of the Indies, he would not thereby be completely independent of the viceroy, 'who represents the king in his district and is his image in those dominions'.[1] The Ordinance expressly stated that in military matters the superintendent and his provincial intendants were subordinate to the viceroy, so that in case of invasion or insurrection only the viceroy would be in charge of policy and defence. The necessary financial resources would always be at his disposal, acting jointly with the superintendent. But even if the latter disagreed with any of the extraordinary expenses which the viceroy considered necessary, he was obliged to defray them, informing the viceroy of his dissent in a secret report for his own indemnity. Moreover, in time of war and insurrection, indeed at all times, the intendant must provide the viceroy with statements of treasury funds for his information; conversely it would be the duty of the viceroy to support the superintendent in his work of collection and assignment of revenue, and to suppress fraud and contraband. Finally, in token of the supreme authority which the king vested in his viceroys, they would be the first to countersign (*poner el cumplase*) all the titles of intendants sent by the Ministry of the Indies to the viceroyalty, while the superintendent would have a similar right afterwards, for the provincial intendants were responsible to him in all concerning the royal treasury.[2]

This carefully considered reassurance took the form of a royal order and indicates at once the importance attached to Vértiz's criticism of the new project and the determination of the government to continue with it and assure its success. It clearly shows, moreover, that the division of power devised by the Ordinance was much less than is usually supposed, and removes many misconceptions held on this account. The viceroy would not be without funds in an emergency. Vértiz seems to have been satisfied with this explanation, and remained convinced that the

[1] A.G.I., Aud. de Buenos Aires 354, R.O. to Vértiz, 5 August 1783.
[2] *Ibid.*

viceroy still enjoyed superior authority and that this royal order proved it.[1] His *Memoria* to his successor contained no criticism of the new arrangements and no warning or complaint about the superintendent. Under this viceroy who had voiced his scepticism there was indeed little sign of friction. Later, when the feud between viceroy Loreto and superintendent Sanz was at its bitterest, Sanz claimed with justice that things had been different under Loreto's predecessor:

> Then we lived in the greatest peace with viceroy Vértiz; business was done energetically; together we executed the establishment of the intendancies . . . he did not disdain like this gentleman to receive joint orders and sign joint reports; together we gave our orders and the necessary arrangements for the new intendancies. . . .[2]

The co-operation between Vértiz and Sanz showed in fact that the new system could work, granted the right conditions, namely agents who were ready to co-operate with each other. In any administrative system there are margins of uncertain territory over which jealous officials can dispute, if disputes are sought. If the intendant system was a fertile source of dispute it was primarily because in its formative period two incompatible characters occupied its leading rôles—an intolerant viceroy and a tactless superintendent.

The government spared no pains to ensure the co-operation of the new viceroy. The instructions accompanying his appointment specifically impressed on Loreto the duty of assisting and co-operating with the superintendent:

> I charge you strictly that in conjunction with my intendant-general you accept this new establishment, imposing it and sustaining it with the fullness of your authority, in order that the common good of those provinces may be promoted. . . .[3]

But strife between the viceroy and the superintendent began almost immediately after Loreto took office on 7 March 1784, and extended over a whole series of issues as long as both

[1] Vértiz, 'Memoria de gobierno', 12 March 1784, in Radaelli (ed.), *Memorias de los virreyes del Río de la Plata*, p. 28.

[2] A.G.I., Aud. de Buenos Aires 358, Sanz to Gálvez, Carta muy reservada 1, 30 March 1785.

[3] A.G.I., Aud. de Buenos Aires 44, 'Instrucción de Govierno' to viceroy Loreto, Art. 55, 9 February 1784.

officials were together in the viceroyalty. Although many of these issues ran concurrently, they have to be disentangled, so that the constitutional significance of each can be appreciated.

Superintendent Sanz was soon complaining that Loreto seemed to be interpreting the *omnímodas facultades* assured to him by the Ordinance of Intendants as including affairs of the exchequer granted to the superintendent.[1] On his arrival at Buenos Aires Loreto was confronted with a vast series of reports describing the economic disorder prevailing in the pampas of the Banda Oriental or Uruguay, where the constant and reckless slaughtering of cattle for the hide industry threatened to exterminate the herds. Sanz had already inquired into this matter in conjunction with the previous viceroy. Now, with the agreement of Loreto, he commissioned the *comandante de resguardos*, Don Francisco Ortega, to conduct an inquiry into the origin of and possible remedy for the irregularities in this territory. Ortega furnished a competent report based on his own experience and information, but meanwhile the viceroy had drawn up a report of his own which he passed to Sanz. To resolve the issue, a private council was held composed of the viceroy and the superintendent with their assessors, comandante Ortega, and the *contador general de propios*, Don Pedro Ballesteros. After both reports had been read, the causes of the trouble were agreed upon but the remedies were disputed. Sanz thought that it was useless to go over the past and try to discover who had been guilty of illegal buying and selling of cattle; rather should they concentrate on future remedies, initiate a stricter inspection of ranches, insist on branding of cattle and reclaim royal land for the treasury. Above all they should control the indiscriminate slaughter of herds. This point of view was supported by all the committee except the viceroy who maintained that any regulations made should also include the discovery and punishment of past offences. This caused confusion in the council and no decision was reached.[2]

Unable to get the support of the council for his policy, Loreto began secretly to appoint his own commissioners, informing

---

[1] *Ord. Ints.*, art. 2.

[2] A.G.I., Aud. de Buenos Aires 358, Sanz to Gálvez, Carta muy reservada 1, 30 March 1785.

neither Sanz nor the other members.[1] He ordered the governor of Montevideo to make an inquiry into the conduct of Don Antonio Pereyra, commander of the military garrisons of the missions, whose conduct was also engaging the attention of the commissioner sent by Sanz. But Loreto soon became dissatisfied with the work of the governor and substituted Colonel Josef Reseguín, intendant-elect of Puno, for the purpose of the inquiry, with secret orders not only to examine the probity of Pereyra, but also to report on the state of the pampas. Loreto argued that this appointment was made simply to aid the agent of Sanz in covering such a vast territory. But Sanz was more justified in regarding it as a slight on himself, for Reseguín was intendant-elect of Puno; instead of proceeding to his post or explaining the causes of his delay to Sanz, he was exercising treasury jurisdiction in Montevideo, searching ships, examining luggage, interfering in the customs, harrassing the coastguards, and finally establishing a private prison in his own house, which the public nicknamed the Inquisition, where he imprisoned criminals and held trials. These proceedings were all the more intolerable to Sanz as Reseguín was only acting by express and private order of the viceroy, while the public construed his conduct as evident insubordination to his own superintendent.[2] Meanwhile Loreto appointed yet another agent and instituted yet another inquiry, all without notifying Sanz. An exasperated Sanz complained to Gálvez of the useless duplication of effort.[3]

Gálvez forwarded both versions of the affair to the Council of the Indies. The Council was of the opinion that Loreto's measures had in fact impeded the reform of the cattle industry by his secretive procedure and by his appointment of Reseguín whose behaviour had been quite irregular. Far from improving matters, he had merely caused unnecessary conflict with the superintendent, and impaired the reputation of both authorities.[4] The viceroy should take care not to violate the powers of the superintendent and should forward to him immediately all the material he had collected on the matter. A royal order to

[1] A.G.I., Aud. de Buenos 333, Consulta del Consejo, 3 June 1786.
[2] A.G.I., Aud. de Buenos Aires 359, Sanz to Gálvez, Carta muy reservada 9, 26 October 1785.
[3] *Ibid.*
[4] A.G.I., Aud. de Buenos Aires 333, Consulta del Consejo, 3 June 1786.

this effect was issued to Loreto on 3 June 1786, reaffirming that
omnímodas facultades did not include management of treasury
business, all cognizance of which was the exclusive province of
the superintendent. The guarding of the countryside, in so far
as it was directed to avoiding contraband and fraud, whether of
export of hides and other prohibited goods to Portuguese
territory or of import of tobacco from Brazil, pertained to the
office of superintendent, while the viceroy must take care of
public order and security there. Reseguín was to be withdrawn
and sent to his intendancy. As for the superintendent the
government merely noticed a certain lack of vigour and
efficiency in his policy towards contraband.[1]

So the first round was won by Sanz, but already another issue
had developed, combining a clash of policy and a dispute over
jurisdiction. In agreement with the superintendent, viceroy
Vértiz had followed a policy of admitting useful foreign goods
under strict government control, and he had allowed in November 1779 the entry of tobacco and negroes from Portuguese
ships, collecting profitable duties. This procedure was approved
by royal order of 8 June 1780 and permission was granted for
similar entries in the future on the decision of the viceroy.[2]
Under this arrangement Vértiz conceded to Manuel Cipriano
de Melo, *segundo comandante del resguardo*, licence to introduce
slaves and wood from Brazil to the amount of 32,000 pesos held
in credit by Spanish merchants. Loreto was completely opposed
to this policy, arguing that, under cover of concessions such as
these, other goods were introduced at prices which made it
impossible for Spanish merchants to compete.[3] Loreto based his
position on the royal order of 20 January 1784 which forbade the
admission of any private foreign vessel. On 13 June 1784 the
governor of Montevideo wrote to the viceroy asking him how,
in view of this royal order, he ought to act towards the permits
granted to Cipriano de Melo. Before coming to a decision
Loreto reported the whole matter to the superintendent on
26 June. After a delay of five months, Sanz replied on 1 December 1784 advising that permits should be continued; otherwise

---

[1] A.G.I., Aud. de Buenos Aires 333, R.O. 3 June 1786.
[2] Vértiz, *Memoria*, pp. 109–10.
[3] A.G.I., Aud. de Buenos Aires 70, Loreto to Gálvez, 21 August 1785.

the trade would only be diverted into clandestine channels. Nevertheless Loreto cancelled the licence and expressed the hope to Sanz that this difference of opinion would not prevent their co-operation in the future.[1]

But Cipriano de Melo continued his importations with the support of Sanz, whereupon Loreto's agent, Reseguín, arrested him and charged him with the smuggling of various contraband goods from Portuguese and French ships and the admittance of a Portuguese merchant, Antonio Juan de Acuña, into Montevideo.[2] On these charges Cipriano de Melo was tried and imprisoned for eleven months. Sanz complained to Gálvez that this was an implicit attack on his own authority by means of a prosecution of one of his subordinates who was merely executing a policy authorized by himself and the previous viceroy.[3] At a more general level he was accusing Loreto of repeated interference and usurpation of authority peculiar to the superintendent. 'Lately this viceroy has tried-to manage this kingdom and its business as though it were his own domestic affair.'[4]

For his part Loreto admitted that he would normally have no cognizance of such an affair, but claimed that this was an exceptional case in that it involved admittance of a foreigner which brought the matter within the sphere of public security and therefore within the scope of the viceroy. And he complained that his efforts to curb contraband were being frustrated by the superintendent whose conduct was openly encouraging it.[5] But the Council of the Indies decided that there was a clear distinction between the Acuña affair and the much more important matter of contraband in general. Loreto could have dealt with the former and left the latter to the proper jurisdiction of the superintendent. This he must do in future. Cipriano de Melo should be freed and restored to office, while it should also

[1] A.G.I., Aud. de Buenos Aires 69, Loreto to Sanz, 22 December 1784.
[2] A.G.I., Aud. de Buenos Aires 69, Loreto to Gálvez, Carta reservada 254, 24 May 1785.
[3] A.G.I., Aud. de Buenos Aires 359, Sanz to Gálvez, Carta muy reservada 6, 6 June 1785.
[4] A.G.I., Aud. de Buenos Aires 358, Sanz to Gálvez, Carta muy reservada 1, 30 March 1785.
[5] A.G.I., Aud. de Buenos Aires 69, Loreto to Gálvez, Carta reservada 243, 1 April 1785.

be made known that it was Sanz's reluctance to control his subordinate officials that led viceroy Loreto to step in.[1]

These recommendations were embodied in a royal order of 29 July 1786 which approved Loreto's policy of suspending the import licences, but clearly stated that all matters of commerce whether internal or external were the business of the superintendent and ordered the viceroy to hand over all the material on this case to Sanz.[2] At the same time the superintendent was authorized to issue licences and passports for those travelling within his own province of Buenos Aires: those wishing to travel to other provinces or to other viceroyalties ought to apply to the viceroy for licences and passports, though they must also procure from the superintendent a certificate declaring that they were not in debt to the exchequer.[3]

So far, therefore, Sanz had gained a favourable decision on all the points in dispute, and the authority assured to him by the Ordinance of Intendants was maintained to the letter. This was all the more significant in that the policy of Loreto as distinct from his legal rights had much to recommend it to the government. Contraband activity in the viceroyalty of the Río de la Plata was indeed on a vast scale, a fact of which the government in Madrid was well aware. Its ramifications were sufficient to justify the intransigence of Loreto. The administrator of the customs of Buenos Aires was shortly to declare complete bankruptcy of public funds and to be charged with malversation of revenue in a scandalous trial in which many highly placed people were involved.[4]

Loreto, therefore, had facts in his favour. But he did not have legal rights, and the government was prepared to uphold these in all their detail. In the same year, 1786, Loreto had received a further reproof, following a complaint by Sanz to Gálvez of 3 June 1785 that the viceroy was holding up a supply of mercury (504 *quintales*) urgently needed in Upper Perú by forbidding the ship to leave Buenos Aires for Arica. He was told

---

[1] A.G.I., Aud. de Buenos Aires 333, Consulta del Consejo, 3 June 1786. Cipriano was freed by R.O. of 3 June 1786.

[2] A.G.I., Aud. de Buenos Aires 333, R.O. 29 July 1786.

[3] A.G.I., Aud. Buenos Aires 333, R.O. 30 June 1786.

[4] Cf. J. M. Gutiérrez, 'El virreinato del Río de la Plata durante la administración del marqués de Loreto', *Revista del Río de la Plata*, viii (1874), pp. 236–40.

to leave the superintendent in the free exercise of his legitimate and exclusive powers in the department of mines and mercury.[1] Loreto's plea that he had in fact issued the licence for disembarkation was left hanging in the air.

The above incidents did not exhaust the argumentative capacity of these two men. In pursuit of his policy of reorganizing and improving the streets of Buenos Aires, the superintendent needed to publish proclamations having the force of law in order to enforce street hygiene and tidiness on an unwilling public. Under the régime of Vértiz the submission of these proclamations to the viceroy for approval was a mere formality, done either orally or by means of a brief note; the proclamation itself was not submitted and the viceroy's reply was merely to provide the customary military escort which accompanied the posting of a proclamation.[2] But when Sanz issued a proclamation in May 1785 to enforce street drainage Loreto challenged the traditional procedure by witholding his reply to Sanz's request for a military escort.[3] The latter immediately complained to Gálvez that Loreto's action was holding up street works in Buenos Aires, a sphere of policy clearly assigned to the intendant by the Ordinance, and was causing scandalous rumours to circulate that the viceroy had withdrawn a proclamation issued by the superintendent.[4] Loreto maintained that there was much popular resistance to Sanz's public works, and that he himself had insufficient information as to what was going on; in any case Sanz had not forwarded the proclamation, and he could not pronounce on something the terms of which he had not seen.[5] At this point the argument degenerated into a petty squabble over the use of words; for Sanz submitted the proclamation, but in reluctant terms which made it appear that he was not sending it for approval but only asking for a military escort.[6] Loreto construed this as a refusal to recognize the superior authority of the viceroy as such and as only acknowledging his

[1] A.G.I., Aud. de Buenos Aires 72, R.O. 6 January 1786.
[2] A.G.I., Aud. de Buenos Aires 359, Sanz to Gálvez, Carta muy reservada 8, 14 June 1785.
[3] A.G.I., Aud. de Buenos Aires 70, Sanz to Loreto, 3 June 1785.
[4] A.G.I., Aud. de Buenos Aires 359, ibid.
[5] A.G.I., Aud. de Buenos Aires 70, Loreto to Sanz, 4 June 1785.
[6] A.G.I., Aud. de Buenos Aires 70, Sanz to Loreto, 4 June 1785.

superiority as captain-general, to which Sanz rejoined that he had merely followed customary practice.[1]

Once the opening gambits of this dispute have been recognized, it need not be followed into the tortuous play of extremely wordy and largely irrelevant arguments used by both sides.[2] Judgment was given by royal order of 30 June 1786. This declared that the superintendent was free to publish proclamations referring to matters over which he had authority given to him by the Ordinance of Intendants, but he would always be obliged to state in them that they were published with the previous notice and compliance of the viceroy; and in order to obtain the customary military escort he should submit them first to the viceroy before publication. For his part the viceroy was given to understand that he was not free to deny or delay his endorsement, except when it would appear that the proclamation in question might cause public disorder. And so in the present case Loreto was ordered to return the proclamation to Sanz for publication and to furnish the escort, for this was a question of public works over which the superintendent had legitimate control.[3]

In spite of the equivocal terms of this order, it must be regarded as at least a moral victory for Sanz. At any rate both sides withdrew to consolidate their positions and keep a watchful eye open for a suitable occasion to renew the attack. Within two years the truce was broken and tempers flared up once more. On 20 May 1788 Sanz submitted to the viceroy for endorsement a proclamation due for publication on the following day and imposing a new tax on cattle. Loreto refused to give an endorsement at a day's notice, especially on a matter of new taxation which affected the whole public and was weighty enough for joint consultation. Sanz considered that he had fulfilled the conditions of the royal order of 30 June 1786, but Loreto maintained that he was in fact abusing this order by trying to push through controversial measures under cover of a proclamation.[4]

Sanz could never take a hint. A week later he repeated the

---

[1] A.G.I., Aud. de Buenos Aires 70, Sanz to Loreto, 5 June 1785.
[2] A.G.I., Aud. de Buenos Aires 70, *passim*.
[3] A.G.I., Aud. de Buenos Aires 333, R.O. 30 June 1786.
[4] A.G.I., Aud. de Buenos Aires 76, Loreto to Porlier, Carta 55, 1 July 1788.

same procedure. The *junta superior de real hacienda* had agreed on 27 February 1788 to establish a public lottery with the superintendent as controller. On 28 May Sanz applied to the viceroy for an endorsement of a proclamation which would put this scheme into effect on the following day. Once more Loreto decided that one day's notice gave insufficient time for study, but Sanz claimed that this attitude was simply one of resistance, and resistance not only to his authority but to that of the *junta superior de real hacienda*. The feud was infectious. Now the *cabildo* of Buenos Aires opposed the establishment of a lottery, while the *junta* based its action on the authority over municipal revenue conceded to it by the Ordinance of Intendants.[1] Loreto questioned whether the relevant article of the Ordinance was still operative in view of the royal order of 11 November 1787 which declared that only the management and use of already established *propios and arbitrios*, or municipal taxes, was reserved to the *junta de hacienda*. A further order of 12 February 1788 which authorized the viceroy to discover new *arbitrios* to support an orphanage, implied that the imposition of new *arbitrios* was the province of the viceroy.[2]

Loreto was on sure ground at last. A royal order of 24 January 1789 supported his opinion and approved his refusal to sanction the lottery.[3] In this case Loreto had been able to act as guardian of the interest of the *cabildo*. In the same year he was able to cultivate the friendship of the *audiencia* and strengthen his hand still more against Sanz.[4] In April 1788 the ministers of the *tribunal de cuentas* of Buenos Aires approached Sanz as superintendent subdelegate, requesting a change of location of the offices of the tribunal in view of the extreme dampness which was damaging its records, and suggesting that it be removed to a former Jesuit building which was some distance from the *audiencia* but otherwise suitable.[5] Sanz consulted the viceroy who opposed the change, partly on the ground that the price of the new building was excessive, and partly because the Laws of the Indies insisted that the tribunal must be situated next to

[1] *Ord. Ints.*, art. 42. See below, p. 124.
[2] A.G.I., Aud. de Buenos Aires 76, Loreto to Porlier, Carta 56, 1 July 1786.
[3] A.G.I., Aud. de Buenos Aires 77, Loreto to Porlier, Carta 104, 28 May 1789.
[4] A.G.I., Aud. de Buenos Aires 76, Loreto to Porlier, Carta 33, 2 March 1788.
[5] A.G.I., Aud. de Buenos Aires 264, Consulta del Consejo, 22 November 1791.

the *audiencia* so that the ministers of the *audiencia* could attend without inconvenience the meetings of the *tribunal de cuentas*. The inevitable battle soon gained momentum: the fiscal and dean of the *audiencia* aligned themselves with Loreto against Sanz and the *tribunal de cuentas*. The tactless behaviour of Sanz and his capacity for making enemies is well illustrated by an incident in which he invited the fiscal and the dean of the *audiencia* to come and see the actual state of the records in the tribunal's offices. The dean still remained unconvinced and remarked that as it was Holy Week there could be no meeting of the *junta* in any case, and therefore no immediate decision. Sanz hotly replied: 'And does the king not pay your wages in Holy Week?'[1] The matter remained unresolved, but three years later the Council of the Indies sharply criticized Sanz's conduct in this affair.[2]

By now, therefore, Sanz was extremely unpopular in Buenos Aires both with the *audiencia* and with the *cabildo*. The enmity between the viceroy and himself was notorious and an evident hindrance to efficient administration. The past four years had seen a series of undignified squabbles over affairs of day-to-day administration which clearly could not be permitted to continue indefinitely. The government might be expected to transfer the two men and give the new system a fair trial under better conditions. But its remedy was far more radical. It would not change the personnel: it would change the system. This experience in the viceroyalty of the Río de la Plata, together with the opposition to the new system on the part of the viceroy of Perú, caused the king and his ministers to reconsider one of the principal elements of the reform of 1782. The Ordinance of Intendants had changed two centuries' tradition in viceregal government by removing financial and economic affairs from the viceroy's authority and assigning them to the superintendent. In 1788 the Spanish government abandoned this new direction and Spanish colonial institutions returned to their former basis. First in Perú and Mexico, then by royal order of 9 May 1788 in Buenos Aires, the attributes of the superintendent were restored to the viceroy and the separate office of

---

[1] A.G.I., Aud. de Buenos Aires 264, Sanz to Valdés, Carta 72, 1 May 1788.
[2] A.G.I., Aud. de Buenos Aires 264, Consulta del Consejo, 22 November 1791.

the superintendent was abolished.[1] The thesis of viceroy Vértiz appeared to have triumphed. Yet in the viceroyalty of the Río de la Plata the new arrangements had proved unworkable not for the reasons adduced by Vértiz, for the division of executive from financial powers was never in fact put to the test and the government had in any case made ample provisions to ensure that a viceroy would never be without funds to execute a policy. The system failed not for the big reason but for a series of small ones, and was the victim of a personal feud between two incompatible men. These two officials would find causes for dispute whatever the constitutional situation. The proof of this was soon forthcoming. Although the modification of the intendant system restored the viceroy to his former powers, it did not restore peace between the Marqués de Loreto and Francisco de Paula Sanz.

Sanz was appointed intendant of Potosí, regarded as one of the most important posts in South America, and Loreto remained as viceroy in Buenos Aires, whence he continued to pursue Sanz with a persistence which bore all the signs of personal malice and vindictiveness. The struggle between viceroy and superintendent became a struggle between viceroy and intendant.

Part of Sanz's territorial jurisdiction in the intendancy of Potosí comprised a stretch of the Pacific coastline, the coast of the desert of Atacama. On 19 April 1789 his subdelegate in this district reported that a message had come from Tarapacá giving information about the appearance of English ships in this region, one of which had entered the tiny port of Tocopilla, near Cobija, sacked and pillaged stores and shacks, and taken aboard all the dry fish its crew could lay its hands on; the terrified inhabitants fled into the interior. The intendant was concerned about the security of his province. Since Sanz's arrival in Potosí, Loreto had withdrawn from the town the only regular garrison it possessed, a company of the Regiment of Extremadura, thus leaving the whole of the mineral wealth of Potosí without an efficient guard.[2] Sanz protested to Loreto and meanwhile bought arms from the commander of the 2nd

[1] Ravignani, 'El virreinato del Río de la Plata (1776–1810), in *H.N.A.*, IV, i, 228. See also Quesada, *op. cit.*, pp. 465–76. Fisher, *Intendant system*, p. 74, gives the date wrongly as 1789.
[2] A.G.I., Aud. de Charcas 434, Sanz to Loreto, 20 May 1789.

Extremadura Battalion. But Loreto informed him that the intendancy of La Paz had more need of the troops than Potosí; as for the reports from Tarapacá, Sanz's panic-stricken and open dispatch could do far more harm to public security than any supposed English landing on the Pacific coast; Sanz should confine himself to his own affairs and leave the viceroy in charge of these matters.[1] Later, in an extremely sarcastic letter Loreto informed Sanz that recent dispatches from the viceroy of Lima and the president of Chile led him to believe that the reported landing was quite mythical and Sanz's concern quite unnecessary; he should return the arms he had bought, for only the viceroy had authority in such matters.[2]

Sanz now had recourse to the government in Madrid. He criticized a proposal of Loreto's to separate the jurisdiction over the affected coastline from the intendancy of Potosí and assign it to the intendant of Salta, a proposal which he considered showed an alarming ignorance of the geographical conditions of an area which was completely inaccessible from Salta during the winter owing to the *cordillera* between Salta and Atacama. As for Loreto's decision to send a special envoy of his own where military matters were involved, this was in direct contradiction to the Ordinance of Intendants which granted the intendant delegated jurisdiction in military affairs within his own intendancy.[3] Sanz ended his message with the complaint, 'Loreto only criticizes my plans and opinions without ever disclosing his own.'[4]

The issue was never explicitly resolved, partly because the danger of invasion from the Pacific coast was never real, partly because it was lost sight of amidst a grand finale of mutual recriminations which ended the six years' rivalry between the two men. The last act was begun by Loreto when in the *Memoria de gobierno* which he left for his successor on 10 February 1790 he made a number of insinuations against Sanz, asserting by implication that the latter's policy as superintendent had been responsible for much illicit commerce and

---

[1] A.G.I., Aud. de Charcas 434, Loreto to Sanz, 30 May 1789.
[2] A.G.I., Aud. de Charcas 434, Loreto to Sanz, 16 August 1789.
[3] *Ord. Ints.*, art. 272.
[4] A.G.I., Aud. de Charcas 434, Sanz to Valdes, 16 October 1789.

had allowed so much scope to local officials that Loreto had great difficulty in controlling them when things changed in 1788.[1] Sanz's reaction was to complain directly to Madrid of the injury thus done to his good name, and to request an official clearance of these criticisms.[2] The government gave him the benefit of an inquiry: a royal order of 14 May 1791 instructed Loreto's successor, Arredondo, to examine and report on Sanz's complaint. This task was distasteful to Arredondo, but he examined the charges made by Loreto and came to the conclusion that many of the expressions used by the former viceroy in his *Memoria* were offensive to Sanz's good name, some were ambiguous, and some were quite false. He advised that in order to avoid lengthy litigation the government should declare itself well satisfied with Sanz's services both as superintendent and as intendant of Potosí.[3] A royal order was issued to this effect, exonerating Sanz of the 'ill-considered' charges made by Loreto and praising him for his disinterested services.[4] And there the matter rested. Loreto departed from the history of the viceroyalty while Sanz remained in Upper Perú, congratulating himself no doubt on having enjoyed the last word, and assured of the confidence of the new viceroy.

The experience, however, had put the viceroys on their mettle and made them more self-conscious of an authority which seemed to be threatened from many sides. A powerful rival in a superintendent in Buenos Aires had been removed, but they were not satisfied. When Melo de Portugal was appointed viceroy of Buenos Aires in 1794 he tried to procure in advance a royal reaffirmation of what he regarded as the traditional plenitude of jurisdiction belonging to the viceroy. He regarded as indispensable a declaration on two points. First, that the *audiencia* should come and pay respects to the viceroy on the customary days. Secondly, that the *audiencia* only enjoyed judicial cognizance, while government and administration were outside its jurisdiction, as was also the royal exchequer, recently reunited to the viceroy's authority: these belonged to

[1] Loreto, 'Memoria', 10 February 1790, in *Memorias de los virreyes del Río de la Plata*, pp. 261–3.
[2] A.G.I., Aud. de Charcas 434, Sanz to López de Lerena, 30 November 1790.
[3] A.G.I., Aud. de Charcas 434, Arredondo to Gardoqui, 12 June 1792.
[4] A.G.I., Aud. de Charcas 434, R.O. to Sanz, 4 October 1793.

the '*omnímoda jurisdicción*' of the viceroy who determined them by himself with his assessor and the *vista* of his fiscal, and when he thought fit he would consult the *audiencia*.[1] This request the viceroy-elect submitted from Aranjuez before he had left Spain. It was peremptorily rejected. The Minister replied that there was no need for a new order as the existing laws adequately defined the terms and limits of a viceroy's authority. Furthermore he objected that Melo claimed too much: his use of the terms '*omnímoda jurisdicción*' was quite unjustified, for a viceroy did not in fact enjoy this which was something in excess of the '*suprema autoridad*' deposited in him.[2]

The viceroys indeed were claiming more than they could manage. Officialdom remained at peace within itself in the viceroyalty for the next ten years, but administration now suffered from an overburdening of the viceroy, who in addition to the viceregal duties of supervising the whole viceroyalty was now intendant of the city and province of Buenos Aires.[3] Consequently when the reform of the Ordinance of Intendants was undertaken in 1801–3, this question received much attention. It was Jorge Escobedo, former visitor-general of Perú and a recognized expert on colonial affairs, who pointed out that a viceroy had so many higher and weightier preoccupations that he could not himself fulfil all the obligations laid on the intendants by

[1] A.G.I., Aud. de Buenos Aires 39, Melo de Portugal to the King, 21 May 1794.
[2] A.G.I., Aud. de Buenos Aires 39, Duque de Alcudin to Melo de Portugal, 7 June 1794. As has been seen, the *Ordenanza de Intendantes*, art. 2 used the terms '*omnímodas facultades*'.
[3] Quesada, *op. cit.*, pp. 408, 465–83, argues rightly that the abolition of the superintendency did not involve the abolition of the intendancy of Buenos Aires. But who now occupied the latter? Quesada maintains that it was the lieutenant-lawyer, to whom the Ordinance of Intendants had already assigned functions of intendant whenever the latter was absent. It is no doubt true that the lieutenant-lawyer continued to exercise the civil and criminal litigation entrusted to him by the Ordinance, but there is no reason to doubt that it was the viceroy who was his superior governor and who exercised authority over the intendancy of Buenos Aires. Such an interpretation has the authority of the viceroys themselves: '. . . cuando se extinguió la intendencia de Buenos Aires, y se reunió la super-intendencia general subdelegada de real hacienda a este superior gobierno, no se hizo distincion alguna entre la que era superintendencia general y lo que era de provincia, se recibieron y se ejercicieron unas y otras facultades por el señor marques de Loreto, y yo las ejercí tambien en todo el tiempo de mi mando . . .'. Arredondo, 'Memoria de gobierno', 16 March 1795, in *Memorias de los virreyes del Río de la Plata*, p. 450.

the Ordinance. He proposed therefore the creation of provincial intendants in viceregal capitals.[1] A similar suggestion for Mexico had already been made by viceroy Revillagigedo.[2] The idea was incorporated in the New Ordinance of Intendants of 1803. The Ordinance itself was suspended but Article 10 was published by a decree of 29 June 1803, which created a provincial intendant in Mexico, Lima, Santa Fe and Buenos Aires.[3] To the post in Buenos Aires was appointed Domingo de Reynoso by royal order of 20 December 1803. The new official was to enjoy the same powers as the other provincial intendants enjoyed in their intendancies but there was this difference: his powers in the capital were limited, for there the presence of the viceroy might cause a repetition of the old disputes. And so in the capital his functions were limited to the exercise of appellate jurisdiction in matters of treasury and other offices, to assistance at court and at monthly valuations, and to presidency of the *juntas* of auctions. But the government of tribunals and offices in the capital, receipt and expenditure of funds, the control of shipping arriving in port, and all affairs of the *cabildo* remained reserved to the superintendency, i.e. the viceroy, who had to maintain the intendant in his due authority and work in harmony with him.[4]

This was a careful attempt to limit the authority of the restored intendant and to make sure there would be no more conflicts with the viceroy. From now on the viceroy was in undisputed command and the intendant in Buenos Aires kept his place. On 10 February 1807, after his intolerable conduct during the English invasion of the Río de la Plata, viceroy Sobremonte was deposed and the *audiencia* of Buenos Aires assumed political and military authority, temporarily appointing a separate superintendent-general as subdelegate of exchequer.[5] Don Lucas Muñoz y Cubero filled the office from October 1807 to May 1808. When Santiago Liniers was sworn

---

[1] Biblioteca Nacional, Madrid, MS 3073, Jorge Escobedo, 'Manifiesto de las razones en que está fundado cada uno de los articulos de la nueva ordenanza de intendentes de Indias', Madrid, 2 August 1802, fol. 16.

[2] Fisher, *Intendant system*, p. 75.

[3] A.G.I., Indif. Gen. 1713, Real Decreto, 29 June 1803.

[4] A.G.I., Indif. Gen. 1713, R.O. 2 December 1803.

[5] See below, pp. 235, 236.

in office as viceroy on 16 May 1808 the superintendency was reunited to the viceroy.[1]

While the relations between the viceroy and the intendant in Buenos Aires had been settled, there was still room for dispute between a viceroy and his provincial intendants. This could arise either out of personal animosity, as we have seen in the case of Loreto and Sanz, when the latter was at Potosí, or it could arise out of differences of policy. Between 1798 and 1803 the administrative peace of the viceroyalty was disturbed by a vociferous controversy between the intendant of Paraguay and the viceroy of Buenos Aires over the fate of the *pueblos de misiones*, the former Jesuit communities in Paraguay. This case was an example of completely divergent policies both seeking confirmation at court. As will be seen, the problem of the Guaraní Indians received considerable royal attention after the expulsion of the Jesuits, but the results were meagre and produced more plans than remedies.[2] In 1798 a solution was still being sought, and on 30 November of that year a royal order instructed viceroy Avilés to report on the state of the Guaraní communities. After making the conventional accusations against the former Jesuit régime Avilés went on to criticize the civil administrators who had been substituted for the Jesuits and to castigate the intendants, all of whom, he claimed, had simply been occupied in lining their own pockets out of the labour of the Indians. There had been a scandalous loss of cattle and waste of crops. The numbers of the community Indians in the intendancy of Paraguay had fallen from 48,150 in 1767 to 17,415 in 1787; those in the province of Buenos Aires had fallen from 35,358 to 23,148 owing to desertions to Brazil or to Spanish towns. The only remedy for this state of affairs, argued Avilés, was to extinguish the communal property system and establish among the Indians the principle of private ownership. At the same time free and open commerce with Spanish merchants should be encouraged.[3]

This policy was directly opposed by intendant Rivera of Paraguay. The latter had already come into conflict with

[1] A.G.I., Aud. de Buenos Aires 369, Muñoz y Cubero to Soler, 14 May 1808.
[2] See below, pp. 187-92.
[3] A.G.I., Aud. de Buenos Aires 85, Avilés to Caballero, 8 June 1799.

Avilés over rival claims of jurisdiction. The Ordinance of Intendants assigned thirteen of the thirty Guaraní communities to the intendancy of Paraguay and the remainder to Buenos Aires.[1] But on 12 June 1799 a decree from the viceroy ordered that the products produced by the communities, including the thirteen within the boundaries of Paraguay, must in future be sent to the administrator of the *pueblos* in Buenos Aires to be disposed of by him. At the same time a commissioner was sent to Paraguay to administer the new arrangement. Rivera protested to Avilés that this deprived him of his rightful faculties and virtually removed the communities from his jurisdiction, uniting into one entity subject to Buenos Aires that which the king had previously divided into two. Meanwhile the administrator in Buenos Aires was issuing orders to the communities in Paraguay without any consultation with the intendant. However, Rivera resigned himself to the new arrangement until the commissioner in Asunción required him to order the exchequer officials of Asunción to give an account to him of the state of income and expenditure and any other information he would require in the future. Basing himself on the Ordinance of Intendants, Rivera refused to agree to this removal of his own jurisdiction.[2] At the same time he protested to Avilés over the new dispensation for the *bienes de comunidad* of the Indians, which the viceroy had also placed at the disposal of the administrator in Buenos Aires, although the Ordinance clearly stated that they were under the management of the intendant who was in turn responsible to the *junta superior de real hacienda*.[3]

Meanwhile Avilés was going ahead with his new policy. On 18 February 1800 he issued a decree freeing enumerated Indian families from the necessity to work on the communal basis, and allowing them to work for themselves, paying a moderate tribute of one peso a year, and receiving an allotment of land and cattle.[4] Intendant Rivera adhered to the principle of the traditional community system and gloomily surveyed the results of the new policy imposed in the name of liberty. He reported

---

[1] A.G.I., Aud. de Buenos Aires 322, Loreto to intendant of Paraguay, 14 July 1784.

[2] A.G.I., Buenos Aires 322, Rivera to Avilés, 14 October 1800. Cf. *Ord. Ints.*, arts. 118–19.

[3] *Ibid.*   [4] See below, pp. 192–93.

that villages were falling into decay; churches, estates, plantations, all were threatened with complete neglect.[1]

On 8 March 1800 viceroy Avilés sent a more extensive
report to the crown, in which he reaffirmed his opinion that the
only solution was to abolish the community system and allow
the Indians to enjoy the same rights as Spaniards, managing
their own property and trading with whom they pleased.[2]
Avilés' knowledge of the area for which he was legislating does
not inspire confidence,[3] but he went on to attack the intendant
of Paraguay. The persistence of *encomienda* service among the
non-Jesuit communities he attributed to the compliance of the
intendants whom he called 'new despots', absolute lords of the
Indians whom they treated as they pleased.[4] Rivera's new plan
of government for the communities Avilés described as 'hypo-
critical' and designed to ensure that only the intendant of
Paraguay could rob the communities.

The governors of Paraguay have been and will be, unless the
matter is remedied, absolute lords of the ranches and goods of the
communities, and of all the Indians, young and old, men and women;
if they require ten, twenty or thirty thousand pesos annually, they
take them, giving some to the administrators and some to Spanish
favourites. . . .[5]

Finally, he alleged, the intendants had included thirteen
pueblos in their jurisdiction in spite of the fact that after the
expulsion of the Jesuits they were placed under the immediate
authority of the government of Buenos Aires and the supervision
of the administrator there.

This significant attack on the independent policy pursued by

[1] See below, pp. 193–4.
[2] Avilés to Caballero, 8 March 1800, printed in *D.H.A.*, iii, 26–53. See J. C.
González, *Don Santiago Liniers, gobernador interino de los treinta pueblos de las misiones
guaraníes y tapes 1803–1804* (Buenos Aires, 1946), pp. 61–2, 71–4. He twice mistakes
the date of this despatch.
[3] His account of the discovery of Argentina began a battle of historical knowledge
between himself and Rivera in which the latter was able to summon a better array
of sources. Rivera also ridiculed Avilés' notions of the present state of the Indians in
Paraguay. Cf. Avilés to Caballero, 8 March 1800, *D.H.A.*, iii, 27; A.G.I., Aud. de
Buenos Aires 142, Rivera to Caballero, 19 June 1801.
[4] Avilés to Caballero, 8 March 1800, *D.H.A.*, iii, 40–1.
[5] *Ibid.*, p. 48.

the intendant of Paraguay brought forth a determined reply from Rivera.[1] He hotly defended his predecessors in office against these charges from Buenos Aires which he described as inaccurate and ill-informed. He was able to point out that on 29 May 1775 Agustín Fernando de Pinedo, governor of Paraguay, had written a report to the king in which he vehemently denounced the ills of the *encomiendas* and advised their abolition and incorporation in the crown. On 19 May 1798, Rivera himself had reported against the *encomiendas* and proposed various concrete methods to abolish them. As for the charge that the intendants usurped the jurisdiction of the thirteen *pueblos* against previous resolutions of the king, he considered it incredible that a viceroy should make such a charge. 'He agrees that the thirteen pueblos were included in our jurisdiction by the Ordinance of Intendants, yet he wishes at the same time that the will of the king should not take effect.'[2] The results of freeing and hispanicizing the Indians of the *pueblos* of Santo Domingo, Soriano, Quilmes and Batadero had not been too promising, continued Rivera. The limited hopes, lack of ambition and simple character of the Indians made it more appropriate to continue the community system. Avilés had drawn his account of the Indians from the fantasies of the fanatical Las Casas, 'a book which is rightly despised by the whole nation and has only served to adorn the poetic accounts of Raynal and Robertson'.[3] The underlying motive of Avilés was simply to procure for Buenos Aires the thirteen *pueblos* assigned by the crown to Paraguay.[4]

After looking at the case, the Council of the Indies decided in November 1802 in favour of Avilés and agreed that the new system should be adopted for all the thirty *pueblos*. These should be brought under a single political and military government which would include all the missions formerly divided between Paraguay and Buenos Aires. This opinion was given effect by a royal resolution of 28 March 1803.[5]

Hard words had been used on both sides in this dispute. In

---

[1] This rivalry between the governments of Buenos Aires and Paraguay in the colonial period is a foretaste of the future separatism of Paraguay.

[2] A.G.I., Aud. de Buenos Aires 142, Rivera to Caballero, 19 June 1801.

[3] *Ibid.*   [4] *Ibid.*   [5] González, *op. cit.*, p. 75.

November 1801 Rivera had complained to Madrid of the 'spirit of ambition and revenge which dominates the Marqués de Avilés; his abuse of the power entrusted to him; the irreparable damage caused by his arbitrary government'.[1] Avilés had left office in May 1801. But his successor did little to heal the breach of good relations, and a concerted move to get rid of Rivera was now evident. Powerful influences were working against him. Félix de Azara, former head of the boundary commission in the viceroyalty of the Río de la Plata, pursued him unmercifully in a series of reports which he submitted to the government from 1805 onwards on behalf of the *Junta de Fortificaciones y Defensa de Indias*. He advised that the thirty communities ought to be reunited to the intendancy of Paraguay and that Colonel Bernardo de Velasco, governor of the united *pueblos de misiones* since 1803, should be appointed intendant, replacing Rivera, whom Azara alleged was impeding the policy of abolishing *encomiendas* and freeing the Indians enjoined by the crown in 1803.[2] This attack was backed up by a further charge that Rivera was retaining in Paraguay a *banco de guerra*, with considerable funds, supplied by taxes, completely controlled by the intendant, and responsible neither to the viceroy nor to the exchequer.[3]

Rivera also came into conflict with the new viceroy over a tobacco scheme prepared by the Director of Tobacco in the viceroyalty and approved by the viceroy. To increase tobacco production in Paraguay it was planned to contract with individual producers to grow and sell to the government a given amount of tobacco every year, granting the contractors exemption from military service and from other public obligations. Rivera opposed this project, first on the ground that it was no improvement on the previous system of voluntary sale, and secondly because it deprived the intendancy of Paraguay of

---

[1] A.G.I., Aud. de Buenos Aires 48, Rivera to Soler, 25 November 1801.

[2] Félix de Azara, 'Informe sobre las factorias y cultivo de tabaco en el Paraguay', in *Memoria sobre el estado rural del Río de la Plata y otros informes* (Buenos Aires, 1943), pp. 267–8; also 'Informe sobre los tabacos de Paraguay', *ibid.*, pp. 274–5.

[3] Azara, 'Dictamen . . . sobre una exposición del Gobernador Intendente del Paraguay', *op. cit.*, p. 288; also 'Informe sobre los tabacos del Paraguay', *op. cit.*, p. 275. This bank was first created in 1726 to supply funds for maintaining a governor's guard; since then it had been extended but never officially approved by the crown.

necessary militia.[1] In Madrid Azara and the *Junta* criticized the way he reported directly to the king and council on this matter behind the back of the viceroy, and accused him of using disrespectful language about his superior.[2]

Rivera was in fact replaced by Velasco, and he himself, in a defence of his conduct published in Madrid in 1807, attributed his loss of office to Azara's campaign against him.[3] He found a staunch defender in viceroy Liniers, his brother-in-law,[4] who sent a complimentary report on his behaviour to Madrid, and appointed him as envoy in Rio de Janeiro.[5] Liniers also submitted a general defence of Rivera's conduct in the intendancy of Paraguay and attributed his deposition to the personal enmity of Azara and Lastarría, the secretary of viceroy Avilés, who had employed methods of lies and calumny which merited an inquiry.[6] He denied the right of the *Junta de Fortificaciones* to take cognizance of the *real renta de tabaco*, and described Azara and Lastarría as 'miserable flatterers of Godoy'. Far from neglecting the tobacco revenue Rivera worked for its prosperity, forming efficient instructions to improve the cultivation of tobacco, all of which were enumerated by the *Fiscales del Supremo Consejo de la Guerra*. His absence now proved his worth, for the tobacco revenue had dwindled to a pittance.[7] Furthermore, reported Liniers, Rivera had also abolished forty-two *encomiendas*, a task all the more commendable in view of the failure of all the attempts to do likewise ever since the conquest.[8] The general conclusion which Liniers drew from the episode was that it provided 'a terrible lesson for the faithful servants of the crown. What will the other governors-intendant think when they have seen the fate of Rivera, who, employed at the head of the first province of the viceroyalty, and enjoying an excellent reputation for integrity and loyalty, is rewarded with desertion and contempt?'[9]

---

[1] Azara, 'Informe sobre las factorias y cultivo de tabaco en el Paraguay', *op. cit.*, p. 265.

[2] Azara, 'Informe sobre los tabacos del Paraguay . . .', *op. cit.*, pp. 271–2.

[3] Azara, 'Dictamen sobre una exposición del Gobernador Intendente del Paraguay', *op. cit.*, pp. 279–97.

[4] Rivera was married to the sister of Liniers' wife. See E. Udaondo, *Diccionario biográfico colonial argentino* (Buenos Aires, 1945), p. 762.

[5] B.M., Add. MS 32,608, fol. 90, Liniers to Cornel, 21 January 1809.

[6] B.M., Add. MS 32,609, fols. 114–15, Liniers to Cornel, 26 January 1809.

[7] *Ibid.*, fols. 115v–16.   [8] *Ibid.*, fol. 117.   [9] *Ibid.*, fol. 118v.

CHAPTER VI

The Intendant and the Exchequer

FINANCE was the touchstone of Bourbon policy, the common theme running through all the reforming endeavour of Spanish governments in the eighteenth century. Crisis after crisis involved Spain in international situations which forced her to increase her army, to create a navy almost from nothing, and to sustain various costly wars. Her vast overseas dominions, far from contributing to the resources of the mother country, were themselves in need of costly reorganization. From the beginning of the reign of Charles III the pace of policy quickened. Now it was realized that the expansion of Britain overseas and the coveted wealth of the Spanish empire were factors which could almost certainly lead to war, the result of which would decide for a long time to come Spain's position as a world power. 'A war potential capable of meeting the test was the true objective of many of the notable economic reforms of Charles and his enlightened ministers.'[1]

This combination of circumstances caused a progressive increase in public expenditure, which in turn demanded a policy capable of raising correspondingly the national income. Hence the importance which the Bourbon kings attached to the development of the public exchequer, and the care they took to improve its administration. Among the many testimonials to this preoccupation none is more convincing than the well-known *Instrucción reservada dirigida en 1787 por el rey a la Junta de Estado*, an accurate reflection of the political aspirations of Charles III and his government, wherein is set forth the essence of its financial policy, the increase of national production and consumption, the rationalization of taxation, and, as a distant goal, the

---

[1] E. J. Hamilton, 'Monetary problems in Spain and Spanish America, 1751-1800', *Journal of Economic History*, iv (1944), p. 40.

establishment of a single and equitable tax.[1] Such a policy
needed to be applied with greater urgency in Spain's overseas
dominions, where the harnessing of resources was even more
backward, and administration even more corrupt. The colonial
exchequer was modified in all parts of the empire during the
course of the eighteenth century, but particularly under the
stimulus of Charles III and his ministers. The obligations of the
state were increasing: it was necessary to undertake public
enterprises of all kinds in the dominions overseas, the creation of
exchange banks to buy the precious metals from mining
operators, costly experiments in new metallurgical processes,
improvement of communications, and other public works.

Financial administration in the colonies had reached its nadir.
An incredibly primitive method of accounting, loose organization, unskilled officials—each defect alone was sufficiently grave
to cause decay. The royal mints, especially that of Potosí, were
long-standing models of wastage and ignorance. But above all,
the fundamental cause of distress was the dishonesty of under-
paid exchequer officials, an inheritance of the practice of sale of
offices.[2] Although treasury offices were never legally classed as
saleable, the crown was reduced to selling them with increasing
recklessness during the seventeenth century, so that 'the sale of
Hacienda offices, above all of offices in the Tribunals of
Accounts, inevitably opened a breach in the last strongholds of
bureaucratic integrity'.[3] Consequently, treasury posts were
filled with men still trying to pay off the interest on the purchase
price of their office and resorting to treasury funds to do it.
Viceroy Amat of Perú (1761–76) declared that all exchequer
officials traded with public funds, and was able to make concrete accusations of increasing defalcations.[4] The young viceroyalty of the Río de la Plata inherited the corruption of Perú.
The treasury officials of Cochabamba came under the strong
suspicion of visitor-general Areche, who recognized that one of

[1] Printed in A. Ferrer del Río (ed.), *Obras originales del conde de Floridablanca, y
escritos referentes a su persona*, pp. 213–72, see particularly pp. 242–56.

[2] See J. H. Parry, *The sale of public office in the Spanish Indies under the Hapsburgs*
(Berkeley and Los Angeles, 1953), pp. 49–54, 72.

[3] *Ibid.*, p. 54.

[4] Manuel de Amat y Junient, *Memoria de gobierno* (1776) ed. V. Rodríguez
Casado y F. Pérez Embid (Sevilla, 1947), pp. 351–2, 395.

the causes of dishonesty was the low salaries of the officials.[1] Two years later superintendent Fernández was complaining of the same officials, and making a plea for 'exchequer officials of integrity, zeal and purpose'.[2]

Apart from the internal administrative problems, there were other more general ones. The yield of *alcabala* and *sisa* taxes in places like Upper Perú was low not only because officials were dishonest, but because agriculture itself was unproductive. This lack of intensive agriculture was a problem general to the whole of Spanish America.[3] But the economy of Upper Perú was rendered even more unsatisfactory because of the absence of a competent technique for a full exploitation of the mines, and by the poverty of the mining operators, who, lacking capital to invest in new equipment and methods or to attract human skill from Europe, were unable to contribute a substantial amount to the treasury.[4] In addition to the problem of production, there was an equally critical one of circulation, which also seriously affected the treasury. The large scale and systematic evasion of duties on commerce by means of contraband trade was considerable, though its extent was difficult to estimate. Contraband export of Potosí silver via Sacramento and other places to foreign markets where it could be sold at as much as 11 to 14 pesos a mark was estimated by the royal treasurer of Potosí in 1784 to remove the greater part of the precious metals in this way.[5]

To exploit more efficiently the potential wealth of the Indies and make it contribute greater revenue to the domestic exchequer demanded a number of reforms of varying technique. Starting at the top, the higher administrative organs were remodelled in the interests of greater centralization. One of the earliest manifestations of Bourbon centralization was, it has been seen, the creation of *Secretarías de Despacho*, or individual

[1] A.G.I., Aud. de Buenos Aires 356, Areche to Fernández, 22 December 1780. Encl. in Fernández to Gálvez, 12 September 1782, Carta 600.

[2] A.G.I., Aud. de Buenos Aires 356, Fernández to Gálvez, Carta 600, 12 September 1782.

[3] See G. Céspedes del Castillo, 'Reorganización de la hacienda virreinal peruana en el siglo XVIII', *Anuario de Historia del Derecho Español*, xxiii (1953), pp. 329–69.

[4] A.G.I., Aud. de Buenos Aires 21, Informe del Consejo, 1 April 1778.

[5] Ots Capdequí, *El siglo XVIII español en América. El gobierno político del Nuevo Reino de Granada* (Mexico, 1945), p. 28.

ministries, one of which was the *Secretaría del Despacho Universal de Asuntos de Indias*, or Ministry of the Indies. The *cédula* of 16 November 1717 assigned to this ministry 'everything pertaining directly or indirectly to the management of my royal exchequer, war, commerce, and navigation in those kingdoms, as well as appointments to offices and duties'.[1] These powers were increased by a series of subsequent royal orders, which progressively reduced the jurisdiction of the Council of the Indies, leaving to it cognizance of exchequer business only in matters of justice. The Secretary, or Minister, of the Indies came to be the supreme chief, the real superintendent of the colonial exchequer, and in this way the structure of government took on a more unified and a more personal character.

In the colonies themselves the superior control of the exchequer had always been assigned to the viceroy, and involved legal functions such as drawing up ordinances and instructions, as well as financial authority to receive the accounts, order inspections, control financial officials, impose the level of taxation and many other duties.[2] In the eighteenth century, by the same process of unification and centralization which was taking place in Madrid, more and more financial matters were drawn within the scope of viceregal authority. In 1747 and 1751 the viceroy's jurisdiction was endowed with that which the *superintendentes generales* already enjoyed in Spain, a title which they henceforth assumed: from now on they controlled all the financial offices, including those such as the *comisiones de lanzas, media anata, papel sellado*, which had hitherto stood apart from the viceroy's jurisdiction, so that henceforth, without the approval of the viceroy, nothing could be effected in matters of exchequer.[3] At this stage, therefore, in addition to being supreme inspector of exchequer, the viceroy was now one of its most burdened officials, involved in multifarious bureaucratic tasks. And still the administration of public funds, as the testimony of viceroy Amat of Perú clearly showed, did not improve. Further modifications of the system were still required.

[1] *Ibid.*, pp. 29–32. See above, p. 6.
[2] *Recopilación*, III, iii, 2, 55, 57; III, xvi, 17; VIII, viii, 1; VIII, xxvii, 12; VIII, xxviii, 1.
[3] A. García Gallo, *Curso de historia del derecho español* (2 vols., Madrid, 1947), i, 449.

The need was all the greater in the viceroyalty of the Río de la Plata, where a new political, administrative and military system had been created in 1776, and where new financial agencies, independent of Lima, were indispensable. A precursor of the financial autonomy of Buenos Aires, the *contaduría mayor de cuentas*, had been created there in 1767, with jurisdiction in all the business of accounts, including both inspection and appeals in the provinces of Buenos Aires, Paraguay and Tucumán, to the complete exclusion both of the tribunal of accounts in Lima and of the *audiencia* of Charcas.[1] When the viceroyalty was created in 1776, the instructions given to Cevallos, the first viceroy, ordered that the northern provinces of the viceroyalty, those of Upper Perú, should continue to render their accounts to Lima, which meant that only Mendoza and San Juan were incorporated into the financial jurisdiction of the *contaduría* of Buenos Aires.[2] In practice, however, Cevallos ignored the instructions, and his message of 10 July 1777 to the *audiencia* of Charcas ordered that henceforth all the funds and accounts of the subtreasuries of Upper Perú should be remitted to Buenos Aires.[3] In 1778 when the superintendency of army and treasury in Buenos Aires was created, the legal anomaly itself was removed and all the accounts of the new viceroyalty were assigned to Buenos Aires.[4] Superintendent Fernández wrongly interpreted his instructions, and on 1 July 1778 suppressed the jurisdiction of the *contador mayor de cuentas* (chief accountant) of Buenos Aires. When this was known in Madrid, a royal order of 12 August 1779 re-established this official with his former functions.[5] To cope with the heavier burden of work now falling on the tribunal of Buenos Aires with the addition of the new provinces of Upper Perú, ten accountants were transferred from Lima in 1779. Thus in 1780 the *contaduría mayor* of Buenos Aires, founded twelve years previously, was transformed into a *tribunal mayor de cuentas* with the same structure and status as similar organs in the rest of the Spanish empire.[6]

---

[1] J. M. Mariluz Urquijo, 'El Tribunal Mayor y Audiencia Real de Cuentas de Buenos Aires', *Revista del Instituto de Historia del Derecho*, iii (Buenos Aires, 1951), pp. 116–17.

[2] Mariluz Urquijo, *op. cit.*, pp. 117–18, note.

[3] Cevallos to Aud. de Charcas, 10 July 1777, in *D.H.A.*, i, 39–40.

[4] *D.G.I.E.A.*, i, 27.   [5] Mariluz Urquijo, *op. cit.*, p. 118.   [6] *Ibid.*

The primitive method of accounting was itself overhauled in 1784 when an Instruction issued by the *Contaduría General* in Madrid for all the Indies explained to the treasuries and sub-treasuries a standardized system of double-entry book keeping for income and expenditure, which included the drawing up of monthly statements and the rendering of accounts at the end of each year, as well as the keeping of three separate books. The royal officials of each treasury, that is the accountant and the treasurer, were to be held responsible for any discrepancies in the accounts.[1] But the new system was unable to make headway against the hard core of ancient practices, and proved too much for the unskilled clerks who had to operate it. It was withdrawn after three years, and return was made to the old system, although some of the new methods were retained.[2]

Once the viceroyalty of the Río de la Plata had taken root and the port of Buenos Aires was opened to direct commerce with many parts of the peninsula, it was necessary to establish a specialized agency to look after the collection of a rising customs revenue with which the ordinary exchequer officials could not be expected to cope. By royal *cédula* of 25 June 1778 the *aduana*, or customs house, of Buenos Aires was established, and Francisco Ximénez de Meza was appointed its first administrator.[3] From the very beginning the *aduana* had important consultative functions. It was never simply a tax-collecting office but was also an exchequer institution with decisive opinion in the policy of viceroys and superintendents, and was always consulted on important commercial and financial matters. The basis of its importance lay in the fact that it was the customs revenue which covered a large part of the expenditure on administration in the viceroyalty, and that in an age of increasing commerce this revenue was rising remarkably. Before 1777 the customs revenue of Buenos Aires had not exceeded 20,000 pesos a year. In 1778 after the establishment of 'free commerce' the revenue collected

[1] 'Nuevo método de cuenta y razón para la Real Hacienda en las Indias . . .', 9 May 1784, printed in *Revista de la Biblioteca Nacional*, iv (Buenos Aires, 1940), pp. 267–318.
[2] Levene, 'Funciones económicas de las instituciones virreinales', *H.N.A.*, iv, i, 482–3.
[3] Ravignani, 'El virreinato del Río de la Plata (1776–1810)', *H.N.A.*, iv, i, 178–9. Another was created for Montevideo by R.O. 10 February 1789.

by the customs house was 53,974 pesos. Between 1791 and 1795 it had a yearly average of almost 400,000 pesos. In 1804 this had risen to about a million pesos.[1]

One of the methods of financial reform in which Charles III placed great confidence was the *visita*, or general inspection, of the state of a given viceroyalty by a special commissioner of the crown. The work of José de Gálvez in New Spain was the outstanding example of this technique, and, heartened by this precedent, the government appointed in March 1776 José Antonio Areche, fiscal of the *audiencia* of Mexico, as visitor-general of Perú. Most of Areche's attention was directed towards a reform of the exchequer, and he strove to eliminate administrative corruption and evasion of taxation, and to impose a better organization of collection of revenue.[2] The creation of the new viceroyalty at the expense of Perú had caused tension between Buenos Aires and Lima, stimulated by the particularist policy pursued by the former. Yet the greatest financial problems were common to the two viceroyalties and needed a unified solution. In appointing Areche visitor of the Río de la Plata and Chile as well as of Perú, the crown seems to have had in mind some sort of co-ordination. If so, it must have been bitterly disillusioned. From Lima viceroy Guirior waged a relentless war against Areche,[3] while from Buenos Aires Cevallos and Vértiz simply ignored him. Worse than this, superintendent Fernández fought him vigorously. Areche clearly enjoyed the right to take cognizance of the affairs of the superintendent, but Fernández considered himself of equal status to the visitor, and by royal order of 11 June 1779 he cleverly got the entire visitation suspended in the new viceroyalty until Areche himself should arrive in person in Buenos Aires. Areche naturally refused to accept such a humiliating order, which prevented him from acting through his assistants. The Council of the Indies approved his attitude, recognized that the visitation ought to be entirely maintained, and decided that Fernández's conduct

[1] Levene, *op. cit.*, p. 485.

[2] G. Céspedes del Castillo, 'Lima y Buenos Aires. Repercusiones económicas y políticas de la creación del virreinato del Plata', *Anuario de Estudios Americanos*, iii (1946), pp. 826–37.

[3] See V. Palacio Atard, 'Areche y Guirior. Observaciones sobre el fracaso de una visita al Perú', *Anuario de Estudios Americanos*, iii (1946), pp. 269–376.

warranted a strong reprimand.[1] In practice, however, the visitation in Buenos Aires remained suspended, and Areche was replaced in Perú by his assistant in Potosí, Jorge Escobedo.[2]

The superintendent of exchequer had not proved very co-operative. Yet this official was one of the most important elements in the financial reorganization undertaken by Charles III. His establishment was a completely new departure in colonial exchequer organization, whereby the viceroys were reduced to general political and military leadership, while the specialized business of finance was assigned to an independent authority, the superintendents, who were now the royal chiefs of financial and economic affairs within each viceroyalty. The royal *cédula* of 21 March 1778 which granted these faculties to Fernández, explained that the new device was designed to increase the royal revenues and to stimulate agriculture and commerce.[3] The superintendent was assured exclusive cognizance of financial tribunals and treasuries, and was made responsible directly to the Ministry of the Indies. Fernández's activities were multifarious. He played a most prominent part in the establishment of the *aduana* in Buenos Aires, and in the operation of the new *comercio libre*.[4] His appointment of extra clerks to the subtreasuries and reorganization of book-keeping methods and office routine were all a foretaste of the approaching reform.

The new official was in fact a precursor of the full intendant régime established by the Ordinance of Intendants in 1782. This must be regarded as the culmination of the financial reorganization undertaken by Charles III in the empire, for it contained not only a modification of the existing system, but also a redefinition and formalization of the whole hierarchy of exchequer administration. The very length and detail of the financial part of the Ordinance gives it a preponderance over other matters contained there.

The executive side of the financial system was now

[1] A.G.I., Aud. de Buenos Aires 473, Informe del contador general y del fiscal de Nueva España, 9 April 1782.

[2] On this affair see Ravignani, *op. cit.*, pp. 148–50.

[3] R.C., 21 March 1778, printed in *D.G.I.E.A.*, i, 27.

[4] A.G.I., Aud. de Buenos Aires 18, Fernández, Instrucción al Consejo, 27 March 1779. See also *D.H.A.*, vi, 135–6.

strengthened and clearly defined. The Secretary of the Indies in Madrid was confirmed in office as superintendent general of the royal exchequer,[1] and was regarded as delegating authority for the viceroyalty of the Río de la Plata to the superintendent in Buenos Aires, who in turn delegated powers to the various intendants of the provinces within the viceroyalty. To lighten the burden of the superintendent of the viceroyalty, a *junta superior de real hacienda* was created. A *junta de hacienda* had always assisted the viceroys in the colonies, and eighteenth-century viceroys had made considerable use of it to save their responsibility before the government and to reinforce their decisions. Now the Ordinance gave it a new name and composition and defined its powers more closely. Constituted under the presidency of the superintendent, it was composed of officials of various departments. These were the senior ministers of the tribunal of accounts, the accountant-general of the exchequer, the assessor of the superintendency and the fiscal of the exchequer. With the establishment of the *audiencia* of Buenos Aires in 1785 the composition of the *junta* was altered, and it was thenceforth formed of the superintendent as president, the regent of the *audiencia*, one judge (*oidor*), one minister of the tribunal of accounts, the fiscal of the exchequer and an accountant. The *junta* also had two reporters, one notary and a clerk.[2] The *junta* had to meet once a week, or more often if necessary. Its general task was to look after the management of the treasury, and to give uniformity to the administration of justice in financial matters; more particularly, it had to supervise the economic aspect of the war department, and to control the funds of the municipalities, a task which had previously been assigned to the tribunal of accounts.[3] The *junta superior* thus united attributes which had formerly been dispersed between the *junta de hacienda*, the *audiencia* and the tribunal of accounts.

The direction of royal revenue within each province was

[1] *Ord. Ints.*, art. 219.

[2] *Ibid.*, art. 3. As a result of the suggestion of viceroy Revillagigedo of New Spain, the Ordinance of Intendants of 1803 modified the *junta*. It was divided into two parts; one part the *junta contenciosa* to take cognisance of all judicial matters, and the other, the *junta de gobierno*, to deal solely with administrative and financial affairs. But this Ordinance was never operative. See Zamora y Coronado, *Biblioteca de legislación ultramarina* (6 vols., Madrid, 1844–6), iii, 379; iv, 89–94.

[3] See below, pp. 216–17.

under the exclusive jurisdiction of the intendants, who reproduced on a smaller scale in the intendancies the attributes of
their chief, the superintendent. They too were assisted by a
committee, the *junta provincial de real hacienda*, which was composed of treasury officials, administrators and chief accountants.[1] Although this *junta* was supposed to meet once a week,
such was not the regular practice: according to intendant
Sobremonte, in Córdoba it only met when there was special
reason for it.[2] Cognizance of all cases arising out of disputes in
financial matters and payment of taxes, which the Laws of the
Indies had entrusted to exchequer officials, was now transferred
to the intendants in their respective provinces, who were thus
endowed with the sanction to enforce collection of revenue.[3]
In the subdistricts of the intendancies the subdelegates were
judges of first instance in treasury matters, and appeal from
their decisions was always allowed to the intendants, who
determined the cases by means of their assessors.[4] The intendants, therefore, had absolute jurisdiction over financial affairs
within their provinces, to the exclusion of any other court.
Appeals from their decision could be made to the *junta superior* in
Buenos Aires, which was the highest court of appeal in financial
matters in the viceroyalty.[5] In this way the competence of the
audiencia, which had hitherto heard appeals in second and third
instance, was diminished, and the administrative hierarchy was
carefully centralized.

Each intendancy had a *caja principal*, or principal subtreasury,
situated in the capital of the province; these were the centres of
the collecting and accounting of taxes, whence they were submitted to the tribunal of accounts in Buenos Aires. There were
already twelve subtreasuries existing in Buenos Aires, Santa Fe,
Asunción del Paraguay, La Paz, Chucuito, Carabaya, Mendoza,
La Plata, Cochabamba, Oruro, Carangas and Potosí. To these
the Ordinance of Intendants added subtreasuries in San Miguel
de Tucumán, Córdoba, and Santa Cruz de la Sierra. Those of
the intendancy capitals were given the status of principal subtreasuries, and the intendants were authorized to create even

---

[1] *Ord. Ints.*, arts. 214–15. [2] Garzon, *Crónica de Córdoba*, p. 369.
[3] *Ord. Ints.*, arts. 72–3. [4] *Ibid.*, art. 73.
[5] The superintendent could not be present when lawsuits appealed from his
decisions as intendant of province were being heard in the *junta. Ord. Ints.* art. 74.

more subtreasuries if necessary.[1] The subordinate subtreasuries were simply receiving centres which passed on their collections to the principals.

The subtreasuries were staffed by exchequer officials (*oficiales reales*), who were the actual administrators of the system, and formed, as it were, the workers at the face, being responsible for the collection and accounting of the royal revenue. On their competence and honesty ultimately depended the success of the reform. Various laws already existed, such as the prohibition to engage in commerce or receive any other emoluments, laws which were now reaffirmed and which were designed to make officials devote themselves exclusively to the function of their office. In turn the officials had high privileges, such as authority to correspond directly with the king.[2] The Ordinance of Intendants did not significantly modify the position of the exchequer officials, nor did it call a halt to sale of offices. It did, however, standardize the number of officials at two in each principal subtreasury, an accountant and a treasurer, and one in the subordinate treasuries.[3] The wages of these officials were increased to 3,000 pesos in Buenos Aires and 2,000 in the remaining principal subtreasuries.[4] The salaries of the officials of any new subtreasuries were to be determined by the intendants with the advice of the *junta superior*.[5] The *junta* would often in practice consult the government in Madrid about pay increases, as for instance when it forwarded an application from the intendant of La Paz for an increase for his subordinate officials in 1786.[6]

To prevent leakage from treasury funds various checks were imposed. The intendants had to be careful that funds were not paid from subtreasuries by warrants drawn by the officials who administered them, and the superintendent and provincial

---

[1] *Ord. Ints.*, art. 91.

[2] But the *via reservada* was closed to them by R.O. of 20 November 1784. A.G.I., Aud. de Buenos Aires 358, Sanz to Gálvez, Carta 315, 27 March 1785.

[3] *Ord. Ints.*, art. 93.

[4] *Ibid.*, art. 94. Before the intendant system the treasury officials of Jujuy had a salary of 1,000 pesos a year. But the salaries of officials of the subordinate treasuries remained inadequate, e.g. those of Mendoza still only had 200 a year. A.G.I., Aud. de Buenos Aires 358, Sanz to Gálvez, Carta 327, 27 March 1785.

[5] *Ibid.*, arts. 91, 93.

[6] A.G.I., Aud. de Charcas 704, Junta Superior de Real Hacienda de Buenos Aires to Sonora, 11 July 1786.

intendants were forbidden to draw upon the treasury without special royal permission. Any official who issued a warrant without a royal order would be held responsible.[1] Before salaries, pensions or any other expenditure could be paid, the superintendent had to countersign the order, a memorandum had to be made in the tribunal of accounts, and another by the ministers of the treasury. Then the payments had to be authorized by the *junta superior*. In extraordinary expenditures the process was even more complicated. First a provincial junta of the treasury had to be held in the intendancy to discuss and vote upon the matter. Then the provincial intendant gave an account of the decision to the *junta superior* through the superintendent as its president. Finally royal approval had to be obtained.[2]

When treasury officials had any doubts about the making of duly authorized payments, they had to submit the matter to the intendant, who would decide it, in consultation with the *junta superior* in the more serious cases; in this event the treasury officials would not be held accountable, but only the intendant or *junta*, whichever had given the order for payment.[3] Intendants had power to suspend payments and to transfer funds from one treasury to another within their territory, but only the superintendent could convey them from one province to another.[4] For the sake of uniformity in financial administration each intendant had to keep a general account book of the finances of his province, showing income and expenditure; a copy of this was to be sent to the superintendent in order that a general statement for the whole viceroyalty could be drawn up and forwarded to Madrid.[5]

The intendants naturally had to provide for the punctual collection of revenues and for their increase if it could be done fairly. They were enjoined to make sure that lessees of revenues did not oppress the community by collecting too much, and that they paid punctually into the treasury the full amount collected. The intendants heard complaints of those who considered themselves wrongly assessed and had authority to punish tax-collectors who proved to be defaulting.[6]

---

[1] *Ord. Ints.*, arts. 96–7. [2] *Ibid.*, arts. 98–101. [3] *Ibid.*, art. 101.
[4] *Ibid.*, arts. 102–4. [5] *Ibid.*, art. 104. [6] *Ibid.*, arts. 106–15.

The Ordinance enumerated the traditional sources of royal revenue. The royal tribute, paid at the rate of five pesos every half year, was one of the principal ones and was commended to the special attention of the intendants. Formerly the *corregidores* and *alcaldes mayores* had collected this tax, with much incidental peculation. Now it was entrusted to the *alcaldes ordinarios* and subdelegates, who had to enter the money into the treasury twice a year whence it was accounted for in Buenos Aires. In order that the intendants might be well informed about this revenue, the tribunal of accounts and treasury officials were to submit to them any information they had on the subject.[1] *Alcaldes ordinarios* and subdelegates received as remuneration 4 per cent of the amount that entered the treasury from this branch, while Indian tax gatherers received 3 per cent.[2] As the collection of this revenue was based on the number of inhabitants, the intendants had to see that a census of the population of their province was made, and in order to keep this up to date they were ordered to make visitations every five years.[3] The Indians (but not those of the Paraguayan reductions) had to pay tribute between the ages of eighteen and fifty, and the only persons exempted were *caciques*, the eldest sons of *caciques*, Indian *alcaldes* and women. Both in Perú and in the viceroyalty of the Río de la Plata the contribution of the royal tributes was not equitable and it was now established that the quota should be fixed according to the classes of people, the quality of their arable land and the profits from their trade and incomes. The *junta superior* with the advice of the fiscal was to determine a just quota. Intendants were enjoined to ensure that vagabonds of the tribute-paying class should be put to work under good masters who would deduct their wages on a pay-as-you-earn basis.[4]

The other classical sources of income for the crown were the royal fifth and the *alcabala*, or purchase tax, paid at the rate of 6 per cent.[5] Intendants were to take measures to check fraud in the collection of the *alcabala* and to prevent evasion of its payment, and they were always to give an account of their

---

[1] *Ord. Ints.*, art. 119.   [2] *Ibid.*, art. 117
[3] *Ibid.*, art. 121.   [4] *Ibid.*, arts. 123–7.
[5] In frontier districts it was paid at 4 per cent. It was paid at 4 per cent in the province of Córdoba, see 'Memoria de Sobremonte', printed in Garzon, *Crónica de Córdoba*, Appendix I, p. 369.

measures to the *junta superior*.[1] The old royal fifth (reduced since 1723 to a tenth) from gold, silver, copper and other metals, still remained and brought considerable revenue into the treasury. For this reason the intendants were expected to do their best to encourage mining. They were to preside over the mining tribunals in their provinces, and in the smaller towns their subdelegates were to have cognizance of mining cases. Under the centralizing policy of Charles III the *Banco de Rescates* of Potosí had already been incorporated in the crown in 1779.[2] Now, in order to prevent concealment and fraudulent removal of gold and silver in bullion, which needy mining operators often sold to dealers in violation of the laws prohibiting trade in these metals before the fifth was deducted, it was ordered that in all the principal and subsidiary treasuries of the provinces which had mines in current operation there should always be kept enough money for the fair purchase of gold and silver brought for sale by the mining operators. In order that their value could be paid promptly and accurately at the current market price, the offices of melter and assayer of the existing subtreasuries were incorporated in the royal treasury.[3] The efficient distribution of mercury was entrusted to the special care of the intendants.[4]

Intendants also had to supervise the department of revenue from *papel sellado*, or stamped paper required for all legal documents. The superintendent sent the paper to the provincial intendants, who distributed it among the subtreasuries and tobacco administrators. Each intendant had to report his

---

[1] *Ord. Ints.*, arts. 129–30.

[2] This bank existed specifically for the purchase of metals from the miners. Established by royal *cédula* of 12 June 1752 it had an unsatisfactory existence under private enterprise and was bought out by the crown on the initiative of Escobedo, Areche's assistant in Potosí, in 1779. See V. Palacio Atard, 'La incorporación a la Corona del Banco de Rescates de Potosí', *Anuario de Estudios Americanos*, ii (1945), pp. 723–36. The *Casa de Moneda* of Potosí, hitherto operated by a system of semi-private enterprise, was also incorporated in the crown in 1753. The superintendent of the Royal Mint was also superintendent of the bank, and had independent jurisdiction to the exclusion of any other tribunal; appeals from his judgment went to the *junta superior*. On the personnel of the royal mint, see H. F. Burzio, *La Ceca de la Villa Imperial de Potosí y la moneda colonial* (Buenos Aires, 1945), pp. 20–8.

[3] *Ord. Ints.*, arts. 133–4. By R.O. 16 July 1790 the offices of melter and assaye were declared vendible and renunciable. See *D.G.I.E.A.*, i, 58, n. (1).

[4] *Ord. Ints.*, art. 136.

requirements to the superintendent so that shipments from Spain could be made twice a year.[1]

There was a tendency on the part of the Spanish crown in the eighteenth century to administer directly certain taxes hitherto leased to individuals or institutions, and to perform public services which had previously been entrusted to private management. This development of state monopolies gave another impetus to the specialization of officials, so that agencies emerged dedicated exclusively to the administration of certain taxes which involved more specialized methods of collection and management. By this process separate agencies for the royal mint and for the postage service developed, and thus the *casas de moneda* and *correos* made their appearance, incorporated in the crown in 1753 and 1769 respectively. Revenues from the monopolies of tobacco, gun-powder and playing cards had also been brought under treasury administration after having been leased out. Their separate departments were now united under a single administration, but this was still separate from the general exchequer department. The intendant was given judicial cognizance over this revenue, and the superintendent, with the advice of the tribunal of accounts, was to draw up a code of administration for these monopolies, to be approved by the *junta superior*.[2] In 1796 a further stage in the process of centralization and uniformity was marked when it was definitely established that the accounts of the tobacco revenue, which had hitherto been examined by its own accountant-general without the intervention of the tribunal of accounts, should come before the tribunal of accounts.[3] The royal dues from half-annates and titles of nobility were entrusted in all parts of the empire to special commissioners and had their own special accounting office in Buenos Aires; the Ordinance established that these revenues had to be included in the general statement of the treasury and the minister of the accounting office had to submit at the beginning of each year a report of their accounts separately to the superintendent.[4]

[1] *Ord. Ints.*, arts. 142–3.   [2] *Ibid.*, arts. 140–1.
[3] Mariluz Urquijo, *op. cit.*, p. 127.
[4] *Ord. Ints.*, art. 144. Revenues from salt mines and from a tax on grocery stores were also administered by the intendants. Arts. 137–9. Ecclesiastical tithes were also brought under their jurisdiction. Arts. 147 ff.

The intendants had to transmit monthly all the funds (except the tobacco revenue which continued under separate management) from the minor subtreasuries to the principal subtreasury of the province, and finally all the surplus funds of the principal subtreasury to the capital.[1] On the first day of each month intendants and subdelegates attended the very formal ceremony of opening the coffers and checking the contents against the books of the treasury officials. When the coffers were inspected, another statement of receipts and expenditure was given to them. They compared the first one with it and signed the former if it was correct. Each intendant had to send the statements of receipts and expenditure with those from their treasury and other administrative offices of the capital to the principal accounting office of the province where they could all be united into one general and comprehensive statement of all the branches of the treasury in each province. The subdelegates submitted five copies of each of their monthly statements to the intendants. The provincial intendant kept one and sent the rest to the superintendent, who also retained one, and transmitted another to the tribunal of accounts and the other two to the king. From these documents the yearly statement of the whole royal treasury would, it was hoped, be compiled.[2] At the end of the year there was a similar, though more detailed, inspection of the coffers, and annual financial statements were forwarded to the superintendent.[3]

This formidable financial programme began to operate in 1783. It made no revolutionary departure from established financial practice, and it took for granted the continuance of sale of offices, but by harnessing almost all exchequer matters to the intendants and canalizing the accountancy system to the one tribunal of accounts, it gave a unified and vigorous stimulus to honesty and efficiency. The one fundamental modification of the existing system for which the Ordinance legislated did not last long. The division of labour between viceroy and superintendent, whereby the superintendent received all the financial authority hitherto enjoyed by the viceroy, produced an argument between conservatives and reformers, in which all the weight of ancient viceregal institutions and prerogatives was

---

[1] *Ord. Ints.*, art. 202.   [2] *Ibid.*, arts. 206–9.   [3] *Ibid.*, art. 209.

pitted against the innovation. In the viceroyalty of the Río de la Plata the system was rendered practically unworkable by the cold war between viceroy Loreto and superintendent Sanz over matters which were not connected with finance but which were persistent enough to bring the whole device into disrepute.[1] Shortly after the death of José de Gálvez, who had stoutly sustained the reform as long as he lived, former practices triumphed, the independent superintendency of exchequer was abolished and its attributes restored to the viceroy. The viceroy became not only superintendent of the whole viceroyalty but also the intendant of the province of Buenos Aires: thus he now had cognizance in first instance of contentious cases in finance in Buenos Aires and its province, and from his decisions appeals could be made to the *junta superior de real hacienda*, just as they should be made from those of the other intendants.[2]

Meanwhile the provincial intendants went ahead with the work of the exchequer assigned to them, and soon their administration began to bear fruit. The first to produce concrete results was Sobremonte in Córdoba. By a conscientious and unspectacular application of the rules of the Ordinance, he was able to show a striking increase in royal revenue after three years, 'with the satisfaction of not having a single complaint, since the only innovation has consisted in the zeal of the particular and general administration of the branches of the royal treasury. . . .'[3] The figures speak for themselves. In Córdoba the net annual revenue in 1784 was 9,994 pesos. In 1785 this had almost doubled to 19,362 pesos 2¼ reales. In Mendoza the income in 1784 was 10,535 pesos 1¾ reales. In 1785 it had risen to 18,544 pesos 1¼ reales, an amount which could not quite be sustained in 1786 when the total was 16,877 pesos. In Córdoba the total increase over two years was 21,280 pesos 6¾ reales, while in Mendoza it was 8,008 pesos 7¾ reales.[4] This remarkable

---

[1] See above, pp. 95–105.

[2] Arredondo, 'Memoria de gobierno', 16 March 1795, in Radaelli, *Memorias de los virreyes del Río de la Plata*, p. 450.

[3] A.G.I., Aud. de Buenos Aires 363, Sobremonte to Sanz, 5 April 1786.

[4] A.G.I., Aud. de Buenos Aires 473, 'Estado que manifiesta . . . los valores de los ramos de Real Hacienda . . . Provincia de Córdoba', 24 March 1787; a similar account is to be found in A.G.I., Aud. de Buenos Aires 363. See Appendix II, Table A.

effort earned the praise of superintendent Sanz, and was duly reported to Madrid.[1]

The figures available from Potosí show a similar rise which can be dated from 1783.[2] One of the greatest factors contributing to an increase of revenue in Potosí, as in other places, was the royal tribute, which yielded an appreciably larger income in the early years of the intendant system, owing to the administration of intendant Pino Manrique, who established new registers of taxable Indians based on a revised census. The total increase of taxable Indians in the intendancy of Potosí was 6,349, producing a financial rise of 38,570 pesos 1½ reales.[3] In Puno also the Indian tribute was a source of rising financial return.[4] Pino Manrique's administration in Potosí also procured a substantial increase in customs revenue. In the six years before 1782 the customs yielded 297,999 pesos 6¼ reales. In the six years of Pino Manrique's régime they yielded 501,835 pesos ¼ real, thus giving an increase of 203,835 pesos 1½ reales. The intendant's campaign against contraband was obviously bearing fruit.[5]

The *alcabala* tax, so badly administered before the intendant régime, now began to contribute something like its due amount. In Paraguay there is a good example of this, though it should be remembered that its increase in this province lasted longer than it did in most others, owing to the fact that Paraguay enjoyed an almost unbroken line of first-class intendants.[6] In the intendancy of La Paz, on the other hand, the new system produced no automatic improvement, and a comparison of the *alcabala* revenue in a five-year period afterwards shows an actual decrease of 64,265 pesos 3¾.[7]

The financial system in La Paz, it is true was an exceptionally corrupt one, but after the first flush of enthusiasm the system

[1] A.G.I., Aud. de Buenos Aires 363, Sanz to Sonora, Carta 693, 14 June 1787.

[2] See Appendix II, Table B.

[3] A.G.I., Aud. de Charcas 704, Estado Gral del numero de Indios tributarios y valor de sus tasas . . . Potosí, 16 November 1787.

[4] See Appendix II, Table C.

[5] A.G.I., Aud. de Charcas 435, Pino Manrique to Porlier, 16 March 1788. See Appendix II, Table D.

[6] See Appendix II, Table E.

[7] See Appendix II, Table F. It should be remembered however, that these periods were divided by the Tupac Amaru rebellion.

began to falter in all parts of the viceroyalty, and the intendants were faced with a rising tide of inefficiency and dishonesty in the exchequer service. In some cases the intendants and the exchequer officials did not work well together. In Potosí intendant Pino Manrique reported obstructionist tactics on the part of the officials, which he attributed to jealousy over their loss of judicial cognizance of financial disputes, and he complained that they were trying to reassert an independence which they did not legally possess. He named as glaring examples specifically Lamberto de Sierra, and his own assessor, Pedro Vicente Cañete.[1] For their part the exchequer officials of Potosí complained directly to the authorities in Madrid of the intendant's aggressive behaviour.[2] Relations between intendant and the exchequer deteriorated still further in the next few years. In 1787 Pino Manrique established ten primary schools in the subdistrict of Chayanta, and fixed the salary of the master in each one at 100 pesos a year. As this district did not have any community or municipal funds at its disposal, the intendant assigned the charge to the revenue from the royal tribute.[3] Now he was open to attack. The exchequer officials of Potosí opposed the expenditure and reported the matter to Madrid. The accountant-general in Madrid decided that while the intendant's scheme was worthy of approval, his method was not, for he had exceeded his faculties as laid down in the Ordinance of Intendants, which declared that all extraordinary expenses (as this one was) ought to be decided in the *junta provincial de hacienda* and submitted for approval to the *junta superior*.[4] The crown accepted this opinion, and although it approved the education scheme it also decided that such a project must be financed according to the laws.[5]

Uncooperative officials, however, were the least of an intendant's worries: dishonest ones were much more common. In 1791 intendant Pizarro reported on the case of Luis Surlin, administrator-general of the tobacco revenue in the intendancy

[1] A.G.I., Aud. de Charcas 435, Pino Manrique to Porlier, 16 May 1788.
[2] A.G.I., Aud. de Charcas 423, Oficiales reales de Potosí to Valdés, 16 March 1788.
[3] A.G.I., Aud. de Charcas 438, Pino Manrique to Sonora, 6 September 1787.
[4] A.G.I., Estado 76, Consulta del Consejo, 14 March 1790.
[5] A.G.I., Aud. de Charcas 552, R.C. to Gov. Int. of Potosí, 7 April 1790.

of Salta. Surlin had defaulted on 30,000 pesos, for which he was quickly imprisoned. Pizarro looked into the matter on his visit of inspection, and was able to recover two-thirds of the loss,[1] but the case was a warning that all was not well beneath the surface. On his accession to the intendancy of Puno in 1790 the Marqués de Casa Hermosa found the exchequer there in sore straits. In unpaid revenue alone the province was 362,269 pesos in arrears. By a concentrated effort on the part of the intendant, the subtreasuries gathered in three years 156,382 pesos, that is almost half of the arrears, and gained an increase of almost 40 per cent in the royal tribute.[2] This vigorous financial policy created for the intendant many enemies, especially among those who had profited from maladministration, such as the exchequer officials of Carabaya, José Ballivián and Juan de Dios Villamoz, who had fraudulently concealed a bankruptcy of more than 126,000 pesos in which many other officials were involved. The intendant also brought to light the corrupt practices of the administrator-general of tobacco, Miguel de Echerique, and was obliged to suspend from office the subdelegates of Azángaro and Chucuito who were also concealing considerable deficits.[3] All this activity rendered part of the official class discontented and led to a campaign of intrigue and libel against the intendant which unfortunately some of his own imprudent actions rendered the more plausible: his subsequent resignation and embarrassing trial might well have served as a deterrent to other intendants against stirring up similar hornets' nests.[4]

Other cases proved the parlous state of the exchequer affairs in various parts of the viceroyalty. The situation was worst in Upper Perú. In 1794 the subdelegate of the district of Paria in the intendancy of La Plata defaulted on the tribute revenue to the amount of 10,614 pesos 7½ reales, and it was the opinion of the Council of the Indies that this was made possible by slack

[1] Pizarro to Crown, 5 October 1791, printed in J. Torre Revello, 'Relación de la visita . . .', *B.I.I.H.*, xiii (1931), p. 72.
[2] Archivo Histórico Nacional, Madrid, Consejo de Indias, leg. 20406, pz. viii, fol. 2; pz. xviii, fol. 29, Causa del marqués de Casa-Hermosa.
[3] V. Rodríguez Casado, 'Causa seguida contra el marqués de Casa-Hermosa, gobernador-intendente de Puno', *Anuario de Estudios Americanos*, III (1946), pt. ii, pp. 959–60.
[4] See below, pp. 251–53.

accounting by treasury officials.[1] Rumours and complaints of financial corruption in La Paz became more and more persistent. An anonymous complaint of 1796, written under the name Alberto Pérez and addressed to fiscal Villava, accused the subdelegate of Achacachi of serious peculation and of trading with treasury funds, and claimed that he enjoyed the direct protection of the intendant, who, it was alleged, was ready to sell any subdelegacy for hard cash.[2] In September 1798 Villava drew the viceroy's attention to the state of affairs in La Paz, and in October 1801 he reported that the subtreasuries in the city of La Paz were more than a million and a half pesos down, while those of Oruro were more than a million in default.[3] Villava considered that the fiscals of the *audiencias* should have more influence in exchequer affairs. Formerly the fiscals had appointed the *defensores de real hacienda* in the provinces of their district, but since the establishment of the intendant system these appointments had been made by the intendant. Villava considered that this made the *defensores* too dependent on the intendants, and that they should be appointed once more by the fiscals.[4] The government eventually adopted this suggestion: on 5 June 1801 a royal order was issued, declaring that in future *defensores de hacienda* of the provincial capitals of the viceroyalty of the Río de la Plata should be appointed by the viceroy from three candidates presented by the fiscals of the *audiencias*.[5]

Meanwhile the treasury officials in Potosí blamed the tribunal of accounts in Buenos Aires for confusion and incompetence in the settling of accounts. The basis of their complaint was that the methods of the central tribunal lacked order and fairness, showed ignorance of the law and were over-burdened with legal niceties. They submitted their complaint to intendant Sanz, who, grateful for any opportunity to embarrass his enemies in Buenos Aires, forwarded it with his support to the government in Madrid as well as to the viceroy in Buenos Aires.[6] But he got

---

[1] A.G.I., Aud. de Charcas 424, Consulta del Consejo, 14 March, 1798.

[2] A.G.I., Aud. de Charcas 446, 'Alberto Pérez' to Villava, 16 December 1796.

[3] Levene, *Vida y escritos de Victorián de Villava*, pp. cxxiii, xxxvii–xxxviii.

[4] A.G.I., Aud. de Charcas 446, Villava to Acuña, 24 May 1793.

[5] A.G.I., Aud. de Charcas 424, R.O. 5 June 1801.

[6] A.G.I., Aud. de Charcas 440, Sanz to Diego de Guardoqui, Potosí, 26 September 1794. Also in A.G.I., Aud. de Charcas 705.

little encouragement: the complaints were rejected as completely unfounded, their lack of respect was condemned, and Sanz himself was reprimanded for lending his support to them.[1]

The government's view of the tribunal of accounts was an unrealistic one. It is impossible to give a completely circumstantial account of the state of the exchequer in the viceroyalty of the Río de la Plata and of its contribution to the revenue of the mother country precisely because of the negligence of the tribunal of accounts. According to the Ordinance of Intendants, general accounts for the whole of the viceroyalty should have been regularly drawn up in Buenos Aires. But the viceroys themselves were unable to obtain such material. The tribunal of accounts in Buenos Aires had been in arrears in its work ever since its establishment. Extra officials were appointed without avail. When he entered office in March 1799, viceroy Avilés tried to procure a general statement of the finances of the viceroyalty, but this proved almost impossible:

... the tribunal of accounts ... informed me that it was unable to prepare it, because it lacked the necessary information, for from the year 1780, in which it was established, to the present time, it was unable to calculate the accounts for any five year period, nor even for a single year, and could only inform me that the treasuries and other offices had failed to send their special and general accounts.[2]

From this it must be inferred that the blame did not lie entirely with the tribunal but also with the provincial exchequer offices and subtreasuries. For such a wholesale neglect of the Ordinance of Intendants viceroy Avilés blamed not only the tribunal but also all the intendants, as well as the previous viceroys. The government ordered Avilés to take the strictest measures against any officials failing in their duties, and although he himself did little to arrest the decline, he did at least make known more information about the true state of affairs, and revealed that the situation was unsatisfactory not only in La Paz but even in places like Potosí, Salta and Paraguay.

In Spain itself the treasury was in desperate straits, as was

[1] A.G.I., Aud. de Charcas 704, R.O. to intendant of Potosí, 12 January 1796.
[2] Marqués de Avilés, 'Memoria de gobierno', 21 May 1801, in Radaelli, *Memorias de los virreyes del Río de la Plata*, p. 523. See Levene's figures in *Investigaciones acerca de la historia económica del virreinato del Plata*, ii, 28.

revealed by the appointment of a special Junta to seek measures for repairing it.[1] This domestic urgency, combined with the situation in the Río de la Plata, led the government to attempt some remedies. By royal dispatch of 22 February 1802 Pedro José Ballesteros and Juan Andrés de Arroyo, accountants of the tribunal of accounts in Buenos Aires, were retired. Diego de la Vega, hitherto accountant in Lima, was appointed *contador decano* in Buenos Aires and visitor-general of all the subtreasuries and other exchequer offices of the viceroyalty of the Río de la Plata.[2] Undeterred by the experience of Areche, the government once more put its faith in the device of the general visitation. Vega was given power to suppress useless offices, remove corrupt officials, appoint new ones; and neither the viceroy nor the *audiencias* could annul or suspend his measures.[3] It was not an enviable task. He had to attack a hard core of interest, officials who could not be expected to co-operate, and without the moral support of the viceroy on whose financial supremacy he was encroaching.

Vega opened his programme with a general diagnosis of the financial ills of the viceroyalty. Not only were accounts not rendered from the provinces to the capital, but surplus funds remained undue time in the subtreasuries, instead of being sent to the head treasury in Buenos Aires for their remittance to Spain; this accounted partly for the extent of peculation, for officials began to use these conveniently available funds for their own commerce. Erring officials were too often left unpunished. There had been no registers of taxable Indians made for the last ten years. According to the accounts of the tobacco and playing-card monopoly for the previous five years, accounts which Vega himself had ordered to be made and which were the first since its very establishment, the yearly net revenue was only 173,533 pesos. 'Here everything lies in a profound lethargy,' was his conclusion.[4]

A royal order of 1 October 1803 authorized him to go ahead with vigorous inquiry and punishment. After stirring up the

[1] A.G.I., Indif. Gen. 844, 'Dictamen de la Junta creada para buscar los medios de atender a las urgencias de la Corona, 1798'.

[2] Mariluz Urquijo, *op. cit.*, p. 120.

[3] *Loc. cit.*   [4] A.G.I., Aud. de Charcas 710, Vega to Soler, 25 May 1803.

tribunal of accounts in Buenos Aires, he strictly enjoined the intendants to look to their duty, threatening the exchequer officials with serious consequences if they did not render their accounts by return of post. This produced some response, but when he ordered the subtreasuries to remit their funds every two months he had less success, and had to report that when expenses had been deducted there was usually little left over to be sent.[1] Moreover the administrators of the tobacco revenue in La Paz, Cochabamba, Salta, Córdoba, and Montevideo had dissipated great quantities of royal revenue and endeavoured to cover up their deficiencies in interminable and voluminous litigation.[2]

One of the greatest difficulties facing Vega was the fact that he had to proceed against an official class which was firmly entrenched and had much to lose. He hesitated to stir up this interest, or to proceed to wholesale dismissals, though he judged it indispensable that some officials should be removed and others transferred. Least of all did he feel confident of proceeding without the co-operation of the viceroy. He therefore proposed to viceroy Pino that when any financial office fell vacant, he should communicate the names of the applicants to Vega who would vet them.[3] It was now evident, however, that the visitor-general could not count on the support of the viceroy,[4] and Vega came to the conclusion that the viceroy's criterion for filling exchequer offices was not one of competence and aptitude but consisted in a desire to satisfy friends with offices, many posts being left vacant for years until a protégé of the viceroy presented himself. An example of this was the post of senior official of the accounting office of the Banco de San Carlos of Potosí, which had been vacant for two years.[5]

It was inevitable that the largest single item on Vega's programme would be the notorious exchequer in La Paz and Oruro. An official attempt to grapple with affairs in this remote province had already misfired. In 1796 the intendant of La Paz

[1] A.G.I., Aud. de Buenos Aires 370, Vega to Soler, Carta 17, 24 December 1802.
[2] *Ibid.* Vega removed the provisional administrator of the tobacco revenue in Córdoba, Manuel de Alfaro, and replaced him by Martín Josef de Goyeoechea.
[3] A.G.I., Aud. de Buenos Aires 39, Vega to Viceroy Pino, 3 August 1803.
[4] A.G.I., Aud. de Buenos Aires 370, Vega to Soler, Carta 80, 28 December 1803.
[5] A.G.I., Aud. de Buenos Aires 39, Vega to Soler, 28 December 1803.

protested against the behaviour and the measures of Pedro Vicente Cañete, *teniente letrado* of the intendancy of Potosí, who had been appointed in 1794 visitor of the principal subtreasuries and customs house of La Paz. In this capacity Cañete revived many *alcabala* taxes and took many other restrictive measures which the intendant alleged were disturbing commerce. The intendant argued that a lesson was to be learned from the fact that one of the principal causes of the Tupac Amaru rebellion lay in the resentment aroused by the imposition or threat of new customs taxes, and claimed that the people of La Paz were in no position to pay heavy taxes after the destruction wrought by this rebellion. The *hacendados* of the province sent a deputation to the intendant requesting more moderate procedure from the visitor. The intendant took the side of the ranchers, land owners and mining operators, and reported to the government that the commissioner should be limited to making inquiries and should desist from grandiose schemes. Cañete, however, was undeterred by the opposition of the intendant and actually tried to extend the jurisdiction of his visitation. He became so troublesome that his commission was eventually suspended, having effected singularly little.[1]

Vega proceeded with more prudence, and soon discovered that at the end of June 1802 the subtreasuries of La Paz owed 1,333,601 pesos 6 reales, and that the officials had not rendered accounts for the last seven years; those in Oruro owed 565,306 pesos $3\frac{1}{4}$ reales up to 31 December 1801, and lacked accounts for the eight previous years. Under the stimulus of Vega, the debts of La Paz were reduced by 1 April 1803 to 951,348 pesos 5 reales, and those of Oruro to 520,934 pesos 7 reales.[2] The exchequer officials in La Paz and Oruro were arrested and their goods confiscated. In reporting these affairs to Madrid, Vega pointed out that this large-scale peculation could easily have been discovered in its early stages if the intendant at that time, Fernando de la Sota, had insisted on regular accounts, as he was obliged to do by the Ordinance.[3]

---

[1] A.G.I., Aud. de Charcas 440, Fernando de la Sota (Intendant of La Paz) to Crown, 7 June 1796.

[2] A.G.I., Aud. de Buenos Aires 370, Vega to Soler, Carta 24, 25 May 1803.

[3] A.G.I., Aud. de Buenos Aires 40, Vega to Soler, 28 December 1803.

Further smaller defalcations were discovered.[1] The minor subtreasury of Carangas, in the charge of Juan Muñoz Villegas, had a deficit of 84,968 pesos 6 reales. Villegas made little effort to cover up his crime. From 1792 he had been drawing on treasury funds: to cover this he had invested more public funds in a mining operation, but the venture failed. The tribunal of accounts had never insisted on remittance of regular accounts, and naturally Villegas had not volunteered them, so the loss was not stopped in its early stages.[2]

The subdelegate of the district of Omasuios was charged with a deficiency of more than 70,000 pesos in the royal tribute and other branches over a period of four years' administration during which he lost the greater part of the royal revenue in fruitless mining ventures. Intendant Burgunyo removed him, and he retaliated by accusing Burgunyo of being an accomplice, with such persistence that the viceroy appointed on 25 September 1800 one of the judges of the *audiencia* of Charcas to proceed to La Paz and investigate the affair. Burgunyo protested against this affront to his prestige in La Paz, but in any case the inquiry accomplished nothing.[3] Burgunyo's subsequent opposition to Vega, taking the form of evading his orders and rejecting his commissioner, González de Prada, as unnecessary, once more drew suspicion on to the intendant himself, but Vega was unable to prove anything.[4] After Burgunyo's death, Vega recommended Gonzáles de Prada, hitherto senior accountant of the tribunal of accounts in Lima, for the intendancy of La Paz, hoping that the administration of a financial specialist would cure the ills of the body politic in La Paz. The viceroy granted Prada the intendancy, but only in the department of exchequer, reserving political and judicial affairs to the *teniente asesor*, Tadeo Dávila. This unworkable arrangement was completely overthrown by Dávila, who proceeded not only to exclude Prada from financial authority but even to resist his visitation, an attitude in which he was supported by the exchequer officials and the multitude of treasury debtors. As a

[1] A.G.I., Aud. de Buenos Aires 40, Vega to Soler, 30 April, 1804.
[2] A.G.I., Aud. de Charcas 710, Vega to Soler, 30 April 1804.
[3] A.G.I., Aud. de Charcas 441, Burgunyo to Crown, 17 April 1804.
[4] A.G.I., Aud. de Charcas 441, Vega to Soler, 28 February 1808.

compromise the viceroy then appointed Antonio Álvarez de Soto Mayor as intendant, and suspended the visitation of González by a dispatch of 23 June 1809, despite the protests of Vega. Meanwhile Dávila continued and so did treasury losses in La Paz.[1]

Vega had been fighting a losing battle. His appointments of delegate visitors for the provinces of the interior were consistently opposed by viceroy Pino, who considered he had no authority to appoint commissioners. Resistance to Vega was so powerful that his enemies succeeded in obtaining a royal order of 23 March 1804 which disapproved of his appointment of commissioners for the interior and which limited the visitation of the viceregal exchequer system to one city, Buenos Aires, and to one office, the tribunal of accounts.[2] In practice, however, Vega was able to disregard this and carry on with the work he had begun. He drew up a very efficient *Instrucción para el Tribunal de Cuentos de Buenos-Ayres* (23 October 1805), a code of instruction for every official of the tribunal which was still in use after the colonies had won their independence from Spain.[3] He managed to procure a small amount of the revenue owed from La Paz but had to report in 1809 that the debts existing at the end of 1808 in the subtreasuries and customs amounted to 1,178,772 pesos 1 real.[4]

In the realm of finance, therefore, the intendant system after early signs of promise, did not fulfil the high hopes held of it. The intendants were unable to reform a treasury service corrupted by sale of offices and official patronage. They themselves were often remiss in insisting on regular rendering of accounts. Moreover the province of La Paz suffered from the fact that it never had an intendant for a full term of office and had to endure a series of short and often temporary appointments. It is true that the situation was not so sombre in every part of the viceroyalty; in the province of Córdoba fair progress was maintained almost to the end of the Spanish régime.[5] It is also true

---

[1] A.G.I., Aud. de Charcas 441, Vega to Francisco de Saavedra, 30 June 1809. González de Prada was appointed intendant of Tarma in Perú in 1809 and took office there in 1810. See Manuel de Mendiburu, *Diccionario Histórico-Biográfico del Perú* (2nd edn., 11 vols., Lima, 1931–4), vi, 115–16.

[2] Mariluz Urquijo, *op. cit.*, pp. 121–2.   [3] *Ibid.*, pp. 123–4.

[4] A.G.I., Aud. de Buenos Aires 369, Vega to Saavedra, 30 June 1809.

[5] See Appendix II, Table G.

that many of the factors reducing the yield of the new vice-royalty to the Spanish exchequer were beyond the control of the intendants. For it could not be expected that expenses would remain stable, even though income might be rising. There was first of all the expense of military defence, especially that connected with the defence of the Portuguese frontier and the establishment of the viceroyalty itself. And while wages were themselves rising in this period, the total amount of revenue paid in wages was increasing inasmuch as each step in the reforms of Charles III involved the creation of new officials, the new *audiencia* of Buenos Aires, the customs houses, tobacco department, and finally the intendants themselves.[1] But the greatest single drag on the progress of the viceregal exchequer must be attributed to the epoch of the paralysation of external commerce caused by the war with Britain 1796–1802. The colonies suffered great scarcity of goods from Europe and were unable to export their national products: during this great economic crisis, the prices of foreign articles tripled in value, and exports which in 1796 had amounted to 5,470,675 pesos dropped in 1797 to 334,708 pesos, with consequent loss to the treasury.[2] In this situation, damaging to the subject as well as to the state, the *cabildo* sought permission from the viceroy to export produce and import merchandise in neutral vessels; and in 1797 as a result of the intervention of Ángel Izquierdo, administrator of the customs, foreign goods transported in neutral vessels were allowed entry into Montevideo and Buenos Aires. After 1802 the customs revenue increased, but the British invasions of the Río de la Plata (1806–7) struck a blow at the royal exchequer from which it never recovered. By February 1807 the funds in the general treasury of Buenos Aires were completely exhausted in the cost of the defence of Montevideo, and specialized branches of the exchequer, such as the tobacco revenue and even the postage revenue, had to be exploited to their limits. When all these funds were exhausted, the *cabildo* of Buenos Aires came to the rescue not only with its own funds but also with substantial

---

[1] By 1801 the salaries of all the officials in the intendancy of Potosí amounted to six million pesos. See Pedro Vicente Cañete, 'La Intendencia de Potosí, 1802', printed in *La Revista de Buenos Aires*, xxiv (1871), p. 174.

[2] Levene, 'Funciones económicas de las instituciones virreinales', *H.N.A.*, iv, i, 484.

loans from the commercial community, which had to be repaid by treasury remittances from the interior provinces. The superintendent of the exchequer estimated that even the two remittances from Potosí, which were then on their way and which amounted to about a million pesos, would hardly be sufficient to repay these debts. There was little hope of improvement, for it was necessary to preserve and extend the defences.[1]

Nor did the intendant system effect any substantial increase in the output of precious metals. It is true that in the second half of the eighteenth century the production of Potosí was reviving somewhat, but production costs were also increasing since the sinking of a costly new tunnel begun in 1757, and the content of the ore was deteriorating.[2] Nevertheless, according to one contemporary estimate, between 1761 and 1774 Potosí was still producing an average of 366,343 marks of silver a year; each mark left to the exchequer about one peso in the duties of royal tenth and *cobos*, and the annual royal revenue from this branch came to 350,000–400,000 pesos.[3]

In Potosí the intendant system was designed to concentrate the direction of the mining and minting system in the hands of the intendant: united to his authority was the superintendency of mines, *mita*, Banco de San Carlos, and the royal mint, so that all economic and legal jurisdiction in affairs of precious metals were unified under one authority.[4] But administrative reorganization could not touch the basic problem of Potosí, which was one of technique. Intendant Pino Manrique recognized that a terrible ignorance of mining and lack of technical instruction were holding back the industry. He reported that although Potosí was the 'most important mining district in

---

[1] A.G.I., Aud. de Buenos Aires 40, Lucas Muñoz y Cubero (Regente Superintendente subdelegado de Real Hacienda de Buenos Aires) to Soler, 4 August 1807. In 1807 the annual budget of the viceroyalty showed that income was 2,047,248 pesos, expenses amounted to 3,372,709 pesos, leaving a deficit of 1,325,461 pesos. See *D.G.I.E.A.*, i, 195–6.

[2] According to Humboldt production in 1779–89 amounted in value to 3,676,330 pesos, compared with 1,850,230 pesos of 1740–50 and 1,299,800 of 1720–30. See A. von Humboldt, *Ensayo político sobre el Reino de la Nueva España* (6th Spanish edn., 4 vols., Mexico, 1941), iii, 354.

[3] M. de Amat y Junient (Viceroy of Perú, 1761–6), *Memoria de gobierno*, p. 540.

[4] See P. V. Cañete, 'La intendencia de Potosí' (1802), *La Revista de Buenos Aires*, xxiv (1871), p. 178.

America, it is the most abandoned because of the lack of the techniques required to mine and refine the metals'. As there were no adequate books or technical courses available for the miners, he proposed that a special tax be levied on all mercury used at Potosí, for the purpose of bringing from Europe three competent instructors.[1] His own reforms were trifling in their effects, and his long and verbose reports as well as those of his successor, Sanz, could not disguise the fact that lack of satisfactory technique for operating the mines of Potosí was never overcome under the intendancy system.[2] Intendant Sanz welcomed the services of the Nordenflicht mission which the Spanish government sent out to improve mining methods in Perú, and which halted in Potosí on the journey to Lima, but although the German scientists erected some new machines their stay was too short to effect anything permanent. The German mineralogist, Anton Zacharias Helms, who visited Potosí in 1789–90 with this mission, was contemptuous of the methods used there. Absence of satisfactory drainage prevented proper exploitation. Primitive methods of amalgamation wasted at least two-thirds of the silver, and methods in the royal mint were equally unscientific. Intendant Sanz encouraged Helms to do what he could. A metallurgical laboratory was erected and Helms lectured officials on better methods of amalgamation in order 'to dispel the incredible barbarism and ignorance that prevailed in the mint and mining departments there'. But Helms and the whole mission were extremely unpopular with the Spanish mining class in Potosí, who resented being taught by foreigners and intrigued against them in spite of the enthusiasm of the intendant.[3]

---

[1] Pino Manrique to Gálvez, 16 February 1783, printed in G. René-Moreno, 'El Alto-Perú en 1783', *Revista Chilena*, viii (1877), pp. 207–34; see particularly, pp. 223–5.

[2] For an example of Pino Manrique's activity see B. M. Egerton MS 1813, fols. 58v–59, 'Informacion producida por el Sindico Procurador General de Potosi relativamente a los felices progresos de su Intendencia, 1786', which describes an invention for easier crushing of metals. Sanz instituted a more rigorous yearly inspection of mines. See A.G.I., Aud. de Buenos Aires 78, Sanz to Arredondo, 30 July 1790, encl. B in Arredondo to Lerena, 30 September 1790.

[3] See A. Z. Helms, *Travels from Buenos Ayres by Potosí to Lima* (London, 1807), pp. v, 21–3. See also A.G.I., Aud. de Charcas 439, Sanz to Lerena, Carta 10, 16 November 1791.

The acute shortage of mercury was another basic cause for the crisis in the metal industry. This was responsible in 1802 for a decline in monetary production, though previous to this production in the royal mint had been maintained at a reasonable level and even increased.[1] Such improvement in the running of the mint was an eloquent testimonial to the administration of the intendants, but it could not affect the basic problem of production. Potosí could not in fact fulfil the demands made on it from Spain. An urgent call by royal order of 2 June 1785 for as much silver as possible drew from superintendent Sanz the reply that the exigencies of the viceregal exchequer and the demands of the mint of Potosí only left 100,000 pesos worth of silver for yearly remittance to Spain.[2] In addition to this Potosí supplied the exchequer in Buenos Aires with fairly regular supplies of money for viceregal expenses.[3]

Much of the potential revenue from the new viceroyalty was lost through contraband. As far as the precious metals were concerned Humboldt estimated that perhaps not more than one-third of the production of Potosí was registered and paid the royal tenth.[4] The intendant of Buenos Aires was specifically enjoined by the Ordinance to take precautions against the notorious contraband at Buenos Aires and Montevideo.[5] In addition, superintendent Sanz was instructed to institute a system of patrol guards to board ships, foreign and national, entering the harbour, and to prevent any clandestine commerce, a system which he entrusted to the customs and coast guards of Buenos Aires and Montevideo.[6] But Sanz's record in the matter of contraband was not a good one. Viceroy Vértiz and Sanz himself followed a liberal policy in the admittance of foreign goods, but Loreto reversed this and refused to allow trade with any foreign ships. In this he did not get the co-operation of the superintendent, and had to struggle against officials who condoned it and a public who welcomed it. The principal offenders were the coast guard commandant, Francisco de Ortega y

[1] See Appendix II, Table H.
[2] A.G.I., Aud. de Charcas 363, Sanz to Sonora, Carta 659, 27 March 1787.
[3] See Appendix II, Table I.
[4] Humboldt, *Ensayo político*, p. 354.
[5] *Ord. Ints.*, arts. 211–12.
[6] A.G.I., Aud. de Buenos Aires 357, Sanz to Gálvez, Carta 171, 5 June 1784.

Monroy, his second-in-command, Cipriano Melo, and the administrator of the customs of Buenos Aires, Francisco Ximénez de Meza. Loreto complained that they were all (Meza on his own confession) trafficking in public funds, and shielding their activities behind the support of their chief, superintendent Sanz. Meza supplied neither accounts nor funds, and when, after the suppression of the independent superintendency, Loreto looked into the matter himself, he discovered that Meza had in his keeping no more than 49 pesos, though he should have had at the very least 130,000 pesos.[1]

But the viceroys themselves were to prove no more efficient in the supervision of financial affairs. In the epoch of viceroys Avilés (1799–1801) and Pino (1801–4) contraband was still rampant, in spite of the orders of 20 April and 27 November 1799 excluding neutral ships from the ports of the viceroyalty. Rumours circulating in Buenos Aires compromised the names of the highest administrative and judicial officials, and in a secret report sent to Madrid viceroy Pino confirmed much of this scandal. He agreed with the opinion of Avilés and reported that

this Junta de Real Hacienda, erected by the Ordinance of Intendants to help the superintendent, is more a means of hindrance than of improvement, for it is inclined arbitrarily to dispense private favours to the detriment of public interest. . . .[2]

In spite of the contraband, however, customs revenue in the viceroyalty had increased remarkably.[3] This must be attributed to the new policy of *comercio libre* rather than to the activity of the intendants.

[1] Loreto, 'Memoria de Gobierno', 10 February 1790, in Radaelli (ed.), *Memorias de los virreyes del Río de la Plata*, pp. 259–62.
[2] R. H. Caillet-Bois, 'Un informe reservado del virrey Joaquín del Pino', *B.I.I.H.*, xi (Buenos Aires, 1930), p. 74.
[3] See above, pp. 121–22.

CHAPTER VII

The Intendant and Public Administration

I

THE two most prominent features of the reforms of Charles III were finance and defence. This was as true of the Ordinance of Intendants as it was of other legislation. Both objectives were pursued in the interests of the mother country, commercial and exchequer reforms in order to increase the financial returns from the colonies, political reforms in order to consolidate a sprawling empire and equip it to resist foreign pressure. This orientation of Spanish policy in the eighteenth century has invited the obvious charge of colonial exploitation, and the whole basis of the Bourbon reorganization has been criticized on the ground that it failed to take account of the peculiar interests of the colonies themselves. From the point of view of political devolution or self-government the criticism is a valid one. There was, however, a third element in Spain's reorganization of her overseas possessions which merits a category of its own. This took the form of a genuine desire for improvement in the government and administration of the colonies, a policy which had fruitful, if spasmodic, results, and was inspired by the paternalist and humanitarian ideas of the age of 'enlightened despotism'. Such a policy was encouraged in many royal dispatches, and it was undertaken by various viceroys; the record of viceroy Vértiz in Buenos Aires was the outstanding one in the later period of Spanish colonial history, and embracing as it did public building, social service and the promotion of culture it set a standard for similar work by other officials. But the policy was also legislated for by the Ordinance of Intendants: what viceroys did in their capitals intendants were expected to do in their provinces. Under the division of *policía,* or general administration, ideals were set and instructions given, designed to secure 'the greater advantage of my subjects'.[1] Any judgment on the justice of Spanish colonial rule in the last days of the empire will depend upon the measure in which the intendants succeeded in fulfilling this policy.

The attempt to improve the standard of living in the colonies followed two main lines, encouragement to colonial industry and agriculture, and improvement of the conditions of urban life, duties which were specifically assigned to the intendants.[2] But action had to be preceded by inquiry, and it was hoped that the intendants would furnish fuller information than had hitherto been available about the resources of the provinces under their command. Ignorance of the potentialities of Spanish possessions overseas had been one of the greatest obstacles to satisfactory legislation in the past, and of the far-flung provinces of the southern continent Spanish authorities knew even less than they did of the rest of the empire. Now, one of the most important duties imposed upon the intendants was that of inspection and report, and they were expected to furnish information on climate and natural phenomena, communications, agriculture, industry and commerce, and mineral resources, and to submit suggestions for the better exploitation of the country. These data were to be submitted in annual reports and in order to obtain them the intendants were to make regular and personal visitations of their intendancies.[3]

Visits of inspection had always been part of the duties of colonial governors, constantly enjoined by royal orders but inadequately fulfilled.[4] The Ordinance of Intendants specifically ordered the intendants to visit their provinces every year in order to further economic progress; only in the event of being entirely prevented themselves could they send subdelegate commissioners.[5] Although this order gave a new impetus to the practice of provincial visitations, it was never observed to the

---

[1] *Ord. Ints.,* art. 53. [2] *Ibid.,* arts. 57–66.
[3] *Ibid.,* arts. 53–4. They were to be illustrated by topographical maps drawn by competent engineers.
[4] An example of pre-intendant visitation is that of governor Mestre of Tucumán who in 1778 inspected the frontier of Jujuy and the reductions of the Tobais Indians. See A.G.I., Aud. de Buenos Aires 37.
[5] *Ord. Ints.,* arts. 21–2.

letter. The correspondence of the intendants preserved in the Archive of the Indies in Seville shows that visitations were made only irregularly: there is, in fact, no unbroken series of annual reports. This is not surprising, for the task was an impossible one. In the first place, the burden of administrative work, especially in times of crisis, would often demand the continued residence of the intendants in the capital of their intendancy. This problem was put to Minister Gálvez in 1787 by intendant Viedma of Cochabamba who explained that on his appointment as intendant he had had to decide between making a visitation, a task which in a province like Cochabamba would take two years, and pushing ahead with immediate problems of administration, such as the appointment of competent subdelegates, the regulation of municipal finance and the compilation of a register of taxable Indians.[1] Viedma chose the latter course and postponed his tour of inspection, but when he did make it the result was a thorough inquiry and report. Apart from this difficulty, the unfavourable climatic and geographical conditions of some provinces rendered a yearly visitation a most physically arduous task beyond the capacity of many of the intendants.[2] In spite of this, however, more inspections were now made, and the resulting reports were much more informative.

A good example of inquiry, diagnosis and suggestion was that of intendant Pino Manrique of Potosí, who inspected the province of Tarija in 1784–5, after which he sent a report to Gálvez in August 1785.[3] His description of Tarija supplied information on one of the most remote and little known areas of the southern continent. Populated by Chiriguan Indians, this province had been neglected and ignored by the *corregidores* of Chicha and left to the devices of the *cabildo* of Tarija, which appointed military commanders to conduct expeditions against the frontier Indians, and gave them a free hand to run affairs in their own interests. Pino Manrique submitted his own plan for reforms: a military government in the town of Tarija, with a garrison of 40–50 soldiers and militia, forbidden to wage any

[1] A.G.I., Aud. de Buenos Aires 140, Viedma to Sonora, 6 May 1787.
[2] The difficulties in the way of visitations were recognized by viceroy Revillagigedo of New Spain in his report on the intendancy system. See Fisher, *Intendant system*, p. 93.
[3] Pino to Gálvez, 16 August 1785, in Angelis, *Colección*, ii, 267–71.

war against the Indians except in defence of an area of 20 or 30 leagues around the town. Thus the country would be open to receive new settlers, and a fertile land could be exploited for the first time.[1] Two years later intendant Pino reported on the state of Potosí, and furnished interesting information on its social structure.[2] As for agriculture, he urged the development of the wool of the *vicuña* which abounded in the district of Lipes.[3]

Another notable visitation was that of intendant Pizarro of Salta who toured his province in 1791-2, travelling 500 leagues in all to visit the towns of Salta, Tucumán, Santiago del Estero and Catamarca, as well as several Indian reductions. In a careful report he described the state of his intendancy and the measures he had taken in the four departments of government. In his progress through these towns he composed peace among the citizens, heard the complaints of disaffected subjects, encouraged the establishment of primary schools, established *alcaldes de barrio* and gave them official instructions to look after public order in their areas and assist the ordinary magistrates to do so. He encouraged farmers and landowners to improve and intensify agricultural production, appointed a director of forests in various subdistricts of the intendancy, and promoted the production of indigo and sugar at Jujuy. The province needed more roads, especially to improve communications between the capital and the outlying districts. Pizarro took active measures for the repair of old roads and for the opening of new ones where necessary. In order to give permanence to these measures, he appointed in each rural *curato* a commissioner of roads who would ensure that each year repairs were made to damaged roads.[4]

Among the best reports submitted by intendants were those of Sobremonte of Córdoba, whose close observation and accurate description of his province were a model of what the government required. Nevertheless, active as Sobremonte was, he only made three provincial inspections during the fourteen years of his

[1] *Ibid.*
[2] Pino to Loreto, 6 December 1787, in Angelis, *Colección*, ii, 7-8, 20-1.
[3] *Ibid.*, 16-17.
[4] Ramón García Pizarro to Crown, 5 October 1791, printed in J. Torre Revello, 'Relación de la visita hecha a la intendencia de Salta del Tucumán', *B.I.I.H.*, xiii (1931), pp. 69-70.

tenure at Córdoba. In 1785, the year after his appointment, he spent almost a whole year in a visitation of Cuyo. In 1787 he made yet another inspection of Cuyo. In 1794 he was absent more than a year from Córdoba on a tour of the southern frontier, where, among other activities, he founded the town of Concepción del Río Cuarto.[1] The fruit of his visitation was an extensive report to viceroy Loreto in which he made a detailed analysis of the state of the province in the four departments of government, proposing a scheme of action which he pursued in the course of his administration.[2] From this report it was evident that apart from its capital city the province of Córdoba enjoyed no great prosperity. It was a poor region, most of whose inhabitants lived in miserable shacks in an inhospitable countryside to which royal authority hardly extended; what education there existed was supplied by the local parish priests, and the only industry which had made any progress was that supplied by hereditary family looms. Sobremonte's policy, as will be seen, did much to improve this state of affairs and to raise the standard of living in his province. In addition to his reports, Sobremonte left an extensive *Memoria de gobierno* to his successor in 1797, constructed in the style of the traditional viceregal *Memoria*, but far more informative than most of those written by the viceroys of Buenos Aires.[3] A model of its kind both in form and matter it gave a comprehensive account of the problems and prospects of the province, a description of the policy and accomplishments of Sobremonte himself, and a pointer to his successor.

In 1793 Francisco de Viedma, intendant of Cochabamba, completed a long and detailed account of his territory; covering as it did topography, natural resources, administrative organization, obstacles to progress and methods for overcoming them (the report was accompanied by maps drawn up by an engineer,

---

[1] J. Torre Revello, *El marqués de Sobre Monte* (Buenos Aires, 1946), p. 20. In addition to this Sobremonte took advantage of his journey to Córdoba on assumption of office in 1784 to make a visitation of the territory through which he passed; the information which he then gathered was included in his first extensive report. See Sobremonte to Gálvez, 6 January 1785, in Torre Revello, *op. cit.*, pp. lxxxvii–lxxxix.

[2] The report, dated 6 November 1785, is printed in *ibid.*, pp. xci–cviii.

[3] Printed in Garzon, *Crónica de Córdoba*, pp. 350–91.

José Bureta), this report constituted an important contribution to the study of one of the lesser known provinces of the Spanish empire.[1]

It was evident, however, that not all of the intendants were submitting reports of the quality of those of Pizarro, Sobremonte and Viedma. Consequently a royal order of 6 May 1792 instructed the intendants that in their final dispatches of each year they should send to the Ministry a brief and circumstantial account of the measures they had taken in the department of *policía* with an estimate of the results obtained. As there was no reminder of the necessity of a yearly visitation, this can be construed as a tacit acknowledgment of its impossibility. It drew from intendant Alós of Paraguay two very significant reports in 1793 and 1794. Already in 1788 Alós had made a thorough visitation of the thirteen *pueblos de misiones* situated in his intendancy, in the course of which he inspected their accounts, examined agricultural production, investigated the conduct of the administrators and the treatment accorded to the Indians, and visited the schools. The result of this visitation was a report covering sixty-four manuscript pages; its picture of the Paraguayan reductions after the expulsion of the Jesuits is a depressing one, but it is an invaluable commentary on the situation of the Guaraní Indians under the new administration.[2] The report submitted by Alós in 1793 contained further material on the Indian communities and an account of his reforms there—his measures against alcoholism, a scheme for the renting of more land, and regulations promoting the increase of cattle. Payment of Indian labour also received his attention. Hitherto the labourers had been paid twice monthly at a very low rate. Now Alós raised it to three pesos a month, half of which they retained for their own use, while the other half went to the community funds; at the same time he removed the abuse whereby they had been paid in kind with high-priced goods. In the same report Alós sent examples of the different types of wood of the province, as well as of other flora and fauna, all of

---

[1] Printed under the title 'Descripción de la provincia de Santa Cruz de la Sierra', in Angelis, *Colección*, ii, 418–516.

[2] A.G.I., Aud. de Buenos Aires 142, Alós to Crown, 20 October 1788. See below, pp. 188, 192.

which were accompanied by a commentary on their practical value.[1]

An important influence on the spread of economic and statistical information, especially within the viceroyalty itself, was provided by the newspapers and periodicals published in Buenos Aires at the beginning of the nineteenth century.[2] In 1802 the *Semanario de Agricultura, Industria y Comercio* made its appearance, under the direction of Hipólito Vieytes and the patronage and encouragement of viceroy Joaquín del Pino, having as its object the increase of production through the dissemination of information on the resources of all parts of the viceroyalty. To encourage the circulation of the new periodical, the viceroy sent a circular to all the intendants, enclosing copies of the prospectus, with a suggestion that they promote its sale in their respective provinces. The significance of the *Semanario* was that it consistently advocated a policy of free exportation of the produce of the country from Buenos Aires. Many intendants encouraged its circulation. Intendant Rivera of Paraguay, for example, enthusiastically passed on the advice of the viceroy to the *cabildo* of Asunción, declaring that such a periodical deserved encouragement and that he himself was going to subscribe.[3]

Nevertheless, in spite of the labour of the intendants, and later of the *consulado*, or chamber of commerce, of Buenos Aires, much still remained to be done. In April 1810 the *Correo de Comercio* complained of the prevailing ignorance about all branches of the economy of the country, its geography and natural resources; it blamed, however, only the *consulado*.[4]

II

The impetus to the improvement of urban life and culture in the colonies came from the movement in Spain itself, where care for the cities was a prominent part of the policy of Charles III, a care of which there is abundant evidence even to this day in the

---

[1] A.G.I., Aud. de Buenos Aires 19, Alós to Crown, 19 January 1793.
[2] See J. D. Echagüe, 'El periodismo', *H.N.A.*, IV, ii, 79–93.
[3] Rivera to Cabildo of Asunción, 27 September 1802, in A. Zinny, *Historia de los gobernantes del Paraguay 1535–1887* (Buenos Aires, 1887), pp. 205–8.
[4] *Correo de Comercio*, 14 April 1810, in *Documentos del archivo de Belgrano* (7 vols., Buenos Aires, 1913–17), ii, 67–9.

streets of Spanish cities and towns. The Ordinances of Intendants of 1718 and 1749 had provided for improvement in the
hygiene and appearance of the cities as well as for public order
therein, but it needed a government of the ability and purpose
of that of Charles III to carry such a policy into effect.[1] This
endeavour spread to the colonies, where the intendants, acting
on the instructions given to them in their Ordinance,[2] played
a prominent rôle in the progress of urban life in all its aspects.
In the viceroyalty of the Río de la Plata, their activity took two
forms, the establishment of new towns and the improvement of
existing ones.

The creation of new urban settlements by the intendants was
part of a general attempt by the Spanish authorities in the late
eighteenth century to effect a more intensive colonization of the
new viceroyalty. This policy had as its object the defence of
frontier territory against the attacks and encroachments of
savage Indians, the absorption into community life of the
multitude of scattered settlers living on the fringes of the law,
and the establishment of centres of production which could
increase the yield of the country and furnish new income to the
royal exchequer. In this way the new immigrants, now arriving
in increasing numbers in search of prosperity, could be properly
assimilated to the country. The movement was launched in the
colonization of Patagonia as well as of the Banda Oriental. None
of the individual attempts of the intendants was on such a
scale as this, but the cumulative effect of their activity was considerable. A typical example was that of intendant Pizarro in
the province of Salta. Taking into account the strategic situation and the natural fertility of the valley of Ceuta which he
observed on his visitation of 1792, Pizarro decided to found a
city there, which would serve the threefold purpose of exploiting
a territory rich in pasture and running water, absorbing landless Spaniards and mestizos, and reducing the distance between
frontier forts, thereby improving supplies and lines of communication. He procured the approval of the viceroy and of the

[1] See L. M. Torres, introd. to *D.H.A.*, IX, xlviii–xlix. The intendants were themselves conscious of their debt to Spanish urban examples. See *ibid.*, xviii–xlix.

[2] *Ord. Ints.*, arts. 64–6. Plans for churches and other public buildings had to be
submitted to the *junta superior de hacienda* for approval of style and expense. See
ibid., art. 66.

junta superior de hacienda, and issued decrees inviting landless subjects in all parts of the province to submit their names for settlement in the valley of Ceuta. He was soon able to report that 808 settlers had presented themselves, 'algunos de notoria Hidalguia'. The town itself he planned in classical Spanish colonial style: a central plaza bounded by the church and town hall, parallel streets, convents, monasteries and hospital. He named it Nueva Oran, after his birthplace in North Africa, and secured royal approval for the foundation on 16 July 1794.[1] Pizarro then endowed the town with civil government, appointing a subdelegate according to the terms of the Ordinance of Intendants, and setting up a *cabildo* to which he gave a municipal constitution.[2] Finally he equipped the settlement for military defence by forming the citizens into three companies and organizing them into a militia for defence against the Indians of the Gran Chaco.[3]

In the province of Córdoba there was an even greater need for urbanization and for the introduction of the amenities of a civilized life. The necessity for a new policy in this matter was one of the greatest impressions left on the mind of intendant Sobremonte by his first visit of inspection:

> The general defect of the whole province is the lack of organized towns, for the people are accustomed to live in isolation, with no inclination to assemble themselves in communities. Seeking reasons for this defect, I find that it usually derives from a passion for liberty: such dispersion keeps these settlers from the eyes of the magistrates and of the priests who would otherwise pursue them for their cattle robberies and other crimes to which they are so given. . . .[4]

This situation, apart from preventing any education, secular or religious, also made for great difficulty in the collection of taxes and tithes. Nevertheless Sobremonte realized the obstacles in the way of urbanizing these people: violence would only

---

[1] There is a reproduction of Pizarro's map of the town in P. Torres Lanzas, *Relación descriptiva de los mapas, planos etc. del virreinato de Buenos Aires, existentes en el Archivo General de Indies* (2nd edn., Buenos Aires, 1921), p. 141.

[2] A.G.I., Aud. de Buenos Aires 81, Pizarro to Minister of Grace and Justice, 4 Aug. 1795, encl. No. 8 in Melo de Portugal to Llaguno, Carta 19, 12 November 1795. [3] *Ibid.*

[4] Sobremonte to Loreto, 6 November 1785, in Torre Revello, *El marqués de Sobre Monte*, p. c.

alienate them, while in any case they had certain economic facts on their side, namely that for some of them country houses formed the centres of their ranches and left them no incentive to live in towns. Sobremonte had a plan for forming one town every year.[1] This was too ambitious, and in spite of his efforts Sobremonte was unable to fulfil it. He was, however, able to achieve some concrete results. In 1786 he visited the district of Río Cuarto and decided that in order to bring together scattered settlers and give security to the frontier and to the ancient road from Cuyo to Chile, the village of Concepción could usefully be consolidated into a town. He assembled there thirty-one scattered families and organized the building of new houses. By decree of 1794 he authorized the distribution of land among the new settlers, and to the jurisdiction of the town he added the *pueblos* and forts of Santa Catalina, San Fernando and San Bernardo.[2] On 16 February 1795 he submitted a report to the king asking for royal approval and requesting the title of *villa* and authorization for the creation of a *cabildo* and other privileges for the new town. This was granted by Charles IV in a royal *cédula* of 12 April 1797.[3]

Sobremonte's activities did not stop here. In the mining district of La Carolina he began the establishment of a town of sixty-four houses and the construction of a church. He also founded the towns of San Carlos de Mendoza (264 inhabitants), La Carlota (926 inhabitants), Corocorto and Fortín de San Carlos (110 inhabitants).[4]

This account of town building in the viceroyalty of the Río de la Plata cannot be completed without mention of the record of viceroy Vértiz, who devoted considerable energy to the foundation of new settlements, in order, as he reported, 'to reduce to a Christian, civil and social life the many people dispersed in these territories [the Banda Oriental] and to curb in this way the robberies, murders and other disorders which arise because the criminals are not under the observation of the authorities'.[5]

[1] *Ibid.*, pp. c–ci.
[2] A.G.I., Aud. de Buenos Aires 282, Sobremonte to Crown, 16 February 1795.
[3] See A. C. Vitulo, introd. to *Actas capitulares de la villa de Concepción del Río Cuarto* (Buenos Aires, 1947), pp. 14–23. [4] Torre Revello, *op. cit.*, pp. 43–5.
[5] Vértiz, 'Memoria de gobierno', 12 March 1784 in S. Radaelli (ed.), *Memorias de los virreyes del Río de la Plata*, p. 62.

Between the rivers Paraná and Uruguay he founded the towns of Gualegay, Concepción del Uruguay and Gualeguaychu. In the Montevideo district he founded the towns of San Juan Bautista, San José and others.[1] Apart from the creation of new towns, intendants were concerned with the improvement of existing ones, and the new régime witnessed a revival of public building. In Asunción del Paraguay a new hospital was built and the cathedral restored, streets were repaved and new ones built, walls erected to prevent floods, street lamps introduced, and two offices added to the town hall for the use of the *alcaldes ordinarios*. To sustain and give continuity to this policy of public works, six *alcaldes de barrio* were appointed.[2] In Salta del Tucumán, intendant Mestre earned the praise of the *cabildo* for 'the magnificent building of the town hall', where for the first time there were decent offices for the dispatch of municipal business.[3] In La Paz the temporary intendant Fernando Sota built a new bridge, organized street lighting, and constructed a new theatre.[4] This policy was continued by intendant Burgunyo, who improved the drainage and water supply of the city, and repaired the hospital of San Juan and the bridge of San Sebastián.[5] In Potosí the vigorous administration of intendant Pino Manrique brought new life to public works, road construction and restoration, street planning and bridge building.[6] President-intendant Joaquín del Pino was responsible for a vast improvement in the appearance of Chuquisaca, where he installed underground drainage, beautified the streets and enforced rules for the whitewashing of houses.[7]

It is true that public works could not always be organized directly by the intendant, for he could only reside in the capital

[1] *Ibid.*, pp. 62–4.
[2] A.G.I., Aud. de Buenos Aires 19, Consulta del Consejo, 24 July 1796, summarizing Alós to Crown, 19 January 1793.
[3] A.G.I., Aud. de Buenos Aires 143, Cabildo of Salta to Crown, 29 July 1789.
[4] A.G.I., Aud. de Charcas 436, Cabildo of La Paz to Godoy, 31 August 1796.
[5] A.G.I., Aud. de Buenos Aires 37, Cabildo of La Paz to Crown, 11 December 1798.
[6] B. M. Egerton MS 1813, fols. 45–71, Testimony of Joaquín Yañes *alcalde ordinario* of Potosí, 17 January 1786, in 'Informacion producido por el sindico procurador general de Potosí'.
[7] A.G.I., Aud. de Charcas 439, Relación de Pino, 30 December 1793.

of his province. Thus in the provincial towns it was the *cabildos* which generally directed public building under the surveillance of the intendant. In Luján, for example, it was the *cabildo* which took the initiative in interpreting the Ordinance of Intendants and issued a proclamation on 9 October 1787 which imposed on the citizens under pain of fines various obligations to keep their streets and houses in order and repair.[1] Nevertheless, it was the intendants who achieved the most striking results in this field, and once again intendant Sobremonte outshone the rest. He worked tirelessly to improve the material amenities of Córdoba and to make this provincial capital a model of the Spanish cities he knew.[2] In the very first *cabildo* session after his appointment he formed plans for the enlargement of the town water supply which were to bear fruit in a fine aqueduct and two public fountains, financed by voluntary contributions from prominent citizens.[3] In the same session he initiated a scheme for the enlargement of the local prison in the interests of better sanitation for the inmates. Apart from this he reinforced the river banks and improved the streets, constructed a beautiful public *paseo* and introduced street lighting.[4] On the institutional side he created *comisarios de barrio*, copied from his experience under viceroy Vértiz in Buenos Aires: six *comisarios de barrio* were appointed to supervise the execution of his orders for the progress of the public life of the town, public building, internal security, control of private building and enforcement of traffic regulations.[5]

It was in Buenos Aires, however, that the most impressive results were obtained under the intendant régime. Until the mid-eighteenth century Buenos Aires presented to the world an appearance of unrelieved shabbiness: a main square full of untidy market stalls, bounded by the royal fortress, an unfinished cathedral, a nondescript town hall and an episcopal palace which belied its grandiose name. Ill-paved and often

[1] E. Udaondo, *Reseña histórica de la villa de Luján* (Luján, 1939), pp. 282–3.

[2] The basic account of this work is his own 'Memoria de gobierno' to his successor, printed in Garzon, *Crónica de Córdoba*, pp. 353–68.

[3] Torre Revello, *op. cit.*, pp. 39–40.

[4] Garzon, *op. cit.*, pp. 6, 29.

[5] Sobremonte, 'Informe de gobierno', 12 February 1785, in Garzon, *op. cit.*, pp. 341–5.

impassable streets were lined by unimpressive houses. Here was abundant work for the intendants to do. They were set an inspiring example by viceroy Vértiz who already as governor had set about promoting the material progress of the capital and initiating its reorganization by his proclamation of 21 May 1772.[1] Superintendent Sanz served his apprenticeship under Vértiz and took over where the master left off. His double objective was to beautify the town and to improve commerce by better communications, 'giving to it a level of civilization, culture and cleanliness which corresponds to its present status as capital of a vast kingdom and port for national and foreign commerce'.[2] The financial basis of such a policy was not neglected: Sanz set up a *junta municipal de propios* and issued a constitution (22 January 1785) for its operation.[3] His *Instrucción* of 4 February 1784 included rules for the uniform composition of the streets and a systematic method of street naming, and was distributed to the *alcaldes de barrio* with instructions that they inform the residents of their districts to regulate their streets accordingly. Those who could not afford this work were to be subject to a careful means test and then could qualify for assistance from the rest of the district or, if necessary, from the public funds.[4] The actual work was to be supervised by *diputados* chosen by the residents in each *barrio*, and would be under the technical control of a qualified engineer. This instruction was followed by a proclamation of 18 February which ordered the removal of any refuse obstructing street drainage under pain of twenty pesos fine, and forbade workmen to practise their trades in the streets.[5] Another proclamation of 17 March 1784 fixed the wages of workmen engaged on public works and controlled prices of building materials.[6] Yet a further proclamation of 23 December 1784 implemented Vértiz's decree of 5 December 1783 which had forbidden the passage of heavy vehicles in the centre of the city.[7] The administrative agents for the enforcement of public order and for the application of the public policy

[1] Bando publicado 21 de Mayo de 1772, in *D.H.A.*, ix, 3–7.
[2] Instrucción, 4 February 1784, in *D.H.A.*, ix, 24.
[3] See *D.H.A.*, ix, pp. cxxix–lxxx.
[4] *Ibid.*, p. 26.
[5] Bando sobre el arreglo y trazado de calles, 18 February 1784, in *ibid.*, pp. 32–7.
[6] *Ibid.*, pp. 121–9. [7] *Ibid.*, pp. 18–21, 21–2.

of the intendant or the viceroy were the *alcaldes de barrios*; elected annually in *cabildo*, they were magistrates in their districts and were entrusted with immediate vigilance over the fulfilment of the *bandos de policía*.[1]

The progress of urban life under the intendants was not confined to public building. It also included a type of social service which found expression in the establishment of hospitals,[2] the instalment of public granaries,[3] and above all the provision of better educational facilities. There is scattered evidence that in some places education progressed under their care. During the first two centuries of colonization all the work of education with the exception of a few private schools of primary grade was performed by the Church. But during the reign of Charles III, at a time when secular education was a favourite theme of reformers in Spain, many public and municipal schools were established in America as well as in Spain, the former financed mainly from the funds left by the Jesuits, the latter from the municipal treasuries.[4] The intendants played some part in this movement, for apart from the faculty of granting titles of teachers which was assigned to them by the Ordinance of Intendants, they were also allowed to establish new schools wherever they were necessary.[5] In Asunción del Paraguay intendant Rivera established a primary school where Indians and Spaniards were educated in the reading and writing of Spanish and instructed in the Catholic religion.[6] The school was directed by lay teachers, and parents were obliged to send their sons from the age of six.[7] In the city of Córdoba Sobremonte founded a new school which he called *Escuela Gratuita y de Gobierno*, directed by Franciscan lay brothers. More significant still were the rural primary

[1] *Ibid.*, p. cvii.

[2] A.G.I., Aud. de Buenos Aires 88, Rafael de la Luz to Crown, 3 May 1802, encl. in Pino to Caballero, Carta 145, 11 June 1802. See also Sobremonte, 'Memoria de Gobierno', in Garzon, *op. cit.*, p. 362.

[3] A duty assigned to the intendants by *Ord. Ints.*, arts. 68–9, in order to eliminate the extortions of middlemen. See Viedma to Arredondo, 12 March 1793, in Angelis, *Colección*, ii, 427–8.

[4] See J. Probst, introd. to *D.H.A.*, xviii, xxiii: and 'La enseñanza primaria desde sus origenes hasta 1810', *H.N.A.*, iv, ii, 157–8.

[5] *Ord. Ints.*, art. 28. This faculty had been hitherto held by the *cabildos*.

[6] A.G.I., Aud. de Buenos Aires 48, Cabildo of Asunción to Saavedra, 19 November 1798.

[7] See Zinny, *Historia de los gobernantes del Paraguay 1535–1887*, pp. 201–2.

schools which he created in districts which had been hitherto completely bereft of educational facilities.[1] He had no illusions about the difficulty of sustaining such schools against the opposition of parents who had no desire to send their sons to be educated.[2] In spite of this he managed to open and maintain twenty schools in different localities of the intendancy of Córdoba.[3] Intendant Pino Manrique of Potosí established ten primary schools in the subdistrict of Chayanta 'to promote the progress and civilization of the area', and assigned them lay teachers with a salary of 100 pesos a year.[4]

The intendants made little impression on university education, though in this sphere it is worthy of mention that it was largely due to the representations of Sobremonte that viceroy Arredondo established a Chair of Law in the University of Córdoba in 1791, thereby freeing parents from the necessity of sending their sons to Chuquisaca or Santiago de Chile.[5]

III

The profound changes in the economic situation of the River Plate provinces introduced by the regulations of free commerce of 1777–8 have already been noticed. Liberated from the economic and political domination of Lima, the country was at last in a position to exploit the advantages of the more direct route to markets through the port of Buenos Aires. The removal of laws prohibiting interprovincial trade resulted in a rapid increase of commerce. There was a considerable decrease in import prices and a simultaneous appreciation of the value of commodities destined for overseas markets. For the first time the country was in a position to make full and free use of the vast cattle resources which had accumulated in the past two centuries. It was less obvious, however, that it would

[1] Garzon, *Crónica de Córdoba*, p. 14.
[2] Sobremonte, 'Memoria de Gobierno', in Garzon, *op. cit.*, p. 365.
[3] Torre Revello, *El marqués de Sobre Monte*, pp. 43–5.
[4] A.G.I., Estado 76, Consulta del Consejo, 21 March 1790; see also Aud. de Charcas 438, Pino Manrique to Sonora, 6 September 1787, and Aud. de Charcas 552, R.C. to Intendant of Potosí, 7 April 1790. On the legal and financial difficulties of this project see above p. 134.
[5] Garzon, *op. cit.*, pp. 22, 346.

also be able to exploit its agricultural and industrial potential, and thus replace a single-export system by a more balanced economy.

The intendant system in its economic aspect can be regarded as complementary to the regulations of free commerce: the intendants were expected to promote agriculture and industry so that the colony could profit from the commercial expansion now open to it. But between the hope and the fulfilment there was an immense void. It has often been suggested that the intendants did in fact fulfil the economic rôle expected of them.[1] There is, however, little evidence for such an assumption, and it must be concluded that in the economic sphere, unlike the urban, good intentions did not mean good results. It is true that in the viceroyalty of the Río de la Plata the intendants did not have very promising material on which to work. Far removed from the main highways of transatlantic commerce, and sacrificed by the Spanish government in the interests of Perú, the under-populated lands of the River Plate had suffered from two centuries' neglect which could not be remedied in thirty years.

Nevertheless it will be recalled that the agricultural capacity of this region was not insignificant.[2] With the addition of Mendoza to the colony it was even increased. In Mendoza and San Juan a favourable climate, good irrigation and abundance of native labour had facilitated the progress of a varied agriculture: here almost all crops and fruits were cultivated except rice,[3] though the vine was the principal source of wealth and the wine of San Juan always had a market in Buenos Aires.[4] In the provinces of the interior there were centres of handicraft production, while places like Córdoba were in close commercial relations with Buenos Aires and with Lima as termini and as transit points for the extensive mule trade between the River Plate region and

[1] See e.g., C. E. Corona Baratech, 'Notas para un estudio de la sociedad en el Río de la Plata durante el virreinato', *Anuario de Estudios Americanos*, viii (1951), pp. 71–2.

[2] See E. A. Coni, 'La agricultura, ganadería e industrias hasta el virreinato', *H.N.A.*, iv, i, 362–5. See above, pp. 27–29.

[3] Sobremonte to Loreto, 6 Novembér 1785, in Torre Revello, *op. cit.*, p. xciii.

[4] B.M., Add. MS 17, 592, fol. 412, 'Description of Perú, Chile, and Buenos Aires compiled by members of an expedition fitted out in 1783–4 by the Spanish government'.

Perú.[1] Their industries were able to develop owing to an abundance of native Indian labour which the littoral provinces did not enjoy, and owing to a plentiful supply of raw material. At the same time the forced abstinence from consumption of foreign articles had afforded protection and a favourable commercial balance for more than two centuries, which allowed the provinces to accumulate considerable financial reserves.

The fundamental modification to this existing economic situation was made not by the intendant system but by the creation of the viceroyalty as an autonomous unit in 1776 and by the regulations of free commerce in 1777–8.[2] The complementary rôle expected of the intendants bore little fruit. But this was often due to factors outside their control. The province of Paraguay can be taken as an example. This was a zone rich enough in natural resources which produced, among other things, sufficient yerba, tobacco, sugar and honey for export to Buenos Aires, whence it circulated to the rest of the viceroyalty; in exchange Paraguay imported from Buenos Aires clothes and other consumer goods. But Paraguay's economy, potentially healthy, was actually floundering. Its merchants were at the mercy of their wealthier counterparts in Buenos Aires: lacking capital reserves, they traded on money borrowed in Buenos Aires at a rate of 8 per cent of their earnings for a given transaction. But this was a minor obstacle compared with others. Paraguay enjoyed a natural monopoly of yerba, a drink which was consumed in almost the whole of South America. In good years the province exported as much as 300,000 arrobas of yerba, and never less than 200,000. Yet this was far below the productive capacity of the region, for in the face of the crippling taxes to which this product was subject there was no incentive to a more intensive cultivation: first it went to Santa Fe whence it was distributed to Buenos Aires, Tucumán, Potosí, Perú and Chile,

---

[1] This mule trade, though of great importance, was subject to considerable fluctuations. In the period 1776–81 exports to Perú comprised 70,000 mules at 8–9 pesos each; 1790–1800 it had dropped to 30,000 a year at 13–16 pesos; by 1803 it was oscillating between 40,000–50,000 a year. See R. R. Caillet-Bois, 'Apuntes para una historia económica del virreinato. Gobierno intendencia de Salta del Tucumán', *Anuario de Historia Argentina*, iii (1941), p. 112.

[2] This was recognized by superintendent Sanz himself. See A.G.I., Aud. de Buenos Aires 357, Sanz to Gálvez, 17 October 1784.

taxed all the way from post to post, by provincial as well as by *alcabala* taxes.[1] At the same time the tobacco industry was retarded by primitive methods of production; in 1783 the superintendent reported that Paraguay could not produce enough tobacco for consumption in the whole of the viceroyalty which had to rely on exceptional imports from Seville.[2] Analysing the economic state of Paraguay in 1798, intendant Rivera drew a vivid comparison between the potential wealth of the province and the evidence of poverty which he met on all sides. Out of a population of about 100,000 more than 5,000 were living, according to Rivera's estimation, below the level of subsistence. Seeking an explanation of this phenomenon, he drew attention to yet another factor impeding the economic progress of Paraguay—the shortage of man power, arising out of the antiquated military system with which the province was saddled. Surrounded by hostile and predatory Indians the region had to be in a constant state of defence. But instead of a system of regular garrisons, all the settlers were obliged to give militia service, a plan suitable for the pioneering days of the time of the conquest when it was formulated but one which no longer responded to the economic needs and potentialities of the province, or facilitated a full exploitation of its resources.[3]

The case of Paraguay is significant because it was typical of the sickness of the viceroyalty as a whole and shows that what was needed was not individual efforts on the part of the intendants but a new policy and direction from the central government, which they could then apply. Faced with a situation born of the policy and practice of centuries, an intendant could do little more than Rivera did in Paraguay—report and suggest. It is true that there were concrete obstacles to agricultural progress, particularly in technique, which the intendants might have been expected to remedy. Writing in 1801 Félix de Azara, the Spanish geographer, pointed out that agricultural equipment was still primitive in all parts of the viceroyalty: in Paraguay, for example, the use of the metal plough was still

[1] A.G.I., Aud. de Buenos Aires 322, Agustín Fernando de Pinedo (governor of Paraguay) to Crown, 29 January 1777.

[2] A.G.I., Aud. de Buenos Aires 356, Fernández to Gálvez, Carta 684, 15 February 1783.

[3] A.G.I., Aud. de Buenos Aires 322, Rivera to Saavedra, 19 May 1798.

unknown.[1] Moreover the efforts of intendants like Alós in Paraguay and Sobremonte in Córdoba to improve communications by the provision of new and better roads could well have been imitated by others.[2]

But what the intendants could not be expected to change was policy: they were simply administrators and policy was formed in Buenos Aires and Madrid. The root cause of agricultural backwardness in the territory of Buenos Aires was land policy. This was recognized by the Ordinance of Intendants itself, for the intendants were granted explicit authority to distribute unoccupied royal land or even private domains, if the owners were unable or unwilling to cultivate them (with, of course, proper compensation from public funds)—

for it is my royal will that all the natives shall enjoy an adequate endowment of landed property, and that the lands apportioned for the purposes provided, whether bought with public funds, or waste or royal lands, shall pass into the control of those who desire them, whether they be Indians or other castes, but with only the right of possession, since direct ownership is reserved for the crown and for the public treasury respectively.[3]

On this matter, however, royal policy was equivocal. It is true that the size of estates in the Río de la Plata has been exaggerated and that the fifty leagues quoted by Lastarría must have been an exception for a single holding.[4] Nevertheless, the existing legal system of land acquisition was at once favourable to the creation of large estates and detrimental to full exploitation. In the first place, in spite of the directive quoted above, the law was that land could only pass to those who bought it and the price was prohibitive. Apart from this, the ritual of acquisition was tedious

[1] F. de Azara, *Memoria sobre el estado rural del Río de la Plata en 1801 y otros informes*, p. 8.

[2] For the record of Alós, in this respect see A.G.I., Aud. de Buenos Aires 19, Alós to Arredondo, 8 April 1790, and Alós to Arredondo, 12 September 1794; Aud. de Buenos Aires 295, Alós to Llaguno, 5 November 1794. For Sobremonte see Torre Revello, *op. cit.*, p. 44.

[3] *Ord. Ints.*, art. 57. All grants issued under the Ordinance of Intendants required the approval of the *junta superior de hacienda*. In 1796, the land question was transferred to the viceroys. See Fisher, *Intendant system*, p. 42.

[4] Lastarría, 'Colonias orientales del Río Paraguay ó de la Plata' [1805,] in *D.H.A.*, iii, 245. See Levene, *Investigaciones acerca de la historia económica del virreinato del Plata*, ii, 115.

and costly. A prospective buyer had to apply to the government in Buenos Aires, where he had to pay 50 pesos for a first decree and for the opinion of the fiscal of the *audiencia*. He then had to pay the cost of a judge to review the territory and of a surveyor to measure it; this amounted to one peso a league each and four pesos a day. The legal formalities took two and often as much as eight years.[1] In Paraguay, it is true, the intendants had divided up the lands by ignoring the legal niceties and thus the province was populated with *estancias*, but this rejection of the law was hardly desirable and had led to much arbitrary occupation based on no legal title.[2] The general situation was that only the rich could buy, and as it cost almost as much to buy a small amount as a large one, they bought huge areas which they could not themselves exploit, but rented to the poor. Thus these provinces were reproducing the familiar features of huge estates farmed by men who lacked the incentive of absolute possession. Manuel Belgrano, secretary of the chamber of commerce of Buenos Aires and a man destined to play a brilliant rôle in the future independence movement, considered that the chief obstacle to agricultural progress lay not in poor communications, nor in discrimination against export, nor in heavy taxation, though all these things existed, but in the simple fact that the farmers lacked ownership and thereby lacked incentive.[3]

Nevertheless, it can be argued that the lack of an overseas market by the denial of free export for colonial agricultural produce was at least as great a hindrance to development as was the lack of ownership. Colonial agriculture was retarded by a burden of taxation which it could not bear—tithes, *alcabala*, and municipal dues. It was also damaged by municipal protectionism, for the *cabildos*, looking after the interests of the cities, prevented the export of grain in order to maintain a supply of cheap bread for their own locality; thus the farmers were forced to sell at a fixed price so that the cities could buy their products at the figure they wanted.[4] The road which was thus blocked by

---

[1] Azara, *op. cit.*, pp. 13–14. Levene, *op. cit.*, ii, 116, depreciates this argument, but cannot deny that the process was costly.

[2] Azara, *op. cit.*, p. 15.

[3] *Correo de Comercio*, 23 June 1810, in *Documentos del Archivo de Belgrano*, ii, 197–9.

[4] But in Cochabamba there was apparently no price control. See Viedma to Arredondo, 2 March 1793, in Angelis, *Colección*, ii, 427.

taxation and by municipal restriction was completely closed by
the policy of the Spanish government which prohibited a direct
intercourse with foreign markets.[1] This was yet another example
of the lack of harmony between the instructions given to the
intendants and the outmoded general policies pursued by the
crown. Lack of a price incentive crippled colonial agriculture.
In 1792 the price of wheat fell to 10–17 reales a *fanega*, a figure
which could not cover the simple cost of production. The
situation was so desperate that in the following year it drew from
the farmers of the province of Buenos Aires a petition in which
they begged the crown not to prohibit the free export of their
products, arguing that in spite of the opportunities offered by a
temperate climate and fertile land their position was critical
because of the lack of a market in the absence of free commerce
and exportation.[2] After 1796, when the war with Britain began,
the situation became even more desperate.

The backwardness of agriculture was accentuated by the
economic rivalry between commerce and land. The creation of
the *consulado*, or chamber of commerce, in Buenos Aires in 1794,
with its double character of a judicial tribunal in mercantile
cases and a board for the protection and development of commerce, represented a government attempt to integrate the two
interests, for the new tribunal was specifically instructed to give
its attention to the progress of both.[3] But in this very attempt at
co-ordination merchant and landowner soon clashed, and to
avoid further conflict the crown had to resolve that the *consulado*
should be composed of an equal number of merchants and landowners, sharing offices alternately, 'in order to avoid any kind of
superiority on the part of either profession. . . .'[4] But this rivalry
was only a reflection of the deeper division within the economy
of the viceroyalty, a division arising out of the predominant

[1] On the other hand the cultivation of hemp and flax, encouraged by the *Ord.
Ints.*, art. 57, was protected and these commodities were exported to Spain
free of duties—but precisely because they were raw materials which the Spanish
market badly needed. See Levene, *op. cit.*, ii, 110.

[2] V. G. Quesada, 'Representación al Rey de los labradores de Buenos Aires
(1793)', *La Revista de Buenos Aires*, xvii (1868), p. 17.

[3] Real Cédula de Erección del Consulado de Buenos Aires, 30 January 1794,
art. xxii, in *D.H.A.*, vii, 62.

[4] Valera to Prior and Consuls of the Consulado of Buenos Aires, 31 March 1797,
in *D.H.A.*, vii, 127–8.

position occupied by the cattle industry, the only part of the agricultural resources of the viceroyalty to profit from the opening of the port of Buenos Aires.

The province of Buenos Aires was the most important producer of the country's prime exportable commodities—hides and meat. Under the expansion afforded by the regulations of 1777–8 the export of hides increased phenomenally. Before 1778 the annual export of hides was 150,000. Between 1778 and 1783 it rose to 800,000.[1] After the Peace of Versailles which terminated the war with England in 1783 the number of hides exported annually amounted to 1,400,000.[2] The ease of production and the lucrative nature of the export trade, legal or clandestine, created problems of diminishing cattle stock which were difficult to overcome. From the middle of the eighteenth century many decrees were enacted to control the slaughter of cattle and to prevent their illegal exit to Brazil.[3] The Ordinance of 1783 specifically ordered the intendants to prevent excessive slaughter for hides.[4] Superintendent Sanz submitted a scheme for the establishment of guard posts and patrols in the Banda Oriental, and for the compulsory branding of cattle to facilitate identification and prevent rustling. But nothing came of this and in 1796 it was still being complained, now by the *consulado* of Buenos Aires, that the lack of security for the cattle stocks in the Banda Occidental needed a remedy.[5]

The greatest economic problem presented by the grazing industry, however, was not that of declining stocks. There was a lack of homogeneity in the economic structure of the viceroyalty of the Río de la Plata. While the cattle industry responded quickly to the opening of the country to foreign trade, for the provinces of the interior, Córdoba, and Salta, free commerce was a disaster which spelt the doom of their industries. These industries, as has been seen, were nurtured on an isolation and

---

[1] Levene, *op. cit.*, ii, 73.

[2] B.M., Add. MS 17, 604, fol. 129v, Francisco de Ortega, 'Informe sobre la Banda Oriental', 23 October 1784. The export of salt meat was also begun, but this owed most not to the intendants but to viceroy Loreto.

[3] Levene, *op. cit.*, ii, 74–5.

[4] *Ord. Ints.*, art. 59.

[5] A.G.I., Aud. de Buenos Aires 21, Report of the consulado of Buenos Aires on the economy of the viceroyalty, 1796.

protection no less effective because it was involuntary. Now, as a result of the regulations of free commerce, the goods of the interior provinces were forced out of the Buenos Aires market. Spanish and foreign goods were easy victors in the competition against domestic products in the River Plate area, and threatened to invade the interior provinces themselves. This situation was yet another example of the lack of integration between the intendant system and the other reforms introduced by Charles III and his government. In spite of all the stimulus which intendant Sobremonte might give to the wine industry in the province of Córdoba, he could not cope with the economic facts created by the legislation of 1778; the local wine, hampered by excessive cost of freight, could not compete with the cheaper and superior foreign liquors, which now flooded Buenos Aires.[1] It was in fact singularly inept to advise the intendants to promote local industry and at the same time create conditions which would rapidly stifle such industry.[2]

Any interruption or diminution of foreign commerce, on account of war for example, enabled the home industries to recuperate. In the period of the war with England, 1796–1802, the provinces again supplied the towns with cloth and other products. Those of Cochabamba and Cuzco sold even in Buenos Aires, in spite of the enormous distance of 600 and 800 leagues respectively. And in 1802 wine from San Juan was once more finding its way in increasing quantities to Buenos Aires, Santa Fe and Salta.[3] If in fact Buenos Aires could consume the products of the interior wealth would circulate evenly in the viceroyalty. But such was not the case: in normal times the Buenos Aires market, satiated with European goods, was closed to its own interior provinces. And the dominant cattle interests, *estancieros* and meat packers, in Buenos Aires and its province, demanded yet freer commerce and a direct market in Europe.

---

[1] Levene, *op. cit.*, ii, 133–4, 138.

[2] It is true that industry in the interior was also impeded by a tendency to monopoly (e.g. sale of brandy in Tucumán), which was liable to become inefficient, and also by curious labour practices, such as in Salta the refusal to work unless wages were paid three months in advance. See Caillet-Bois, 'Apuntes para una historia económica del virreinato', *Anuario de Historia Argentina*, iii (1941), p. 119. But the main cause of decline was undoubtedly that of foreign competition.

[3] Levene, *op. cit.*, ii, 134–5, 139.

In 1809 they were pressing for permission to trade with Britain. The opposition of Fernández de Agüero, agent for the *consulado* of Cádiz, to such a proposition was far from disinterested, but his words were none the less apposite:

> The most grievous and most pressing evil is that our interior provinces are going to suffer intensely from the entry of English goods into our ports: they will suffer inevitable ruin and perhaps even ignite among themselves the fires of division and rivalry.[1]

In order to reply to these arguments of the agent of Cádiz the landowners of the eastern and western banks of the Río de la Plata commissioned Mariano Moreno to put their point of view, which he did in the famous *Representación de los Hacendados*.[2] In this he convincingly stated the proposition that it was politic for the country to allow the free importation of products which it did not itself produce, and the export of home products of which there was a surplus. In the first instance the consumer would profit by lowering of prices, and in the second case the farmer by security of a large market. But this did not answer the problem of the dislocation of the economy of the country or solve the dilemma of the division between the littoral and the interior. This clash of interests, already clearly apparent under the colonial régime, was handed on to the independent republic, where 'the economic problems became a political issue in which states' rights were pitted against centralization. Around this issue centred the political and social struggles of the first four decades of Argentina's independence'.[3]

---

[1] *D.G.I.E.A.*, i, 222. Another staunch defender of the old régime, viceroy Abascal of Perú, wrote in 1816: 'Las manufacturas del Reyno tubieron una época mas floreciente antes de expedirse el Real Decreto de . . . Octubre de 1778, o de libre Comercio . . . Despues de aquella fecha empezaron a decaer los de lana por la mejor calidad y baratura de los paños ordinarios Españoles y ultimamente los de Algodón por el Contrabando: de suerte que no teniendo salida han venido a arruinarse a un tiempo las Estancias, y obrages que cosechaban las primeras materias y disponian los texidos', Abascal, *Memoria de gobierno* [1816], ed. V. Rodríguez Casado y J. A. Calderón Quijano, (2 vols., Sevilla, 1944), i, 218–19.

[2] Printed in *D.G.I.E.A.*, i, 228–47.

[3] M. Burgin, *The economic aspects of Argentine federalism, 1820–1852* (Cambridge, Mass., 1946), p. 17.

CHAPTER VIII

The Intendant and the Indians

I

SPANISH policy towards the Indians was conditioned by the motives which drove them to colonize. 'We came here to serve God, and also to get rich'; the famous phrase of Bernal Díaz, soldier and chronicler of the Cortés expedition to Mexico, underlined the economic and religious impetus behind Spanish enterprise in the New World. This twofold endeavour was reflected in the agencies which formalized relations between Spaniards and Indians, the *encomienda* and the *reducción*, and was responsible for the strange ambivalence in Spanish policy, wavering between close association of Spaniards and Indians on the one hand and complete segregation on the other.

The Spaniards needed Indian labour, but the Indians, accustomed to a subsistence economy which many Spaniards even to the end of the colonial régime confused with idleness, were unwilling to work for outside employers. Consequently, although the Indians were declared to be free, they were clearly less free than their conquerors. An *encomienda* was a native settlement, or part of a settlement, or a group of settlements, 'commended' by royal grant to the care of an individual Spaniard who was entitled to collect for himself the tribute of the Indians and in return assumed obligations for the spiritual and temporal welfare of the Indians and for the military defence of the area.[1] The *encomienda* easily became a means of forced labour, for in place of tribute most *encomenderos* preferred personal service from the Indians; but even when this was no longer so, the primitive labour-*repartimiento* (allocation of Indians to the

---

[1] *Recopilación*, VI, ix, 1–23. On the *encomienda* see S. Zavala, *La encomienda indiana* (Madrid, 1935); L. B. Simpson, *The encomienda in New Spain* (Berkeley and Los Angeles, 1950).

necessary tasks of cultivation and building for the benefit of Spaniards) remained in existence, and all Indians, whether held in *encomienda* or not were subject to the labour-*repartimiento*, which thus became synonymous with the Peruvian word *mita*. Each village was called upon to provide a fixed quota of labourers every week; a local magistrate assigned the labourers to their task, whether to public works or to private employers. The *repartimiento*, however, was not strictly a labour tribute, for in New Spain at least the employers, private or public, paid their Indian wages at a rate fixed by law.

The *encomienda* system invited many abuses and was the object of many legislative attacks, partly to prevent the rise of a powerful feudal class in the colonies and partly to protect the Indians, but these attacks were not always effective and the system managed to strike deep root. The problem has been well summed up by a modern historian:

The colonial authorities were required to suppress the abuses of the *encomienda*, slavery and personal servitude, without infringing the rights of deserving conquerors and settlers; to ensure an adequate supply of hired labour for the Spanish settlements, while protecting the Indians in their possession of land, which relieved them of the necessity of working for wages. The task was an impossible one.[1]

It was a problem, with which the colonial authorities were still trying to deal in the Río de la Plata in the eighteenth century.

In the district which became the viceroyalty of the Río de la Plata the indigenous population was divided between those who lived freely alongside the Spaniards, those subject to the *encomienda*, and the mission Indians.[2] The Indians who lived freely with the Spaniards were so few in number that they do not enter the Indian problem of this period. The *encomienda* Indians were to be found in the provinces of La Paz, Cochabamba, Potosí, Paraguay and the districts to the north of the Río de la Plata. The life of most of these Indians did not differ in kind from that of *encomienda* Indians in other parts of the empire.

[1] J. H. Parry, *The audiencia of New Galicia in the sixteenth century* (Cambridge, 1948), p. 55.
[2] See C. E. Corona Baratech, 'Notas para un estudio de la sociedad en el Río de la Plata durante el virreinato', *Anuario de Estudios Americanos*, viii (1951), pp. 82–104.

But from the beginning of the eighteenth century there began a notable transformation in *encomiendas* in certain parts of these provinces. In Tucumán the Spanish *encomenderos* declined in number to 167 and the Indian *encomendados* to 1,550. The decline was most evident in the Córdoba district where there were only 17 *encomenderos* with 94 *encomendados*. In Catamarca and La Rioja there were more *encomenderos*, but each had only one Indian.[1] This phenomenon has been explained by the suggestion that the interest of the Spanish settlers tended to be directed more and more to the direct cultivation of the land and less to the use of *encomienda* Indians who were becoming unfit for work and even extinct; at the same time the settlers began to expropriate the land of the Indians in the fertile zones.[2]

In Paraguay, however, the *encomienda* system was firmly entrenched and its abuses were even greater than elsewhere. In this province there were two types of *encomienda* Indians, the *originarios* and the *mitayos*.[3] In the early days of colonization the Spaniards, who had already suffered from the implacable hostility of the Indians in the region of Buenos Aires, settled in Asunción where the Indians were friendly, and formed an alliance with certain Guaraní chiefs. During the first twenty years of settlement the permanent assignment of lands and establishment of *encomiendas* was not considered, because the Spaniards still hoped to move on elsewhere in search of gold and silver mines. In the absence of *encomiendas*, the Spaniards acquired large numbers of Guaraní women as wives, concubines and servants; the relatives of these women also helped to provide food and labour for the Spaniards, just as they customarily provided them for their own chiefs, an arrangement which they evidently considered a normal consequence of the alliance. This informal, casual relationship gradually hardened, and as the hopes of discovering mines faded and the colonists became resigned to permanent settlement at Asunción, the original system of personal service by Indian women and their relatives came to be regarded as an *encomienda*, and was called the

[1] M. Lizondo Borda, 'El Tucumán de los siglos XVII y XVIII', in *H.N.A.*, iii, 505-6.
[2] *Ibid.*, p. 415.
[3] See E. R. Service, 'The *encomienda* in Paraguay', *H.A.H.R.*, xxxi (1951), pp. 230-52.

encomienda originaria. Then in 1556, acting on orders from the crown, governor Irala divided the Indians in the vicinity of Asunción into formal *encomiendas* and turned the attention of the colonists from the mirage of precious metals to the humdrum task of permanently settling the land. Such a reorientation led to a rapid extension of the *encomienda* system to new areas of Paraguay, and even beyond, so that Spanish control spread to villages of Indians at some distance from Asunción. This system, created by decree, was called the *encomienda mitaya*, because the Indians were brought to Asunción periodically as labourers; hence *mitayo* after the *mita* labour system of Perú. These differences of origin help to account for the different conditions endured by the *originario* and the *mitayo* Indian. The *originarios* were not grouped into any town, had no lands or goods except those allowed to them by their masters, and were in effect nothing more than slaves; living permanently on the lands of their Spanish masters for whom they performed domestic and agricultural service, they were paid no wages and were simply rewarded by food and clothing, all of which was notoriously inadequate: they were badly treated and the religious side of the *encomienda* was entirely neglected. The mitayo *encomienda* derived from the Spanish legal concept of *encomienda* but differed from it in certain respects. The Indians paid no tribute but had to serve as an unpaid, part-time labour force, working in the service of their masters about a third of the year; for this they received only their sustenance, and were treated just as inhumanly as the *originarios*. But unlike the latter they lived and worked in their own villages for the rest of the year; here they had fixed residence, with priests who looked after their spiritual welfare and Spanish administrators who took care of their material wants, feeding and clothing them out of the community funds; they also had their own *cabildos* and magistrates whom they themselves appointed every year.[1]

From the beginning of the seventeenth century the crown made many attempts to regulate *encomiendas* in the Río de la Plata, Tucumán and Paraguay, particularly to prevent the taking of personal service instead of tribute,[2] but local pressure from the

[1] A.G.I., Aud. de Buenos Aires 322, Augustín Fernando de Pineda to Crown, 29 January 1777.   [2] See, e.g., *Recopilación*, VI, xvii, I.

interested parties always prevented the colonial authorities from putting them into effect. A royal *cédula* of 15 October 1696 ordered the governor not to grant any further *encomiendas*, and to incorporate existing ones in the crown, but there were so many protests from the colonists, mainly in the form of representations from the procurators and the *cabildos*, that the order was never implemented. Another *cédula* of 4 April 1776 ordered the governor of Paraguay to report on the advisability of incorporating in the crown all the *encomiendas* of Paraguay, but in spite of the governor's support of such a policy nothing was then accomplished. Meanwhile the abuses continued, and the effect of this spectacle on the surrounding hostile Indians, the Payaguas, Guanes and Abipones, was to make them resist more fiercely than ever all attempts to 'reduce' them, while many of the Christian Indians deserted to these tribes. And not only did the *encomenderos* fail to fulfil their obligations towards the Indians: they even evaded their obligations to the crown, neglecting to perform the military service in defence of the province which was an essential part of the *encomienda* contract.[1] But the *encomienda* laws most consistently ignored in Paraguay were those designed to prevent unpaid, unregulated exploitation of native labour, whether *originario* or *mitayo*. The nature of the Paraguayan economy contributed towards this situation. Lack of mineral wealth, isolation, and limited commerce meant that the only commodity the Spaniards could take from the natives was their labour; consequently this was exploited in terms of a subsistence economy, because tribute of money, agricultural produce, or a native trade ware could not develop in the absence of any export market of importance.

The *encomiendas* continued undiminished during the early years of the intendant régime. In 1784 viceroy Loreto was ordered to enforce the prohibition of personal service, but to ensure that the Indians worked for wages.[2] There is no evidence, however, that this produced any better results than previous injunctions. Writing in 1800 viceroy Avilés reported that royal policy had made practically no progress for the past 190 years,

[1] A.G.I., Aud. de Buenos Aires 322, Pineda to Crown, 29 January 1777.
[2] A.G.I., Aud. de Buenos Aires 44, Crown to Loreto, 9 February 1784, 'Instrucción de govierno'. arts. 36–7.

and that the *encomienda* system in Paraguay still existed with all its abuses.[1] Referring to recent years Avilés blamed the intendants for permitting and even conniving at this state of affairs,[2] A royal *cédula* of 17 May 1803 reiterated the many previous orders that all *encomiendas* should be incorporated in the crown, an indication that the situation had so far not been substantially changed by the intendants. Nevertheless, the only real inroad on the *encomienda* system in Paraguay was effected by intendant Rivera; on 19 May 1798 he reported to the government on the problem and followed this up by incorporating 39 *encomiendas* in the crown.[3]

In Upper Perú the Indian labour question assumed a different form and the intendants had a more acute problem to tackle. As has been seen, the *repartimiento*, or the allotting of Indians as labourers and dependants to the colonists, had been an essential feature of the Spanish system since very early colonial times, and had later received some degree of legal definition. All Indians, whether held in *encomienda* or not, were liable to the labour-*repartimiento*. In Perú, however, the labour organization was known as the *mita*,[4] a term which derived from a Quechua word signifying 'turn'. The Indians were forcibly conscripted in turn by the local authorities, and set to work for the State, the Church or private employers in return for wages and under regulated conditions of employment. Only the authorized number of conscripts was to be taken, no more than one-seventh of each village; after their term of service they had to be returned to their villages immediately and not engaged on any other work; they had not to be worked longer hours than was within their capacity; they had to be well treated, and provisions and clothes were to be sold to them at moderate

[1] Avilés to Caballero, 8 March 1800, in *D.H.A.*, iii, 27–9.
[2] *Ibid.*, pp. 40–1.
[3] A.G.I., Aud. de Buenos Aires 142, Rivera to Caballero, 19 June 1801; Aud. de Buenos Aires 48, Rivera to Crown, 19 January 1804. Writing in defence of Rivera in 1809 (see above Chapter V), viceroy Liniers reported that the intendant had recommended this in view of the strong resistance in the past. B.M., Add. MS 32609, fol. 117, Liniers to Cornel (Minister of War), 26 January 1809. Azara insinuated that Rivera obstructed incorporation, but Azara was a prejudiced and even untrustworthy witness. See Azara, *Memorias . . . y otros informes*, pp. 267–8.
[4] See J. Basadre, 'El régimen de la mita', *Letras* (Univ. of San Carlos, Lima), 1937, tercer trimestre, pp. 325–64.

prices.[1] The *mita* was mainly, though not exclusively, associated with service in the mines. In the provinces of the Río de la Plata, where there were no significant mines, the term *mitayos* was used, as has been seen, to describe those *encomienda* Indians who performed *servicio personal* for their masters for a certain period of every year. It was in Upper Perú, however, that the *mita* system assumed its most essential characteristics and became an economic institution and social phenomenon of the first importance; the fabulous mines of Potosí absorbed the Indian labour of 139 Indian villages whose inhabitants were worked one week and rested two weeks, labouring during a year four months altogether, in the most appalling conditions and subject to the most brutal treatment.[2]

The mortality rate was high. Once the service was done a high proportion of the natives never returned home: those who did not die were often forcibly retained under various pretexts. The *Mercurio Peruano* described the *mita* conscription in sombre terms:

The Indians who go to the mines of Potosí depart from their villages somewhat disconsolate, for they know quite well that they may contract in the mines asthma or *choco* which may quickly prove fatal. Their day of departure is extremely sad: the conscripts parade before the priest who awaits them at the church door holding a cross and blesses them with the customary prayers; then he says Mass, for which they pay, in order to ask the Almighty a happy end to their journey. Afterwards they go out to the square accompanied by their priests, relations and friends; and amidst mutual embraces and tears they bid farewell, and followed by their children and wives, they sadly take the road. The grimness and melancholy of this scene is increased by the beating of the drums and the sound of the church bells tolling for prayers.[3]

There was another category of Indians in Upper Perú, differing from the ordinary *encomienda* Indians as the *originarios* differed from the *mitayos* in Paraguay. These were the *yanaconas*,

[1] *Recopilación*, VI, xii, 20 ff. They were not to be employed in dangerous parts of the mines except voluntarily. *Ibid.*, VI, xv, 11.

[2] G. René-Moreno, *Bolivia y Perú* (Santiago, 1907), p. 288; P. V. Cañete, 'Intendencia de Potosí', printed in *Revista de Buenos Aires*, xxiv (1871), p. 179.

[3] *Mercurio Peruano*, 1792, i, 208, quoted in René-Moreno, 'La mita de Potosí en 1795', *Revista Chilena*, viii (1877), p. 392.

or Indians who were bound to the land of certain estates, without freedom to leave or work on their own account, and liable to be transferred with the property to a third party: many royal *cédulas* declared them free, but this legislative principle still remained to be implemented.[1] Nevertheless, desperate as was the state of the *yanaconas*, it was infinitely better than that of the *mitayos*, and to escape the *mita* many Indians became *yanaconas* and worked on estates. There was thus a conflict of interests between those contending for the labour of the Indians, between the miners, protesting that the mines would be ruined, and the farmers, complaining about loss of crops and consequent food shortage. This social discord was a fundamental characteristic of the colonial history of Upper Perú, but whatever the conflicts of interest on that account, one thing was permanent and unchanging—the demand for conscript Indian labour; any attempts to reform the system or remove the labour altogether met with a hard core of resistance. On this problem the *audiencia* of Charcas had a record of indifference.[2] Before 1776 the only hope for reform had been appeal to the viceroy in Lima, but little had been accomplished there. With the transfer of Upper Perú to the new viceroyalty of the Río de la Plata in 1776, Potosí and its social problems became a matter for the viceroy at Buenos Aires, and, from 1783, for the intendants of Upper Perú.

The new masters showed little inclination to reform abuses. The viceroy at Buenos Aires was too distant an authority to do anything. The intendants on the spot were too complacent even to analyse the conditions. Only intendant Viedma of Cochabamba was sensitive to the sufferings of the *mita* Indians of Potosí. In a report of 1793 he described their situation in Potosí—wages below the high cost of living there, insecurity of food and clothing, appalling housing conditions, unjust labour practices, work without pay on Sundays. The labour quota which went from Cochabamba was made up of Indians accustomed to the temperate climate of the valleys of Cochabamba, and easy victims to the harsh and rigorous climate of Potosí and

[1] René-Moreno, *Bolivia y Perú*, pp. 255–6.
[2] René-Moreno, *Bolivia y Perú*, pp. 260–2; Ruiz Guiñazú, *La magistratura indiana*, pp. 31–2.

the cruel work there. Viedma estimated that usually about a third of those conscripted from Cochabamba did not return, a process which would eventually exterminate the whole *mita* population of Cochabamba. Yet Viedma had no plan for reform, beyond a cursory suggestion that the laws should be strictly enforced.[1]

The official complacency was rudely shaken in 1793 by the appearance of a remarkable work entitled *Discurso sobre la Mita de Potosí*.[2] Its author was the recently appointed fiscal of the *audiencia* of Charcas and defender of the Indians, Victorián de Villava.[3] Villava arrived in Upper Perú at a time when the state of the *mita* Indians, far from improving, was actually becoming more desperate. As the profits from the Potosí mines were diminishing, so the Indian labourer was exploited more ruthlessly than ever and the *mita* system applied with little regard to the law. The sight of this injustice and the knowledge that the intendant of Potosí with the support of the viceroy at Buenos Aires had made constant requests for the increase of the *mita* moved Villava to write his *Discurso* in which he combined legal acumen with a warm humanitarianism; the result was a lucid condemnation of the whole *mita* system on economic, legal and social grounds. He argued that work in the mines was legally not of a public nature; it was provided simply for private employers, for the mines were not the property of the state but belonged to those who first discovered them, the royal fifth being no more than a tribute in recognition of the supreme territorial jurisdiction of the crown. But even granted that the work was public it gave no right to force the Indians to perform it or to exploit their labour in appalling conditions: only voluntary labour should be sought. Villava then went on to affirm the rationality of the Indians against those who regarded them as mere machines, and did not hesitate to blame Spanish officials for reducing the Indians to a state of apathy. Human liberty must always be respected, and no one should ever be forced to work. The cause of the *mita* had triumphed simply because of the wealth and influence of the vested interests

[1] Viedma to Arredondo, 2 March 1793, in Angelis, *Colección*, ii, 494–5.
[2] 9 March 1793, printed in Levene, *Vida y escritos de Victorián de Villava*, pp. xxx–xxxiv.   [3] See below, pp. 247–50, 253–55.

behind it: 'la causa de los ricos siempre tiene muchos abogados y la de los infelices apenas halla procuradores'.[1]

The vested interests now found their advocate precisely in the intendant of Potosí, Francisco de Paula Sanz, who reacted indignantly against the theories of Villava and published an extensive *Contestación* (19 November 1794) in which he attacked Villava point by point.[2] Work in the mines of Potosí, he maintained, was different in kind from private work and was properly styled public. He admitted that the Indians were not differently constituted from the rest of mankind and they were perhaps capable of education and improvement, but in fact they had made no progress since the days of the conquest and were no less lazy and stupid than they had been then. Granted this idleness, the *mita* service was useful and expedient to the Indians, for it brought them into contact with civilized society and made them work for a wage. No doubt the system had produced abuses, but many of them had been exaggerated in the style of Las Casas. Moreover the *mita* was useful not only to the Indians but also to the state, and as such must be compulsory.

Sanz asserted that numerous copies of Villava's paper had circulated in Upper Perú, but Villava denied this and claimed that he had taken abundant precautions to remit it secretly to the Council of the Indies in Madrid. It seems likely, however, that copies were made and found their way to various parts of the country, but, even if this were not so, Sanz's reply and the fiscal's subsequent conduct transferred the official dispute into a public spectacle. When Villava discovered that his original suspicions were justified and that in the new mining code on which Sanz and his assessor were working it was proposed not only to change various points of *mita* law but also to add four or five thousand more Indians to the service, he wrote another lengthy paper, defending his original position against the attacks of the intendant.[3] The legal points were made with his usual sureness of touch, though he himself realized that they would have little effect against the existing facts. Nonetheless, he made the telling observation that the lot of the Indian had in no way

[1] Levene, *op. cit.*, p. xxxviii.   [2] *Ibid.*, pp. 21–2.
[3] 'Contrarréplica a la "Contestación" de Paula Sanz', 3 January 1795, in *ibid.*, pp. xxxix–liv.

been improved by the recent political changes associated with the Ordinance of Intendants:

> The fact is that the names have been changed but the substance remains the same: it matters little whether the officials are called Governors, Subdelegates, Assessors, or *Corregidores* nor whether the unjust exactions [made on the Indians] are termed *fiestas, viajes, revisitas,* or *repartos.* . . . It is certain that the lot of the Indian has not improved with the new code of Intendancies.[1]

This somewhat academic debate was given more substantial content by events which changed it into a bitter conflict between authorities and a struggle of rival interests. In December 1794 some missionary priests of the subdistrict of Chayanta protested before the *audiencia* of Charcas against the action of the subdelegate of Chayanta, Pedro Francisco de Arizmendi, who, acting as commissioner of the intendant of Potosí, was about to send 184 Indians to a new *mita* conceded by royal order of 5 May 1793 to two mining operators, Luis de Orueta and Juan Jauregui. Fiscal Villava pointed out that no notice of the new quota had been given to the *audiencia,* and that labour conscription of this nature was contrary to right reason and fair law; he requested the subdelegate be forbidden to introduce a new *mita.* The *audiencia* concurred and by a resolution of 28 March 1795 suspended the dispatch of the new *mita,* permitting only the traditional ones. The viceroy confirmed this decision on 29 April 1795, and ordered full information to be submitted to him on the matter.[2]

The news caused an uproar in Potosí. The *gremio de azogueros* and the officials of the tribunal of accounts took sides with the intendant and denounced Villava in the strongest terms. Support of the new *mita* was described as 'the voice of reason and of justice', while the fiscal and the *audiencia* were criticized for interfering in matters of government; intendant Sanz was eulogized in exaggerated terms.[3] On 1 March 1795 Sanz him-

---

[1] *Ibid.,* p. xliii.

[2] A.G.I., Aud. de Buenos Aires 81, viceroy Melo de Portugal to Gardoqui, carta reservada 13, 3 July 1795.

[3] 'Representación Apologética de la Muy Noble Imperial Villa de Potosí, sus Tribunales, Oficinas y Gremios, al Exmo. S. Virrey, sobre los acaecimientos de la Provincia de Chayanta, 1796', in René-Moreno, 'La mita de Potosí en 1795', *op. it.,* pp. 407–30.

self took the offensive, protesting that the *audiencia* exceeded its competence in taking cognizance of purely government affairs and arguing that the dispatch of Indians to the mines freed them from the illegal services which they would otherwise have to perform for the priests.[1] In reply to this Villava issued on 12 March the first of his striking series of *vistas*, in which he attacked the legal basis of his adversary's position, arguing that laws ought to be modified as circumstances varied and as the reasons which originally justified them ceased to exist.[2]

The issue was becoming less theoretical. On 21 March sub-delegate Arizmendi informed the *audiencia* that there had been an attempted native insurrection in the village of Pocoata, led by an Indian, Victoriano Ayra, and due to seditious statements put out that there was no royal order for the establishment of the new *mita*, which was simply the result of an intrigue between the intendant of Potosí and himself, the subdelegate.[3] Meanwhile, both sides appealed to the higher authorities, but the viceroy and the crown had no clear policy. Remembering that in 1780 native rebellions had originated in Chayanta, the viceroy was perturbed by the new developments there, and he ordered the intendant to arrest the instigator, Ayra, and send him to Buenos Aires. He was able to report in July 1795 that Chayanta was tranquil.[4] A year later Sanz denied that any such rebellion had taken place, and reported that on his visitation of the district the only disturbing things he discovered were ecclesiastical abuses and exploitation of the Indians by the priests,[5] a statement which provides more evidence for the prejudices of the intendant than for the actual state of affairs. In August 1796 the crown sent a compromise decision, suspending the new decrees of the intendant of Potosí and allowing no alteration of the old *mita* system or labour quota.[6] Neither the advocates of abolition nor those of extension were satisfied.

[1] Levene, *op. cit.*, pp. 26–7.
[2] 'Vista del fiscal sobre la servidumbre de los indios,' 12 March 1795, in *ibid.*, pp. cvi–lxiv.
[3] *Ibid.*, p. 29.
[4] A.G.I., Aud. de Buenos Aires 81, Melo de Portugal to Gardoqui, carta reservada 13, 3 July 1795.
[5] A.G.I., Aud. de Charcas 440, Sanz to Gardoqui, 26 June 1796.
[6] A.G.I., Estado 76, Real Resolución, 2 August 1796.

Nevertheless, the practical effects of the fiscal's anti-*mita* campaign were striking. In March 1796 Sanz reported that 745 Indians had deserted from those assigned to that year's *mita*, without counting the 1,000 who had never turned up at all: those who had arrived were working extremely badly.[1] Later the seeds of doubt sown by Villava bore further fruit. In 1803 the intendant of Puno, Josef González, refused on humanitarian grounds to send his *mita* quota from the Indians of the sub-district of Chucuito. González argued that apart from the damage done to the Indians by the unfavourable climate of Potosí, their exploitation and corruption in the mines and in the town, where they were treated as though they were irrational and defrauded of their rightful wages, was completely unjustified: by its violation of the laws Potosí had forfeited its right to the *mita*. In spite of the requests of the intendant of Potosí and the orders of the viceroys at Buenos Aires and Lima González witheld his quota, and he remained unmoved even by a royal order. The viceroy at Buenos Aires and the intendant of Potosí automatically denied the charges he had made, but the Council of the Indies, to which the matter was remitted, observed that some of the abuses reported by González were the same as those described by Villava and advised that · a decree should be issued to the viceroy, the *audiencia* of Charcas and the intendant of Potosí ordering that if such abuses existed they should be ended immediately. But the time had passed when any firm directions could be expected from the central government, and this decree was never issued.[2] While central inspiration was lacking, local administration was unenlightened. It was one of the tragedies of the intendant system that for most of the years of its operation the intendancy of Potosí was occupied by a man who, whatever his merits as an administrator, had little awareness of the Indian problem or sympathy for native suffering. Apart from the report of Viedma and the action of González, the record of the intendants in defence of the *mita* Indians cannot be described, as it has recently been, as one of 'celosa vigilancia'.[3]

---

[1] A.G.I., Aud. de Buenos Aires 82, Sanz to Melo de Portugal, 26 March 1796.

[2] A.G.I., Aud. de Buenos Aires 21, Consulta del Consejo, 30 September 1806.

[3] C. E. Corona Baratech, 'Notas para un estudio de la sociedad en el Río de la Plata durante el virreinato, *op. cit.*, p. 143.

The *mita* system continued unabated until the end of the colonial régime.[1]

II

Spanish policy sought not only to maintain an adequate supply of native labour, but also to persuade the frontier Indians to settle down in permanent communities and live in towns or villages, so that the work of bringing them under royal control and converting them to Christianity would be made easier. For this purpose it was considered necessary to keep the Indians isolated from contact with Spaniards, and such communities, or reductions, were under the management of missionary priests; the Indians could be included in *encomiendas* but they could not lose their right to own lands; to cover common expenses and to guarantee payment of tribute certain lands were set aside and cultivated to produce community funds (*bienes de comunidad*).[2] The most highly organized system of reductions had been those of the Jesuits in Paraguay. In little more than 150 years the Jesuits had gradually extended their spheres of influence over the tribes of the upper Amazon, eastern Bolivia, Chiquitos, the Chaco, Paraguay and the Pampas. The most favourable subjects for Jesuit government were the Guaraní Indians of the middle and upper Paraguay and Uruguay Rivers, and the thirty missions established in this area were characterized by a high degree of collectivism and a unique political position; the Jesuits were able to reject the colonists' demands for Indian labour, and the communities comprised a kind of garrison at the disposal of the Spanish authorities as laid down in the regulations of 1649, in return for which their freedom from *encomienda* was confirmed and a reduction of tribute conceded.[3] A basic condition of the whole system was complete isolation of the Indians from contact with any whites except the Jesuit fathers

---

[1] It continued until 1819 in spite of the decree of the Cortes of 1812. See René-Moreno, *Bolivia y Perú*, p. 289. Native conditions in Potosí did not improve after the collapse of the Spanish empire. Modern Bolivia has still not solved its native problem. For a vivid description of this see Germán Arciniegas, *The state of Latin America* (London, 1953), pp. 121–2.

[2] See M. Mörner, *The political and economic activities of the Jesuits in the La Plata region. The Hapsburg era* (Stockholm, 1953), p. 36.

[3] *Ibid.*, pp. 199–201.

themselves. The value of the Jesuit experiment has been extensively debated: its most recent historian concludes that

It is probable that the Guaranís in the reductions at least enjoyed much better material conditions after the initial period of adaptation . . . than if they had been left to their own resources.[1]

But with the expulsion of the Jesuits from the Spanish dominions in 1768 the system was abruptly disrupted. Henceforth the condition of the Indians in Paraguay and Uruguay was a constant preoccupation of the central authorities in Madrid and of the viceregal government in Buenos Aires. Until the very end of the Spanish régime an unceasing flow of reports came from the pens of the viceroys and intendants, analysing the situation, suggesting reforms and outlining new schemes. But none of these produced the desired results. The Jesuit system, absolutely paternal, had at least solved the problem of the material subsistence of the Indians. Now, however, it was argued that this had been done at the expense of their liberty. The reaction of the Spanish authorities against the community system established by the Jesuits thus had a theoretical as well as practical side. Arguments were used in favour of individual liberty and private property, and such concepts became common currency among the viceroys and intendants when referring to the communities.[2] Ironically enough they were out of tune with the leaders of the Age of Enlightenment. Even opponents of the Jesuit order such as Voltaire, d'Alembert, Montesquieu and the ex-Jesuit Raynal commended the 'Jesuit State' as a rationalistic sociological experiment.[3] The liberal-minded fiscal of the *audiencia* of Charcas, Victorián de Villava,

[1] *Ibid.*, p. 204. The communism of the Guaraní reductions is often exaggerated: 'The Jesuits had no desire to create a communistic state; on the contrary they did their best to develop a sense of individual property among the Indians by encouraging them to plant a surplus trade in the Spanish towns and by giving them cattle to build up herds of their own,' A. Métraux, 'Jesuit missions in South America', *Handbook of South American Indians* (6 vols., Washington, 1946–50), v, 652.
[2] Intendant Viedma of Cochabamba exclaimed 'Nada es mas preciosa al hombre que la libertad con que Dios le ha criado' and advocated the freeing of the Indians of Mojos and Chiquitos from their tutelage; they should be given their own property and pay the alcabala tax and the royal tribute. Viedma to Arredondo, 2 March 1793, in Angelis, *Colección*, ii, 499–500. Viedma's ideas were vetoed by the *audiencia* of Charcas because of lack of financial means for implementing them. See A.G.I., Aud. de Buenos Aires 140, Viedma to Acuña y Malvar, 10 January 1793.
[3] See Mörner, *op. cit.*, pp. 194–5.

praised the reductions as 'simple, industrious communities, free from communication with Spaniards and consequently from European corruption, and in short a model of political perfection which will perhaps be the admiration of future thinkers'.[1]

At first the unaccustomed rôle of Spanish authorities as advocates of freedom was more theoretical than practical. In default of any alternative plan the Jesuit system of government had to be continued and the community system maintained. Three lieutenant-governors were appointed for the thirty *pueblos* with the same authority as the Jesuit Superior of the Missions and the same ordinary jurisdiction as the *corregidores* and *alcaldes mayores* in other parts of the empire. There was a secular administrator for each village who conducted the economic activities of the community, received the fruits of production, assigned to the community what was necessary for its subsistence, sold the surplus, and paid the royal tribute. Each village was supposed to have two priests, though in fact most of them only had one, whose functions were strictly confined to the spiritual, and who were under the jurisdiction of a vicar-general. In Candelaria there was a chief governor for all the thirty *pueblos* with the same faculties as the governors of Tucumán and Paraguay, assisted by a legal assessor and an exchequer accountant, while in Buenos Aires there was an administrator-general who centralized the economic life of the communities and to whom were submitted cases for his approval.[2] Each village had its subordinate Indian officers—two *alcaldes*, four *regidores*, an *alcalde provincial*, two *alcaldes de Santa Hermandad*, and a secretary, but the administrator presided over all municipal *juntas*. The Indians continued working for the community except for a few days spent on their own small plots.

This secular system of administration, theoretically not far removed from the Jesuit régime, was in practice disastrous.[3] The new officials were not only less efficient than the Jesuits but were also less disinterested, and regarded their task as a means of personal profit. The administrator of each village was

[1] 'Discurso sobre la mita de Potosí' (1793), in Levene, *op. cit.*, p. xxxvi.

[2] A.G.I., Aud. de Buenos Aires 353, Real decreto, 25 July 1777.

[3] See Pablo Hernández, S.J., *El extrañamiento de los jesuitas del Río de la Plata y de as misiones del Paraguay por decreto de Carlos III* (Madrid, 1908), pp. 270–8.

assigned a salary of 300 pesos and strictly forbidden to engage in commerce on his own account; this salary was quite inadequate and only attracted a low type of official who augmented it by illegitimate means.[1] Ill-defined instructions gave rise to conflicts between officials.[2] Particularly damaging were the conflicts between the secular officials and the priests, for the latter, inheriting the religious authority of the Jesuits and something of their influence over the Indians, aroused the jealousy and resentment of the local administrators,[3] while the Indians, accustomed only to the unitary command of the Jesuits and incapable of understanding this new conflict of jurisdiction, were uncertain whom to obey.

Moreover the new system afforded the Indians no economic guidance or protection. They were ruthlessly robbed of their cattle by savage Indians and by gangs of Portuguese and Spanish rustlers: the decline in livestock after the expulsion of the Jesuits was recorded by intendant Alós in 1788:[4]

	Number of Cattle		
	1768	*1769*	*1788*
Department of Santiago:			
Santa Maria de Fe .	60,287	33,492	15,338
San Ignacio Guazú .	16,037	10,121	15,511
Santa Rosa . .	80,044	78,797	26,313
Santiago . . .	36,432	32,422	32,390
San Cosme . .	42,914	39,983	18,705
Department of Candelaria:			
Ytapúa . . .	32,500	32,500	31,755
Candelaria . .	25,809	158,23	18,288
Santa Ana . .	50,751	35,313	23,559
Poreto . . .	34,975	40,660	12,916
San Ignacio Miní .	37,695	33,630	12,145
Corpus . . .	20,423	10,331	23,362
Trinidad . . .	25,567	6,286	3,525
Jesús . . .	52,937	42,811	10,099
	516,371	412,169	243,906

[1] A.G.I., Aud. de Buenos Aires 323, Bishop of Paraguay to Gálvez, 13 December 1784. The bishop had recently made a visit of inspection.

[2] Hernández, *op. cit.*, p. 274.

[3] Avilés to Caballero, 8 March 1800, in *D.H.A.*, iii, 42–5.

[4] A.G.I., Aud. de Buenos Aires 142. Joaquín Alós, 'Estado de los ganados . . . que quedaron el año de 1768 . . . 1769 . . . 1788'.

The economic decline was reflected in the decay of the houses and other buildings of the villages which soon fell into ruin and remained unrepaired.[1] The desertion of the natives was the natural consequence of the new state of affairs, and the mission population declined rapidly as the Indians began to make their way to Brazil, Buenos Aires, Montevideo, Paraguay, Santa Fe, Entre Ríos and Corrientes.[2] Many of them joined the swarms of criminals in the Montevideo territory where they earned a living smuggling for the Portuguese. Others obtained work in the towns or as labourers in the country, and in spite of the alleged demoralizing effects of the Jesuit régime were capable enough of earning a living and working for a wage.[3] From 1768 to 1800 the population dropped from 96,381 to 42,885.[4] But the law forbade Indians to leave their reductions,[5] and consequently many attempts were made to turn back the tide of desertions: for example, a decree published by viceroy Vértiz on 17 August 1780 forbade anyone to take into his service Indians from Uruguay or Paraguay under pain of 200 pesos fine, with a reward of 50 pesos to anyone reporting such cases.[6] These efforts met with little success, for Spanish employers needed the labour thus released. Eventually it was realized that the law was now unrealistic, and in 1802 a viceregal resolution of 14 June officially recognized the facts and freed the Indians from the necessity of return.[7]

The disintegration of the Indian communities after the expulsion of the Jesuits was not confined to Paraguay. From Tucumán there were immediate complaints of maladministration of Jesuit estates and funds.[8] For Cochabamba the situation was recorded by intendant Viedma. The decline could be seen, he reported, in cases of Jesuit estates bought up by private management, most of which were now going to ruin.[9] The same

[1] See Avilés, 'Memoria de gobierno', 21 May 1801, in Radaelli, *Memorias de los virreyes del Río de la Plata*, p. 507.
[2] See J. M. Mariluz Urquijo, 'Los guaraníes después de la expulsión de los jesuítas', *Estudios Americanos*, vi (1953), pp. 323–3.
[3] A.G.I., Aud. de Buenos Aires 21, Informe de Melo de Portugal, 23 July 1794.
[4] Avilés, *op. cit.*, p. 507.   [5] *Recopilación*, vi, iii, 18.
[6] *D.H.A.*, i, 312–13.   [7] Mariluz Urquijo, *op. cit.*, p. 329.
[8] A.G.I., Aud. de Buenos Aires 143, Matorres (Governor of Tucumán) to Crown, 3 March 1770.
[9] Viedma to Arredondo, 2 March 1793, in Angelis, *Colección*, ii, 450–1.

thing happened under the rule of secular priests: on one estate improvident slaughter of cattle had dangerously reduced the stock left by the Jesuits. Financial exploitation by some priests rendered the Indians incapable of paying the royal tribute or of maintaining their families and forced them to flee and live a life of vagrancy and robbery. At the same time there was the more permanent problem of the maldistribution of land which had arrived at a state where many natives had been completely dispossessed by the occupation of community lands by Spaniards.[1] The state of the Indians of Mojos and Chiquitos was equally disastrous.[2] The lay administrators were just as unsatisfactory as they were in Paraguay; the secular priests were ignorant of the language and usually despotic; the governors exploited the Indians either on their own account or in the interests of the royal exchequer.[3] Innumerable plans for reform were drawn up by governors and intendants, but none was implemented. Intendant Pizarro of Salta drew attention to the state of the Indians of his province in 1791 after his visitation of the reductions. The Indians of San José de Petacas, he reported, had neither church nor village and possessed no cattle; they were dispersed among Spaniards whom they served as peons. The Abipones of Nuestra Señora de la Concepción had suffered such a decline in their cattle that they had no means of subsistence and as a result of this they had given themselves over to pillage and robbery and infested the highways and roads.[4]

The concern of the government, of the viceroys, and of the intendants, over the Indian problem caused by the expulsion of the Jesuits testified to the good intentions rather than to the actual ability of Spanish administrators. In the search for a policy, and for the administrative machinery to effect it, little progress was made, and a native problem which was essentially cultural

[1] *Ibid.*, pp. 467–8, 492, 495–6.
[2] *Ibid.*, p. 500; A.G.I., Aud. de Buenos Aires 140, Melchior Rodríguez (Governor of Chiquitos) to Acuña (Minister of Grace and Justice), 30 January 1783. See also G. Desdevises du Dezert, 'Les missions de Mojos et des Chiquitos de 1767 a 1808', *Revue Hispanique*, xliii (1918), pp. 365–430.
[3] On the lay administrators see Viedma, *ibid.*, p. 506.
[4] Pizarro to the Crown, 5 October 1791, in 'Relación de la visita hecha a la intendencia de Salta del Tucumán por el governador intendente Ramón García de León y Pizarro en 1791 y 1792 con una noticia biográfica', *B.I.I.H.*, xiii (1931), p. 70.

consistently evaded solution. As far as administrative machinery was concerned the Ordinance of Intendants, far from improving the situation, actually caused more confusion. The new code, while preserving the office of governor of the missions, assigned thirteen of the thirty *pueblos* to the territorial and financial jurisdiction of the intendant of Paraguay and the remainder to Buenos Aires,[1] and it was a fair inference that the intendant should govern the *pueblos* on the same terms as the rest of his district according to the rules of the Ordinance.[2] But the relation between the intendant of Paraguay, who had jurisdiction over thirteen of the *pueblos*, and the administrator-general in Buenos Aires, who had previously been assigned economic control of all the *pueblos*, was never defined. Viceroy Avilés tried to clarify this situation by a decree of 12 June 1799 which clearly subjected the Paraguayan reductions to the economic and financial control and direction of the administrator in Buenos Aires; at the same time he sent a commissioner to Paraguay to implement the arrangement. This naturally drew from intendant Rivera a strong protest against what he considered was a manoeuvre to deprive him of his rightful faculties. Meanwhile the administrator in Buenos Aires was issuing orders to the communities in Paraguay without any consultation with the intendant and as though the whole district of the *pueblos de misiones* were one administrative entity. Rivera resigned himself to the new arrangement until the commissioner in Asunción required him to order the exchequer officials in Asunción to give him an account of the state of income and expenditure and any other information he might require in the future. Rivera refused to comply with this and protested to Avilés over the new arrangement for the Indian community funds, which the viceroy had also placed under the control of the administrator-general, although the Ordinance stated that community funds were to be under the management of the intendant and the higher control of the *junta superior de hacienda*.[3]

In default of a positive policy and of precise administrative

[1] *Ord. Ints.*, art. 1, implemented by viceroy Loreto in 1784. See A.G.I., Aud. de Buenos Aires 322, Loreto to Intendant of Paraguay, 14 July 1784.

[2] *Ord. Ints.*, art. 7. See above, pp. 68, 110–11.

[3] A.G.I., Aud. de Buenos Aires 322, Rivera to Avilés, 14 October 1800. See *Ord. Ints.*, arts. 118–19.

definitions the intendants could accomplish little, beyond reporting on the evils of the new dispensation. The exhaustive survey of the communities under his jurisdiction made by intendant Alós in 1788 affords an admirable account of the state of the *pueblos*. The books in which the local administrators were supposed to keep the accounts of the community funds were in general 'in the greatest disorder and confusion'; because the administrators were only interested in the financially productive *yerba*, agriculture was almost completely abandoned, especially in the villages of the department of Candelaria, where community grain stocks were extremely low; cotton and tobacco were quite neglected; the Indians were shamefully cheated by the merchants, though Alós tried to enforce the regulation that trade contracts had to be reviewed and approved by the intendant; the distribution of food and clothing was inadequate, education almost non-existent. Alós drew up rules for the keeping of community accounts, gave orders for the rebuilding of ruined churches and houses, and tried to control the Spanish merchants, but, conscious of the fact that previous plans for the rehabilitation of the communities had broken against the disinclination of the administrators to execute them, he feared that his own measures would be similarly ignored.[1] His fears were justified; the decline of the communities continued apace.

It was now obvious that secular administration could supply neither the efficiency nor the integrity of the Jesuits and that a new direction would have to be sought. The solution adopted was an admission of defeat, though it was dressed up in the language of liberty and humanitarianism. It was decided to move not the administrators but the Indians, not to change the agencies but simply to abolish the communal system itself. It was proposed to grant the Indians the enjoyment of the same liberty and the protection of the same laws as the Spaniards themselves, assigning them land, abolishing *encomiendas*, and authorizing freedom of commerce between Spaniards and Indians. A royal order of 30 November 1799 requested from viceroy Avilés a report on the state of the Guaraní communities. After condemning the Jesuit system as one of slavery, and the

[1] A.G.I., Aud. de Buenos Aires 142, Alós to Crown, 20 October 1788.

civil administration which replaced it as one of exploitation and inefficiency, Avilés proceeded to his main point, which was that the community system and the principle of communal owner-ship should be abolished and replaced by individual freedom and mutual commerce.[1]

Avilés soon began to implement his policy. On 18 February 1800 he issued a decree freeing 300 enumerated families from communal work and authorizing them to work on their own account; to enable them to do this lands were assigned to them and their families in perpetuity, and sufficient cattle were also granted; the Indians thus liberated were to pay a moderate tribute, either in money or in kind, of one peso a year.[2] There was some hesitation in the application of this drastic policy, and Avilés had to issue a further order on 19 August 1800 in order to clarify it. The enumerated families were to be assigned definite lands and cattle and to have the use of the community oxen and carts; artisans were to be given the necessary tools to practise their crafts; until the end of 1801 the families were to be assisted with food supplies from the community stocks.[3] The scheme was extended to include altogether 6,212 persons in Paraguay and twenty-six families from the three *pueblos* of the Corrientes dis-trict, with the intention of extending it ultimately to all the *pueblos* and abolishing all *encomiendas*. Finally it was hoped to encourage intermarriage between Spaniards and Indian women by offering them ownership of land; an order of 1 December 1800 did this for four Spaniards and one mestizo of the *pueblo* of Concepción.[4]

Intendant Rivera, a firm supporter of the traditional com-munity system, regarded with dismay the results of this novel policy, which he claimed had resulted only in worse confusion: 'Priests, Indians, administrators, subdelegates, all do what they please and they all claim direct authority for their action from the viceroy.'[5] He reported that villages were falling into worse

---

[1] A.G.I., Aud. de Buenos Aires 85, Avilés to Caballero, 8 June 1799. See above, pp. 110–13.

[2] A.G.I., Aud. de Buenos Aires 322, Providencia de virrey Avilés, 18 February 1800. See also *D.H.A.*, iii, 47, 54.

[3] *D.H.A.*, iii, 55.

[4] *Ibid.*, iii, 58–9.

[5] A.G.I., Aud. de Buenos Aires 322, Rivera to Avilés, 19 November 1800.

decay; churches, plantations, estates, all were threatened with complete neglect. Previously the Indians may have had no liberty but now they had no food. Rivera argued that Avilés had no first-hand knowledge of the community Indians. For example the viceroy maintained that even to this day the Indians on being castigated had to fall on their knees to give thanks for it, otherwise they would be punished again.[1] Rivera, who was on the spot and who had made visits of inspection to the reductions, denied this, and denied also the charges of drunkenness and indecency in the living habits of the Indians. He argued that the limited hopes and timid character of the Indians made it necessary to continue the community system. With less justice he accused Avilés of instituting the new plan simply to obtain more effective control over the thirteen *pueblos* assigned by the Ordinance to the intendancy of Paraguay.[2]

The two points of view were submitted to the judgment of the Council of the Indies, which decided in favour of Avilés and agreed that his system should be extended to all the thirty *pueblos*: these should be united, as Avilés proposed, under one single political and military government which would include all the missions formerly divided between Paraguay and Buenos Aires.[3] This opinion was embodied in the royal decree of 28 March 1803 and royal *cédula* of 17 May 1803 which confirmed the principle of liberty for the Indians, describing the community system as 'the most ruinous one for them'. These orders approved the measures taken by Avilés and authorized the appointment of lieutenant-colonel Bernardo de Velasco to a united command of the thirty *pueblos de misiones*, totally independent of Paraguay and of Buenos Aires. At the same time it was ordered that any *encomiendas* still existing in Paraguay be immediately incorporated in the crown, and Spaniards were forbidden to acquire *haciendas* in the territory of the *pueblos de misiones*.[4]

The scheme failed as all other schemes had failed. Félix de Azara and the *Junta Consultiva* set up in Madrid to report on the

---

[1] Avilés to Caballero, 8 March 1800, in *D.H.A.*, iii, 34.
[2] A.G.I., Aud. de Buenos Aires 142, Rivera to Caballero, 19 June 1801.
[3] A.G.I., Aud. de Buenos Aires 322, Consulta del Consejo, 23 November 1802.
[4] R.C., 17 May 1803, in *D.H.A.*, iii, 67–71.

defence of the Indies accused the intendant of Paraguay of pur-
posely obstructing the new plans,[1] but even if Rivera did not
co-operate there were more significant reasons than this for
their failure. There were flaws inherent in the scheme itself.
Theoretically it was admirable to distribute the community
lands, cattle and other property to the Indians in individual
ownership, but in practice this encountered considerable difficulties owing to the fact that community property was now
burdened with considerable debt after the disastrous administration of the secular officials.[2] But the most crippling blow to
the scheme was the fact that its author, viceroy Avilés, did not
continue in office to carry it out, and he himself admitted that
little had been done before he left Buenos Aires.[3] His successor,
Joaquín del Pino, made little attempt to execute it. In September 1805 Velasco was appointed intendant of Paraguay in place
of Rivera, and the administrative arrangement was modified
once again: all the *pueblos de misiones* were included now in the
jurisdiction of the intendancy of Paraguay.[4] But this continual
reshuffling of offices had no significance for the Indian problem,
and the decline of the missions was never arrested nor any
adequate alternative invented.[5]

III

Although the Ordinance of Intendants did not deal precisely
with the specialized problems of *encomiendas, mita*, and missions,
it did attempt to grapple with the general question of Indian
administration. The old officials were replaced and in each
Indian town where there had been a *corregidor* a subdelegate

---

[1] Azara, 'Informe sobre los tabacos del Paraguay . . .', in *Memoria . . . y otros
informes*, pp. 274–5.

[2] *Ibid.*, pp. 251–2.

[3] Avilés, *Memoria*, p. 513.

[4] R.O., 12 September 1805. Velasco asked for two salaries but was granted only
one, that of intendant. See A.G.I., Aud. de Buenos Aires 48, Lucas Muñoz, 29 May
1807.

[5] By 1814 the population of the missions had dropped to 21,000. In 1801 seven
of the pueblos had been lost to the Portuguese; fifteen were destroyed in the wars of
emancipation, some by Francia in 1817. For the rest the community system was
finally abolished by President López of Paraguay in 1848. See Hernández, *op. cit.*,
p. 276, and G. Furlong Cardiff, S.J., 'Los misiones Jesuíticas', in *H.N.A.*, iii, 602–4.

was appointed whose duty it was to administer justice, maintain the Indians in good order, and manage the lands and other properties of the native communities and the funds accruing therefrom.[1] At the same time the Ordinance preserved for the Indians the ancient right, wherever it existed, of choosing every year among themselves the governors or *alcaldes* and other public officials authorized by the laws for their purely economic administration, such as collecting the royal tribute. The meetings of these officials naturally had to be presided over by the subdelegates, but elections also had to be supervised and reported to the intendant for his approval.[2] The latter was expected to direct the natives how to vote:

He should prefer those who know the Spanish language and are most skilled in the worthy vocations of agriculture and industry; and by means which he considers most tactful he should try opportunely to influence the natives to follow these conditions for the elections.[3]

It is evident, however, that these rules were not uniformly observed. Intendant Viedma of Cochabamba reported that in the Chiriguan reductions the local officials were appointed by the priests, without even his approbation. These priests, he asserted, managed affairs with indifference to the royal authority vested in the intendant and with no regard for the dignity and prestige of the Indian officials whom they depreciated and ridiculed; they often punished them in public or suspended them at their will.[4]

But the main Indian question with which the Ordinance was concerned was the *corregidor-repartimiento* issue. Because direct commerce between Spanish merchants and the Indians was discouraged, goods had been distributed to the Indians by the *corregidores*, who, being their political governors, and enjoying a legal monopoly, were able to charge excessive prices and force the Indians to accept a greater quantity of goods than that permitted by the law. The vicious nature of the system can be judged by the intermittent fury of the Indian reaction in Upper Perú. In 1770 in the *pueblo* of Checacupe, province of Tinta, they rebelled and set fire to the house of the *corregidor*; in 1771 in

[1] *Ord. Ints.*, arts. 9, 38.   [2] *Ibid.*, arts. 10–11.   [3] *Ibid.*, art. 11.
[4] Informe de Viedma, 15 January 1788, in Angelis, *Colección*, ii, 527–8.

the province of Pacajes the *corregidor* and his escort of twelve men were killed; in 1775 in the *pueblo* of Santiago de Guamachucos the Indians rose against their *corregidor* and murdered three of his servants, while the *corregidor* himself barely escaped with his life in a riot which had to be quelled by military force.[1] This discontent culminated in the well-known rising in Upper Perú in 1780–1. After the Tupuc Amaru rebellion, although several *corregidores* were reprimanded none was removed; it is true that Miguel de Urbiola, *corregidor* of Carabaya, was removed by inspector-general Joseph del Valle, but the crown ordered his reinstatement, apparently on the petition of local Spaniards.[2] Nevertheless, while it was ready to defend its own servants, the crown was also anxious to jettison the system which had produced so many abuses. *Repartimientos* of goods were explicitly forbidden by the Ordinance of Intendants which authorized that 'the Indians and my other vassals of these dominions are consequently free to trade wherever and with whomsoever it suits them, in order to provide themselves with everything they may need'.[3] This new principle, however, needed to be implemented. In his critique of the Ordinance viceroy Vértiz asked what system would replace the *repartimientos*; he thought it was not sufficient to leave the matter to private commerce, for as the Indians were lazy by nature and given to drunkenness they would never have the money to pay for the goods; it would be difficult to force them to work as the *corregidores* had done.[4] The government itself had second thoughts; in order to ease the period of transition it was decided to establish government stores, financed out of the royal exchequer, in the provinces and villages where they were necessary; these would provide tools, agricultural implements and mules to Indians and other needy castes on a credit basis, the terms of which were to be worked out by the intendants and the *juntas provinciales de hacienda*. The stores would operate until such a time as the

---

[1] B.M., Add. MS 17,601, fols. 191v–192v, 'Quatro informes hechos al Exmo. Señor Don Pedro Cevallos, Virrey de los provincias del Río de la Plata, por un apasionado'.

[2] A.G.I., Aud. de Buenos Aires 44, Vértiz to Gálvez, 12 July 1783.

[3] *Ord. Ints.*, art. 9.

[4] A.G.I., Aud. de Buenos Aires 354, Vértiz and Fernández to Gálvez, Carta 684, 15 February 1783.

Indians were able to provide themselves with these essentials; meanwhile instalments could be paid in money or in kind. The new system was to be called *socorros*, and the term *repartimientos* was never to be used.[1]

The intendants were requested to forward their opinions on the new scheme. Their replies were unenthusiastic.[2] As a result of this information the crown restricted the scheme with cautious conditions to those natives whom it considered needed assistance. Thus the intendancy of Buenos Aires was excluded, as it was thought that there ordinary commerce could supply what was needed. Córdoba and Salta was also excluded, on the grounds that there had been no *repartimientos* in these provinces and that consequently there was nothing needing replacement. Charcas, Potosí, La Paz and Puno were omitted because it was argued that here the natives had sufficient resources to buy directly from the merchants. In the intendancies of Paraguay and Cochabamba the scheme would operate, as well as in needy districts outside the intendancies, but it would be restricted to equipment and tools necessary for agriculture and industry and exclude other merchandise.[3] Superintendent Sanz was still sceptical of the scheme, considering it open to abuses and expense, and viceroy Loreto postponed the publication of the order and secretly asked the intendants for their opinions.[4] The intendants were unanimously unfavourable towards the scheme and considered it unnecessary.[5] The only opinion in support of it was given by Jorge Escobedo, visitor-general of Perú, who argued that government relief would raise the standard of living of the Indians by providing them with equipment for work, while he discounted the financial difficulties raised by the intendants; he also drew attention to the fact that already the financial intrigues between the subdelegates and the *hacendados*

[1] R.C., 5 August 1783, art. 7, in *D.G.I.E.A.*, i, 33, n. 2r.

[2] The intendant of Salta considered it unnecessary for his province as there had never been any *repartimientos* there and the Indians were industrious and able to provide for themselves. B.M., Eg. MS 1815, fols. 135–6, intendant of Salta to viceroy, 14 December 1783 (copy).

[3] B.M. Eg. MS 1815, fols. 109–12, Gálvez to the viceroy and intendant of Buenos Aires, 8 June 1784 (copy).

[4] *Ibid.*, fols. 115–19, Sanz to Loreto, 14 September 1784; fols. 121–2, Loreto to Sanz, 16 September 1784 (mistakenly copied as 1785).

[5] *Ibid.*, fols. 127–76.

were raising the price of mules for the Indians.[1] Having scrutin-
ized all these reports, Sanz noted that apart from Escobedo
the consensus of opinion was against the application of the
scheme; he himself simply recommended that the intendants
only needed to stimulate commerce, distribute lands fairly, and
encourage industry, for which purpose a reduction of the *alcabala*
on iron, as suggested by the intendant of La Paz, would be
effective.[2] The viceroy thus suspended the royal order of 8 June
on the grounds that the conditions demanded by it were not
operating.[3] And there the matter rested. On the advice of local
officials a promising reform broke down, and the Indians were
left to negotiate their purchases with interested merchants under
the general supervision of the intendants. An example of such
supervision was the decree of intendant Viedma of Cochabamba
(23 September 1784) which laid down rules to control the commerce between Spaniards and Indians. Any merchant trading
with the missions in his intendancy had to obtain a licence from
the subdelegate of the district, in default of which they would be
liable to confiscation of merchandise; on no account were they
to sell liquor.[4] Nevertheless there were complaints from the
missionary priests of the Chiriguan reductions that merchants
from Santa Cruz were abusing their position and were responsible for the drunkenness and debauchery of the neophites.[5] No
doubt this was a common enough phenomenon in all parts of
the viceroyalty and one very difficult to control.

This is not to say that the intendants were completely in-
different towards the Indians. It is true that they had a dis-
concerting habit of indulging in theoretical discussions on the
nature of the Indians, using terms and concepts which had not
changed since the sixteenth-century discussions of the same
topic. But there were examples of sanity. Viedma's policy
towards the Indians of the Chiriguan reductions, for example,
was quite humane. By the Laws of the Indies natives who had

[1] *Ibid.*, fols. 177–93, Escobedo to Loreto, Lima, 16 December 1784.
[2] *Ibid.*, fols. 205–12, Sanz to Loreto, 9 May 1795.
[3] A.G.I., Aud. de Buenos Aires 70, Loreto and Sanz to Gálvez, carta reservada
318, 21 August 1785.
[4] Fray Antonio Tomaguacosa (Comisario y Prefecto de Misiones) to Intendant
of Potosí, 26 February 1800, in Angelis, *Colección*, iv, 220.
[5] 'Informe de Viedma', 15 January 1788, in *ibid.*, ii, 528–30.

voluntarily embraced the Catholic faith were exempt from tribute for ten years.[1] Some of the *pueblos* under Viedma's jurisdiction had gone far beyond this time without paying, but he did not consider it wise to levy the tribute: 'It is first necessary to advance them from their simplicity, making them skilful and industrious in agriculture and crafts under a prudent régime and wise direction, governing them with love and zeal.'[2] In the economic sphere Viedma vigorously executed the Ordinance of Intendants and arranged a fair distribution of lands among the Indians. He appointed land commissioners for the intendancy of Cochabamba. These officials clarified the rights of the Indians to a great deal of land of which they had been dispossessed. In the districts of Tapacau, Arque and Mizque land was distributed.[3] Community funds were also increased under his administration.[4]

But these efforts were piecemeal and depended upon the quality of the individual intendant. What was lacking was a clear policy emanating from the central authorities which would give a new direction to Indian affairs. In 1802 a report of Josef de la Iglesia, *oidor* of the *audiencia* of Charcas, once more called the attention of the government to the state of the Indians, to the decline of their community funds and to the continuance of personal service. The matter was passed to the Council of the Indies—an ominous sign. The Council spent until 1808 getting more information, and then finally evaded the issue.[5]

[1] *Recopilación*, VI, v, 3.
[2] 'Informe de Viedma', 15 January 1788, in Angelis, *Colección*, ii, 531.
[3] Viedma to Arredondo, 2 March 1793, in *ibid.*, ii, 496.
[4] A.G.I., Aud. de Buenos Aires 140, Viedma to Marqués de Bajamar, 18 May 1792, for details.
[5] A.G.I., Aud. de Charcas 426, Consulta del Consejo 12 March 1808.

CHAPTER IX

The Intendant and the Cabildo

IN December 1807 the *cabildo*, or town council, of Buenos Aires, conscious of the prestige it had earned in the recent defence of the region against the British expeditions which had invaded the Río de la Plata, petitioned the crown to grant it the title of 'Defender of South America and Protector of the *Cabildos* of the Viceroyalty of the Río de la Plata'. The petition was written by its assessor, or legal representative, Mariano Moreno, and the eloquent document which he submitted to the court contained a remarkable request by the *cabildo* to act as the recognized leader and mouthpiece of the other *cabildos* of the viceroyalty, the channel through which they could direct their complaints to higher authorities.

We learn by bitter experience in these dominions the constant practice followed by governors in general of humbling and depreciating the *cabildos*. Ignorant of their noble origin ... they openly boast of villifying them, and there is hardly a governor or subdelegate who does not consider it a supreme demonstration of his authority to scorn and despise the *cabildos*.[1]

An earlier criticism of the treatment accorded to the *cabildos* in the era of the intendants had been made by viceroy Croix of Perú in 1789 when he argued that the intendants had completely alienated the municipalities by an intolerant intrusion into their affairs.[2] These assertions were echoed by later writers, and historians have generally agreed that the centralization of authority imposed by the Ordinance of Intendants, whatever its results at

---

[1] M. Moreno, *Escritos* (ed. R. Levene, 2 vols., Buenos Aires, 1943), i, 162–3. The following pages have appeared in a shortened form in *H.A.H.R.*, xxxv (1955), 337–62.
[2] A.G.I., Indif. Gen. 1714, Croix to Valdés, 16 May 1789. See Fisher, *Intendant system*, pp. 87–8.

the level of efficiency, was a retrogressive move from the point of view of municipal self-government. The administration of public works and even of justice, it is argued, was almost completely assumed by the intendants,[1] while the financial autonomy previously enjoyed by the *cabildos* was radically diminished by the complex exchequer system which was now established.[2]

But even if it is granted that the great reforms of Charles III gave the intendant the initiative in town government, it does not follow that he took this initiative from the *cabildos*, for he could not take what they did not have. By the beginning of the eighteenth century the heroic age of the *cabildos* was a thing of distant memory in all parts of the Spanish empire, and not least in its southernmost provinces. The days when the *cabildo* of Buenos Aires could offer vigorous and successful opposition to its governors were over.[3] By now the discrepancy between theory and practice, between legal rights and actual conditions, was striking.

It is extremely difficult to generalize about the *cabildos*, particularly about municipal appointments, in the Spanish empire: conditions differed from period to period and from town to town. It is known that the *cabildo* consisted of twelve *regidores*, town councillors, in large towns, while in others there were generally six. But how those councillors were chosen is another matter. Popular election was not to be contemplated, at any rate in large and important towns. Viceroys and governors were expected to exercise close control over municipal affairs, and from the earliest days the crown sought to appoint a majority of the councillors. Moreover, in the seventeenth century, a growing number of municipal posts were offered for sale or made hereditary. Crown-appointed officials such as *corregidores* were told to preside over *cabildo* meetings. But the crown was not so

---

[1] W. W. Pierson, 'Some reflections on the cabildo as an institution', *H.A.H.R.* v (1922), p. 595. See also Haring, *The Spanish empire in America*, p. 177; this work contains a good account of the colonial *cabildo*, pp. 158–78. For fuller accounts see C. Bayle, S.J., *Los cabildos seculares en la América española* (Madrid, 1952), and J. Preston Moore, *The cabildo in Peru under the Hapsburgs* (Durham, N.C., 1954).

[2] E. Ravignani, *Historia constitucional de la República Argentina* (2nd edn., 3 vols., Buenos Aires, 1930), i, 75–7.

[3] For examples of earlier municipal vigour and independence see A. Garreton, *La municipalidad colonial* (Buenos Aires, 1933), p. 345–88, a work which deals with Buenos Aires from its foundation to mid-seventeenth century.

sensitive about local government in less important and less populated parts of the empire. In Buenos Aires, for example, *regidores* could nominally be elected by the people, though it was taken for granted that elections were under the control of the governor. In some towns the *regidores* in their turn annually nominated the various municipal officials, such as the city attorney, the chief constable and the inspector of trade. The most important of these officials were the two *alcaldes ordinarios*, or chief municipal magistrates, one of whom, the *alcalde de primer voto*, acted as mayor. According to the Spanish tradition of combining judicial and administrative functions in the same office, the *alcalde* was both an administrator and a judicial officer of first instance, though appeals in more important cases went from him to the governor or *corregidor* and thence to the *audiencia*.

Theoretically, then, within the framework and limitations of an absolute monarchy, the legal position of the *cabildos* was sufficiently defined. The city appointed its judges, administered its property and exercised its moderate local functions. But in practice the legal theory was infringed by the very authority which was supposed to maintain it. By law municipal elections and nominations had to be submitted to the confirmation of viceroys, presidents, governors, or *corregidores*, who were ordered not to hinder the free election of any *cabildo* members either by interference or by influence.[1] Governors, however, abused this right of confirming elections by using it as an opportunity to revise or annul them, and they even adopted the habit of filling vacancies directly by their own appointments. In 1706 the *cabildo* of Buenos Aires complained to the king that governor Maldonado had filled six vacancies in this way. Another governor, Valdés Inclán, dissatisfied with the legal municipal elections, appointed his own *regidores* without even consulting the *cabildo*, and in spite of a royal resolution sustaining the rights of the *cabildo* he threatened to fine those councillors who resisted him.[2] The practice of sale of office completed the ruin of the municipal system and, in the words of a modern historian, 'undoubtedly contributed to the apathy and incompetence of

[1] *Recopilación*, v, iii, 10; iv and ix, 7.
[2] J. A. García, *La ciudad indiana* (Buenos Aires, 1900), pp. 164–5.

municipal government in many of the towns of the Indies'.[1] In Buenos Aires the proprietary councillors formed the majority of the *cabildo* and this was precisely the faction which allied itself to the governors.[2] At the same time exchequer officials, in direct defiance of all the laws, frequently got themselves or their friends elected to *cabildo* offices. The abuses became so extreme that the governor of Buenos Aires in 1739 requested the king to abolish altogether the elections of *alcaldes* in Santa Fe, Corrientes and Montevideo, for the meagre functions they performed did not justify the electoral disputes which they caused.[3]

A vigorous local policy could not be expected from such bodies. Even in their modest local functions—the administration of their funds, public works, price regulations, inspection of prisons—their authority was subordinate to that of the governor. It was no part of the policy of an absolute monarchy to nurture vigorous municipalities, and neither in fact nor in theory was independence countenanced. The legal rôle of the *cabildo* was that of a counsellor:

It is only to give its advice to those who have the supreme authority, and it has neither power nor competence to order or determine or put into execution its opinion or deliberations, but has to refer all these to the corregidor. . . .[4]

This dependence on higher authorities induced a subservience and inertia that can be read in every line of the minutes of the *cabildos*. The *cabildo* of Santiago del Estero frequently received messages from the governor of Tucumán ordering a certain line of action, and invariably these directives were received with submission.[5] Its *actas capitulares*, barbarously written, are full of

[1] Parry, *The sale of public office in the Spanish Indies under the Hapsburgs*, p. 70. Parry refers to the Indies in general, and considers 'The real dereliction of royal duty lay not so much in making *regimientos* saleable, as in making them renunciable, and so turning many *cabildos* into closed and hereditary oligarchies, inadequately supervised and irresponsible.' *Ibid*. See particularly pp. 33-47.

[2] García, *op. cit.*, pp. 168-9.

[3] R. Levene, *Los orígenes de la democracia argentina* (Buenos Aires, 1911), pp. 124-5.

[4] G. Castillo de Bobadilla, *Política para corregidores* (2 vols., Madrid, edn. of 1775), ii, 172. This work, written by a great Spanish jurist and first published in Madrid in 1597, went through many editions and was a much used legal handbook for *corregidores*. Consequently Bobadilla's view of the status of the *cabildo* was a longstanding one.

[5] *Actas capitulares de Santiago del Estero* (4 vols., Buenos Aires, 1942-6), ii, 41, 45, 60, 119, 122, 279, 280, 319, 329, 336, 434, for examples.

the most humdrum routine such as prison inspection and licence granting, and are often brought to a fruitless close with the monotonous formula 'and there being no business to attend to . . .' Any fundamental work, such as the reconstruction of the town reservoir, would take years to accomplish, and Santiago suffered from periodic shortages of water between 1748 and 1778 precisely because problems of this magnitude were so dilatorily tackled.[1] In Buenos Aires, it is true, the *cabildo* showed a spasmodic energy in looking after the interests of its citizens. It often bestirred itself over food supplies, but it was powerless to regulate them on its own and needed to seek the co-operation of the governor to enforce decisions.[2] Even in Buenos Aires, however, initiative was the exception, passivity the norm.

In most provinces *cabildo* meetings were not well attended. For example, in Buenos Aires on 10 March 1758 it was resolved to call an extraordinary meeting for the following day because there were many matters pending and the majority of members had not responded to two previous summonses.[3] Absence of its members was a persistent worry of the *cabildo* of Buenos Aires and even led it to ask the governor to take action.[4] But an even more fundamental weakness was the reluctance of citizens to serve on the *cabildo* or undertake municipal offices. The *cabildo* had frequently to fine unwilling citizens who refused to accept the posts to which they had been elected.[5] If the situation was bad in towns like Buenos Aires, it was even worse in smaller and more backward places. San Luis and La Rioja in the province of Tucumán had no *regidores* at all and were merely composed of two *alcaldes ordinarios* and a procurator, for no one could be induced to buy proprietary offices.[6]

The fatal condition of the *cabildos* can be traced to two basic causes: they lacked any firm basis of popular representation, and they lacked adequate financial resources. The direct

[1] *Ibid.*, iii, 197.
[2] *Acuerdos del extinguido cabildo de Buenos Aires* (47 vols., Buenos Aires, 1907–34), Serie III, tom. i, pp. 405–7, acuerdo del 22 de Abril 1754.
[3] *A.C.B.A.*, iii, ii, 301, 10 March 1758.
[4] *Ibid.*, iii, ii, 399, 26 March 1759.
[5] *Ibid.*, iii, i, 56–61, 65, 108–11, for examples in 1751.
[6] Sobremonte to Gálvez, 6 November 1785, in Torre Revello, *El Marqués de Sobremonte*, Appendice iii, p. cii.

intrusion of governors in municipal elections has already been noticed; this burden was if anything increasing on the eve of the intendant system.[1] At the same time the viceroy was reaffirming in unambiguous terms his right of confirming elections, and assuring similar rights to his subordinate governors.[2] But the oligarchic composition of the *cabildos* themselves was an even greater drag on municipal development. There were not infrequent complaints that the councillor class was itself 'fixing' elections. Moreover, any ideas the *cabildos* had of changing the electoral system were liable to be retrogressive. The *cabildo* of Buenos Aires, for example, would have liked more than the three proprietary *regidores* which it already had. But there was no incentive for citizens to buy the office, for in return for sacrifice in time and money there was no prospect of their lining their own pockets from the empty municipal coffers. It was suggested, therefore, that those *regidores* who were elected should be elected for a term of six years,[3] and that the *alcaldes* should be allowed re-election before their first term of office had been judged in *residencia*.[4] The idea was submitted to the governor and there it died a natural death, but the incident shows that, far from desiring a greater representative character, the *cabildos* of this period were actually inclined to make themselves a closer oligarchy than they already were.

They were also losing what little control they had over their own membership. A governor could in theory and often did in practice suspend a councillor whom he considered guilty of a civil misdemeanour.[5] This was unquestioned. But the *cabildo* had long enjoyed the right of granting its members licences of leave of absence of up to one year or even longer with the approbation of the governor. This right was used without challenge throughout the first half of the eighteenth century, but it was summarily rejected by a *real provisión*, issued by the *audiencia* of Charcas in 1774, which prohibited any *cabildo* member from taking leave of absence without the express licence of the governor or the *audiencia*.[6]

---

[1] *A.C.S.E.*, iv, 60–3, 152, 155, for examples in Santiago in 1779, 81.
[2] *A.C.S.E.*, iv, 225–7; *A.C.B.A.*, iii, v, 617–31.
[3] *A.C.B.A.*, iii, iv, 244, 25 February 1771.
[4] *Ibid.*, iii, iv, 247, 28 February 1771.
[5] *Ibid.*, iii, v, 148, 5 October 1774.   [6] *Ibid.*, iii, v, 327–32.

The *cabildos* might have been able to withstand this increasing pressure on their position had they enjoyed a strong economic foundation, but lack of any financial influence was itself probably the most fundamental cause of their sterility in this period. The poverty of the *cabildos* was endemic. What income they had was limited to the *propios*, or rents from municipal land and property,[1] and a few local taxes derived from the granting of licences of various kinds. Direct taxation could only be imposed for some specific public object, and was limited to 55 pesos except by consent of the *audiencia*, which could raise it to 200 pesos; otherwise the approval of the crown was required.[2] In 1708 the rent from the municipal *propios* of Buenos Aires amounted to no more than 320 pesos a year. By 1751 this had increased to 844 pesos, but, as the procurator pointed out, this was still an inadequate fund for local government, and in February the *cabildo* asked the Council of the Indies for permission to increase the amount of rentable land.[3] By a royal *cédula* of 1760 authority was given to charge five pesos on all built-up sites on the common ground in the city. But to go ahead and collect these taxes was another matter. The *cabildo* had to make repeated requests to the governor to issue the necessary order to implement the *cédula*, but such was his unconcern that it was 1766 before the first rents were collected;[4] and for many years their collection was surrounded with difficulties and hindrances.[5] Further proposals were made by the *cabildo* to increase its *propios*, but royal permission was difficult to obtain. Meanwhile municipal activity was brought to an almost complete standstill.[6] In February 1768 the *cabildo* was still lamenting its notorious lack of funds, 'since with the *arbitrios* which it now has it can hardly cover the bare and essential yearly expenses'.[7] Eventually it was reduced to asking for voluntary contributions from citizens.[8] The response was not very promising, and in December 1777 it asked the viceroy for a loan of 8,000 pesos to cover various expenses, but met with a refusal.[9] A similar tale of

[1] *Recopilación*, IV, vii, 7, 14.   [2] *Ibid.*, IV, xv, 3.
[3] *A.C.B.A.*, III, i, 28, 15 February 1751.   [4] *Ibid.*, III, ii, 652.
[5] *Ibid.*, III, iv, 25, 27, 32.   [6] *Ibid.*, III, ii, 179, 284 (year 1758).
[7] *Ibid.*, III, iii, 587–8.
[8] *Ibid.*, III, iii, 528, 549–53, 25 September 1767.
[9] *Ibid.*, III, vi, 155–6, 160, 15 December 1777.

poverty emerges from the pages of the council meetings of the *cabildo* of Santiago del Estero, and the story can be supplemented from the records of other provincial *cabildos*. In the province of Tucumán the *sisa* tax was never fully paid before 1783.[1] The yearly income of Mendoza from *propios* in the third quarter of the eighteenth century was only 400 pesos, that of San Juan 200, while San Luis had none at all.[2] In the province of Cochabamba in Upper Perú only the *cabildos* of Cochabamba and Mizque enjoyed *propios* and *arbitrios*; other towns were completely void of this income.[3]

Financial control means little when there are little finances to control. But not only was municipal revenue meagre; its appropriation was for the most part prescribed.[4] The very management of their own funds was so hedged around with restrictions that it is impossible to speak of the 'financial autonomy' of the *cabildos* in the period before the intendants.[5] Without previous consent of the *audiencia* or of the provincial governor, extraordinary appropriations or assignments of wages from revenue were limited to the minute figure of 3,000 maravedis.[6] Governors were quick to pounce upon any deviations from this law. When the *cabildo* of Buenos Aires appointed a paid archivist in April 1772, assigning him 200 pesos a year, the governor decreed that it was legally incapable of disposing of its own funds in this way, and the *cabildo* had no alternative but to submit to the law.[7]

Municipal accounts had to be inspected every year by the local exchequer officials,[8] but the governor could also demand to see the accounts whenever he wished.[9] These were necessary restrictions, for although the *cabildos* had charge of the collection

---

[1] A.G.I., Aud. de Buenos Aires 356, Fernández to Gálvez, 15 May 1783, Carta 714.

[2] Torre Revello, *op. cit.*, Apéndice III, pp. xci, xciii, xcv.

[3] A.G.I., Aud. de Buenos Aires 140, Viedma to Marqués de Bajamar, 18 May 1792.

[4] García, *op. cit.*, pp. 195–8.

[5] Both Levene and Ravignani use this expression. See Levene, *La revolución de mayo y Mariano Moreno*, i, 131–2, and Ravignani in introduction to *Actas capitulares de Concepción del Río Cuarto* (Buenos Aires, 1943), p. 9.

[6] *Recopilación*, IV, xiii, 2.

[7] *A.C.B.A.*, III, iv, 285–6, 422, 459–60.

[8] *Recopilación*, IV, xiii, 3.

[9] *A.C.B.A.*, III, iv, 173, 175, 178.

and custody of their own funds, this was not always efficiently done. There was a *mayordomo*, or treasurer of *propios*, chosen by the *cabildo*, who collected the rents and kept the accounts which he submitted to the *cabildo* for approval after his year's administration, but the treasurers were not necessarily competent or even honest men. In 1771 the office in Buenos Aires was filled by a certain Juan de Ossorio, who produced neither the accounts nor the funds at the end of the year. In view of this the procurator suggested that the office of treasurer should be a fulltime occupation, appointed by the *cabildo* but not from among its members.[1] But the *cabildo* did not agree, and decided instead to inform the governor of the Ossorio affair.[2]

The picture presented by the *cabildos* in the third quarter of the eighteenth century was not, then, an impressive one. An occasional cry of protest indicated that a flame of independence still flickered, but it was a cry of despair and signified impotence. It can be read in the words of the *cabildo* of Santiago del Estero:

We debated the best way to seek a remedy against the despotisms of the chiefs of this province and their absolute government, the outrages they inflict on officials and other subjects . . . their complete immunity from punishment. . . .[3]

They decided to complain to the king through their attorney in Madrid, and no more is heard of the matter. Three years later, in 1776, the *cabildo* of Asunción del Paraguay submitted a long list of complaints against Agustín Fernando Pinedo, governor of Paraguay, accusing him of oppression, nepotism, maladministration of royal revenues, private commercial activities and many other crimes.[4] But Gálvez did not offer an opinion and it was not until 1785, that is precisely in the period of the intendancies, that the complaints against Pinedo were really entertained.[5] While Santiago and Asunción were complaining of despotism, from Upper Perú came a faint plea for more government. In 1781 the *cabildo* of La Plata petitioned the crown to move the seat of the viceroyalty there because of the lack of

---

[1] *Ibid.*, III, iv, 460, 8 August 1772.   [2] *Ibid.*, III, iv, 467–9, 14 August 1772.
[3] *A.C.S.E.*, iii, 365–6, 29 November 1773.
[4] A.G.I., Aud. de Buenos Aires 48, Cabildo of Asunción del Paraguay to Gálvez, 29 July 1776.
[5] *Ibid.*, R.O., 24 November 1785.

government in the province and its propensity to disorder, so great was its distance from Buenos Aires. Not surprisingly, the request was coldly received in Madrid, where it was pointed out that the president of the *audiencia* had adequate authority for dealing with the problems of Upper Perú.[1]

Any evidence of strength or independence on the part of the *cabildos* was abnormal and ephemeral. Yet twenty years later, between approximately 1800 and 1810, in almost all the main cities of the viceroyalty of the Río de la Plata vigorous *cabildos* were in conflict with the local political authorities and challenging them on many issues. Sometime between the 1770's and the end of the century the *cabildos* found a new lease of life. This coincided precisely with the period of the intendancies.

It is true that the centralizing policy pursued by Charles III and his ministers did not augur well for the *cabildos*. The municipality of Buenos Aires showed a clear desire to share in the increase of political powers assigned to the area with the creation of the new viceroyalty in 1776, a desire which was encouraged by Cevallos, the first viceroy, who relied on the support of the *cabildo* for initiating his new policy, and who responded completely to its demands for freer commerce.[2] But five years' experience under superintendent Fernández before the Ordinance of 1782 inaugurated the full intendant system dashed any hopes the *cabildo* may have had of the arrival of a new period in municipal government. Fernández kept *cabildo* activity carefully confined. There was in Buenos Aires a war fund amounting to more than 25,000 pesos and used for maintaining three militia battalions in the province. This fund was administered by the exchequer, but it had originally been collected and managed by the *cabildo* of Buenos Aires. When Fernández heard that the *cabildo* was pressing the viceroy to return the fund to its jurisdiction, he immediately sought confirmation from Madrid of his own exclusive control of this revenue as head of the exchequer of the viceroyalty.[3] This was granted to him by royal order of 9 March 1779.[4] A further pretension of the *cabildo*

[1] A.G.I., Aud. de Buenos Aires 151, Cabildo of La Plata, 15 February 1781.
[2] A.G.I., Aud. de Buenos Aires 157, Cabildo of Buenos Aires to Cevallos, 22 July 1777.
[3] A.G.I., Aud. de Buenos Aires 473, Fernández to Gálvez, 1 December 1778.
[4] *Ibid.*, R.O., 9 March 1779.

of Buenos Aires to cognizance in revenue matters received an even sharper rebuff. In 1778 the procurator-general requested the superintendent to forward for the information of the *cabildo* a copy of the royal order relating to the establishment of the tobacco monopoly and other duties in the viceroyalty. In a message dated 25 November 1778 Fernández refused this request and denied the *cabildo* any access to exchequer business. This was orthodox doctrine and received the full support of the crown in a royal order of 12 March 1779 which condemned the action of the procurator and declared that he 'had no right or competence to interfere in or object to these matters for they are peculiar to the supreme authority.[1]

The *cabildo* of Buenos Aires had political as well as financial pretensions. In April 1778, claiming to speak on behalf of all interests and classes in the city, it uttered a genuine cry of distress at the impending departure of viceroy Cevallos to whom it attributed all the recent progress made in the affairs of the province, and implored him to remain in office while an extension of his appointment was sought from the crown.[2] This representation was made after the publication of the appointment of viceroy Vértiz and was therefore interpreted in Madrid as an affront to the prestige and reputation of the new viceroy and as setting an extremely dangerous precedent. Superintendent Fernández was instructed to examine the minutes of the *cabildo* and take note of all the events of the incident and the names of the members who were its promoters. As a result of Fernández's inquiry and advice two councillors, Judas Josef de Salas and Bernardo Sancho de Larrea, were banished to the Falkland Islands for a year, after which they were to reside in Mendoza, while the other nine *cabildo* members who had signed the representation were prohibited from exercising office for seven years.[3]

The *cabildos*, therefore, had no reason to welcome any extension,

[1] *D.H.A.*, i, 85–6; *A.C.B.A.*, iii, vi, 303–5, 380–1.

[2] *Ibid.*, iii, vi, 204–5, 9 April 1778.

[3] A.G.I., Aud. de Buenos Aires 308, Fernández to Gálvez, 5 February 1779; R.O. Reservada, 28 May 1779; *A.C.B.A.*, iii, vi, 427–9, 10 September 1779. Vértiz secured royal pardon for the offenders (R.O., 10 March 1780) and the two exiles were brought back. *Ibid.*, iii, vi, 572–4; A.G.I., *loc. cit.*, Fernández to Gálvez, 20 October 1780.

still less formalization, of the intendant system by the Ordinance of Intendants of 1782. Yet it was obvious that they themselves were incompetent to deal with the type of administration which local government lacked and which the new system was meant to supply. The colonial municipal oligarchy treated and resolved the affairs of the city according to the same criterion as they dealt with their own personal affairs. This was not surprising in these small, closed communities. But, with the extension of commerce and increase in population, this simple domestic machinery was no longer adequate to cope with the new administrative problems which were arising, nor were merchant-councillors competent to resolve them. The time had passed when they could miss sessions because there was nothing to do. Building, public works, hygiene, finance and justice were all clamouring for prompt attention and needed a treatment for which the *cabildos* had no precedent and their members no skill.[1] This is the context in which the intendancy system must be judged. In view of the evidence showing the legal and practical weakness of the *cabildos* on the eve of the intendancy system, it is unreal to consider the problem in terms of local institutions being absorbed by centralizing officials. The criterion of any judgment on the *cabildos* in the new era will be whether the intendants made the *cabildos* more active and whether they allowed them to co-operate in the work they were doing.

It has been maintained that the *cabildos* lost part of their authority because the *alcaldes* and *regidores* appointed by them had to be confirmed in office by the intendant.[2] In fact there was no substantial change. By the Laws of the Indies the ultimate authority for confirmation of municipal elections was the viceroy.[3] This law was expressly annulled by the Ordinance of Intendants, and the power of confirmation was reserved exclusively to the intendants who were to ensure that 'the said offices be assigned to individuals who are judged most suitable for the fair administration of justice and for the proper security of the revenues of my royal treasury. . . .'[4] This system operated until

---

[1] R. de Lafuente Machain, *Buenos Aires en el siglo XVIII* (Buenos Aires, 1946), pp. 10–11.

[2] Ravignani, *Historia constitucional*, i, 75.   [3] *Recopilación*, v, iii, 10.

[4] *Ord. Ints.*, art. 8. The intendant presided over the *cabildo* of his capital; when he could not attend meetings his *teniente asesor* had to preside. *Ord. Ints.*, art. 15.

1787 when by royal *cédula* of 29 November it was annulled and the right of confirming the election of *alcaldes ordinarios* was restored to the viceroy. In cities where there were *audiencias*, and for fifteen leagues around them, the president of the *audiencia* was to confirm the *alcaldes* in office. In small towns viceroys could authorize intendants to do this with subsequent central confirmation.[1] But whatever changes were made the *cabildos* themselves neither lost anything nor gained anything from the point of view of legal rights.

In practice, however, there were far less abuses under the new régime. Between 1784 and 1789 the intendants of Salta regularly confirmed the elections in Santiago del Estero without any intrusion. In 1790 the intendant annulled the election of Juan José Iramaín as junior *alcalde* on the ground that he was already subdelegate of exchequer and as such was precluded from municipal office by the Ordinance of Intendants.[2] He ordered the *cabildo* to make a new appointment, which was done without demur and this time approved.[3] In the event of a disputed election the *cabildo* of Santiago would voluntarily offer the case for solution to the intendant.[4] In general, the intendants only cancelled elections on strictly legal and not on political grounds. For example, intendant Rodríguez of Córdoba approved the 1806 elections in Concepción except that of Josef Francisco Tisera as *alcalde ordinario* on account of the distance he resided from the city and of the fact that he had a tobacco *estanco* which would suffer from lack of attention to the detriment of royal revenue. The *cabildo* agreed without comment and proceeded to elect another *alcalde* whom the intendant confirmed.[5] In fact whenever royal authority was brought to bear on *cabildos* in these matters it was likely to be in the interests of purer elections; a *residencia* on councillors of Santiago who had served between 1778 and 1790 disclosed that some *regidores* were very susceptible to bribery and would sell their votes to aspirants to office. Punishments in these cases varied from deprivation of votes to monetary fines.[6]

[1] A.G.I., Aud. de Buenos Aires 76, Loreto to Porlier, Carta 41, 1 May 1788. See Fisher, *Intendant system*, p. 94, 107.

[2] *Ord. Ints.*, art. 73.   [3] *A.C.S.E.*, iv, 504–6, 511.

[4] *Ibid.*, iv, 423–5, 25 January 1788.

[5] *A.C.C.R.C.*, 230, 232.   [6] *A.C.S.E.*, iv, 557–68.

In Santiago any diminution of the already weak representative basis of the *cabildo* came not as a result of pressure from the intendant but on the initiative of the *cabildo* itself. At the end of the year the *cabildo* met to choose six citizens 'of education and intelligence' who were admitted to the council to assist in the election of the new *cabildo*.[1] This system was followed until 1786 when, on the pretext of avoiding dissension which the admission of citizens was alleged to cause, the existing *cabildo* omitted this first stage and itself made the elections for the following year.[2] This procedure was then approved by the intendant.[3] On the other hand, when in 1797 intendant Sobremonte created the town of Concepción del Río Cuarto and endowed it with a *cabildo* he did this in a more democratic manner than earlier founders of towns had followed. Instead of founding the *cabildo* by direct appointment,[4] Sobremonte authorized the citizens themselves to make the first elections, and instructed his commissioners only to supervise.[5] His two commissioners summoned the most suitable and substantial citizens on 1 January 1798: these elected the *regidores* who in turn chose the *alcaldes*.[6]

But it was the *cabildo* of Buenos Aires which maintained most vigilance over its own composition, and came to resent interference not only from the intendant but also from higher political authorities. In the elections of 1788 it elected Manuel Antonio Warnes as senior *alcalde*. Superintendent Sanz approved all the other appointments but annulled that of Warnes and ordered the *cabildo* to make another one.[7] Sanz's real objection to Warnes was personal dislike combined with a political distrust of what he called his '*espíritu revoltoso*'.[8] The *cabildo*, however, would not retreat and appealed to the *audiencia*, which upheld their election and confirmed Warnes in office.[9] In the election of 1792 it was viceroy Arredondo who forbade the election of Warnes, but this was on the legal grounds

---

[1] *A.C.S.E.*, iv, 53–5, 99 and *passim*. [2] *Ibid.*, iv, 349–50.
[3] *Ibid.*, iv, 353, 23 June 1786. [4] *Recopilación*, iv, iii, 10.
[5] A. C. Vitulo, 'Fundación de la villa de Río Cuarto', *B.I.I.H.*, xvii (Buenos Aires, 1933–4), pp. 156–7.
[6] Vitulo, *A.C.C.R.C.*, p. 37, n. 2. [7] *A.C.B.A.*, iii, viii, 439–43.
[8] A.G.I., Aud. de Buenos Aires 364, Sanz to Porlier, 2 January 1788.
[9] A.G.I., Aud. de Buenos Aires 445, Warnes to Porlier, 8 January 1788. *A.C.B.A.*, iii, viii, 454–5.

that there was a law suit against him, and although the *cabildo* protested vigorously it had to obey.[1] Nevertheless, it carried its protest to the crown and received a royal *cédula* of 24 December 1795 disapproving Arredondo's exclusion of Warnes from the elections as being against the spirit of the municipal ordinances of Buenos Aires.[2]

At the same time the *cabildo* was securing more control of its own members. A royal *cédula* of 8 May 1789 conceded to the *cabildos* the privilege of hearing renunciations of office. When, therefore, Martín Alzaga, procurator elect for 1790, obtained exemption from office from the viceroy, the *cabildo* of Buenos Aires insisted on its rights and enforced his acceptance.[3] On 21 August 1794 Benito González de Rivadavia, *regidor* and *depositario general* of the *cabildo* of Buenos Aires, was exiled by the *audiencia* to Córdoba. On the 22nd the *cabildo* protested that he had been banished on no more specific ground than that of public security, and, what was more significant, that no notice had been given to the *cabildo* on a matter affecting its own members; in particular it was complained that Rivadavia had been forced to leave without giving an account of the municipal deposits he held. These objections were made to the viceroy, who was supporting the action of the *audiencia*, and were continued unremittingly—three representations were made between 22 August and 3 September—until the viceroy issued an order on 26 October authorizing the return of Rivadavia so that he could give an account of his deposits to the *cabildo*.[4]

The municipalities neither before nor after 1782 questioned the right of a higher political authority to inspect and confirm their elections. Even after the fall of the Spanish colonial régime, the *cabildos* continued to submit their elections to the appropriate authority. In November 1810 the *cabildo* of Concepción submitted its elections to the *junta*-appointed intendant of Córdoba, Juan Martín Pueyrredón.[5] In November they went to the *Superior Junta Provincial* of Córdoba for confirmation.[6]

While *cabildo* elections were subject to less intromission by higher authorities during the first stages of the intendant period,

[1] *Ibid.*, III, x, 9–13.
[3] *Ibid.*, III, ix, 246, 26 January 1790.
[5] *A.C.C.R.C.*, 370–1, 375.
[2] *Ibid.*, III, xi, 76–7.
[4] *Ibid.*, III, x, 363, 424–5.
[6] *Ibid.*, 409–10.

their financial basis was also becoming more secure. It is true that the Ordinance of Intendants circumscribed the already slender control they had over their own finances. These were now subject to inspection by the *junta superior de hacienda* in Buenos Aires, which could ask the intendants for information concerning municipal finance and communicate its measures to them through the accountant-general of municipal finance. The intendants were instructed on taking office to ask each of the cities and towns within their jurisdiction for an exact account of their funds and of the municipal taxes. From this information the intendants were to draw up a provisional ordinance for municipal finance and submit it to the *junta superior*, which in turn was to report it to the crown. A municipal *junta* was to be established in each Spanish city and town for the control of financial matters; this was composed of the senior *alcalde ordinario*, who was to preside over it, two *regidores* and the procurator-general, but it was supposed to be a distinct body from the *cabildo*, which was forbidden to interfere with it in any way. The business of the *junta* was to conduct the sale of offices connected with municipal *juntas* in order to prevent abuses. In their capitals they could do this directly or through their *tenientes asesores*, and in the smaller towns by means of the justices. Each municipal *junta* annually appointed a steward to take charge of all funds on hand and he received as remuneration $1\frac{1}{2}$ per cent of what he collected. At the end of the year he made a report of the revenue intake to the municipal *junta*. If a favourable balance was shown the steward deposited the funds in the 'coffer of the three keys' in the presence of the members of the *junta*. The account was certified by a notary and signed by all the members of the retiring *junta*. The certified account was then presented to the town council and, if approved, was returned to the *junta*, which sent the original with the certified records to the intendant. The municipal *juntas* were to obey promptly any orders from the intendant for drawing up documents relating to municipal finance. If they ever had complaints against the intendant's measures they could appeal directly to the *junta superior*. All the funds of the local treasuries except those needed for current expenditure were to be sent to the treasury of the province. The Spanish subdelegates in the

smaller divisions of the provinces had much the same supervision over municipal finance as the intendants had in the
capital.[1]

The financial authority of the *cabildos* was circumscribed to
this moderate degree not from any conscious anti-municipal
policy, but simply in the interests of greater efficiency and by the
creation of a more detailed administrative machine. They were
not completely deprived of financial powers. The *cabildos* chose
from among their own members the two *regidores* who were to
serve on the municipal *junta*, and the *alcaldes* were already
cabildo appointees.[2] The rule of submitting the accounts to the
cabildo was adhered to.[3] In a small town like Santiago del Estero
the two bodies were virtually identical and the *cabildo* simply
turned itself into the finance committee for certain purposes:

> We the *cabildo* . . . having assembled as president and members of
> the municipal *junta* of *propios* and *arbitrios* of this city to treat of
> matters pertaining to it, determined to consider the business of
> bringing the taxable wine-stores at the disposal of this city up to the
> number of eight. . . .[4]

It is clear, in fact, that the *cabildo* of Santiago considered its own
interests and that of the *junta* identical, and, far from regarding
it as a rival, it was as ready to defend it as it was to defend itself
whenever there was unwarranted interference from the subdelegate.[5]

By the new system the interests of efficiency were better
served than they had previously been. At the same time the
most important single fact in the life of the *cabildos* in this period
was the increase in their funds. This can be ascribed in many
cases precisely to the activity of the intendants. The quickest
results were obtained in Córdoba and owed their existence to
intendant Sobremonte, who was able to report in November
1785:

> The *propios* of this city have risen in the past year to 1,040 pesos:
> the year previously they only amounted to 525 pesos. And according

---

[1] *Ord. Ints.*, arts. 23–44. The accountant-general of municipal finance was also
secretary of the junta.
[2] *A.C.B.A.*, III, viii, 282.
[3] *Ibid.*, III, vii, 401–2.
[4] *A.C.S.E.*, iv, 340, 23 August 1785.
[5] *Ibid.*, iv, 300–1, 4 August 1784.

to what I have proposed to the *junta superior* for their increase, sufficient quantities can now be assigned to meet its needs, to complete the municipal buildings and other useful and decorative works.[1]

He also had proposals for increasing the *propios* of the other towns of his province. His methods did not involve any spectacular creation of new taxes but simply a more thorough collection of existing ones, a thing which the *cabildo* had never been able to accomplish on its own. By this method he was able to triple the *propios* of Córdoba in his first five years of office there.[2] The result in practicable terms was seen in the new growth of public building in Córdoba.

Buenos Aires had completely outgrown its existing financial resources, and there the situation required not only a rigorous collection of existing taxes but also the creation of completely new ones. Superintendent Sanz spared no pains to increase municipal revenue. He kept the *cabildo* on its toes by periodically demanding a statement of revenue accounts.[3] And soon after he took office he requested a formal statement from the *cabildo* containing its precise requirements in matters of taxation. This was the opportunity the *cabildo* had been waiting for all during the century. In a long and far from clear report the *cabildo* outlined its needs: new taxes amounting to more than 11,000 pesos were proposed and a substantial increase in existing *propios* was suggested.[4] The proposals were considered by the *junta superior de real hacienda*, presided over by the superintendent, and on 29 February 1788 it conceded new taxes on a scale which the *cabildo* had been demanding in vain for years. Authority was granted for taxes on hawkers' stalls, gaming saloons, weights and measures and at an increased rate on built-up areas on the common land.[5] Twenty-two taxable wine stores were added to the eight which were already assigned to the *cabildo*, at the rate of 25 pesos each one.[6] Moreover, the *junta* tackled the chronic inability of the *cabildo* to collect its own taxes by prodding it to a

---

[1] Sobremonte to Loreto, 6 November 1785, printed in Torre Revello, *Sobre Monte*, Apéndice, p. xcix.

[2] A.G.I., Aud. de Buenos Aires 363, Sobremonte to Sanz, 5 April 1786. Revello, *op. cit.*, p. 33.

[3] *A.C.B.A.*, III, vii, 473, 22 January 1785.   [4] *Ibid.*, III, viii, 196–219.

[5] *Ibid.*, III, viii, 496–7.   [6] *Ibid.*, III, viii, 363.

stricter sense of duty in this respect. For instance, it demanded an explanation from the *cabildo* for its failure to collect the duty on the *corredores de lonja* (a sort of merchant exchange) to which it had been entitled ever since the foundation of the city.[1] But the *cabildo* was even dilatory in collecting the taxes so long demanded and now at last conceded. On 4 March it requested a proclamation from the superintendent to ensure the obedience of the public. The reply of the *junta* was a curt admonition to proceed with the work immediately.[2]

It was not a tale of unrelieved progress. In January 1792 at the instance of certain citizens the viceroy suspended the tax on occupiers of common-land, in spite of a strong protest from the *cabildo*.[3] On 17 February the *cabildo* was driven to ask the viceroy for a further increase of *propios* and *arbitrios*, but the financial support they had enjoyed under superintendent Sanz was not so assured after the suppression of the independent superintendency in 1788.[4] Nevertheless, the increased taxative powers conceded by Sanz in the 1780's gradually began to bear fruit, and the funds in the municipal treasury steadily rose.[5]

Year	Pesos	Reales
1798	9,668	3
1799	15,298	$4\frac{1}{2}$
1800	10,674	$1\frac{3}{4}$
1802	15,903	$\frac{1}{4}$
1805	23,431	$1\frac{3}{4}$

But the new municipal prosperity was not shared by every town. The story of Santiago del Estero continued to be one of crippling poverty. When the *cabildo* was organizing road repairs and improving the town hall for the viceroy's visit of inspection in 1789, it had to report that there were no funds available for this work from the regular municipal revenue. Santiago still suffered from what the intendants in Buenos Aires and Córdoba were trying to reform—an inability to collect its own taxes and control its own collectors. The senior *alcalde* for 1788 did not

[1] *Ibid.*, III, viii, 497.
[2] *Ibid.*, III, viii, 523, 9 April 1788.
[3] *Ibid.*, III, x, 30. But by the 25 September 1792 this must have been restored, for the *cabildo* was requesting powers to increase it. *Ibid.*, III, x, 129-33.
[4] *Ibid.*, III, x, 47.　　　　[5] *Ibid.*, III, xi, 79, 497; IV, i, 41, 279; IV, ii, 685.

collect the *propios* for that year, so that in 1789 the *cabildo* had to inform the intendant of Salta that it had nothing with which to defray the expenses of public administration ordered by him.[1] The administration of the tax on wine stores was also les-efficient in Santiago. Under the intendant system the *cabildo* was assigned eight wine stores. But on the 18th August 1784 intendant Mestre had to remind it to collect from all the eight, as only four were being taxed. Again on 23 August 1785 it had to make up the number to eight, and it was reported that there were still many wine stores on the outskirts of the town paying no taxes at all. Meanwhile the town hospital was falling into ruin because its revenue had not been collected since 1783, and it was reported that *alcaldes* had to defray costs of public ceremonies out of their own pockets.[2] In short, Santiago had no steady fund for administration in general, but only paltry amounts raised for specific objects. The inference to be drawn is that only the immediate presence of the intendant in his provincial capital was sufficient to stimulate the *cabildos* and that the others fared ill under the subdelegates.

Revenue in Potosí was in a much healthier state. In April 1787 the town *propios* had a fund of 7,960 pesos. In 1788 the annual revenue was 2,139 pesos from the *sisa* tax and 2,314 pesos 2½ reales from the *propios*. In all, therefore, the municipal treasury was in possession of 12,413 pesos 2½ reales.[3] To put this income to profitable use 'intendant Pino Manrique, in consultation with the *cabildo*, proposed to the *junta superior de real hacienda* in Buenos Aires a scheme for investing it in a public store, which would relieve the town of the necessity of buying its most essential foodstuffs in so-called *canchas* at exorbitant prices.[4] This sort of financial activity was authorized by the Ordinance of Intendants which advised that 'the amount which each town may possess as an annual surplus from the proceeds of municipal finance, or from the community funds, shall, after meeting the obligations determined in its special ordinance, be invested in the purchase of lands and the imposition of rents which, becoming sufficient for paying their public debts and

---

[1] *A.C.S.E.*, iv, 452–3, 7 January 1789.   [2] *Ibid.*, iv, 308–9, 18 August 1784.
[3] A.G.I., Aud. de Charcas 439, Pino Manrique to Porlier, 16 March 1788.
[4] *Ibid.*

providing for communal needs, will allow the *arbitrios*, which are always burdensome to the public, to be suppressed'.[1] But in spite of the repeated applications of intendant Pino Manrique, the *junta superior*, took no resolution on the matter and he was forced to report to the government.[2] The result of his complaint was a salutary devolution of power. By royal *cédula* of 14 September 1788 it was decided that in order to avoid such delays to useful projects the investment of municipal funds in all the colonies should in future be made on the proposal of the intendants and with the approbation of the *audiencia*, to which, and not to the *juntas superiores*, the proposal should be submitted.[3]

With the validity of their elections more assured, and their finances clearly if fitfully improving, the *cabildos* entered upon a period of greater activity in public administration. The initiative generally came from the intendant, but this was not a question of removing the faculties of the *cabildo*; rather was it the necessity of making them do things which they should have done before but had neglected. In January 1779, for example, superintendent Fernández made the *cabildo* of Buenos Aires undertake an inspection of weights and measures in the interests of the consumer. This task had, of course, always been open to the procurator, but only now was it undertaken.[4] Superintendent Sanz pushed the *cabildo* along even more vigorously, consulting it on various points of public interest, and inviting a profusion of reports on matters such as the regulation of supplies and prices, public works, taxes, rights of citizens, economic affairs.[5] On 24 November 1785 he sent a message to the *cabildo* drawing its attention to the shortage in the wheat crop and consequent price problems, and asking its opinion. The *cabildo* suggested that the price of corn should be six pesos a *fanega*, under penalty of confiscation and fine if exceeded.[6] On 28

---

[1] *Ord. Ints.*, art. 41.   [2] A.G.I., Aud. de Charcas 439, *loc. cit.*
[3] A.G.I., Aud. de Buenos Aires 77, Loreto to Porlier, Carta 85, 20 January 1789; *A.C.B.A.*, III, ix, 21; *A.C.S.E.*, iv, 471-2. But apparently this order was not efficiently enforced. See A.G.I., Aud. de Buenos Aires 152, Mata Linares (*regente* of the *audiencia*) to Porlier, 21 May 1791, and Aud. of Buenos Aires to king, 15 June 1803.
[4] *A.C.B.A.*, III, vi, 491-2, 5 February 1780; 500-1, 3 March 1780.
[5] *A.C.B.A.*, III, viii, *passim*.
[6] *Documentos para la historia del virreinato del Río de la Plata* (3 vols., Buenos Aires, 1912-13), i, 187-8, 190-2.

November Sanz requested the *cabildo's* opinion on the shortage of salt. It agreed that licences should be granted to those offering to bring it from Paraguay, and suggested that the price should be fixed and taxes charged for municipal funds.[1] In 1786 Francisco Maziel applied for a licence to bring meat from the Banda Oriental to the Buenos Aires market. Sanz consulted the *cabildo* which recommended that the licence should be granted and a tax of ½ real on each head of cattle charged for the municipal funds. This proposal was adopted.[2]

Meanwhile the *cabildo* pursued its own work of inspection in the service of the public, but there were many instances where by the nature of things, it could not act alone but needed the assistance of higher authority. That assistance was generally forthcoming, and the vigilance of the *cabildo* would be implemented by a proclamation from the superintendent or the viceroy. In March 1791, for example, the *cabildo* of Buenos Aires informed the viceroy that many ranchers were slaughtering infected cattle for consumption and requested a prohibition of this activity. Arredondo issued a proclamation ordering the ranchers to take adequate precautions and detailing the *ministros de los corrales* to undertake inspections.[3] Similarly the *fiel executor* needed the assistance of the viceroy to prohibit the sale of bread in the countryside and enforce its sale in open market in the town.[4] In 1803 the *cabildo* requested a proclamation declaring illegal corn monopolies which by causing a bread shortage were artificially raising prices. Viceroy Joaquín del Pino issued such a proclamation and the *cabildo* put it into operation, declaring

> The cabildo can always count on the help of the superior orders of Your Excellency, particularly in matters like these which affect the common good of the city. . . .[5]

But this mutual co-operation between *cabildo* and governor did not extend to every branch of municipal administration. It did not extend to town planning and public works. By an order issued in agreement with the viceroy in February 1785, superintendent Sanz removed all competence from the municipal

---

[1] *Ibid.*, pp. 188–9, 29 November 1785.
[2] *D.H.A.*, iv, 30–4.
[3] *D.H.A.*, iv, 119, 31 March 1791.
[4] *Ibid.*, iv, 209–11, 7 February 1781.
[5] *Ibid.*, iv, 318, 16 June 1803.

officials in matters of street regulation and public building and reserved all executive power in these affairs to himself and his officials.[1] His motives were greater efficiency and speed, and he specifically maintained the right of the *cabildo* to render advice and ideas. When the superintendency was suppressed in 1788 the viceroy did not go back on this order, and he himself assumed the faculties of the superintendent. But the concentration of work was too much for him, and it was inevitable that the *cabildo's* own *diputado de policía* (generally the third *regidor*) should in practice assume more power in this field. But this could not make good the need for a full-time official in charge of public works. Consequently on 1 August 1799 the viceroy appointed Martín Boneo *intendente de policía* in Buenos Aires, subject to the viceroy and charged with street registration, enumeration and censorship, duties which were later extended to more general public works.[2] He soon came into conflict with the *cabildo* when he requested that its *mayordomo* should be placed at his orders and disposal. The *cabildo* bluntly refused and carried its point.[3] But its real objection was the very principle of the new establishment, and it was not slow to take its protests to the viceroy. The occasion was the publication of the instructions drawn up by the viceroy for the intendant, dated 13 May 1801, and passed to the *cabildo* for its information. The *cabildo* protested that it was 'prejudicial to ordinary royal jurisdiction, and to the faculties of the *cabildo*', and requested its suspension.[4] The viceroy rejected this request and reported to the government that the intendant was doing useful work.[5] Meanwhile the *cabildo* obstructed Boneo's work and appealed to Madrid with such success that a royal *cédula* of 16 January 1804 ordered Boneo to resign his post and return to Spain, singular evidence that South American *cabildos* were not without influence in the metropolis.[6] The viceroy replaced him by Antonio de las

[1] *Ibid.*, ix, 181–2, Sanz to Cabildo, 14 February 1785. This had already been the practice since the beginning of 1784. *Ibid.*

[2] *A.C.B.A.*, iii, xi, 471–2, iv, i, 162.

[3] *Ibid.*, iii, xi, 493–4, 3 October 1799.

[4] *Ibid.*, iv, i, 39–40, 28 May 1801.

[5] *Ibid.*, iv, i, 46–7, 7 July 1801. A.G.I., Aud. de Buenos Aires 14, viceroy to Minister of Indies, 22 August 1801.

[6] A.G.I., Aud. de Buenos Aires 14, cabildo to king, 26 May 1803; R.C., 16 January 1804, *A.C.B.A.*, iv, i, 402–18.

Cagigas. The *cabildo* now implicitly recognized that a full-time official in charge of public works was essential, for it reported to the viceroy that it had no objection to this appointment, but insisted that the appointee 'ought to proceed in his commission with the intervention and knowledge of this illustrious *cabildo* or of the *junta municipal* . . .'[1] Its persistence was rewarded, for it was now allowed to appoint two councillors to audit the income and expenditure of funds destined for public works, and Cagigas had to regulate his account with them.[2] Even in the sphere of public works, therefore, the *cabildo* was never completely excluded in this period. Furthermore, growth of business was shown by the fact that it had to decide in January 1790 to increase its meetings to two each week.[3]

The history of Córdoba under the rule of its first intendant, Sobremonte, reveals a similar tale of invigoration and mutual co-operation. Until the advent of Sobremonte, the *cabildo* consisted of eight members. He enlarged it to twelve, and initiated a subscription among members, heading it himself, to pay for repairs to the town hall. Drawing on his experience as viceregal secretary under Vértiz in Buenos Aires, he instituted the system of *comisarios de barrios*; six of these were appointed by the *cabildo* from among the citizens to see to the execution of orders for the improvement of the city, police and security, control of beggars, and traffic supervision.[4] Already in 1786 the *cabildo* was remarking on the zeal of the new intendant.[5] Sobremonte worked well with the municipality, which in turn gave him support and co-operation.[6] Through the initiative of Sobremonte, the *cabildo* contracted with the *hacendados* of the province to supply an adequate amount of meat every year at fair prices, free of *alcabala* and all other taxes.[7]

In the neighbouring intendancy of Salta del Tucumán a similar effort on the part of the intendant to stimulate municipal activity can be discerned, though the plans were less well defined and the policy less vigorous. In December 1785 he

[1] *A.C.B.A.*, IV, i, 436, 3 July 1804.

[2] *Ibid.*, IV, i, 499–500, 11 October 1804; IV, ii, 12, 7 January 1805.

[3] *A.C.B.A.*, III, ix, 259–60, 29 January 1790.

[4] 'Informe de Sobremonte', 12 February 1785, printed in Garzon, *Crónica de Córdoba*, pp. 341–5.

[5] Garzon, *op. cit.*, p. 15.   [6] *Ibid.*, p. 43.   [7] *Ibid.*, p. 14.

requested from the *cabildo* of Santiago del Estero a report on its various activities.[1] The *cabildo* was apparently becoming more conscious of social problems in the town, and was developing a scheme of poor relief, the details of which are not clear.[2] Two years later the intendant requested the remittance within two months of statistics of the size of the town, its population and racial composition, its agricultural and mineral products. Without waste of time, the *cabildo* collected and forwarded the required information.[3] Thus, in their task of collecting data and information for submission to Spain, the intendants had to seek the collaboration of the *cabildos*. In turn, the intendants passed on general news and information to the *cabildos*, which thereby became a means of distributing to the people constitutional and political news from Spain.[4] And for all the predominance of the intendant in the economic affairs of his province, the *cabildo* of Santiago could still look after its own economic interests: in January 1786 it forbade the export of grain from the district because of the bad harvest.[5]

By means of the *alcaldes ordinarios* and the *alcaldes de la Santa Hermandad*, the *cabildo* exercised not only administrative but also judicial functions.[6] This municipal justice was quite distinct from royal justice in that it was exercised by magistrates who were appointed by the town council, while all the other judges received their appointments directly or indirectly from the crown. But this judicial localism was limited in scope, for it was confined to minor civil and criminal cases and was liable to appeal before the *audiencia*. Moreover, governors and *audiencias* were instructed to watch over the activities of the *alcaldes* in order to ensure that they did their duty.[7] The Ordinance of Intendants modified the attributes of the *alcaldes* in various ways.

[1] *A.C.S.E.*, iv, 344.
[2] *Ibid.*, iv, 463, 12 March 1789.   [3] *Ibid.*, iv, 405–6.
[4] *Ibid.*, iv, 406, 24 November 1787.
[5] *Ibid.*, iv, 351–2, 7 January 1786.
[6] Ruiz Guiñazú, *La magistratura indiana*, pp. 285–8, gives an account of the judicial attributes of the *alcaldes*. See also J. M. Ots Capdequí, 'Apuntes para la historia del municipio hispano-americano del período colonial', *Anuario de historia del derecho español*, I (Madrid, 1924), pp. 93–157.
[7] Zorraquín Becú, *La organización judicial argentina en el período hispánico*, pp. 52–4. The office of *alcalde* was never vendible. Alcaldes were appointed annually by the out-going councillors. See above p. 203.

Their term of office was extended from one to two years, one *alcalde* being appointed each year so that the senior *alcalde* could instruct the new one in his duties.[1] This provision was universally opposed by the *cabildos*. First to protest was that of Buenos Aires, which claimed that the duties of the *alcaldes* were already too heavy to be extended.[2] In March 1790, in a strongly argued petition supported by viceroy Arredondo, the *cabildo* of Santa Fe requested a return to the former practice of a one year term of office.[3] Córdoba made a similar request in February 1792.[4] Individual concessions were made to certain *cabildos*. A royal order of 19 September 1788 allowed the *cabildo* of La Plata to appoint its *alcaldes* for one year only.[5] A similar privilege was granted to Buenos Aires in July 1787 and to Santa Fe in September 1790.[6] In February 1797 the *cabildo* of Asunción del Paraguay asked for the concession which so many other *cabildos* were now enjoying, arguing that as most people in Paraguay lived in the country on their estates, from which they derived their livelihood, it was unfair to expect them to desert their affairs for two years.[7] Similar complaints were coming from other parts of the empire, particularly from Perú and Mexico. It was therefore ordered by royal *cédula* of 11 September 1799 that *alcaldes ordinarios* should only serve for one year, and that this rule should apply to all America.[8]

The Ordinance of Intendants also altered the faculties of certain *alcaldes*. Previously the jurisdiction of these magistrates had been additional to that of the governors. Under the new system the competence of the governors in civil and criminal litigation passed entirely to the *tenientes asesores* of each intendancy, but only in respect of the capital of the intendancy and its territory.[9] At the same time the deputies of the governors in

---

[1] *Ord. Ints.*, art. 8.   [2] *A.C.B.A.*, iii, ix, 20, 19 January 1789.

[3] A.G.I., Aud. de Buenos Aires 78, Cabildo of Santa Fe to the Crown, 6 March 1790, enclosed in Arredondo to Porlier, 31 March 1790.

[4] A.G.I., Aud. de Buenos Aires 79, Arredondo to Bajamar, 9 June 1792.

[5] A.G.I., Aud. de Buenos Aires 77, Loreto to Porlier, Carta 87, 20 January 1789.

[6] A.G.I., Aud. de Buenos Aires 78, Arredondo to Porlier, Carta 43, 21 January 1791; *A.C.B.A.*, iii, ix, 199.

[7] A.G.I., Aud. de Buenos Aires 142, Cabildo of Asunción del Paraguay to King, 6 February 1797.

[8] A.G.I., Indif. Gen. 1706, R.C., 11 September 1799.

[9] *Ord. Ints.*, art. 12.

the other cities of the province were suppressed. Thus in these areas the *alcaldes ordinarios* came to exercise ordinary jurisdiction in civil and criminal cases without the interference of any other magistrate, a clear increase of power.[1] It was the custom in Buenos Aires for appeals from the *alcaldes* to go to the governor or to his deputies. The creation of the intendants modified this, for the judicial faculties of the governors passed to the *tenientes letrados* in each intendancy, but only in the capitals; hence, elsewhere appeals went to the *audiencia*.[2]

Cabildo justice, at least in Buenos Aires, made great technical advance in the era of the intendancies, but this must be attributed to an inevitable response to the increase of population and the greater complexity of judicial problems rather than to the direct stimulus of the intendants. Consultation of lawyers became more and more frequent, and from 1784 the *cabildo* of Buenos Aires had its own *asesor letrado*. In 1784 the viceroy ordered that in the capital no document coming before a judge should be considered valid without the signature of a lawyer. With this increase of skill, justice improved, and in 1787 the *alcaldes ordinarios* of Buenos Aires earned the praise of the *regente* of the *audiencia* for the way they accomplished their judicial duties.[3]

The increase of population in the country territory of Buenos Aires made necessary an increase in the number of *alcaldes de hermandad*, for two were no longer adequate. On 31 December 1777 viceroy Cevallos had authorized the *cabildo* to appoint eight.[4] In December 1784 superintendent Sanz authorized the *cabildo* to appoint as many as they considered necessary. In the elections of 1 January 1785 the *cabildo* availed itself of this to appoint sixteen for the Buenos Aires countryside, and six for the Banda Oriental.[5] By 1810 the number had grown to twenty-four.[6]

---

[1] Zorraquín Becú, *op. cit.*, p. 60. But the *cabildo* of La Plata complained of unwarranted interference on the part of the *audiencia* of Charcas in the work of its *alcaldes*. See A.G.I., Aud. de Charcas 589, R.C. to *audiencia* of Charcas, 26 July 1794.

[2] Zorraquín Becú, *op. cit.*, pp. 67–70.

[3] J. M. Mariluz Urquijo, 'Las memorias de los regentes de la Real Audiencia de Buenos Aires', *Revista del Instituto de Historia del Derecho*, i (Buenos Aires, 1949), p. 21.

[4] Zorraquín Becú, *op. cit.*, p. 63.

[5] *A.C.B.A.* iii. vii, 445, 446–7, 453–9.   [6] *Ibid.*, iv, iv, 6.

The *cabildos* themselves were not slow to show their appreciation of the intendants, and during the first fifteen years of the régime there flowed from the municipalities an impressive stream of eulogies of their political superiors. The *cabildo* of Mendoza described Sobremonte as its '*nuevo fundador*', and in August 1788 sent a long and glowing account of his services, requesting from the crown his retention in office, 'because his extraordinary activity and tireless zeal combined with his integrity and enlightened political ideas have contributed advantageously to the general prosperity, progress and administration of these remote and loyal dominions'.[1] In 1790 the *cabildo* of Córdoba decided to send a testimonial of Sobremonte's merits and services to the king.[2] The good impression left by Sobremonte lasted long. When he was appointed temporary viceroy on the death of Joaquín del Pino, the *cabildos* of Córdoba, San Juan, Mendoza and San Luis petitioned the crown (18 May 1804) to confirm him permanently in office.[3] And even after his conduct during the first British invasion of the Río de la Plata in 1806,[4] the *cabildo* of Córdoba defended him in a message to the king dated 29 August 1806.[5]

In 1789 the *cabildo* of Salta del Tucumán reported on the good services of intendant Mestre in all branches of government, and asked the king to prolong his term of office. Particular praise was given to his completion of a 'magnificent town hall' and its division into decent and comfortable offices where the *alcaldes* and other officials could work with proper formality.[6] The *cabildo* of Potosí reported on the new system of government in 1786, and, in terms disappointingly vague, declared that the intendancy system had had beneficial results in restoring public peace, stimulating industry, and formulating new municipal legislation. Special praise was given to intendant Pino Manrique's administration in public works, commerce, mines and

---

[1] A.G.I., Aud. de Buenos Aires 50, 'Memorial del Cabildo de Mendoza', 26 August 1788; part of this is printed in Revello, *op. cit.*, p. 35, who misdates the dispatch.
[2] Garzon, *op. cit.*, p. 23.
[3] *Ibid.*, p. 78.
[4] See below, p. 235.
[5] *Ibid.*, pp. 90–4.
[6] A.G.I., Aud. de Buenos Aires 143, Cabildo of Salta to Crown, 29 July 1789.

exchequer. The *cabildo* was of the opinion that only the intendancy system had been able to provide a strong government in unruly Potosí.[1] In 1793 the *cabildo* of La Plata informed the crown of the good services of president-intendant Joaquín del Pino, his zeal in reorganizing the hospital and personally visiting the sick, his reform of prison conditions, his efforts to promote public works, and his success in increasing royal revenues.[2]

The *cabildo* of La Paz showed a particular readiness to support the intendancy system, and was in fact concerned that it was not operating to full advantage in this distant province. The *cabildo* was quite alive to the fact that what La Paz suffered from was a lack of permanency in its governors: there was a continual change of appointments, and no intendant completed a full term of office. In 1795 La Paz was enjoying the rule of a temporary intendant, Fernando Sota, a naval captain and a man whom the *cabildo* considered intelligent, experienced and well versed in the affairs of the province and of the viceroyalty. So concerned was the *cabildo* to retain his services that it offered 25,000 pesos to the Spanish treasury for the war fund on condition that Soto's appointment be confirmed and prolonged.[3] In August of the following year the *cabildo* sent a further and more substantial account of Soto's administration and renewed its previous request and offer.[4] It was supported by the *audiencia* of Charcas, but it failed to move the home government.[5] Nevertheless his successor, intendant Burgunyo, also earned the support of the *cabildo* and its gratitude for an increase in municipal revenue.[6]

The *cabildo* of Asunción del Paraguay forwarded in 1798 a long report on the services of intendant Rivera, whom it described as a 'prudent and zealous governor', and supplied a detailed account of his administration and policy in military,

[1] B.M., Egerton MS 1813, fols. 76v–78, Cabildo of Potosí to Crown, 4 February 1786.
[2] A.G.I., Aud. de Buenos Aires 45, Cabildo of La Plata to Crown, 28 January 1793.
[3] A.G.I., Aud. de Charcas 436, Cabildo of La Paz to Crown, 17 December 1795.
[4] *Ibid.*, Cabildo of La Paz to Principe de la Paz (Godoy), 31 August 1796.
[5] *Ibid.*, Aud. de Charcas, 25 December 1795.
[6] A.G.I., Aud. de Buenos Aires 37, Cabildo of La Paz to Crown, 11 December 1798.

frontier, Indian and financial affairs, concluding with an appreciation of his régime in no uncertain terms.[1]

This reaction of the *cabildos* of the viceroyalty of the Río de la Plata to the activity of the intendants could be supported by an even more striking body of evidence from the viceroyalty of Perú. In 1786, for example, the *cabildo* of Lima submitted a report on the work of the superintendent and on his treatment of the *cabildo*, which is convincing both in its generalizations and its particulars, and which augured extremely well for future co-operation between the two bodies.[2] Grateful testimonials came also from the *cabildos* of Huancavelica and Arequipa.[3]

A *cabildo* which criticizes intendants is likely to be giving its real opinion when it praises them, and thus these testimonials are convincing precisely because they are not indiscriminate. The very *cabildos* which praise the intendants with whom they can work, do not hesitate to protest against those whom they oppose. In the 1780's and 1790's esteem and co-operation were the norm. But in the first decade of the nineteenth century in almost every part of the viceroyalty of the Río de la Plata the *cabildos* were at loggerheads with their intendants. The revival of political consciousness and public spirit which was evident in the municipalities in this era was then turned against the very intendants who had helped to nurture it, or rather against their successors. This apprenticeship in opposition was in turn an invaluable preparation for the approaching revolution for independence. The change from collaboration to distrust resulted from two causes. In the first place the quality of the intendants appointed to the colonies declined in proportion as the quality of patronage in Madrid declined: the difference between Sobremonte and González in Córdoba is the measure of the difference between

---

[1] A.G.I., Aud. de Buenos Aires 48, Cabildo of Asunción to Francisco de Saavedra, 19 November 1798.

[2] A.G.I., Aud. de Lima 802, Cabildo of Lima, 31 March 1786. 'Desde qu. el Sor. Intendente se posesionó del empleo empesó a dirigir oficios a este Illo. Ayuntamiento para que se meditase, y confiriese todo lo que exigía su atencion, y providencias consultandolo inmediatamente para expedirlas con prontitud, y oportunidad.' These remarks are the aptest commentary on the criticisms of viceroy Croix mentioned above, p. 201 and below, p. 280.

[3] *Ibid.*, Cabildo de Huancavelica, 11 April 1788; Cabildo de Arequipa, 30 December 1788. I owe this and the preceding reference to the kindness of Professor J. Preston Moore.

the government of Charles III and Gálvez and that of Charles
IV and Godoy. Moreover, the *cabildos*, their confidence restored
by fair treatment from the early intendants, came to resent any
intrusion into their electoral affairs, and tried to extend their
control over the increasing municipal funds.

Hostilities in Chuquisaca began as early as 1796. In November of that year the *cabildo* submitted to Madrid a lengthy complaint against what it described as the violation of its authority
and usurpation of its jurisdiction by president-intendant
Joaquín del Pino, whose conduct it had commended only three
years previously. Pino was in fact a fair-minded administrator,
and in this case the initiative came from the *cabildo*. It protested
that its right of appointing the town doctor had been violated by
the intendant, who, with the support of the fiscal of the *audiencia*
of Charcas, Victorián de Villava, had removed its nominee and
appointed his own. In the sphere of public works the intendant
had rejected a contract given by the *cabildo* to one of its *regidores*
for the repair of a bridge at an estimate of 500 pesos and commissioned a contractor of his own at 600 pesos, which the *cabildo*
considered an exorbitant charge on the town funds. The intendant had also overruled the *cabildo* in a scheme for improving
the water supply of the city and had usurped its right of granting
licences to doctors and chemists. Generalizing from these particulars, the *cabildo* made an eloquent appeal for independence
and municipal liberty, for freedom of votes and acceptance of
majority decisions, ending with the remark: 'We now feel that
the city is no longer represented in its *cabildo* but in the vote of
the fiscal and the will of the president.'[1]

The *cabildo* asked the crown for a judgment, and a royal *cédula*
of 15 September 1787 requested the *audiencia* of Charcas to
collect information and forward its opinion.[2] The *audiencia*
accepted the intendant's case that he had authority in matters
of public welfare, such as appointment of doctors, and that
in any case the candidate appointed by the *cabildo* did not have
valid degrees. Traditional practice was that the *cabildo* appointed
doctors and surgeons and submitted them to the intendant for

---

[1] A.G.I., Aud. de Charcas 589, Cabildo of La Plata to Crown, 20 November
1796.
[2] A.G.I., Aud. de Charcas 589, R.C., 15 September 1797.

approbation. On all the points at issue the *audiencia* took the side of the intendant and judged that the complaints of the *cabildo* were unjustified.[1]

It would be a mistake to regard the attitude of *cabildo* in this case as entirely progressive, or the result of the intendant's policy entirely oppressive. The *cabildo* regretfully reported that its authority and prestige had suffered so much from these rebuffs that the offices of *regidores* could no longer find purchasers and had consequently depreciated greatly in value. Thus there were no longer any proprietary councillors, and they all had to be elected annually.[2] The intendant had unwittingly liberalized the municipal régime, but the *cabildo* of Chuquisaca was quite unconscious of the irony.

In Córdoba the happy period of co-operation between intendant and *cabildo* came to an end in 1798, when the first election which took place after the Sobremonte régime was annulled by the temporary intendant, Pérez del Viso. The *cabildo* appealed to the *audiencia*, which ordered a new election, but this also was annulled. The *cabildo* was reduced to three proprietary *regidores*, until the *audiencia* of Buenos Aires decided that the councillors of 1797 should elect those of 1799. But the councillors of 1797 who elected the enemies of the governor in 1798 did the same in 1799. Consequently, with the installation of this *cabildo* a period of administrative sterility began in Córdoba.[3] The situation worsened with the arrival of the new intendant, José González, a man of choleric disposition and domineering temperament. He was sworn into office on 4 December 1803 and one of his first acts was to demand that all the records of the municipal archive should be copied so that he could be precisely informed about the privileges of the *cabildo*. The latter considered that its province was being invaded and yielded with such reluctance that the intendant dropped the matter. A few days later the *cabildo* took the initiative and demanded that the intendant pay the 10,000 pesos security to which he was bound by the title of

[1] *Ibid.*, Pino to Crown, 25 May 1797; Informe de la Audiencia de Charcas, 25 July 1800.

[2] *Ibid.*, Cabildo of La Plata to Crown, 20 November 1796.

[3] Garzon, *op. cit.*, pp. 61–3. See also 'expediente iniciado por don Ambrosio Funes y otros capitulares sobre anulación de elecciones', 1798, *ibid.*, Apéndice 5, pp. 391–406.

his appointment. González retorted that 'it ought not to waste the precious time of its sessions in useless affairs'. Nevertheless the *cabildo* stuck to the point and informed the viceroy repeatedly until by September 1805 the intendant had fulfilled his obligation.[1]

In a note of 11 June 1804 González informed the *cabildo* that it was 'no more than a representative economic body, incapable of determining anything itself without the intervention of the governor'.[2] The reply of the *cabildo* was to draw a comparison between the régime of Sobremonte and the present fractious state of affairs. But there was no improvement under the next intendant, Gutiérrez de la Concha, who was appointed in September 1806 and took office on 28 December 1807. An immediate election dispute ensured that for the whole of 1808 a *cabildo* dominated by Ambrosio Funes and his political associates would form a party hostile to the intendant and his assessor Rodríguez.[3] This feud was nourished by an excessive legal formalism and petty disputes over public ceremonial and precedence which were a perennial breeding ground of bad feeling in Spanish colonial society, especially in the small isolated communities of the interior.[4] Then, in the elections of January 1809, the two *cabildo* nominees for senior *alcalde* and procurator were refused confirmation by the intendant who appointed others in their place. In the subsequent appeal the *cabildo's* case was defended by Mariano Moreno, then a lawyer in Buenos Aires and *relator* of the *audiencia*. He declined to labour the point that a majority vote decided municipal elections and that this obliged the superior authorities to confirm the choice of the *cabildo* unless there were legitimate legal objections, and went on to argue that 'the most precious prerogative of the *cabildos* is the private right of electing the councillors who are to compose it', a privilege too important to remain exposed to capricious usurpation or to a 'stroke of despotism'.[5]

Considerable opposition to the intendant of Córdoba was stirring in Buenos Aires, inspired largely by Martín Alzaga. At

[1] *Ibid.*, pp. 75–80.   [2] *Ibid.*, p. 78.   [3] *Ibid.*, pp, 107–8.
[4] *Ibid.*, pp. 85–6 n., 103–4, for examples.
[5] Moreno, *Escritos*, i, 302, 311. In a similar case in Corrientes in January 1808 Moreno used like arguments on behalf of the *cabildo*. *Ibid.*, i, 171–80.

the time of the British invasions viceroy Sobremonte had fled to Córdoba. The *cabildo* of Buenos Aires suspended him. Gutiérrez de la Concha bitterly opposed this suspension. Tense relations were rendered worse when in 1810 the *alcaldes de barrio* in La Rioja were suppressed on his orders, a measure which gave rise to an appeal to the viceroy.[1] Meanwhile ill-feeling developed between the intendant of Córdoba and the *cabildo* of Concepción during 1808,[2] and in 1808 Gutiérrez took exception to the fact that the *cabildo* of Mendoza made a direct financial contribution to Buenos Aires without his permission.[3]

Comparable tension also existed in La Paz, where the genesis of the revolution of 1809 which deposed the intendant lay largely in *cabildo* activity.[4] But the most vigorous defence of municipal liberty and opposition to arbitrary government came from the *cabildo* of Buenos Aires. Its relations with the new intendant, Reynoso, were not significant, because the powers of the latter were so circumscribed that only the viceroy stood in direct relation with the *cabildo* and continued to preside over its sessions, confirm its elections and supervise its funds. And it was generally the viceroy and not the intendant who communicated with the *cabildo*.[5] But relations between the viceroy and the *cabildo* deteriorated precisely under the régime of Sobremonte, whose character and behaviour underwent a strange metamorphosis after his appointment as viceroy in April 1804.

The feud was started in May 1805 by an ill-tempered dispute over etiquette and precedence, in which Sobremonte publicly insulted the *cabildo* and the latter retaliated by declining the invitation to attend the burial of his son.[6] Relations were not improved when the viceroy granted the title of *villa* to the town of Las Conchas, near Buenos Aires, and authorized the election of a *cabildo*, for the metropolis, showing more than a touch of municipal jealousy, protested to the crown against this grant and claimed that it was beyond the competence of viceroy to bestow

---

[1] Levene, *La revolución de mayo y Mariano Moreno*, i, 109.
[2] *A.C.C.R.C.*, pp. 268–9.
[3] *A.C.B.A.*, iv, iii, 53–4, 27 February 1808.
[4] M. M. Pinto, *La revolución de la intendencia de La Paz en el virreynato del Río de la Plata, con la ocurrencia de Chuquisaca* (Buenos Aires, 1909), p. 57. See below, pp. 271–3.
[5] *A.C.B.A.*, iv, ii, 244, 27 March 1806, for example.
[6] *Ibid.*, iv, ii, 82–6, 92.

the title and privilege of a *villa*. The Council of the Indies annulled the grant on the grounds that such a concession was peculiar to the sovereignty of the crown.[1]

The part played by the *cabildo* in the critical events of the summer of 1806 when Buenos Aires was invaded by a British expedition, and its rôle in the reconquest, gave it a moral ascendancy over the viceroy which it was able to turn to good account.[2] The viceroy refused to confirm the elections of 1807, arguing that in the critical circumstances of another imminent invasion experienced councillors should remain in office yet another year. The *cabildo* rejected this argument and on 9 January repeated its request, only to find the viceroy adamant.[3] An appeal was therefore lodged with the *audiencia* on the 22 January, and as Sobremonte was nowhere to be found at the time the *regente* confirmed the elections within two days.[4] The viceroy sent a lame approval later.[5] Sobremonte's reaction to the British invasion of the Río de la Plata bore all the marks of panic; he deserted the capital and made for Córdoba on the pretext of going to raise troops. In 1807 he was arrested by deputies of the *cabildo* of Buenos Aires near Montevideo and detained in a monastery in Buenos Aires. He was then deposed by the *cabildo* and the *audiencia*, and the latter was left temporarily as the depositary of royal authority.

The *cabildo*'s denouncement of maladministration became more and more outspoken. Already on the 3 July 1806 it had written to its attorney in Madrid reporting Sobremonte's conduct in the crisis of 1806.[6] Then in secret dispatches to Madrid in May and July 1807 it instructed its attorney to impede the appointment of Liniers, the hero of the reconquest of Buenos Aires, as viceroy, for it considered him ill-suited for the command of the viceroyalty.[7] In a representation to the government dated 13 September 1808 it requested the appointment of a worthy viceroy, and stated its opinion that

[1] Torre Revello, *Sobre Monte*, pp. 76–88.

[2] J. M. Saenz Valiente, 'Los alcaldes de Buenos Aires en 1806', *B.I.I.H.*, xvii (1933–4), pp. 105–18. In the *cabildo* of 1806 Europeans formed the majority; only four were creoles. *Ibid.*, p. 101.

[3] *A.C.B.A.*, IV, ii, 389, 396.   [4] *Ibid.*, pp. 402, 407.

[5] *Ibid.*, p. 421.   [6] Saenz Valiente, *op. cit.*, p. 105.

[7] *A.C.B.A.*, IV, ii, 533, 21 May 1807; IV, ii, 643, 29 June 1807.

Corruption in all departments of government has arrived at its extreme. . . . Justice is administered without any subjection to the laws; administration knows no rules; the exchequer is managed without economy and with criminal indolence; . . . for many years America has had to suffer corrupt and despotic leaders, ignorant and venal ministers, inefficient and cowardly soldiers.[1]

The vigorous example set by Buenos Aires in these years appealed to the other towns of the viceroyalty, and a growing consciousness of their rights and duties radiated to the other *cabildos*. Buenos Aires came to be regarded as a leader and protector in municipal politics. When the *cabildo* of Asunción del Paraguay planned to form a constitution for itself modelled on that of Buenos Aires, and submitted its scheme to the *audiencia*, the latter requested the *cabildo* of Buenos Aires to furnish a copy of its ordinances and constitution for its information.[2] On 23 December 1805 the *audiencia* ordered the *cabildo* to submit a similar record to the municipality of Córdoba.[3] In April 1807 the *cabildo* of Asunción was in conflict with the newly appointed temporary intendant of Paraguay, and naturally sought the patronage of the *cabildo* of Buenos Aires for its appeal before the *audiencia*.[4] For their part almost all the *cabildos* in the viceroyalty, and many beyond, rallied round Buenos Aires with generous gifts of money in 1807 for the repulse of the English invasions.[5] By now the metropolis was conscious of its ascendancy, and in December 1807, in requesting the title of 'Defender of South America and Protector of the *Cabildos* of the Viceroyalty of the Río de la Plata', it posed as the leader of municipal life in the viceroyalty, the benefactor who could help its poor neighbours, 'the organ whereby the complaints of the *cabildos* reach Your Majesty and through which they receive Your graces'.[6] Buenos Aires was already prepared for its rôle in the revolution for independence.

[1] A.G.I., Aud. de Buenos Aires 157, Cabildo de Buenos Aires, 13 September 1808.

[2] *A.C.B.A.*, IV, ii, 151, 16 October 1805.

[3] *Ibid.*, IV, ii, 192, 24 December 1805.

[4] *Ibid.*, IV, ii, 529, 18 May 1807.

[5] *Ibid.*, IV, ii, 490–650.   [6] Moreno, *op. cit.*, i, 162–4, 30 December 1807.

CHAPTER X

The Intendant and the Audiencia

JUAN DE SOLÓRZANO, one of the greatest of Spanish jurists, described the *audiencias* in the Indies as 'the rock and defence of those kingdoms, where justice is done, where the poor find their defence from the oppression of the great and powerful, and where every man may claim his own in law and in truth'.[1] In less idealistic terms a modern historian of the Spanish colonial system has concluded that of all the administrative hierarchy in the Spanish dominions 'the *audiencia* or court of appeal was the most essential and characteristic institution'.[2] Combining three classes of functions, judicial, administrative, and consultative, its services to crown and people in keeping watch over the activities of viceroys and governors, and in checking the private conduct of colonists were invaluable at all times and in all parts of Spanish America. Where the seat of an *audiencia* was also a viceregal capital as in Mexico and Lima and later in Buenos Aires, the viceroy presided over the *audiencia*, but he had no vote in its judgments, unless he happened to be a qualified lawyer. During an interregnum, or a prolonged absence of the viceroy, the *audiencia* temporarily exercised all his powers. It always had the right to hear appeals against the viceroy's actions, and could draw up corporate complaints against his administration. Many special powers, reserved in Spain for the royal councils, were delegated in America to the courts. The *audiencias* there exercised a general supervision over the conduct of inferior justices. They were empowered to review the *residencias* of retiring *corregidores* and other officials. They might send out special commissioners to make additional investigations where necessary.

[1] Juan de Solórzano Pereira, *Política indiana* [1647] (5 vols., Madrid, 1930), v, iii, 7.

[2] J. H. Parry, *The audiencia of New Galicia in the sixteenth century*, p. 2. For a general account of the colonial *audiencia* see Ruiz Guiñazú, *La magistratura indiana*, pp. 13-255. On the *audiencia* as a court of appeal see C. Ferres, *Época colonial. La administración de justicia en Montevideo* (Montevideo, 1944), pp. 101-24.

Each *audiencia* was to sit regularly in *acuerdo* to discuss and propose measures concerning the administration of its province, and in *acuerdo de hacienda*, jointly with the royal treasury officials, to determine urgent questions of financial administration. Finally the supervision of Indian affairs was assigned to the especial care of the *audiencias*.[1]

These political functions of the royal courts were no mere accidental accretions, for the very creation of an *audiencia* was often occasioned by political exigencies in a given area of the dominions.[2] And by the eighteenth century they had hardened with long usage, so that the establishment of any new political agency was bound to cause resentment. This was particularly noticeable in the viceroyalty of the Río de la Plata.

To its already formidable constitutional equipment, geographical remoteness and historical circumstances added even further *de facto* power to the *audiencia* of Charcas. It is true that the Laws of the Indies clearly assigned superior authority in the district of this *audiencia* to the viceroy of Perú, and that the *audiencia* was explicitly forbidden to intrude in the government of the district.[3] Nevertheless, by various means the *audiencia* of Charcas came to assume all the appearances of an organ of government and to enjoy an indeterminate power in its vast territory. Its presidents and judges (*oidores*), generally men of higher intellectual quality than the majority of colonial officials, adopted the practice of corresponding direct with the Council of the Indies, and even with the crown, on a profusion of matters many of which had only the most tenuous juridical significance.[4] The viceroys often had to entrust the *audiencia* with the execution of resolutions issued from Lima, while in times of crisis, such as disturbances in Potosí or Paraguay, the viceroy never exercised immediate authority over official operations, but invariably delegated it to the *audiencia*.[5]

[1] Solórzano, *op. cit.*, v, iii.

[2] Pío Ballesteros, 'La función política de las Reales Chancillerías coloniales', *Revista de Estudios Políticos*, xv (Madrid, 1946), p. 47.

[3] *Recopilación*, II, xvi, 1; III, iii, 6.

[4] E. Cardozo, 'La audiencia de Charcas y la facultad de gobierno', *Humanidades*, xxv (La Plata, 1935), pt. i, p. 141.

[5] G. René-Moreno, *Bolivia y Perú*, pp. 242–5. The chapter on the *audiencia* of Charcas is a reprint of his article 'La *audiencia* de Charcas 1559–1809', *Revista Chilena*, viii (1877), pp. 93–142.

The *audiencia's* writ ran in a district which was the most extensive of all the Americas. Before the creation of the viceroyalty of the Río de la Plata in 1776 its jurisdiction stretched from the Atlantic to the Pacific, from Arica to Montevideo, embracing the governments of Tucumán, Buenos Aires and Paraguay, bounded by Brazil, Cuzco and Arequipa on one side and by Atacama and Cuyo on the other.[1] It is not surprising that this tribunal enjoyed immense political and social prestige and was regarded as the highest professional grade after that of Lima, and one to which an ambitious judge would aspire after service in others. The salaries of the *oidores* were actually the same as those in Lima, though this was offset by a higher cost of living in Chuquisaca.[2]

The independence of the *audiencia* of Charcas had arrived at such an extreme by the mid-eighteenth century that the viceroys at Lima made desperate efforts to curb it.[3] In 1753 the viceroy reaffirmed his exclusive cognizance over exchequer affairs. In November 1761 the *audiencia* suffered an actual loss when the viceroy forbade it to review the *residencias* of governors and *corregidores* in its district. He had already curtailed the judicial faculties of the tribunal in May 1750 when he informed it that appeals from *alcaldes ordinarios* and other inferior judges in Tucumán should be heard before the governor of Tucumán without the intervention of the *audiencia*. The *audiencia* appealed, but the viceroy maintained his position.[4]

On the whole, however, the *audiencia* stuck stubbornly to its ground. On the eve of the establishment of the intendant system the extent of its jurisdiction had actually increased, for with the expulsion of the Jesuits the provinces of Mojos and Chiquitos came under the administration of the *audiencia*. The creation of the viceroyalty of the Río de la Plata, while it

[1] *Recopilación*, ii, xv, 9, 14 and 15. Legally the *audiencia* only had cognizance of affairs in Tucumán in so far as they related to '*cuentas y buena distribución de las sisas*'. Cardozo, *op. cit.*, p. 147.

[2] A.G.I., Indif. General 843, 'Nota de la producción y utilidad en que conceptuan las Plazas de Ministros de las Audiencias de Indias', Tomás Ortiz de Landazuri, Madrid, 30 October 1772.

[3] The *oidores* of Charcas also had a reputation with the authorities in Madrid 'por el desarreglo de su conducta enlaces y negociaciones de Minas, y Comercios ilicitos en Potosi'. A.G.I., Indif. Gen. 843, *loc. cit.*

[4] Cardozo, *op. cit.*, pp. 150–2.

diminished the influence of the *audiencia* in the eastern provinces, had little effect on its position in Upper Perú. This was clearly demonstrated during the rebellion of Chayanta in 1780–1, when viceroy Vértiz had to report that:

> The oppression and despotic procedure of the *corregidor* certainly provoked this rising, and if the *audiencia* had paid more attention to the instructions sent to it by this government then these conflicts, in which they were caught by apathy and inattention to such important matters, would not have arisen. . . . But the *audiencia*, far from obeying government orders, actually sent orders to this government and issued decrees. . . .[1]

Yet within a few years two new institutions were challenging the power and pretensions of this historic tribunal. The creation of the intendants in 1782 and of the *audiencia* of Buenos Aires in 1785 opened a new era in the history of the *audiencia* of Charcas. Charcas now had to share appeals with the *audiencia* of Buenos Aires, for the new tribunal took from it the provinces of Buenos Aires, Paraguay, Tucumán and Cuyo. But its greatest loss was to its political authority in Upper Perú itself, and this was effected by the intendants who were posted out to the provinces of Potosí, La Paz, Cochabamba and La Plata. Responsible directly to the central authority of the viceroy and the superintendent in Buenos Aires, the new officials had strictly defined powers in the four government departments of justice, finance, war and general administration, a system which removed by mere definition and assertion the claims of the *audiencia* which had hitherto flourished on vagueness and precedent. Now, the simple presence of these powerful political figures filled the gaps in the government of Upper Perú which the *audiencia* had had to supply and made this territory much less politically remote than it had been. While the *audiencia* lost by the Ordinance of Intendants, its president gained, for he also was assigned the four faculties of government, but strictly as intendant of the province of La Plata.[2] The *audiencia* retained its plenitude of power as court of appeal, but in a considerably reduced area.

Although the *audiencia* of Charcas thus lost its traditional ascendancy, it discarded neither its ambitions nor its social

---

[1] Vértiz to Gálvez, 24 October 1780, in Angelis, *Colección*, iv, 474.
[2] The judicial power of the president now became purely nominal.

prestige. 'The toga which [the *oidores*] now wore', Mariano Moreno remarked, 'had lost its Roman majesty but retained all its despotism.'[1] This was not a fair verdict. It is truer to say that the introduction of intendants into Upper Perú provoked a reaction on the part of the *audiencia* which completely shattered the united front of Spanish government in this part of the empire, and created a tension which contributed in no small part to the undermining of the colonial régime in Upper Perú.

The Ordinance of Intendants recognized the possibility of conflict between the two authorities when it enjoined the *audiencias* to aid the intendants and to put no opposition in their way.[2] It defined the limits and the relations of the two authorities in careful terms. Each intendant had a deputy, a lawyer (*teniente asesor*), who exercised for the intendant contentious civil and criminal jurisdiction in the capitals of the intendancies. This lawyer, appointed by the crown, had to be duly examined and approved by the *audiencia*.[3] Appeal could be made against the political acts of intendants or their subdelegates to the *audiencia* of the district according to the Laws of the Indies, as well as against the legal decisions of the intendant or his lawyer.[4] But for a certain type of appeal a careful distinction was drawn: if an intendant prosecuted any treasury official on a purely political or civil matter, then the accused could appeal to the *audiencia*, but if on a financial issue then the appeal had to go to the *junta superior de hacienda* which was the highest court of appeal in financial affairs to the absolute exclusion of any other tribunal.[5] The *audiencia* thus lost all power of intervention in exchequer cases.[6]

Disputes rapidly developed between the intendants and the *audiencia* of Charcas: in some cases these were legal squabbles over boundaries of jurisdiction, but more often they were simple

---

[1] Quoted by the Bolivian historian, Gabriel René-Moreno, who in even more exaggerated language concludes, 'desde su retiro, o por mejor decir jubilación política y administrativa, el regio tribunal lidiaba por ser, si cuando mas no fuese en aperiencias, lo que ya no era. Hubierase dicho que había perdido la apostura severa y desenvuelta de la virilidad, y que mostraba su decrepitud entre contorsiones de altivez e impaciencia'. *Ultimos días coloniales en el Alto-Perú* (Santiago de Chile, 1896–8), pp. 133–4.   [2] *Ord. Ints.*, art. 270.
[3] *Ibid.*, art. 12.   [4] *Ibid.*, arts. 5, 14.   [5] *Ibid.*, art. 84.
[6] But in a viceregal capital, as will be seen, one *oidor* and the regent would be members of the *junta superior*.

clashes over policy and were born of the *audiencia's* jealousy over the loss of its political monopoly in Upper Perú. In Chuquisaca the system faltered from the very beginning. The extraordinary appointment of a creole as its first president-intendant was grist to the *audiencia's* mill and gave it a convenient opportunity to reassert itself. The *oidores* in the colonial *audiencias* formed an exclusive class of peninsula-trained lawyers, completely closed to creoles and intensely conscious of its European origin. Viceroy Vértiz's unexpected appointment of colonel Ignacio Flores, a native of Quito, as temporary president of the *audiencia* of Charcas and intendant of La Plata in reward for outstanding services in the recent rebellion of Tupac Amaru was regarded as a direct affront to the European elements in Upper Perú, and the resentment was increased when Flores appointed another creole, Juan Josef de Segovia, as his *teniente asesor*. The *audiencia* was thus assured of a certain measure of outside support, while it also knew it could count on the encouragement of the new viceroy, the marqués de Loreto, whose attitude to Flores was manifestly hostile. Loreto actually set the neighbouring intendant of La Paz to spy on Flores.[1] He himself reported unfavourably to Madrid on the competence of the new president, whom he described as confused and tactless.[2] As a result of this critical report the government decided to relieve Flores as soon as possible and appointed Vicente de Gálvez in his place by royal order of 7 March 1785.[3] But before the new incumbent arrived, the *audiencia* had already opened a more immediate attack on Flores.

During the Tupac Amaru rebellion the *mestizos* of Chuquisaca had been armed and organized into a *cuerpo de patricios*. After the crisis they were disbanded and replaced by Spanish regular troops, the Extremadura Regiment, who were extremely unpopular with the *mestizos* of Chuquisaca.[4] On the night of 21 July 1785 a soldier of the 2nd Extremadura Battalion killed a *mestizo* in a brawl, an incident which provoked a popular and

---

[1] Aud. de Buenos Aires 72, Loreto and Sanz to Sonora, Carta reservada 422, 19 January 1786; A.G.I. Aud. de Buenos Aires 354, Segurola to Loreto, 6 December 1785.

[2] A.G.I., Aud. de Buenos Aires 68, Loreto to Gálvez, 8 October 1784.

[3] A.G.I., Aud. de Charcas 434, R.O., 7 March 1785.

[4] René-Moreno, *Ultimos días coloniales*, pp. 57–8.

spontaneous riot in which crowds filled the streets for two days and tried to effect summary justice upon the troops. Flores and Segovia acted with coolness. Accompanied by the fiscal of the *audiencia*, they met the rioters and managed to disperse them without force of arms.[1] But as a security measure Flores decided to re-establish and rearm the *mestizo* militia company, which he then set to patrol the streets.[2] The situation was thus brought under control but a storm of criticism now broke over the head of the unfortunate Flores. On the one hand he was attacked because he did not act vigorously enough against the rioters and failed to consult all the local authorities. On the other hand his policy of rearming the creoles was bitterly resented by the *audiencia* and by European opinion in general.[3] The resentment in La Plata was echoed in Buenos Aires where viceroy Loreto deplored 'the bad example caused in the kingdom in putting arms in the hands of those whose motives are not to be trusted in such circumstances. . . .'[4] Evidence of the circulation of subversive literature in La Plata heightened the general concern,[5] and the intendant had to defer to Loreto's orders, disband the *mestizo* company and summon another company of regular troops from Potosí.[6]

Flores was well aware of the *audiencia's* animosity towards himself as a creole, and in reports to the government he took the offensive against the tribunal. On 15 August he wrote to the authorities in Madrid via Loreto protesting against the attempts of fiscal Arnaiz and *oidor* Ciceron to discredit him, describing the former as 'cargado de deudas, y con un genio tétrico,

[1] A. Costa du Rels, 'Un precursor inesperado de la emancipación americana', *Boletín de la Academia Nacional de la Historia*, xvii (Buenos Aires, 1944), pp. 217–18. For a brief account of the rising see L. Paz, *Historia general del Alto-Perú, hoy Bolivia* (2 vols., Sucre, 1919), i, 469–70.

[2] A.G.I., Aud. de Buenos Aires 70, Flores to Loreto, 24 July 1785, encl. 1 in Expediente sobre el tumulto acaecido en la Ciudad de la Plata, 22 Julio 1785', fols. 1–7. See above, pp. 77–8.

[3] A.G.I., Aud. de Buenos Aires 70, Domingo Arnaiz (fiscal of the *audiencia*) to Loreto, 2 August 1785, in 'Expediente . . .', fols. 44–9.

[4] A.G.I., Aud. de Buenos Aires 70, 'Libro de Autos Reservados', 31 August 1785, Copia.

[5] A.G.I., Aud. de Buenos Aires 72, Expediente sobre el motín en la Plata, Testimonio del 3° Cuerpo, fols. 1–2, 86.

[6] A.G.I., Aud. de Buenos Aires 72, Flores to Loreto, 29 August 1785, *ibid.*, fol. 13.

embrollador, y faláz', and the latter as 'turbulente, maligno, e injusto'.[1] In further reports he defended himself against the *audiencia*'s criticisms of his conduct in the disturbance in Chuquisaca, and claimed that his re-arming of the *mestizo* company had in fact brought a speedy end to the riot. With some bitterness he remarked:

> The *mestizos* (who are very different from the *cholos*) do have a modicum of honour. They too venerate the king's name, and have proved their loyalty in the recent rebellion [of Tupac Amaru].[2]

He rejected the testimony of the fiscal, protested against the general attitude of the *audiencia* towards himself, and ended by pointing out that if he were removed on account of his creole policy, it would be an ominous sign to Americans.[3]

On 29 August the viceroy ordered Flores to divide the town of Chuquisaca into *barrios* or quarters, and to place each division under the supervision of a citizen of repute who could organize patrols and report on the situation. Flores thereupon summoned a *cabildo abierto* of principal citizens which was held on 7 October and decided to appoint *alcaldes* for the *barrios*, and to urge the *audiencia* to pursue the inquiry into the riot in order to arrive at the facts and to clear the good name of honourable citizens who were under suspicion; it was also agreed to request the viceroy to allow a fair hearing to anyone accused.[4] This incident, especially the summoning of a *cabildo abierto*, naturally aroused the suspicions of the viceroy and *audiencia* still further.

Meanwhile the fiscal had been informing the king and the viceroy that Flores was animated by anti-Spanish sentiments, and was particularly prejudiced against Andalusians. Flores denied this and affirmed that he had in fact made a special point of being fair and friendly to Europeans, particularly in appointing them to posts, and that he had always lived a reclusive life, precisely in order to avoid social connections which might compromise him, facts which were corroborated by many Europeans

---

[1] A.G.I., Aud. de Buenos Aires 69, Flores to Loreto, 15 August 1785.
[2] A.G.I., Aud. de Buenos Aires 72, Flores to Loreto, 15 October 1785. Expediente sobre el motín en la Plata., Testimonio de 4° Cuerpo, fol. 5.
[3] *Ibid.*, fols. 7–12.
[4] A.G.I., Aud. de Charcas 555, R.C. para la Audiencia de Buenos Aires, 15 July 1789.

themselves, including the archbishop of La Plata.[1] More positively, he claimed that in conducting an inquiry into the recent occurrences the *audiencia* was in fact using faculties which properly belonged to the intendant in whom was deposited *jurisdicción ordinaria*.[2] In a highly sarcastic and contemptuous reply the fiscal pointed out that the highest civil and criminal cases required the highest tribunals, and that as riots and uprisings were essentially an affront to legitimate authority they came into this category; moreover Minister José de Gálvez's approval of their cognizance of the Tupac Amaru rebellion afforded an effective precedent.[3]

The dispute was ended by the departure of Flores. In spite of his popularity with the creoles of La Plata,[4] his appointment had never been permanent, and already on 7 March 1785 his successor, Vicente de Gálvez, had been appointed. By September the latter had arrived in Buenos Aires, and Loreto hurried him out to his post with instructions to investigate carefully the state of government in La Plata.[5] Flores was summoned to Buenos Aires to answer for his conduct. On 16 December 1785 the *audiencia* of Buenos Aires censured his conduct in the affair of the *cabildo abierto*, and he was detained pending the result of the full inquiry into the riot in La Plata. He died in Buenos Aires on 5 August 1786 before the inquiry was terminated.[6] By now the *audiencia*'s campaign against Flores had merged with its persecution of his former assessor, Juan Josef de Segovia. Segovia, a close friend of Flores, was already vice-rector of the University of Chuquisaca, and now he stood as candidate for the rectorship in December 1785, assured of the support of all the creoles. There was, however, considerable European opposition to his candidature, and when he was elected by a resounding majority

[1] A.G.I., Aud. de Charcas 438, Flores to Loreto, 15 September 1785, and enclosures 4 and 6.   [2] *Ibid.*
[3] A.G.I., Aud. de Charcas 438, Vista del Fiscal, 29 August 1785.
[4] A.G.I., Aud. de Charcas 434 'La Ciudad de la Plata y todos sus principales y honrados vecinos informan a V.M. de los importantes servicios, que ha hecho en la Provincia de Moxos, en la revolucion de los Indios, y en su Intendencia y Presidencia de Charcas', 20 January 1786. Seventy-seven signatures.
[5] A.G.I., Aud. de Buenos Aires 69, Loreto to José de Gálvez, Carta reservada 343, 18 October 1785.
[6] A.G.I., Aud. de Buenos Aires 73, Loreto to Sonora, carta reservada 556, 3 September 1786.

fiscal Arnaiz stirred up such a campaign against him that Loreto ordered Segovia's arrest and remission to Buenos Aires, where he was imprisoned with Flores.[1]

The *audiencia* of Charcas itself was hardly efficient in the discovery and punishment of the instigators of the riot of 1785 and soon incurred the displeasure of the viceroy and of the government in Madrid for its dilatory procedure in the case. A royal order of 4 November 1787 instructed Loreto to urge the president to terminate the case as quickly as possible in conjunction with the regent of the *audiencia*. But in March 1788 Loreto had to report that the matter still remained in abeyance, an implicit confession of his inability to bring effective pressure to bear on the *audiencia*.[2]

But an even more glaring example of the self-will of the *audiencia* in relation to the political authorities had already increased the tension between Upper Perú and Buenos Aires. In April 1785 subversive and anti-government leaflets had been posted up in Cochabamba. The intendant arrested and imprisoned the two brothers, Domingo and Josef Arias de Argüello, and a priest, Miguel Yquize, 'men notoriously subversive'. The *audiencia* assumed cognizance of the case and issued an order that the prisoners be handed over to the tribunal. The intendant ignored this, as the viceroy had already claimed the case for his jurisdiction. The *audiencia* insisted and demanded the transfer of the accused on two further occasions. With the appointment of Vicente de Gálvez as president-intendant Loreto believed that he would have a more trustworthy servant in Chuquisaca, and he instructed Gálvez to take a firm line with the *audiencia*, whose conduct he regarded as 'a confirmation of the sad state and constitution of that tribunal'.[3] Loreto had the support of a royal order of 4 March 1786 which authorized him to take cognizance of the case to the exclusion of any tribunal. The *audiencia*, however, remained unimpressed, and when the wife of Josef Arias appealed before court it issued a royal writ ordering the intendant of Cochabamba to remit the prisoners and the case. The

[1] A. Costa du Rels, *op. cit.*, pp. 219–22.

[2] A.G.I., Aud. de Buenos Aires 76, Loreto to Valdés, 2 March 1788.

[3] A.G.I., Aud. de Buenos Aires 72, Loreto to Sonora, Carta 446, 17 March 1786.

intendant was in a dilemma, but matters were forcibly taken out of his hands by the escape of Arias, who presented himself before the *audiencia* in Chuquisaca and meanwhile remained at liberty.[1]

These initial skirmishes between intendants and the *audiencia* were but the prelude to large-scale hostilities. With the arrival of a new fiscal in 1791 the tension between the two authorities entered a new and decisive stage. Victorián de Villava would have been a credit to the Spanish colonial service in any period of its history. A former professor of law in the University of Huesca in Aragon, he combined erudition and an instinct for reform to a remarkable degree.[2] In August 1789 he was appointed fiscal of the *audiencia* of Charcas and protector of the Indians,[3] and his arrival in Chuquisaca initiated a direct conflict between the intendants and the *audiencia* in which the subject-matter, as has been seen, was the Indian problem in Upper Perú.[4] The sight of the *mita* slavery inspired Villava to write his *Discurso sobre la Mita de Potosí* (9 March 1793), in which he attacked the basis of the whole system, and condemned it on legal, economic and moral grounds.[5] Intendant Sanz of Potosí, horrified by the theories of Villava, which obviously struck at the root of the whole economic and social structure of Upper Perú, wrote an extensive *Contestación* (19 November 1794), in which he sharply attacked Villava and defended the *mita* system in its entirety. This began a public controversy in legal and political ideas, and caused a profound stirring in government circles in Upper Perú and Buenos Aires.

The crucial question was, would the *audiencia*, a tribunal which had no reputation for liberal views, align itself with its fiscal? Eventually it was won partly by his arguments and personality, but still more by the desire to profit from a supreme opportunity to embarrass the intendant of Potosí. The miners and the tribunal of accounts, on the other hand, took sides with

---

[1] A.G.I., Aud. de Buenos Aires 73, Loreto to Sonora, carta reservada 538, 8 July 1786. Domingo Arias had already died in prison.

[2] Levene, *Vida y escritos de Victorián de Villava*, pp. 9–13.

[3] A.G.I., Aud. de Charcas 442, Titulo de Fiscal de la Audiencia de Charcas, 8 August 1789.

[4] See above, pp. 180–4.

[5] Printed in Levene, *op. cit.*, Appendix 12, pp. xxx–xxxiv.

the intendant in community of economic interests and denounced Villava vociferously.[1] As has been seen, the dispute was continued in bitter and personal terms, offering to the public of Upper Perú a spectacle of political disunity which the crown was unable or unwilling to control.

Moreover, Villava began to question the financial probity of intendant Sanz. In March 1799, reporting on the state of the exchequer in Upper Perú, he commented on

. . . the persistent bankruptcies experienced and the indolence or complicity of the intendants, especially arising out of the revelations of Pedro Altolaguirre, treasurer of the Casa de Moneda of Potosí, who on his death declared that he had usurped many thousands of pesos at the expense of the exchequer, which he could not repay, asserting, moreover, that the governor-intendant of Potosí owed him more than 5,000 pesos, of which he had excused him half.[2]

To correct this state of affairs Villava suggested that the fiscals of the *audiencias* should have more influence in exchequer affairs: the power of appointing the *defensores de real hacienda*, assigned to the intendants by the Ordinance of Intendants, should be restored to the fiscals who had previously exercised it, a method which would relieve these exchequer officials of any dependence on the intendants who appointed them and enable them to fulfil their functions with greater freedom.[3] The government eventually adopted his suggestion, and in June 1801 issued an order that in future *defensores de hacienda* of the provincial capitals of the viceroyalty of the Río de la Plata should be appointed by the viceroy from three candidates suggested by the fiscals of the *audiencias*.[4]

Intendant Sanz came to the conclusion that 'it appears that Villava came from Spain to America only to conflict with the intendants'.[5] Certainly during Villava's term of office disputes between the *audiencia* and the intendants extended to further

---

[1] Levene, *op. cit.*, pp. 25–6.

[2] A.G.I., Aud. de Charcas 446, Villava to Pedro de Acuña, 24 May 1793; Aud. de Charcas 424, Consulta del Consejo, 27 May 1801.

[3] *Ibid.*

[4] A.G.I., Aud. de Charcas 424, R.O., 5 June 1801. The same order gave notice to the viceroy to effect the collection of the whole of Sanz's debt.

[5] A.G.I., Aud. de Charcas 426, Consulta del Consejo, 27 February 1798.

issues and to other intendants. A quarrel over a legal case
between the *audiencia* and the intendant of La Paz ruined
relations between these two authorities from 1792 onwards. The
matter arose out of a dispute over the execution of a will. The
intendant's decision in the case was appealed before the
audiencia, but he refused to remit the case to the court and
ignored six writs issued by the *audiencia* ordering him to do so.[1]
The general argument which then developed is more important
than the original case itself. Intendant Álvarez asserted that the
fiscal was refusing to recognize the faculties lawfully assigned to
the intendant.[2] This drew from the *audiencia* a sustained attack
in which it pursued the unfortunate Álvarez with all the force of
its superior polemical powers. In a very revealing passage
Villava interpreted the authentic attitude of the *audiencia*
towards the new system:

> The fiscal is not an enemy of the intendants, nor of their establish-
> ment, but since he has taken office he has had abundant evidence to
> support his opinion that the combination of authorities and power
> which they have been assigned makes each one of them a petty
> viceroy in his district. . . .[3]

The *audiencia* followed this up with a declaration that intendant
Álvarez was working to destroy the authority of the royal
tribunal and deride its most serious decisions, ignoring a royal
provision on a matter of justice, and persisting in an attitude
which if allowed to go uncorrected would make the intendants
even greater despots in their provinces.[4] The tribunal went so
far as to request a government order authorizing the military
commandant at La Paz to provide the *audiencia* with troops
necessary to enforce its writs.[5] Villava was convinced that the
very powers given to them by the new system encouraged the
intendants in a despotism which could only be corrected by
subordinating them in all military and financial matters to the

---

[1] A.G.I., Aud. de Charcas 446, Audiencia of Charcas to viceroy Arredondo,
25 August 1792, encl. 3.
[2] A.G.I., Aud. de Charcas 446, Informe de Álvarez, 16 June 1792, encl. 2 in
Audiencia of Charcas to marqués de Bajamar, 25 September 1792.
[3] A.G.I., Aud. de Charcas 446, Vista del fiscal Villava, 19 July 1792.
[4] A.G.I., Aud. de Charcas 446, Audiencia of Charcas to Crown, 25 July 1792.
[5] A.G.I., Aud. de Charcas 446, Audiencia of Charcas to Crown, 25 July 1792.

presents of the *audiencias*; subdelegates should be appointed by
the *audiencias*, and church patronage should return to viceroys
and presidents.[1]

In July 1792 Villava received an anonymous complaint from
the Indians of certain villages of La Paz against the extortionate
behaviour of priests, subdelegates and the intendant himself.
The fiscal submitted this to the *audiencia*, which decided that
such an opportunity could not be missed, and sent it off to the
viceroy with a few pertinent remarks.[2] At the same time the
audiencia submitted a general criticism of intendant Álvarez. His
temperament was violent, his talents were meagre. His province,
one of the best on the continent, could with proper attention be
made extremely productive, but in fact its subjects suffered from
misgovernment; lacking public security and fair justice, they
lacked confidence in their leaders, while the natives were dis-
gusted to see the resources maladministered. The *audiencia*
doubted whether a decree of the viceroy would be useful, for he
was not so well instructed in this issue as the *audiencia*. The only
effective remedy would be to remove the intendant, and this
would have the support of a discontented public. The *audiencia*
concluded its report in general terms:

The frequent altercations with the intendants and the reports
which we have of their administration have convinced the *audiencia*
that if it is considered advisable to continue this system, then it
would be better to separate the political from the military command
and if this should prove impracticable on account of the heavier cost
to the exchequer in multiplying offices, then the faculties of the
intendants (who, with ecclesiastical patronage also in their possession, consider themselves independent of everyone) should be
curtailed. Moreover, they should be made to appreciate the powers
of the royal *audiencias*, especially in matters of insurrection and
indeed in all priority cases, and they should cause no delay in appeals
to the viceroy. . . .[3]

[1] A.G.I., Aud. de Charcas 446, Villava to marqués de Bajamar, 25 September
1792.
[2] A.G.I., Aud. de Charcas 446, Aud. of Charcas to Crown, 25 September 1792.
[3] A.G.I., Aud. de Charcas 446, Audiencia of Charcas to marqués de Bajamar,
25 September 1792, encl. 1 in Aud. of Charcas to Crown, 25 September 1792.
Relations did not improve and in 1798 the *audiencia* described the intendancy of La
Paz as 'the reef on which our authority has been wrecked'. A.G.I., Aud. de Charcas 446, Aud. of Charcas to Crown, 25 September 1798.

The *audiencia* did not get its way, but two years later it was loudly denouncing despotism in the intendancy of Puno. The intendant there, the marqués de Casa-Hermosa, had taken office in 1790, and had been confronted with a network of corruption in the exchequer. His strenuous efforts to root this out and to improve royal revenue naturally created enemies among those who had profited from the old system.[1] Protests were put out, instigated by his own subdelegates, and denunciations were sent to viceroy Arredondo, accusing Casa-Hermosa of indulging in private commerce, practising forced *repartimientos* on the Indians, imposing arbitrary taxes, and in general of pursuing a policy of extortion and oppression. The viceroy ordered the *audiencia* of Charcas to conduct preliminary inquiries (27 February 1794).[2] The *audiencia* had to admit that there was not enough substantial evidence on every point, but had no hesitation in declaring that everything pointed to the fact that the intendant of Puno was of 'a ruthless, despotic and self-interested character', that his conduct was another confirmation of the absolutism of the intendants and the impotence of the *audiencias*, and that the viceroy ought to proceed against him immediately.[3]

Viceroy Arredondo hesitated to begin extraordinary proceedings against the intendant because of the bad effect they would have on public opinion in such an unstable area, and was inclined to leave judgment to the ordinary process of the *residencia*, especially as Casa-Hermosa's term of office would soon be completed.[4] But a royal order from Madrid ordered an impartial inquiry and relieved Casa-Hermosa of office.[5] Arredondo thereupon appointed Antonio de Villaurrutia, *oidor* of the *audiencia* of Charcas to conduct a secret inquiry. From the

[1] Archivo Histórico Nacional, Madrid, Consejo de Indias, Legajo 20406, pieza 7, fols. 7–30; pieza 8, fols. 2–5; pz. 18, fol. 29. See V. Rodríguez Casado, 'Causa seguida contra el marqués de Casa-Hermosa, gobernador intendente de Puno', *Anuario de Estudios Americanos*, III (1946), pt. ii, pp. 959–60. See above, p. 135.

[2] A.G.I., Aud. de Buenos Aires 80, Arredondo to Llaguno, carta reservada 18, 18 September 1794.

[3] A.G.I., Aud. de Buenos Aires 80, Aud. of Charcas to Arredondo, 25 May 1794, encl. in Arredondo to Llaguno, 18 September 1794. See also A.H.N., Consejo de Indias 20406, pz. 16, fol. 36.

[4] A.G.I., Aud. de Buenos Aires 80, Arredondo to Llaguno, 18 September 1794.

[5] A.G.I., Aud. to Buenos Aires 85, R.O., 19 February 1795.

material thus obtained he decided the case required a formal trial, and the following charges were brought against Casa-Hermosa in 1796: forced *repartimientos*, frequent visits of inspection to Indian *pueblos* at exorbitant costs to the *caciques*, employing Indians and mules of the *caciques* without paying, political nepotism, employment of forced Indian labour on the work of the parish church of Puno, employment of forced Indian labour in the transport of large quantities of wood to Puno by rough and difficult roads for which he paid them no more than 1 real, forcing of the *caciques* of the *partido* of Chucuito to build the town hall at their own expense, appointment of Spanish *alcaldes* in many Indian *pueblos* in order to extract the 12 pesos appointment fee, appointment of inexperienced and incompetent persons to the subdelegacies of Anagro and Carabaya.[1]

As the attorney of Casa-Hermosa pointed out, the number of witnesses supporting these charges was meagre, and most of the charges were made without specifying who was making them.[2] Casa-Hermosa himself pleaded not guilty, and his nephew and representative in Puno, José García y Mesa, forwarded a long and documented testimonial, together with the evidence of witnesses who vouched for the conduct of his uncle, in which each accusation was systematically rebutted; he demanded acquittal and rehabilitation of the accused and punishment of the calumniators.[3] Witnesses for the defence included various subdelegates, the junior *alcaldes* of Puno and Chucuito, exchequer officials, mine owners, merchants and priests.[4] In this war of witnesses Casa-Hermosa put his faith in numbers. He was not disappointed. *Oidor* Villaurrutia gave judgment on 11 September 1798 in Chuquisaca. The accused was acquitted on all major charges, but on some of the minor ones he was given warning that his conduct had been compromising. For this reason he had to pay costs, but it was declared that the minor blemishes ought not to prejudice his future career in government service. In 1800 Casa-Hermosa appealed against the sentence to the Council of the Indies, which confirmed Villaurrutia's judgment,

---

[1] A.H.N., Consejo de Indias 20406, pz. 2, fols. 33v–39, pz. 1, fol. 40.
[2] *Ibid.*, pz. 16, fols. 4v ff.
[3] *Ibid.*, pz. 16, fols. 1–44; pz. 18, fols. 27–47.
[4] *Ibid.*, pz. 2, fols. 24–44, 49–58, 59–77, 78; pz. 5.

but assigned the costs to the accusers, who were also fined 100 pesos each on account of the contradictions in their evidence.[1]

Potosí, La Paz, Puno, all these intendancies had felt the sting of the *audiencia's* hostility. From 1795 the intendant of Cochabamba incurred its displeasure. Arising out of a judgment given in a law suit by the intendant in a *partido* of the intendancy, Villava pointed out that the intendant had no ordinary jurisdiction in the subdelegate districts, for these had their own *justicias mayores* in whom resided entirely the legal jurisdiction for that area without the intervention of any other judge. Consequently in the subdistricts the intendants had supreme power only in the departments of war and finance, and had no power to interfere in matters of ordinary justice even on a visitation.[2] This opinion caused a hot-tempered reaction from intendant Viedma:

This system [of intendancies] has produced the most advantageous results for the state in the course of thirteen years, yet at the moment it has no more dangerous enemies than the very ministers who are supposed to sustain it, that is, those who form the tribunal of the royal *audiencia* of Charcas, and principally your fiscal, Victorián de Villava. Either because they are jealous in seeing the authority they used to exercise in exchequer cases decline, or because they resent the power assigned to the intendants, they have declared, especially the fiscal, the most ruthless and bitter war against them, with the object of suppressing their faculties by depreciating their office and opposing it to the limit.[3]

Viedma appealed to article 8 of the Ordinance of Intendants, which declared that 'the royal jurisdiction must devolve upon the respective intendants as the chief justices (*justicias mayores*) of their provinces', and interpreted the attitude of Villava and the *audiencia* as an 'attack on one of the most fundamental bases of the intendant system, ascribing to the subdelegates the authority of chief justices of their districts and leaving the intendant confined to the narrow precincts of his capital'. He requested a royal *cédula* confirming the intendant's complete jurisdiction and affirming that the subdelegates were not chief justices but

[1] Rodríguez Casado, *op. cit.*, pp. 967–8.
[2] A.G.I., Aud. de Charcas 436, Villava, Vista fiscal, 22 May 1796.
[3] A.G.I., Aud. de Charcas 436, Viedma to Crown, 14 January 1798.

subordinate to the intendants whom they must obey not only in affairs of war and exchequer but also in those of justice and administration.[1]

Nevertheless Villava's was the correct interpretation of the Ordinance, which had in fact made a distinction between the district of the capital and that of the rest of the province.[2] Consequently, when the government confirmed the intendant's judgment in the particular case which had given rise to the dispute, it was careful to point out that in future he had to leave cognizance of cases in the subdistricts to their respective territorial judges.[3]

On many other issues did the *audiencia* harry the intendant of Cochabamba,[4] and after a long series of desultory skirmishes relations between the two completely collapsed in 1801. On 13 July 1801 the bishop of Santa Cruz, Don Manuel Nicolás de Rojas y Argadana, preached a sermon which the subdelegate of the district of Clisa alleged was depreciative of royal government. He collected evidence of those present at the sermon, and forwarded it to the intendant.[5] Viedma accepted this and passed it with his support to the *audiencia* of Charcas, at the same time accusing the bishop of sowing discord and unrest and of failing to give the king due power in the temporal sphere. He requested the *audiencia* to approve the action of the subdelegate and condemn that of the bishop. Another political war thus broke out, in which the bishop ex-communicated the subdelegate and in which the *audiencia* naturally aligned itself with the bishop against the intendant and the subdelegate and procured many witnesses to testify that the words of the bishop, innocent in content and intention, had been completely distorted by the subdelegate.[6] The case called from fiscal Villava a devastating series of *vistas* at the expense of the intendant, all evidently read with relish by an interested public in copies which were

[1] A.G.I., Aud. de Charcas 436, Viedma to Crown, 14 January 1798.

[2] For an explanation of this point, see above p. 82.

[3] A.G.I., Aud. de Charcas 436, Auto del Regente en Real Sala, n.d.

[4] A.G.I., Aud. de Buenos Aires 21, Informe sobre la Audiencia de Charcas y el Gobernador Intendente de Cochabamba, Madrid, 29 August 1804; A.G.I., Aud. de Charcas 436, Informe de Viedma, 23 December 1793; *ibid.*, Villava to Viedma, 8 August 1798, Viedma to Olaguer Feliú, 12 August 1798.

[5] A.G.I., Aud. de Charcas 727, Auto de subdelegado, 19 June 1801.

[6] A.G.I., Aud. de Charcas 728, Expediente 17.

distributed in taverns and other public places.[1] Forays and counter-attacks continued for four years. In 1803 the Council of the Indies approved the action of the subdelegate, and reprimanded the bishop for exceeding his functions in excommunicating a public official.[2] Two years later a royal *cédula* apprehensively ordered an end to this case, and forbade further appeals to the *audiencia* on the matter.[3]

The tension between the *audiencia* and the intendants in Upper Perú can be dated from the very beginning of the intendant system, and continued with increasing momentum and acrimony, extending to every intendancy and over a variety of topics, and often characterized by sheer political opportunism on the part of the *audiencia*. During the régime of fiscal Villava, however, the argument was raised to a higher level, and the intendants had the worst of the matter, for none of them was intellectually equipped to reply in kind to the series of *vistas*, accurate and satirical, issued by Villava. Meanwhile the American public observed and noted. The point of departure in the estrangement between *audiencia* and intendants had been its dispute with its own president from 1783 to 1785. This was also the *terminus ad quem*, for in 1804 a second conflict between the *audiencia* and its president began a dispute which was to culminate in the overthrow of the president in 1809 and was to play an important part in the general struggle for independence in Upper Perú.

After the removal of the creole Flores, the *audiencia* had regarded its presidents with less disfavour, and in 1797 it actually recommended the policy and conduct of president-intendant Joaquín del Pino.[4] But this situation changed with the accession of Ramón García de León y Pizarro, octogenarian and intractable. Hostilities opened in December 1804 over financial policy. Pizarro had assigned funds to combat frontier encroachments by hostile Indians, an action which the *audiencia* opposed. Pizarro, however, persisted, and with the support of the viceroy was able to resist the opposition of the *audiencia*.[5] This incident was

[1] A.G.I., Aud. de Charcas 727, Viedma to Crown, 13 July 1801.
[2] A.G.I., Aud. de Charcas 727, Consulto del Consejo, 16 May 1803.
[3] A.G.I., Aud. de Charcas 727, R.C. 19 March 1805.
[4] A.G.I., Aud. de Charcas 433, Aud. of Charcas to Crown, 25 April 1797.
[5] René-Moreno, *Ultimos días coloniales*, p. 142.

followed by a typical squabble over official protocol, in which the *audiencia* demanded, against custom, that the president should appear with his head uncovered whenever he attended the tribunal. The *audiencia* also lost this argument, and in revenge tried in 1806 to persuade the doctors to declare Pizarro physically unfit for office.[1]

Relations grew even more strained with the arrival in Chuquisaca of a new assessor, Pedro Vicente Cañete. A native of Paraguay and doctor of the University of Santiago de Chile, Cañete was a living example of a creole turned against his past. Thrusting and domineering, with a ready pen and a rich wife, he rose from office to office within the limits of those allowed to creoles, balefully regarding his compatriots and losing no opportunity to show his loyalty to the crown and his penchant for authoritarian government[2]. He eventually became assessor of the intendancy of Potosí, but there his activities aroused so much opposition and he showed so little inclination to take orders from the intendant that in 1803 the viceroy transferred him to Chuquisaca thinking that his conduct would be more prudent if he were situated under the very eyes of the *audiencia*.[3] In Chuquisaca, however, he came to exercise a powerful influence on the aged president, and his capacity for making trouble widened the already considerable division between president and *audiencia*. He began to work upon the wavering character of Pizarro, urging him, no doubt, to take a firm stand against the tribunal, whose power and pretensions he clearly opposed[4] His influence over Pizarro was such that in March 1808, although he was no longer assessor, he was able to persuade the president to reimprison Manuel Sánchez de Velasco, secretary of the *audiencia*, whom the *audiencia* had freed after his arrest by the president on a criminal charge. An exasperated

---

[1] René-Moreno, *op. cit.*, p. 142.

[2] On Cañete see René-Moreno, *op. cit.*, pp. 135–6, and Udaondo, *Diccionario biográfico colonial argentino*, p. 213. Cañete was the author of a lengthy description of Spanish administration in Potosí, recently edited, *Guía histórica, geográfica, física, política, civil y legal del gobierno e intendencia de la provincia de Potosí, 1787* (Potosí, 1952). I have not been able to consult G. Mendoza L., *El doctor don Pedro Vicente Cañete y su historia física y política de Potosí* (Sucre, 1954).

[3] A.G.I., Aud. de Buenos Aires 39, Pino to Soler, 29 August 1803.

[4] René-Moreno, *op. cit.*, pp. 135–6; P. V. Cañete, 'Espectáculo de la verdad', printed in René-Moreno, *op. cit.*, documentos inéditos, pp. cxxxi–clii.

audiencia issued a decree ordering Cañete's removal from Chuquisaca, but the viceroy cancelled this and assured Cañete the right to reside wherever he wished.[1]

But an even more powerful influence on Pizarro was that of the archbishop of La Plata, Don Antonio Moxo. It was in the young archbishop, a vigorous prelate and an extreme loyalist, that the intendant sought the support he could not find in the *audiencia*. At the same time, the opposition and hatred which the archbishop was incurring on account of his reform of the clergy in Cochabamba, Chuquisaca, Potosí and Oruro, had the effect of binding him closer to the president.[2] The *audiencia*, aware of the archbishop's influence, grew doubly suspicious of its president, so that by mid-1808 alignments had hardened and relations between the two sides were extremely tense.

Into this situation arrived news in August and September 1808 of the French invasion of Spain and of the bewildering succession of events which followed it, the fall of Godoy, the abdication of Charles IV, the accession of Ferdinand VII, the abdication of Ferdinand in favour of Napoleon, and the formation of the *Junta* of Seville as the self-constituted repository of the rights of the Spanish dynasty and the independence of the Spanish nation. The *Junta* sought recognition and support from the dominions overseas and sent its representative, José María de Goyeneche, to secure this. Goyeneche's credentials were accepted by viceroy Liniers who recognized the *Junta* and ordered all the provincial governors to send similar assurances of loyalty. Pizarro was inclined to accept the manifesto of the *Junta* and the authority of Goyeneche, but the *audiencia* of Charcas remained sceptical and in *voto consultativo* of 23 September 1808 decided that the papers from Seville did not come in proper legal form and that in default of better credentials than this they ought to proceed according to the royal *cédula* of 10 April 1808 and proclaim Ferdinand VII. President Pizarro subscribed to this vote, but on 25 October issued a decree declaring his consent null and void and ordering entire obedience to the orders of the *Junta* of Seville. This caused another outburst of arguments between president and *audiencia*, the tribunal demanding of the president his superior orders authorizing his actions, and the president

<hr>

[1] *Ibid.*, pp. 142–4.　　　　　　　　　　[2] *Ibid.*, pp. 146–53.

replying that he acted by his own authority in a matter of government proper to his own responsibility and that he also had the authorization of the viceroy to obey completely the *Junta* of Seville.[1]

This refusal of the *audiencia* of Charcas to follow the lead given by Buenos Aires was a characteristic act of political insubordination, accompanied by attempts to spread suspicion of Liniers' loyalty. 'The viceroy, though he is French, cannot be ignorant of the fact that Seville is not the capital of the kingdom,' it remarked, and resisted his order for extraordinary taxation for the emergency on the ground that the community could not afford it.[2] Its reports on Pizarro were becoming almost contemptuous. On 26 October it reported, 'His years, his many years, have already weakened the meagre mind and strength which God gave him.'[3] On the same day Pizarro wrote to Liniers that the members of the *audiencia* were animated by aspirations of independence and despotic ambition, and that they were nurturing a party which would have fatal consequences.[4] Alliances were now extending. While the president and the archbishop had received reinforcements in the persons of Liniers and Goyeneche, the *audiencia* began to give its moral support to the government of Montevideo which had repudiated the authority of viceroy Liniers.[5] The *audiencia* was not motivated by any desire for independence in the sense of American emancipation; neither its record nor its composition permit any such interpretation. What it was really doing was claiming to stand directly for the absent Ferdinand VII, to be sovereign representative and depository of the laws in Upper Perú, while the viceroy and the *audiencia* of Buenos Aires ruled in the eastern provinces.[6] Such an attitude is not surprising in view of its past history, particularly of its reaction to the intendant system; and to profit from the present embarrassment of viceregal government was an irresistible temptation. But opportunism savoured

---

[1] B.N., MS 8299, 'Informe del Consejo de Indias', Madrid, 7 March 1820, fols. 54–58v.

[2] René-Moreno, *op. cit.*, pp. 236–8, and docs. inéds, p. c.

[3] *Ibid.*, p. 251.

[4] R. Levene, 'Intentos de independencia en el virreinato del Plata (1781–1809)', *H.N.A.*, v, 648–9.

[5] See below, pp. 267, 273.   [6] René-Moreno, *op. cit.*, pp. 382–3.

of irresponsibility in this period of profound crisis for the Spanish empire. Before it was attacked from without, Spanish government in Upper Perú had already cracked within.

The power of the *audiencia* of Charcas had been checked not only by the establishment of the intendant system in 1782 but also by the creation of the *audiencia* of Buenos Aires in 1785.[1] The jurisdiction of the new tribunal covered the provinces of Buenos Aires, Paraguay, Tucumán and Cuyo, and on 13 August 1785 it sent *reales provisiones* to the intendants of this district, notifying the inhabitants of the installation of the new court, and informing them that appeals from the intendants were henceforth to be submitted to Buenos Aires and not to Charcas.

From the very first the new *audiencia* acquired prestige and by reason of its judicial integrity came to exercise a strong influence in the government of the viceroyalty, acting as a salutary balance to viceregal authority. Many were the examples of its independence and of its conflicts with the viceroys,[2] while in the last years of Spanish rule it vigorously defended Spanish authority and tried to maintain the declining prestige of the monarchy.

In the formative period of the *audiencia* its fiscal displayed resistance to the provision of the Ordinance of Intendants that the fiscal and two *oidores* should attend meetings of the *junta de real hacienda*, a duty which, he argued, impeded their more immediate occupation, but a royal order forbade further opposition on this point.[3] Later the *audiencia* had misgivings about another aspect of the intendant system. In 1789 the regent of the *audiencia*, Benito de Mata Linares, complained to the authorities in Madrid that in practice the tribunal was unable to take cognizance of imprisonments ordered by intendants, and that this resulted in default of justice, for there were many accused whose cases had been suspended and who were

[1] On the *audiencia* of Buenos Aires see Ruiz Guiñazú, *La magistratura indiana*, pp. 161–242 and Levene, *Historia del derecho argentino*, ii, 387–433.

[2] Levene, 'Historia de la segunda audiencia de Buenos Aires' *Revista de Indias*, vii (Madrid, 1946), pp. 247–51. See also Loreto, 'Memoria de gobierno' in Radaelli (ed.), *Memorias de los virreyes del Río de la Plata*, pp. 288–91.

[3] A.G.I., Aud. de Buenos Aires 310, Marqués de la Plata (fiscal) to Gálvez, 8 October 1784; *ibid.*, R.O., 7 August 1785.

kept in prison without trial.[1] But no action was taken on this matter.

In 1804 intendant Rivera of Paraguay raised an issue of considerable juridical importance with the *audiencia* of Buenos Aires. Under the pre-intendant régime the governors of Paraguay had been a first court of appeal, capable of taking appeals on minor matters from judgments of the *alcaldes*, and without hindrance to a further appeal if necessary to the *audiencia*. This practice had been followed for two and a half centuries in this province and had the sanction of the Laws of the Indies.[2] Since the Ordinance of Intendants and the creation of the *audiencia* of Buenos Aires, however, appeals always went directly to the *audiencia*. Rivera argued that the previous practice had never been legally suspended, and that to reconstitute the intendants of Paraguay as first courts of appeal would certainly not be contrary to the Ordinance of Intendants, as was imagined in Buenos Aires. He maintained that article 14 of the Ordinance declared that appeals should be heard in accordance with the laws of those kingdoms. Article 14, however, declared something quite different: 'Appeals and recourse by litigants from the decisions or sentences of the aforesaid lieutenants as ordinary judges must be heard by the *audiencia* of the districts in accordance with the laws of those kingdoms.' But in spite of his poor arguments, Rivera had a not unreasonable case, for, as he pointed out, the poverty of the majority of the citizens made it impossible for them to take an appeal outside the province, least of all to distant Buenos Aires; and this disability was all the more serious in view of the often unsatisfactory administration of justice by the *alcaldes ordinarios*.[3] On the other hand it could be argued that Buenos Aires was at least nearer than Charcas, and that in the interests of judicial speed and efficiency it was better to reduce to two the magistrates capable of intervening in cases. In any case, although the *audiencia* considered the matter, it never arrived at a decision.[4]

[1] A.G.I., Aud. de Buenos Aires 152, Mata Linares to Porlier, 11 May 1789.

[2] *Recopilación*, v, xii, 27.

[3] A.G.I., Aud. de Buenos Aires 140, Expediente sobre apelaciones, 28 September 1804; Rivera to Caballero, 18 November 1804.

[4] *Cedulario de la Real Audiencia de Buenos Aires*, iii, 303-7. The incident is an interesting hint of Paraguayan separatism.

In general, relations between the intendants and the *audiencia* of Buenos Aires were devoid of that tension and political significance which characterized the relations of the intendants of Upper Perú and the *audiencia* of Charcas. The *audiencia* of Buenos Aires did not have a glorious past to preserve, nor a position to maintain against the intrusions of a modern upstart. Both were newly instituted and grew up together, under closer supervision of viceregal authority than their counterparts in Upper Perú. In his *memoria* to his successor written in 1787 regent Manuel Antonio de Arredondo had nothing significant, still less unfavourable, to report on relations between *audiencia* and intendants.[1] The *memoria* of the second regent, Benito de la Mata Linares (1787–1803), himself a former intendant of Cuzco, reveals conflicts with the viceroys but none with the intendants.

One of the few historians who have hitherto commented on the relations between the *audiencias* and the intendants has suggested that 'the *audiencias* of Buenos Aires and La Plata did not interfere in matters of administration. They only judged appeals that were submitted to them and took charge of such administrative affairs as were entrusted to them'.[2] In view of the evidence now assembled this generalization can no longer be regarded as adequate. The introduction of the intendants had vastly different results in Upper Perú from those which it had in the Río de la Plata, and these served to underline even more strongly the contrast of problems and circumstances between two areas brought forcibly together by the creation of the viceroyalty of the Río de la Plata in 1776.

[1] J. M. Mariluz Urquijo, 'Las memorias de los regentes de la Real Audiencia de Buenos Aires', *Revista del Instituto de Historia del Derecho*, i (Buenos Aires, 1949), pp. 21–2.

[2] Fisher, *Intendant system*, p. 90.

CHAPTER XI

The Intendant and the Revolution

THE intendant régime, although it was designed to provide greater political stability and to assert more definitely royal control over Spain's distant possessions, collapsed in 1810 when the provinces of the Río de la Plata threw off Spanish rule and established their independence. The occasion had little to do with the intendant system as such. American aspirations for independence, based on a triple desire for political freedom, economic autonomy and social equality, would have found expression under the intendant system or under another method of administration. Nevertheless, it was under the intendants that the *cabildos*, the vehicles of the revolution, grew to manhood. At the same time the effect of the intendant system on the traditional structure of Spanish colonial government tended to be disruptive. The struggle of creole against Spaniard was preceded by the struggle of Spaniard against Spaniard. The revolt for independence in the Río de la Plata followed rather than preceded the breakdown of the unity of Spanish colonial government.

During the period of the intendants there were spasmodic premonitions of the approaching storm. To describe these phenomena as 'intentos de independencia'[1] is to distort them out of their true proportion, but they are significant in that they show the temper of the creoles. The rebellion of Tupac Amaru in 1780–1 was simply a native reaction to the abuses of the *repartimiento* system and the oppressive practices of the *corregidores*. But while it bore abundant testimony to Indian discontent, it also showed the reluctance of most of the creoles of Upper Perú

[1] Levene, *La revolución de mayo y Mariano Moreno*, i, 249 ff.

to serve the cause of the crown and the readiness of many of them to exploit native discontent in order to embarrass Spanish administration.[1] The rebellion also had repercussions in Mendoza where certain citizens publicly burned a portrait of Charles III and applauded the victories of the rebel chieftain.[2] The subsequent nervousness of Spanish authorities in Upper Perú testified to the shock which the insurrection had given them. In the province of La Paz intendant Segurola vigorously undertook the task of restoring law and order and continued to pursue the leaders of the rising; as late as January 1784 he arrested nine alleged leaders of the Oruro rebellion.[3] Similar activity occupied Pino Manrique in Potosí.[4]

In May 1784 president-intendant Flores of Chuquisaca warned the viceroy of the disaffection of the creoles of Upper Perú.[5] There was soon to be more concrete evidence of this disaffection. It will be recalled that during the critical days of the Tupac Amaru episode some *mestizos* of Chuquisaca had been armed in a *cuerpo de patricios*.[6] After giving good service they were disbanded and replaced by hated peninsular regulars, the 2nd Battalion Extremadura Regiment. The resentment thus caused and the hatred between the regular troops and the *cholos* of Chuquisaca flared into open discontent in July 1785 when a *mestizo* was murdered by a soldier in a brawl. The *mestizos*, wishing to effect summary justice, rose in protest and occupied the streets of Chuquisaca during 22nd and 23rd July, demonstrating against the troops. Many of the Europeans retired to the safety of their homes, but president-intendant Flores, aided by his assessor and the fiscal of the *audiencia*,

---

[1] A.G.I., Aud. de Buenos Aires 143, Mestre to Gálvez, 24 April 1781. Mestre, governor of Tucumán, here reports on the activities in Jujuy of '. . . un traidor criollo de Santiago llamado Josef Quiroga, que seduciendo la maior parte de la Gente comun de la jurisdiccion logro reducir al se quito de sus maquinas mas de doscientos cristianos criollos, que se pasaron a la Reduccion de Tovas y venciendo la rudeza de los Yndios con artificio les hicieron concevir era tiempo oportuno de desprenderse del Yugo y sugesion de los Españoles y facil destruirlos, y apoderarse de sus familias y Caudales. . . .' On the more general creole indifference see A.G.I., Aud. de Charcas 594, Segurola to Gálvez, 1 July 1781.

[2] Levene, *op. cit.*, i, 250–2.

[3] A.G.I., Aud. de Buenos Aires 68, Vértiz to Gálvez, 4 March 1784.

[4] A.G.I., Aud. de Charcas 435, Pino Manrique to Gálvez, 16 June 1782.

[5] A.G.I., Aud. de Buenos Aires 68, Flores to Loreto, 15 May 1784.

[6] See above, pp. 242–4.

264 THE INTENDANT AND THE REVOLUTION

managed to restore order and tranquillity.[1] But the measures of the creole Flores were suspect by the higher authorities.[2] He reorganized and armed a company of native Americans to patrol the streets and enforce a curfew. Eventually he had to submit to the orders of viceroy Loreto, disband the company and strengthen the garrison in Chuquisaca with additional regular troops from Potosí.[3] Obstructed and denigrated by the *oidores* of the *audiencia*, Flores was well aware that his main crime was that of being a creole and occupying a position of responsibility.[4]

The rising in Chuquisaca, however, was not of political significance. It was not a movement of liberty against colonial oppression: there was no attempt to overthrow the authorities. It was simply a violent expression of the hatred of the *mestizos* for the Europeans, especially for the regular army garrison. Nevertheless, secret inquiries into the incident made by the *audiencia* showed a significant increase of association between the creoles and the *mestizos* in relation to the Spaniards.[5] Although public order was restored, the *cholos* remained vociferous: there was evidence of subversive literature circulating in Chuquisaca,[6] and lampoons against higher officials were posted up in public places. As some of these were written in Latin they must have come from the pens of educated creoles.[7]

Reports of disaffection submitted by the intendants became more frequent, especially after the outbreak of the French Revolution. In 1793 it came to the notice of intendant Sobremonte of Córdoba that a certain José María Caballero, a mining engineer employed at La Carolina, was spreading the

[1] A.G.I., Aud. de Buenos Aires 70, Flores to Loreto, 24 July 1785, encl. 1 in 'Expediente sobre el tumulto acaecido en la Cuidad de la Plata. 22 Julio 1785', fols. 1–7, 7–14.

[2] A.G.I., Aud. de Buenos Aires 70, Loreto to Gálvez, carta reservada 324, 1 September 1785.

[3] A.G.I., Aud. de Buenos Aires 72, Flores to Loreto, 29 August 1785, Exped. Testimonio del 4 Cuerpo, fol. 13.

[4] A.G.I., Aud. de Buenos Aires 69, Flores to Loreto, 15 August 1785, 'Quizá me acusan de que como Criollo amo de este Pueblo, porque en los Acuerdos hé propendido a la union de los Veteranos con el . . .'

[5] See René-Moreno, *Ultimos días coloniales en el Alto Perú*, pp. 57–8 and n. 1.

[6] A.G.I., Aud. de Buenos Aires 72, Exped. Testimonio del 3 Cuerpo . . . con motivo del Tumulto en la ciudad de la Plata, fols. 1–2, 86.

[7] René-Moreno, *op. cit.*, p. 59.

ideas of the French Revolution and comparing the Spanish government unfavourably with that of the French. Sobremonte ordered a secret inquiry, whereupon Caballero was arrested and transferred to Córdoba. He denied the charges, but was remitted to Buenos Aires, where the case lapsed.[1]

Literature on events in France was also being spread in the intendancy of La Paz, an area which constituted a continual anxiety to the Spanish authorities by reason of its native discontent. Now, in 1794, there were widespread signs of antipathy to Spanish rule, lampoons posted up in the capital, threats of rebellion noised abroad, a priest in Puno advocating the extension of French revolutionary principles to Spain.[2] La Paz suffered also from lack of permanency in its rulers, and at this moment the absence of the intendant increased the danger, for the temporary officials squabbled over jurisdiction.[3]

From Cochabamba intendant Viedma reported to the viceroy that rumours of a proximate Indian rebellion were circulating from Sicasica and Mohaza in the province of La Paz. Seditious posters against Europeans had been fixed in the main square and on the doors of the subtreasury in Cochabamba, symptoms which he thought were dangerous enough to warrant his preparing arms and supplies of gunpowder, for he feared that the ideas of the French Revolution had enthusiastic followers in the provinces of Upper Perú.[4]

Faced with these indications of unrest, Spanish authorities in Upper Perú were also distracted by internal conflicts of their own which, as has been seen, took the form of a cold war between the intendants and the *audiencia* of Charcas, and which reached their climax in the tension between the *audiencia* and its

---

[1] See P. Grenon, S.J., 'Un mineralogista afrancesado', *B.I.I.H.*, vii (1928), pp. 33–46. Two years later Sobremonte was complaining that the viceroy was not pursuing the matter. A.G.I., Estado 81, Sobremonte to the duque de la Alcudín, 16 February 1795.

[2] A.G.I., Estado 80, Arredondo to conde del Campo de Alange, 19 February 1795. There is an example of a lampoon acclaiming the news from France enclosed in Mosquera to conde del Campo de Alange (Minister of Grace and Justice), 8 April 1795. A.G.I., Aud. de Charcas 589.

[3] A.G.I., Estado 80, Arredondo to conde del Campo de Alange, Carta 604, 26 February 1795.

[4] Viedma to Arredondo, 17 February 1795, in R. R. Caillet-Bois, *Ensayo sobre el Río de la Plata y la revolución francesa* (Buenos Aires, 1929), pp. cxvi–cxx.

own president-intendant in 1808. These conflicts were to grow even worse, and it seemed unlikely that the brittle state of Spanish administration would withstand any serious shocks. Yet it did withstand the effects of the short-lived British capture of Buenos Aires in June 1806. The flight of viceroy Sobremonte and his subsequent deposition by the *cabildo* and *audiencia* of Buenos Aires left the latter as the depositary of royal authority. Writing on behalf of his colleagues, the other intendants of Upper Perú, intendant Sanz of Potosí deplored the unconstitutional deposition of the viceroy but admitted that it was better to obey the *audiencia* of Buenos Aires than to obey nothing:

> I have had the satisfaction of seeing that the chiefs of these intendancies, and even the royal *audencia* of this district, have coincided with my own way of thinking and agreed in accepting the unity of command of the *audiencia* which we ought to preserve, in not making the slightest alteration in our respective provinces, and in assisting Buenos Aires with all possible aid.[1]

A second British expedition was defeated in July 1807 and left in September. Viceregal government was restored in the person of Santiago Liniers, the hero of the reconquest. Soon, however, the intendants were to be put to an even greater test as news of unbelievable events in Spain reached the viceroyalty. In March 1808 Charles IV abdicated in favour of his son Ferdinand. This was rapidly followed by the French occupation of Madrid, the departure of both Charles and Ferdinand to Bayonne where Napoleon persuaded them to renounce their rights, and by the proclamation of Joseph Bonaparte as king of Spain and the Indies. The news reached Buenos Aires in July 1808, and on 17 August viceroy Liniers wrote to all the intendants, informing them of events in Spain and warning them to be prepared to defend legitimate authority and preserve the possessions of the Spanish monarchy, political solidarity, and adherence to the leadership of Buenos Aires.[2] The intendant of Córdoba soon reported that he had proclaimed Ferdinand VII legitimate king with all possible solemnity and that the *cabildo* recognized the like allegiance; the district, he believed, was

[1] A.G.I., Aud. de Charcas 441, Sanz to Soler, 24 April 1807.

[2] B.M., Add. MS 32,608, fols. 32–5, Liniers to the intendants of Córdoba, Salta, Potosí, Cochabamba, La Paz, La Plata and Paraguay, 17 August 1808.

similarly loyal.[1] The intendant of Paraguay reported 'the honourable fidelity and love of the King' displayed by the citizens and affirmed agreement with the objects of the viceroy; Buenos Aires he described as 'the focal point of the defence and security of all the provinces of the Río de la Plata'.[2] From Potosí intendant Sanz described the indignation with which the news from Spain had been received by the citizens and their undoubted allegiance to Ferdinand VII; he had summoned the *cabildo* and it had taken the oath of allegiance.[3]

These examples were typical of the official reaction to the news from Spain. The provinces in the persons of the intendants loyally proclaimed Ferdinand, while the intendants remained faithful to viceregal authority and leadership. But it was soon evident that such an attitude was unreal. Ferdinand was in custody and did not in fact rule in Spain. How then could he rule in America? The so-called 'Junta Central' now governed in his name, though by what legal right and with what popular support was doubtful. In Buenos Aires alignments were still uncertain. On 21 September 1808 Montevideo under its governor Elío repudiated the authority of viceroy Liniers and established, in the name of Ferdinand VII, a governing *junta* of its own. On 1 January 1809, however, a Spanish attempt, led by Martín de Alzaga, a prominent merchant and influential magistrate, to depose viceroy Liniers and replace him by a similar *junta* in Buenos Aires was defeated by creole support of Liniers.[4] This incident followed the pattern of events in Upper Perú; at a critical stage Spanish unity broke and creoles witnessed Spaniard struggling against Spaniard for political power. Alzaga and the *cabildo* acted not only against Liniers—it was useless to pretend he was anything but loyal—but also against the judges of the *audiencia* and the assessor of the viceroyalty. It was an attack by an aspirant to political power against the actual possessors of power. The *cabildo* did not have the political power commensurate with its economic strength and social influence; it was not inclined to pay a secondary rôle in politics. In this domestic

---

[1] *Ibid.*, fols. 45–6, Gutiérrez de la Concha to Liniers, 26 August 1808.
[2] *Ibid.*, fol. 47, Manuel Gutiérrez to Liniers, 18 September 1808.
[3] *Ibid.*, fols. 48–52, Sanz to Liniers, 27 September 1808.
[4] See Levene, *La revolución de mayo*, i, 124–52. Alzaga was exiled.

quarrel there were strange allies: Liniers was defended by creole troops, while his party received the support of such intransigent representatives of colonial authority as intendant Gutiérrez de la Concha of Córdoba and intendant Sanz of Potosí, who deplored the bad example set by the *cabildo* in thus embarrassing the supreme authorities.

Sanz, however, was in no position to preach to Buenos Aires, for the supreme authorities in Upper Perú had long been maligning each other. There, alignments were more definite and the struggle for power more determined. When Goyeneche, the agent of the *Junta* of Seville, reached Chuquisaca in November 1808 he was received with confidence by his supporters, intendant Pizarro and archbishop Moxo. With the assistance of Pizarro he had already arranged for the meeting of a *junta* made up of the *audiencia*, the archbishop and representatives of the *cabildo*, to which he would present the case of the *Junta* of Seville. At first the *audiencia* had resisted such an arrangement, but finally agreed. At the meeting of the *junta* Goyeneche spoke on behalf of the *Junta* of Seville, declaring that if the *audiencia* refused to recognize the latter he had authority to arrest dissident ministers and send them to Buenos Aires.[1] The *audiencia* naturally reacted with hostility to this clumsy threat, which immediately gave it a superior moral position. This position was strengthened when it became known that in addition to representing the claims of the *Junta* of Seville, Goyeneche was also the bearer of letters which were fundamentally subversive. These came from Princess Carlota, daughter of Charles IV and wife of the Prince Regent of Portugal, who had fled before Napoleon's invasion of the peninsula and set up court in Brazil in March 1808. From Rio de Janeiro Carlota broadcast her claims to represent the Spanish royal house, overthrown by Napoleon. Already in August her foreign minister, Souza e Coutinho had approached the intendants of the viceroyalty of the Río de la Plata.[2] Now Goyeneche personally brought dis-

---

[1] René-Moreno, *Ultimos días coloniales en el Alto Perú*, pp. 447–51.

[2] B.M., Add. MS 32,608, fol. 81, Souza e Coutinho to Sanz, 24 August 1808. Sanz remitted this letter to the viceroy as the only true representative of the sovereign. See *ibid.*, fols. 78–80, Sanz to Liniers, 27 January 1809. Intendant Gutiérrez de la Concha of Córdoba did likewise. See Add. MS 32,609, fols. 61–2, Gutiérrez de la Concha to Liniers, 15 January 1809.

patches from Carlota in which she offered to take the four intendancies of Upper Perú under her protection. The *junta* in Chuquisaca did no more than agree to recognize the *Junta* of Seville as the representative of Ferdinand VII,[1] but the *audiencia* made the most of the duplicity of Goyeneche to embarrass the intendant and his supporters still further. It claimed that Goyeneche counted on the full support of Pizarro and Moxo, as well as on that of the intendant and the bishop of La Paz, all of whom, it alleged, were working for Carlota and deferring to the principles expressed in the manifesto of the court of Brazil. In this way the *audiencia* was able to profit from the ambiguous attitude of the intendant and pose as the only authentic defender of the just rights of the Spanish crown. At the same time the tribunal worked to split the ranks of the intendants of Upper Perú: in March 1809 while continuing to denounce the conduct of Pizarro, it commended the vigorous loyal attitude of the intendants of Potosí and Cochabamba in rejecting the proposals of Carlota, and interpreted the silence of the intendant of La Paz as one of loyalty.[2] Meanwhile rumours concerning the intentions of Pizarro became worse, and it was popularly believed that he held prisoners in his house. Similarly the sudden death of the regent of the *audiencia* was attributed to his opposition to the intendant and the archbishop.[3] The tribunal pursued Pizarro ruthlessly: it received a statement from twenty-four witnesses declaring that the president had received more secret information against the ministers of the *audiencia* and various members of the *cabildo*, branding them as traitors against the Princess of Brazil and viceroy Liniers.[4] Popular imagination was further stimulated by the dramatic appearance in Chuquisaca of intendant Sanz of Potosí who arrived secretly at the archiepiscopal palace one night. It was commonly believed that he had come to treat with the president and the archbishop for the implementation of their policy.[5]

[1] B.N., MS 8299, fols. 71v–73v, Informe del Consejo de Indias, Madrid, 7 March 1820.
[2] 'Vista reservada del fiscal de la Audiencia de Charcas sobre el oficio y manifiestos de la corte del Brasil,' 6 March 1809, in René-Moreno, *op. cit.*, documentos inéditos, pp. cv–cxx.
[3] B.N., MS 8299, fols. 73v–74.
[4] *Ibid.*, fols. 81–3.   [5] *Ibid.*, fol. 84.

At this stage the viceroy tried to bring the situation in Chuquisaca under control. On 6 May he ordered Sanz to investigate events there and to inquire into the spread of seditious ideas; he was to discover especially if the fiscal of the *audiencia* was implicated and if so to expel him and any other suspects to Cochabamba. Sanz himself was to remain in La Plata until tranquillity had been restored.[1] But the order was too late to keep pace with events in Chuquisaca. Pizarro was finally stung into action when the fiscal of the *audiencia* declared that for the public good the president-intendant should leave office and depart from Charcas. Pizarro's reply was to order the imprisonment of the fiscal and of five other ministers. This order was to have been executed on the night of 25 May, but like most of Pizarro's measures it was mishandled; only one *oidor* was apprehended. Immediately there was a rush of people to the *intendencia* shouting for the release of the prisoners. They procured the release of the solitary prisoner and went on to demand the surrender of arms. On 26 May the troops were disarmed and on 27th Pizarro was arrested and imprisoned by the *audiencia*.[2] Meanwhile the news that the intendant of Potosí was approaching Charcas with armed forces to help the president convinced people in Chuquisaca that this must have been a premeditated plan, already operating before the events of the 25th and 26th, and they prepared to meet and oppose Sanz. The *audiencia* persuaded Sanz to leave his troops outside and enter the city alone. This he did. He denied any superior order for his coming and maintained that he acted simply on the invitation of Pizarro. By now the *audiencia* was in complete command of the situation in Chuquisaca, and managed to persuade Sanz to withdraw. The tribunal assumed all the functions of government.

The new viceroy, Baltasar Hidalgo de Cisneros, who had replaced Liniers, preoccupied with worries of his own in Buenos Aires and lacking effective resources to do anything in Upper

[1] B.M., Add. MS 32,609, fols. 137–8, Liniers to Cornel, 6 May 1809.
[2] V. Rodríguez Casado y J. A. Calderón Quijano, eds. *Memoria de gobierno del virrey Abascal*, 1816 (2 vols., Sevilla, 1944), ii, 60–1. The viceroy of Buenos Aires described the rising as one of 'bajo pueblo' who deposed the president and declared the *audiencia* the government. B.M., Add. MS 32,609, fols. 144–51, Liniers to Cornel, 25 June 1809.

THE INTENDANT AND THE REVOLUTION

Perú, confirmed the *audiencia* of Charcas for the moment in its functions of government and enjoined it to take measures to restore public order. At the same time he advised the intendants of Upper Perú to obey the orders of the *audiencia* in so far as they did not conflict with the superior orders of the viceroy.[1] As his colleague in Lima pointed out, 'necessity, not choice, dictated this order of the viceroy. . . .'[2] Already on 16 July, the day before the viceroy dictated these orders, the disorder had spread from Chuquisaca to La Paz. There was this difference, however, between the two movements: the incident in Chuquisaca was essentially a domestic struggle between rival institutions and factions of Spaniards disputing for power in the vacuum created by the deposition of the monarchy; the rising in La Paz, on the other hand, was genuinely creole both in personnel and in intent.

La Paz had been in a state of unrest since 1805, and more particularly since February 1809. When news arrived of the measures taken by the viceroy against Alzaga in Buenos Aires there were demonstrations in the streets against Liniers; it was asserted that the viceroy had no right to banish Alzaga, and that the latter had more than sufficient motives for trying to establish a *junta*.[3] In March the intendant reported that the *cabildo* had been occupied in secret nocturnal sessions.[4] Simultaneously the Spanish authorities started squabbling among themselves. Dávila, the temporary intendant, and the bishop of La Paz accused the visitor of the exchequer in La Paz, Josef González de Prada, of engaging in subversive activities and of planning (in conjunction with certain members of the *cabildo*) to remove Dávila from the intendancy and substitute himself.[5] These assertions need not be taken at their face value: it was probable that Dávila was trying to hide financial mismanagement or even peculation and resented the probing of González.[6]

[1] M. Pinto, *La revolución de la intendencia de La Paz en el virreinato del Río de la Plata, con la occurrencia de Chuquisaca 1800–1810*, p. 186. See also B.M., Add. MS 32,609, fols. 153–4, Cisneros to Cornel, 22 August 1809.

[2] *Memoria de gobierno*, ii, 69.

[3] B.N., MS 13150, fol. 1, Francisco de la Torres to Liniers, 16 February 1809.

[4] *Ibid.*, fol. 2v, Dávila to Liniers, 17 March 1809.

[5] *Ibid.*, fol. 5, Bishop of La Paz to Dávila, 27 October 1808; fol. 6, Dávila to Liniers, 17 November 1808; fol. 9, Bishop of La Paz to Liniers, 16 November 1808.

[6] See above, pp. 141–2.

The latter denied the charges and claimed that they arose out of personal malice.[1] But the incident is significant as yet another example of a split in administration at a critical juncture. After the events of 25–26 May in Chuquisaca the creole conspirators came out into the open. Under the direction of a *mestizo* soldier, Pedro Domingo Murillo, the commandant of the fort, the revolutionaries deposed the intendant and the bishop, and the *cabildo* took charge of the government. Later it constituted itself as a *junta*, under the presidency of Murillo. A 'plan of government' was drawn up, and on 27 July the *junta* issued a proclamation asserting 'Now is the time to organize a new system of government, founded upon the interests of our country which is downtrodden by the bastard policy of Madrid. . . . Now is the time, in short, to raise the standard of liberty in these unfortunate colonies. . . .'[2] The insurgents tried to clothe the action of revolt in loyal terms. On 16 September the *cabildo* wrote to the viceroy affirming their loyalty to him and to Ferdinand VII, and assuring him of the continuation of municipal government.[3] Murillo himself reported to Cisneros that he was maintaining the city and the province in subordination to legitimate authorities, while Dávila, whom he described as the instigator of 16 July, had fled to Puno, where he was stirring up trouble among the natives.[4] Finally the *cabildo* of La Paz, calling itself a representative *junta*, initiated proceedings against intendant Dávila and the bishop of La Paz before the *audiencia* of Charcas in order to clarify the events of 16 July and to affirm its loyalty. But this manoeuvre made little progress, nor did the representations deceive anyone in Buenos Aires. As the insurgents had sent emissaries to other provinces, to Potosí, Charcas and Cochabamba, the viceroy instructed intendant Sanz to take measures to stop the insurrection spreading to other parts of Upper Perú. He appointed Antonio Álvarez de Soto Mayor intendant

[1] B.N., MS 13150, fols. 12–15, 16 February 1809.
[2] Levene, *Revolución de mayo*, i, 354.
[3] B.N., MS 13150, fols. 21–2, Cabildo of La Paz to Cisneros, 16 September 1809.
[4] *Ibid.*, fol. 24, Murillo to Cisneros, 16 September 1809.
[5] *Ibid.*, fols. 26–30, Gutiérrez de la Concha to Cisneros, 2 October 1809. The tension can be gauged from the fact that when the authorities in Cochabamba apprehended the agent of the *junta* of La Paz, one Francisco Xavier Patiño, an ex-religious, they were afraid to prosecute him there on account of the evidence of so much sympathy, and the captive was sent to Córdoba. See *ibid.*

of La Paz, transferring him from the governorship of Chiquitos. Meanwhile he advised the *cabildo* of La Paz to maintain government until the arrival of Soto Mayor and to restore the ministers whom they had deposed.[1]

But this mild policy of temporization was simply a cloak for more violent action. On 10 September Cisneros appointed a new president-intendant of Charcas, General Vicente Nieto, on whom he also conferred the military command of the provinces of the interior, with orders to free Pizarro and to restore harmony between Sanz and the *audiencia*.[2] The viceroy of Perú sent an army of 5,000 strong under Goyeneche against the insurgents of La Paz; the two-pronged attack did all that was expected of it. Goyeneche overthrew the *junta* of La Paz by 25 October and pursued the revolutionaries with relentless brutality; Murillo and his companions were put to death without mercy. Nieto, with an army of 1,000, was able to take over his office in Chuquisaca without any opposition and found that Pizarro had already been released. Nevertheless he also took repressive action; five ministers of the *audiencia* and some *cabildo* members, were arrested, their property was confiscated and they themselves were exiled.

The cracks in Spanish government were too deep to be repaired by such measures as these. Repression was temporarily successful in stifling the revolution in La Paz simply because the movement there was local and isolated and drew no strength from a central source or organization. The dissident party in Chuquisaca saw its affinity with the movement in Montevideo and attempted to establish contact with the *junta* there; the *cabildo* of Chuquisaca wrote to Elío on 10 August 1809 requesting his support against Sanz, and in October the *oidores* of the *audiencia* were corresponding with him.[3] But this interesting phenomenon had no practical effects. The revolution of 1809 in Chuquisaca was indeterminate in character: neither completely Spanish nor genuinely creole, it also died in isolation.

[1] B.M., Add. MS 32,609, fols. 157–60, Cisneros to Cornel, 22 August 1809.

[2] Cisneros admitted that he could not restore Pizarro because of the latter's unpopularity in the province. B.M., Add. MS 32,609, fols. 153–5, Cisneros to Cornel, 22 August 1809.

[3] A.G.I., Aud. de Buenos Aires 40, Josef Agustín de Ossoz to Elío, 26 October 1809.

In Buenos Aires, however, men knew what they wanted, and it was from the capital that events were to be dictated. Already before the final disastrous news from Spain arrived, the spirit of revolution had been infused and its methods organized: 'in Buenos Aires, in the early months of 1810, the revolution was already accomplished in the minds and hearts of the creole leaders.'[1] Viceroy Cisneros was aware of the revolutionary temper and felt the approaching storm. In a circular letter sent to all the intendants on 27 April 1810 he exhorted them to co-operate with him in preserving that part of the state for which they were responsible in public order and royal allegiance.[2] Soon, however, communications between the viceroy and the intendants were to be cut. On 18 May news from Spain was published in Buenos Aires: in January Seville had been occupied by the French army, the Central *Junta* which had already fled from Madrid to Seville had now fled from Seville to Cádiz where it dissolved, arranging for a regency to be established in its place. This information was the cue for action. On 25 May, after some opposition from the *cabildo*, the leading creole patriots established a patriot *junta*, with Cornelio Saavedra as its president, Manuel Belgrano and Juan José Castelli among its members, and Mariano Moreno one of its two secretaries.[3] The revolutionaries lacked a convincing political theory. It is true that Castelli argued that sovereign power had disappeared in Spain and had now reverted to the people who could use it to establish their own government, but the *junta* also paid lip service to the sovereignty of Ferdinand VII,[4] just as the insurgents in La Paz had done. The strength of the movement lay not in theory but in action. The leaders tried to preserve a façade of legality, but in fact they were declaring nothing less than independence. Acting as a sovereign body, the *junta* banished the viceroy and the *audiencia* and removed Spanish officials. It sent notes to the intendants and the *cabildos* of the interior inviting them to send deputies to a general assembly which was to meet in Buenos Aires. But the cloven

---

[1] R. A. Humphreys, *Liberation in South America, 1806–1827. The career of James Paroissien* (London, 1952), p. 43.

[2] Levene, *Revolución de mayo*, ii, 24.

[3] *Ibid.*, 55–72.   [4] Humphreys, *op. cit.*, pp. 46–7.

hoof soon appeared. With the exception of the viceroy, the colonial administrative framework still existed. The members had been deprived of their head but they still reacted automatically against the revolution: the intendants remained staunch royalists and prepared to defend traditional authority. The *cabildos* were uncertain, wavering now one way now the other, though it was well known that most of them had been at odds with their intendants for some years past. One thing was certain, however, the *junta* would have to use force to extend the revolution. In Buenos Aires an expeditionary force was prepared in order to carry the revolution to the interior and to assert the authority of the *junta* by force over the whole of the viceroyalty.

It looked as though this would soon be needed. Montevideo, already in schism, rejected the claims of the *junta* of Buenos Aires and recognized the recently established Council of Regency in Spain. Paraguay followed a similar path. It is true that revolutionary propaganda had already been circulating in Paraguay since 1809, and that intendant Velazco had had to take measures to discover and prevent the spread of subversive literature in cafés and other public places of Asunción.[1] Nevertheless in the hour of decision the intendant was able to exploit the traditional localism and the resentment felt in Paraguay towards the political and economic pretensions of Buenos Aires. In *cabildo* of 26 June he summoned a general assembly of prominent citizens to decide upon the relations to be maintained with the *junta* of Buenos Aires. This was held on 24 July and was attended by about 200 citizens. Under the direction of Velazco it was decided to swear obedience to the Council of Regency in Spain, to maintain fraternity with Buenos Aires but without recognizing its superiority, and to form a *junta* of war for the defence of Paraguay.[2] Velazco began to take practical measures for the maintenance of loyalty and for the defence of Paraguay. An expedition sent by the *junta* of Buenos Aires was defeated in 1811 and Paraguay asserted its independence of Buenos Aires on 14 May 1811; it also severed its last connections with the old régime when it deposed Velazco on 9 June and thus put an end

[1] J. C. Chaves, *Historia de las relaciones entre Buenos-Ayres y el Paraguay, 1810–1813* (Buenos Aires, 1938), p. 12.
[2] *Ibid.*, p. 44.

to the royalist movement he was organizing with the conni-
vance of the Portuguese authorities in Brazil.[1]

Córdoba also presented its difficulties. The first message of the
junta had reached the intendant and *cabildo* on 4 June. Intendant
Gutiérrez de la Concha decided not to recognize the claims of
the *junta*, but the cabildo debated the question in the greatest
uncertainty.[2] The intendant presided as usual over the sessions,
but watched the manoeuvrings of the councillors without offering a word. There was a division of opinion in the *cabildo* over
the status of the *junta* and some suspicion of its intentions,
especially of its decision to send troops.[3] By 15 June the *cabildo*
had still not replied to the *junta*, and still the intendant was
silent. The latter, however, was temporizing and reserving his
hand. With Santiago Liniers, the former viceroy, and the bishop
of Córdoba, he was attempting to organize resistance. This
royalist faction counted on adherents throughout the whole of
the interior, and the intendant was assured of co-operation in
Mendoza. He was also in touch with intendant Sanz of Potosí
and president-intendant Nieto of Chuquisaca, arranging for
royalist expeditions to leave Potosí and Chuquisaca and to
assemble at Jujuy for the defence of the province against the
junta and the overthrow of the revolution. Agents of the *junta*
intercepted all the correspondence so that the intentions of the
royalists were fully known in Buenos Aires.[4] The arrival of the
expeditionary force sent by the *junta* ended all resistance in
Córdoba before the royalists had been able to harness their
resources. On 28 July intendant Gutiérrez de la Concha
announced by letter to the *cabildo* his departure for Upper Perú
with royalist troops. He did not get very far. He was captured
and, by orders of the *junta*, shot on 26 August 1810. On 3
August the *junta* appointed Juan Martín de Pueyrredon intendant of Córdoba, and on 15 August the *cabildo* received him in

[1] Chaves, *op. cit.*, pp. 114–17.

[2] See Levene, *Revolución de mayo*, ii, 113. The *cabildos* of Mendoza and San Luis
opted for the *junta*; that of La Rioja preserved a discreet silence, while San Juan
decided to recognize the Council of Regency. See *ibid.*, ii, 116–18. The *cabildo* of
Concepción del Río Cuarto supported the *junta*. See *Actas Capitulares*, 11 August
1810, pp. 358–9.

[3] Garzon, *Crónica de Córdoba*, pp. 120–1.

[4] R. R. Caillet-Bois, 'La revolución en el virreinato', in *H.N.A.*, v, ii, 160–2.

office.[1] With this appointment royal government ceased in Córdoba.

In Salta both the *cabildo* and the intendant, Isasmendi, recognized the *junta*. Isasmendi, however, was simply waiting to see which way the cat would jump, and the *cabildo*, suspecting him of playing a double game, managed to get him replaced by an appointee of the *junta*. Isasmendi was sent to Buenos Aires but he suffered nothing worse than exile.[2] The revolution was accomplished without difficulty in Salta, and Tucumán and Santiago del Estero soon followed suit.[3]

The expedition proceeded to Upper Perú. There, the intendants had longer warning of the intentions of the *junta* and of the progress of the liberating army. But they did not profit from this knowledge. By 20 June news of the events in Buenos Aires had reached Nieto in Chuquisaca. He immediately summoned a congress, to which he invited the intendants of Upper Perú to send deputies, in order to work out a common policy. But only Sanz sent a deputy. The congress consisted of two *oidores* of the *audiencia*, the archbishop of Charcas, representatives of the clergy, two *alcaldes* representing the *cabildo*, and the deputy from Potosí; under the presidency of Nieto it analysed the situation and decided to place the four provinces of Upper Perú under the orders of the viceroy of Lima.[4] Nieto and Sanz then set about uniting their military strength, gathering arms and concentrating forces in Potosí, the obvious target for any attack on Upper Perú. In July Nieto discovered and quashed an attempted insurrection in Chuquisaca.[5] But it was otherwise in Cochabamba; in Cochabamba intendant Gonzáles de Prada supported Nieto and Sanz in opposition to the revolution, but the temper of the town was such that he had to resign on 16 September. On 23 September Cochabamba officially recognized the *junta* of Buenos Aires.[6] This was a serious strategic blow to the royalists, for it meant that the communications of Chuquisaca and Potosí with La Paz and Upper Perú were less secure. The royalists were also having their own domestic

[1] Garzon, *op. cit.*, pp. 124, 128–9.
[2] See Levene, *Revolución de mayo*, ii, 118–19, 121.
[3] *Ibid.*, ii, 119–20.   [4] Caillet-Bois, *H.N.A.*, v, ii, 224.
[5] *Ibid.*, p. 226.   [6] *Ibid.*, p. 231.

troubles. Nieto showed little military ability; moreover he did not work in entire accord with intendant Sanz whom he considered a mere civilian, while his relations with the viceroy of Perú were not harmonious.[1] The decisive blow came on 7 November when the liberating army defeated a royalist force at Suipacha, a victory which was to open the gates of Potosí to the revolution. Intendant Sanz summoned a *junta* on 10 November and decided that the government should remain in his hands and those of the *cabildo*. The reply of the creoles was to arrest him and free the political prisoners. On 25 November the expeditionary force entered Potosí, and on 15 December intendant Sanz was shot by order of Castelli, high commissioner of the *junta* of Buenos Aires. With him also fell Nieto. The *junta* now appointed its own president of Charcas, Juan Martín de Pueyrredon, whom it transferred from Córdoba.[2] La Paz, still reeling under the effect of Goyeneche's rule of terror, waited until the victory of Suipacha before committing itself definitely to the cause of the revolution; then, on 16 November, in the absence of the intendant, a *cabildo abierto* declared itself for the *junta* of Buenos Aires.[3]

Although the intendant régime in Upper Perú thus collapsed in 1810, the area was not yet won to the revolution, and was never to be secured to the provinces of the Río de la Plata. It remained for many years a battlefield, on which royalist and revolutionary forces struggled for control.

---

[1] *Memoria de gobierno del virrey Abascal*, ii, 313–35.
[2] Caillet-Bois, *H.N.A.*, v, ii, 218–28.　　　　　[3] *Ibid.*, v, ii, 235–6.

CHAPTER XII

Conclusion

SPANISH colonial administration had a capacity for self-criticism and adjustment to circumstances which long periods of lethargy and disillusionment could never completely dispel. The vociferous debates and the generous legislation on the problems of labour and race relations in the sixteenth century are possibly the best examples of a readiness to hear complaints and react to pressure which is not usually associated with Spanish government. Although Spain never again experienced the creative impulse which was her glory in the sixteenth century, this tradition was handed on and managed to survive the dark night of stagnation and decay through which she passed under the later Habsburgs. When a new dynasty awakened new aspirations administrators once again emerged who were ready to say what they thought and promote what they desired. Spanish colonial officials were never slow to complain and denounce. Government insistence on frequent reports, the natural litigiousness of many Spaniards, and the spirit of rivalry which animated the various parts of the colonial service, all combined to remove any false façade of harmony and co-operation and to show up the cracks in the overseas administration. Unfortunately this penchant for plain-speaking and this jealousy of neighbouring jurisdictions, while they encouraged a healthy airing of grievances, could also degenerate into noisy and personal squabbles between officials who were often concerned to criticize rather than to construct. The intendant system, which was itself the fruit of official uneasiness, discussion and investigation in the best tradition of the Spanish service, also provoked hostility and inevitably came under fire from those elements in the colonial administration which resented any change in the established order.

The heaviest, and possibly least accurate, rounds were fired in 1789 by viceroy Croix of Perú, who attacked the new régime in a long and highly confusing report.[1] The power and prestige of the viceroy, he argued, had fallen considerably, for an intendant was virtually a viceroy in his own province. Upstarts in the State, the new officials were equally objectionable to the Church; they conflicted with the bishops who resented the exercise of the royal patronage by men ill-fitted to its possession but influential enough to attract the interest of the clergy. In their own special functions, on the other hand, the intendants had failed to justify themselves; it was their duty to promote agriculture, commerce, industry and mining, but not the slightest progress had been made in any of these fields. Nor had the intendants improved the administration of justice in Perú; people still preferred to appeal their cases before the *audiencia*, in spite of the delay, while in the Indian towns most of the cases were petty affairs with which the Indian *alcaldes* were quite capable of dealing. The new officials, it was alleged, entertained more appeals from the *alcaldes ordinarios* than the law permitted, and when the *audiencia* of Lima ordered them to desist they evaded the commands by calling the appeals complaints and resolving them as such. Any improvement in the royal revenue came not from better financial administration on the part of the intendants but from the new system of double-entry book-keeping. Finally, Croix asserted, the intendants' overbearing attitude towards the *cabildos* had completely alienated these bodies.

The monotonous hostility of the report invites scepticism as to its impartiality, while the confusion of its author's thought can be seen in his naïve suggestion that the *corregidores*, by whom he would replace the intendants, should be given the Ordinance of Intendants as their rule. Croix belonged to the old régime of Spanish administration which resented new forms, particularly if they involved any limitation upon its established supremacy. His criticism of the intendant system was, moreover, part of his general reaction to the reforms of Charles III, for he also

[1] A.G.I., Indif. General 1714, Croix to Valdés, 16 May 1789; summarized in Fisher, *Intendant system*, pp. 84–9. See also Luis Santiago Sanz, 'El proyecto de extinción del régimen de las intendencias de América y la Ordenanza General de 1803', *Revista del Instituto de Historia del Derecho*, no. 5 (Buenos Aires, 1953), pp. 142–185.

advocated the suppression of the new viceroyalty of the Río de la Plata, whose existence lowered the status and prestige long enjoyed by Lima. Nevertheless, the complaints of Croix, later reiterated by his successor, viceroy Gil, went before the Council of the Indies; and the latter now began to seek further opinions, thus opening a debate which continued throughout the 1790's.

This provided an opportunity for more balanced counsels to be heard. In the new viceroyalty the intendant system was accepted and welcomed. The provinces of the Río de la Plata had no long tradition of viceregal government; the intendant system was established shortly after the viceroyalty itself and both grew up together. The conflicts between the viceroys and the intendants were conflicts of personalities and not of institutions, and they never involved any criticism of the intendant system itself. The nearest approach to any such criticism came from the *audiencia* of Charcas in Upper Perú, and significantly followed the same pattern as that of the viceroy of Perú— resentment of an old-established institution against the intrusion of a newcomer. From other parts of the empire, notably from New Spain, evidence was sent in support of the intendant system.[1] In Madrid, too, the régime had its defenders. It was the view of responsible elements in the government that the evils of the *corregidor* system were of too recent memory to permit its re-establishment, and that any complaints about the intendants arose simply because the rules were not being observed.[2] The *Contaduría General*, to which the discussion was referred, rejected the arguments of Croix and came out in support of the new dispensation.[3] This opinion was supported by the Council of the Indies which not only defended the régime but also advocated its extension to those parts of the empire where it did not exist; at the same time it suggested certain improvements, and especially recommended the payment of subdelegates.[4] The most authoritative voice in Madrid, however, was that of Jorge

[1] Viceroy Revillagigedo of New Spain, for example, vigorously defended the system; see Fisher, *op. cit.*, pp. 75–82, and Sanz, *op. cit.*, pp. 150–1. Ramón de Posada, fiscal of New Spain, reporting on the intendants, 6 March 1801, gave detailed evidence of the improvement of revenue under their rule, in A.G.I., Aud. de Lima 1119, Informe de la Contaduría.

[2] A.G.I., Aud. de Lima 1118, Extracto de 16 de Enero de 1790.

[3] See Sanz, *op. cit.*, pp. 154–5.

[4] A.G.I., Indif. General 1713, Consulta del Consejo, 2 December 1801.

Escobedo, former visitor-general of Perú, and his report formed a substantial part of conciliar opinion.[1] He ridiculed the contradictions inherent in the proposals of Croix, who advocated the retention of the Ordinance yet pleaded for the restoration of the old *corregidores*; this was to 'denounce the intendants and approve the intendancies'. The greatest defect in the old régime of colonial administration had been inability to implement the laws: on the one hand there had been viceroys and *audiencias* endowed with almost absolute power, yet on the other hand they operated in provinces so extensive that their orders were not obeyed. Now, argued Escobedo, there were powerful officials, bridging the gap between the higher institutions and the mass of the people, who could intervene and enforce obedience. These officials were worth retaining, though that was not to say that further adjustments to the system were not called for: in particular there ought to be a closer definition of the limits of jurisdiction of the various officials and institutions in order to obviate conflicts.

The opinions of Escobedo carried weight in Madrid. Consequently, although there was uncertainty all through the 1790's, by 1802 the issue was not whether the intendant system should be abolished but how it should be reformed. A royal order of 22 March of that year commissioned the Council of the Indies to undertake the reform of the Ordinance of Intendants, particularly to define and delimit the various powers of officials and tribunals; and in view of the heavy nature of the task the crown appointed a special committee of five, headed by Escobedo, to prepare the new legislation, the final form of which was to be submitted to the Council.[2] The committee set about its work and produced a new ordinance which, with certain modifications suggested by the Council of the Indies, received royal approval on 29 June 1803, and became known as the *Nueva Ordenanza de Intendentes*.[3] This was printed and published in the same year.[4]

[1] A.G.I., Aud. de Lima 1119, 'Voto particular del Sor. Dn. Jorge Escobedo en el Expte. de Intendencias', Madrid, 23 November 1801.

[2] A.G.I., Indif. General 1713, R.O., 22 March 1802.

[3] A.G.I., Aud. de Buenos Aires 354, R.O., 29 June 1803.

[4] A.G.I., Indif. General 1713, R.O., 12 November 1803. *Ordenanza General formada de orden de S.M. para el Gobierno e Instrucción de Intendentes, Subdelegados y demas empleados en Indias*, Madrid, 1803.

In general the new ordinance made more precise definitions of authority and incorporated amendments to the system which had been added since 1782. It provided for a provincial intendant in each viceregal capital, but made it quite explicit that the viceroy was to remain superintendent of finance.[1] The powers of the intendants *vis-à-vis* their subordinates were defined more closely in order to sustain the authority of the intendants, especially against the exchequer officials. Financial administration was itself modified. Each *junta superior de hacienda* was divided into two sections, one called *contenciosa* to take charge of all judicial matters in exchequer affairs, the other called *junta superior de gobierno*, of which the intendant of the capital was a member, to supervise the administrative and financial side of the colonial exchequer. Finally, a significant attempt was made to raise the status and the quality of the subdelegates. Henceforth they were to be appointed directly by the crown on the advice of the Council of the Indies; there were to be three grades of subdelegates, with the possibility of promotion from one to the other; and above all they were now to be paid—in the viceroyalty of the Río de la Plata the salaries were to be 2,400 pesos for first-class subdelegates and 1,200 for those of the third class.

The New Ordinance contained no fundamental modifications to the existing régime. The Spanish authorities had, in fact, learned no real lessons: even now in 1803 there was no devolution of government, no prospects offered for the inclusion of creoles in the work of administration. This persistent intransigence is the most valuable evidence to be derived from the episode of the New Ordinance, for the legislation itself was never implemented. Owing to representations from the Ministry of War that the military provisions of the Ordinance were incompatible with recent military regulations the whole Ordinance was suspended by royal order of 11 January 1804.[2] The Council of the Indies protested in vain that the military sections of the new legislation contained no innovations and did not differ substantially from the provisions of the older Ordinance; to sacrifice undoubted reforms in finance, justice and administration on these doubtful grounds would be a grave error. But

[1] See above, pp. 108-9.
[2] A.G.I., Indif. General 1713, R.O., 11 January 1804.

the government remained unconvinced, and then apparently it lost heart, for no further attempt was ever made to reform the Ordinance of Intendants. The publication and then the withdrawal of the New Ordinance served only to cause more confusion, for magistrates and officials did not know how to decide cases, in terms of the old Ordinance or in the light of the new one.[1]

Thus although the episode was abortive, it had significant effects on the operation of the intendant system. The whole preliminary debate, as Escobedo himself pointed out, meant that the intendants had to work under cramped conditions, uncertain of their ultimate fate and hesitant to apply to the full rules whose abolition was being considered.[2] They were not unaware of the campaign being conducted against them, for they sometimes felt its blast, especially when their salaries were lowered and their faculties gradually circumscribed. The fact that the central authorities still lacked complete confidence in their own creation could not but stay the hand of an intendant in many of the enterprises which the Ordinance committed to him.

In spite of this the intendants accomplished work of permanent value in the viceroyalty of the Río de la Plata. In these provinces, now the focus of unaccustomed attention, a new spirit animated administration. There was a reaction against the decrepit system so long associated with Perú: 'It is necessary', reported Pino Manrique, governor and future intendant of Potosí, 'to fight with fire and sword against the spirit of greed which animates Perú. . . .'[3] In the new viceroyalty the intendants had to operate as it were in virgin territory, where the need was not so much better government as more government. The remarkable régime of Sobremonte in Córdoba, outstanding in its social and financial aspects, attracted attention less because he improved a corrupt administration than because he

[1] A.G.I., Indif. General 1707, 'Informe de los Conts. Gs. sobre el expediente de extinción de los repartimientos', 27 November 1806.

[2] There was even hesitation over the filling of vacant intendancies. On the cover of applications for the office of intendant of La Paz on the death of Segurola in 1790 there is this note: 'Pretendtes. a la Intendencia de La Paz. Aunque es cierta la vacante no conviene se provea hasta qe. el conso. consulte si se deven o no extinguir las Intendencias.' A.G.I., Aud. de Buenos 37. The lack of continuity in intendancy administration in La Paz has already been noticed, see above pp. 142, 229.

[3] A.G.I., Aud. de Lima 1118, Pino Manrique to Gálvez, 16 February 1783.

supplied what had never existed. His work was essentially creative, the provision of public works, the establishment of *alcaldes de barrio*, the founding of guilds of artisans, the creation of bodies of militia, the erection of rural primary schools. In short, he gave new things to a neglected area. Such a story of urban progress can be told of most of the towns of the new viceroyalty, though few of the intendants had the energy of Sobremonte: this was the era of public works and the provision of some of the amenities of civilized life. Along with this activity more and better reports were being supplied to the central authorities: this meant that there was now a more efficient exchange of information between lower officials and policy-making bodies. The intendant system gradually acquired prestige, not only with the home government but also with the people of the viceroyalty. It became recognized as a potential means of progress whereby a district could receive the attention which it desired: in 1807, for example, the municipal and commercial community of Montevideo requested that as a reward for the damages it had suffered and the services it had afforded during the British invasions of the Río de la Plata it should be granted exemption from all taxes for a period of twelve years, that a chamber of commerce be erected in Montevideo, and that an intendancy be created out of the district of the Banda Oriental with its capital in Montevideo. From the latter great benefits in agriculture and commerce were expected to accrue.[1] In soliciting this privilege Montevideo was undoubtedly motivated by a desire to preserve its political and economic identity against the supremacy of Buenos Aires, and it is interesting that it believed that the intendant system was a practical means of doing so.

But in hoping for agricultural and commercial progress from the intendant régime Montevideo was looking at the potentialities of the system rather than its performance. The commercial prosperity enjoyed by the Río de la Plata from 1776 came as a result of the regulations of free commerce and not from the action of the intendants. There is little evidence that the

[1] A.G.I., Aud. de Buenos Aires 21, Francisco Viana (Contador general), Madrid, 29 January 1808. The accountant-general recommended the request for an intendancy but it met with no success.

intendants made any significant contribution to the state of agriculture and industry in the viceroyalty of the Río de la Plata. Unable to control policy, they were unable to combat the process whereby the modest industries of the interior were sacrificed to the cheaper imports through Buenos Aires. To this extent the regulations of free commerce were out of harmony with the instructions given to the intendants. The decline of the wine trade of Córdoba dated precisely from 1778, when the free commerce initiated by the decrees of that year meant that Córdoba wine could not compete with foreign imports owing to the disparity in their freightage costs. Nor could the intendants take effective measures to promote wheat production when the essential condition for its success, namely free export, was lacking. The reforms of Charles III, in fact, were not all of a piece, and consequently in many cases the intendants were left helpless.

This lack of cohesion was also evident with regard to the exchequer reform undertaken by the Ordinance of Intendants. After twenty years' operation it was obvious that the system had not produced the results expected of it, and that apart from the early years of the régime no appreciable increase in royal revenue had been procured. The appointment of Vega as visitor-general in 1802 was a reflection on the intendant system in its financial aspect: it was now evident that a mere application of the Ordinance would produce no automatic results. Vega's discoveries showed, moreover, that the intendants had not in fact applied the Ordinance as it should have been applied; they had not, for example, insisted on yearly rendering of accounts by exchequer officials. But the root cause of financial maladministration lay in the fact that the crown was ill-served by its lower officials. The whole class of exchequer officials needed reforming or even replacing. Such a task was beyond the scope of the intendants and of the visitor-general: it could only be undertaken on the initiative of the central government itself and in a form which would abolish the system of sale of offices. The latter would have been a radical departure from existing practice, but it was the only hope for better financial administration. To apply the Ordinance of Intendants and maintain the system of sale of offices revealed a fatal lack of integration in Spanish policy. To give the subdelegates financial responsibilities and leave them without salaries was equally short-sighted.

While the intendant system failed to yield the fruits expected of it, it had effects which were never intended by its authors. The introduction of intendants had a disruptive effect on existing Spanish institutions in the viceroyalty of the Río de la Plata and tended to break the unity of colonial government at a critical period. The first evidence of this was the relations between viceroy Loreto and superintendent Sanz: the new division of power between the two authorities was practised not with the tactful co-operation it required but with a sense of rivalry and jealousy which ruined its chances of success almost from the start. The government managed to repair this damage but only by jettisoning the office of superintendent, one of the most characteristic features of the intendant system, and restoring to the viceroy his traditional powers in financial and economic affairs. Meanwhile in Upper Perú another feud had broken out which the government never managed to control. The intense rivalry between the *audiencia* of Charcas and the four intendants of Upper Perú continued during the whole period of the intendant régime and extended over a variety of issues. Consequently government in Upper Perú was characterized by lack of co-operation between the crown's representatives, which occasionally broke out into open hostility and mutual recriminations. Ultimately it led to the deposition of the president-intendant of La Plata by the *audiencia* at a time when Upper Perú was already seething with discontent and when the viceroy was preoccupied with the situation in Buenos Aires. Thus it is quite clear that the introduction of intendants into Upper Perú caused a reaction on the part of the *audiencia* which made for disunity and weakness. Faced with the revolutionary situation of 1809–10 royal government was already divided against itself; unable to resolve its own problems, it was in no condition to control a revolution.

If the impact of the intendant system on central government in the viceroyalty was unexpected, its effect on local government was even more surprising. It was no part of Spanish policy to strengthen local government in the colonies. The intendant system involved no decentralization: the intendants were precisely agents of royal authority, appointed to subordinate the whole territory to central control. Although they had no specific instructions to circumscribe *cabildo* activity—municipal government in the colonies was too spiritless a thing to require further limitation—it did seem that the intendants over-shadowed the *cabildos*. The intendants certainly took the initiative in administration. But this did not mean that they took the initiative *from* the *cabildos*, for they could not take what the *cabildos* did not have. In fact, indirectly, the intendants aroused the *cabildos* of the viceroyalty of the Río de la Plata from their lethargy. By increasing their revenue and by giving them more work to do, the intendants provided the *cabildos* with a new view of municipal government and a new prospect of urban development. Encouraged by their association with the work of the intendants and by the respect with which the early intendants treated them, the *cabildos* warmed to their new masters and co-operated happily with them. Then, as they became more sure of themselves, they began to resent the tutelage of the intendants: anxious to control the funds which the intendants had made possible and to direct the work which the intendants had initiated, they reacted against their masters and began to claim more share of local government. Such a claim was naturally rejected and thereupon began a conflict between *cabildos* and intendants which characterized local government in almost all parts of the viceroyalty in the last years of Spanish rule and which gave the *cabildos* yet further training in municipal responsibility. Whichever way the problem is re-garded, therefore, the intendants were a force for good in local government; the better ones attracted the co-operation and esteem of the *cabildos*, while the oppressive ones, precisely because they now had more power, stimulated a healthy re-action from local politicians. Already before 1810 the *cabildos* were at loggerheads with the royal agents.

The attitude of the *cabildos* was symptomatic of the general desire of the creoles for a greater share in their own government. This was denied to them by the intendant system. It is true that they were admitted to posts of *tenientes asesores* on principle, and in practice to those of subdelegates; but these concessions merely whetted their appetites and made them the more desirous of greater responsibilities. Revolutions are caused not by the completely oppressed but by those who have tasted liberty and want more. By giving Americans a vision of better government and denying them a significant share in its operation, the reforms of Charles III, both in their administrative and in their commercial aspects, helped to precipitate the collapse of the imperial régime they were intended to prolong. The intendant system, an instrument of absolute monarchy, suffered from the defects of its origin and from the limitations inherent in the careful distribution of reforms by a paternal government. The comments of Victorián de Villava on the intendants of Potosí might well be applied to the intendant system in general, or even to the whole reform programme of Charles III: 'The governors of Potosí may try to maintain affairs on a durable basis without causing any changes, but they merely lighten their epoch with transitory brilliance which is like a flash of lightning, illuminating us one moment only to leave us in greater darkness.'[1]

[1] *Contrarréplica*, 3 January 1795, in Levene, *Vida y escritos de Victorián de Villava*, p. liv.

APPENDICES

I

Intendants of the Viceroyalty of the Río de la Plata

BUENOS AIRES

Manuel Ignacio Fernández	1778–1783
Francisco de Paula Sanz	1783–1788
Domingo de Reynoso	1803–1810

PARAGUAY

Pedro Melo de Portugal	1783–1785
Joaquín de Alós y Bru	1786–1796
Lázaro de Rivera y Espinosa	1796–1806
Bernardo de Velazco y Huidobro	1806–1811

CÓRDOBA

Marqués de Sobremonte	1783–1797
José González	1803–1805
Juan Gutiérrez de la Concha	1807–1810

SALTA

Andrés Mestre	1783–1790
Ramón García de León y Pizarro	1790–1797
Rafael de la Luz	1798–1807
Tomás Arriguraga	1807–1808
José de Medeiros	1808–1809
Nicolás de Isasmendi	1809–1810

POTOSÍ

Juan del Pino Manrique	1783–1789
Francisco de Paula Sanz	1789–1810

LA PLATA

Ignacio Flores	1783–1785
Vicente de Gálvez	1785–1790
Joaquín del Pino	1790–1797
Ramón García de León y Pizarro	1797–1808
Vicente Nieto	1809–1810

COCHABAMBA
Joseph de Ayarga   1783–1785
Francisco de Viedma   1785–1809
José González de Prada   1809–1810

LA PAZ
Sebastián de Segurola   1783–1789
Juan Manuel Álvarez   1791–1792
Francisco de Cuellar   1793–1795
Fernando de la Sota   1795–1796
Antonio Burgunyo   1796–1805
Tadeo Dávila   1805–1809
Antonio Álvarez de Soto Mayor   1809–1810

PUNO
Josef Reseguín   1784–1788
José Joaquín Contreras   1788–1790
Marqués de Casa-Hermosa   1790–1795
José Antonio de Campos   1795–1796

BIOGRAPHICAL NOTES ON THE INTENDANTS*

Joaquín de Alós y Bru
Born Barcelona, 1742, of a noble and distinguished family.[1] Son of the Marqués de Alós y Rius, lieut.-general of the army and captain-general of Mallorca, and later regent of the *audiencia* of Catalonia. Rose to the rank of captain in the Infantry Regiment of Aragon. Appointed *corregidor* of the province of Chayanta in Upper Perú, where his practice of excessive *repartimientos* was partly responsible for the native rising in Chayanta in 1780.[2] Complaints were made of his conduct and he was removed and underwent trial; in 1783 viceroy Vértiz declared him innocent of all charges and a good servant of the crown. Through the patronage of José de Gálvez, Alós was promoted lieut.-colonel and appointed intendant of Paraguay in 1786 (R.C. 4 May 1786).[3] There he proved an efficient administrator, founded frontier forts and opened a new road to Tucumán; submitted an important report on the state of the Guaraní communities.

* The following notes are not exhaustive, and include only those intendants about whom I have been able to find biographical information.

[1] Udaondo, *Diccionario biográfico colonial argentino*, p. 54, says 1742; J. T. Medina, *Diccionario biográfico colonial chileno*, p. 57, gives 1735.

[2] M. de Mendiburu, *Diccionario histórico-biográfico del Perú* (2nd edn. 11 vols., Lima, 1931–4; appendices, 1935–), i, 339.

[3] A.G.I., Aud. de Buenos Aires 48, Alós to Gálvez, 13 September 1787.

In 1796 he was transferred to Valparaíso (Chile) as governor; swore obedience to the *junta* established in Santiago in 1810 but secretly supported the royalist opposition and was deposed in 1811; retired to Perú.[1]

Juan Manuel Álvarez

Officer in the Extremadura Regiment. Native of Spain. Appointed intendant of La Paz in 1790; took office 17 May 1791.[2]

Antonio Álvarez de Sotomayor

Born in Lucena, Andalucía, 1757, of noble family. Entered the navy in 1775 and took part in many actions against the British navy, including that of Cape St. Vincent. Went to the Río de la Plata in 1789, where the viceroy appointed him to the boundary commission for the Matto Grosso region. Remained in this capacity until 1801 when he received administrative appointments in the Mojos territory. In 1808 appointed temporary governor of Chiquitos. In July 1809 viceroy Cisneros appointed him intendant of La Paz.[3]

Antonio Burgunyo

Native of Spain. After twenty-one years' service in the navy, rank of lieut., was appointed intendant of La Paz by royal decree of 8 July 1795 and promoted captain. Took office 17 September 1796. In 1798 the *cabildo* of La Paz wrote to the crown praising his merits and services.[4]

Marqués de Casa-Hermosa

Francisco José de Mesa Ponte y Castillo. Born in the Canary Islands, son of José de Mesa, colonel of Infantry Regiment of Tacorante, Tenerife. Served in this regiment for twenty-four years, reaching rank of lieut.-colonel. Left army to go to America with appointment as *corregidor* of province of Huaylas, Perú (12 October 1766), where he gave evidence of administrative ability. After the establishment of the intendancies, appointed subdelegate of *partido* of Huaylas in 1785. In 1789 promoted colonel and appointed intendant of Puno (7 March 1789); took office 1 January 1790. As *corregidor* of Huaylas he had proposed the extinction of *repartimientos* in return for fixed wages; now as intendant he showed similar awareness of administrative problems, attacking corruption in exchequer offices,

[1] See Udaondo, *op. cit.*, pp. 54–5. Mendiburu, *op. cit.*, i, 338–42, Medina, *op. cit.*, pp. 57–8.

[2] A.G.I., Aud. de Buenos Aires 37, Oficio del Ministerio de Guerra, 4 July 1790; *ibid.*, Álvarez to Lerena, 7 June 1791.   [3] See Udaondo, *op. cit.*, p. 64.

[4] A.G.I., Aud. de Buenos Aires 37, Burgunyo to Verla (Minister of the Navy), 17 Sept. 1796; *ibid.*, Cabildo of La Paz to Crown, 11 December 1798.

increasing royal revenue, suspending guilty officials. This activity earned him many enemies and complaints were made to higher authorities of his alleged extortionate behaviour; he was brought to trial and suspended from office. Acquitted; retired to Spain.[1]

Francisco de Cuellar

Native of Spain. Army career. *Corregidor* of province of Tarma in Perú; in campaign against Tupac Amaru. On the establishment of the intendant system he was suspended from office by order of visitor-general Escobedo, who suspected him of excessive *repartimientos*. Appointed intendant of La Paz by royal order 24 September 1792; took office 17 June 1793.[2]

José González

Native of Spain. Army career in engineers to rank of colonel. Appointed intendant of Córdoba in 1796 but he was still in Cádiz in October 1802, asking that his journey to America be paid at the cost of the royal exchequer and deducted from his future salary. Apparently took office in 1803. Irascible and domineering character, in constant conflict with the *cabildo* of Córdoba. Died in office, 16 or 17 December 1805.[3]

José González de Prada

Born 1751 at Entrepenas, near Sanabria, of gentry class. Many forbears in colonial service. Studied in Madrid. Went to America in 1783 with appointment as accountant of the subtreasuries of Salta; visitor of those of Buenos Aires, Oruro and Carangas. Discharged these offices satisfactorily, effecting considerable increase of revenue. Appointed to Cochabamba in 1788 as accountant of the treasury and administrator-general of revenue, an office which he held for thirteen years. In 1809 received royal appointment of intendant of Tarma in Perú at a salary of 6,000 pesos, but in the critical circumstances in Cochabamba the viceroy at Buenos Aires put him in charge of the intendancy there because of his prestige and experience in that area. On revolution in Cochabamba he returned to the intendancy of Tarma. To Lima in 1820; unmolested by independent government. Died in Cochabamba 1829.[4]

[1] See V. Rodríguez Casado, 'Causa seguida contra el Marqués de Casa-Hermosa, Gobernador Intendente de Puno', *Anuario de Estudios Americanos*, iii (1946), pp. 957–68.

[2] A.G.I., Aud. de Buenos Aires 37, Viceroy Gil (Lima) to Crown, 5 May 1791; *ibid.*, Cuellar to Gardoqui, 17 June 1793.

[3] A.G.I., Aud. de Buenos Aires 50, R.O., 29 September 1796; *ibid.*, González to Crown, 11 October 1802. See Udaondo, *op. cit.*, p. 401.

[4] See Mendiburu, *op. cit.*, vi, 115–17.

Juan Gutiérrez de la Concha

Born at Esles, near Santander, 2 October 1760. Naval career; service in Mediterranean and Central America. In 1805 was commandant of naval station of Ensenada de Barragán, on the southern coast of the Río de la Plata. Took a prominent part in the counter-offensive against the British expedition to the Río de la Plata in 1807, for which the *audiencia* of Buenos Aires recommended him to the king. By royal order, 18 August 1806, appointed intendant of Córdoba; took office 1807. Organized attempted counter-revolution in 1810; captured and shot 26 August 1810. Gutiérrez de la Concha was the author of various unpublished hydrographical works.[1]

Nicolás Severo de Isasmendi

Born in Salta, 8 November 1753, son of General Domingo de Isasmendi y Ormazabal, a native of Guipuzcoa, Spain. Studied at the College of Monserrat in Córdoba. Career part military and part management of his father's estate and mines. Served royal cause during Tupac Amaru rebellion, for which he furnished a company of troops paid and armed by himself. In 1791 intendant Pizarro appointed him collector of the Indian tribute for the districts of Calchoqui, Payogasta and Atacama. A prominent member of the *cabildo* of Salta; 1795, junior *alcalde*; 1796, senior *alcalde*. On journey to Spain in 1804 was captured by a British naval force and held in London. In 1807 he returned to Salta where he was appointed intendant by viceroy Liniers in 1809. When the revolution broke out Isasmendi played a double game, but his real sympathies were evidently with the royalists; he was deposed by the *junta* and sent to Buenos Aires. After a period of imprisonment he managed to find refuge on his extensive estates in the province of Salta. Died 16 December 1837.[2]

Rafael de la Luz

Native of Spain. Military career. Governor of Isla de Carmen for six years; service commended by viceroy Revillagigedo of New Spain in 1794. By decrees of 4 September 1795 promoted colonel and appointed governor of Portobello, where he remained for two years and earned further commendations. By royal dispatch of 11 November 1796 he was appointed intendant of Salta; took office 3 December

[1] See A. Zinny, *Historia de los gobernadores de las provincias argentinas* (2nd edn., 5 vols., Buenos Aires, 1920–1), iii, 22–30; Udaondo, *op. cit.*, p. 429; A.G.I., Aud. de Buenos Aires 556, Audiencia to Crown, 26 July 1807.

[2] See J. R. Yaben, *Biográficas argentinas y sudamericanas* (Buenos Aires, 1938), iii, 186–9; Udaondo, *op. cit.*, p. 456.

1798. In Salta he founded a hospital and made various visitations of his province.[1]

José de Medeiros

Born in Lisbon. Lawyer of the *audiencias* of Charcas and Buenos Aires; from 1802 *oidor* of the *audiencia* of Buenos Aires. Appointed intendant of Salta in 1808.[2]

Pedro Melo de Portugal

Native of Spain; descendant of Dukes of Braganza. Service in navy, to rank of lieut. Then in army, Dragoon Regiment of Sagunto. Appointed governor of Paraguay with rank of lieut.-colonel February 1778; active in colonizing and forming Indian reductions. Appointed intendant of Paraguay in 1783; in office until 1785, after which he returned to Spain. Promoted lieut.-general and in 1795 appointed viceroy of the Río de la Plata. Died 15 April 1797.[3]

Andrés Mestre

Born in Spain and began military career there. Appointed governor of province of Tucumán, April 1776; took office 1777. When the Tupac Amaru rebellion spread to Jujuy, Mestre suppressed it ruthlessly; ordered execution of seventeen prisoners and branding of others. By now had attained rank of colonel. Appointed intendant of Salta del Tucumán, 15 August 1783. A good administrator; he reformed the militia, constructed and repaired many forts, established Indian reductions, and began the construction of a town hall in Salta, partly at his own expense; built many bridges and roads.[4]

Vicente Nieto

Born in Spain in 1769 and followed a military career; fought in campaigns of the Pyrenees and Catalonia against France. Sent to Buenos Aires with rank of captain; in counter-offensive against British expeditions 1806–7; promoted colonel. *Junta Central* at Seville appointed him governor of Montevideo in 1809 but the situation there prevented him from taking office. Promoted brigadier, and viceroy Cisneros appointed him president of the *audiencia* of Charcas and intendant of La Plata after the deposition of Pizarro by the

---

[1] A.G.I., Aud. de Buenos Aires 50, Rafael de la Luz to Jovellanos, 4 December 1798; Aud. de Buenos Aires 88, *idem* to Crown, 3 May 1802.

[2] See Udaondo, *op. cit.*, p. 571.

[3] *Ibid.*, pp. 575–7.

[4] Torre Revello, *El marqués de Sobre Monte*, p. 16 note; Zinny, *op. cit.*, i, 215–18; Udaondo, *op. cit.*, pp. 594–5.

audiencia. Exercised office from December 1809. After the revolutionary victory at Suipacha, Nieto was taken prisoner and shot, 15 December 1810.[1]

Joaquín del Pino

Native of Spain. Army career in engineers; by 1770 lieut.-colonel. 1771 appointed commandant of engineers and director of fortifications in the province of the Río de la Plata. From 1773 to 1790 he was governor of Montevideo. Appointed president of Charcas and intendant of La Plata by royal order of 2 April 1789, and promoted brigadier; took office 1790. Promoted field marshal 1794.[2]

Juan del Pino Manrique de Lara

Of gentry-class family of Málaga. Studied law at University of Granada. Subdelegate to Areche, visitor-general of Perú, 1776–81. When Areche was replaced by Escobedo in 1781 Pino Manrique was given the latter's post of governor of Potosí and superintendent of the mint, the exchange bank and the mines. In 1788 appointed *alcalde del crimen* in the *audiencia* of Lima, and in 1797 promoted *oidor*. As *alcalde del crimen* he served as vice-protector and legal representative of the periodical *Mercurio Peruano*. Held various other legal posts in Lima before his death in 1814.[3]

Ramón García de León y Pizarro

Born in Oran, Africa 1730; son of colonel José García de León. Army career until 1777 when appointed temporary governor of province of Río de la Hacha by viceroy of New Granada (31 March); by royal decree of 28 August same year appointed governor of Maynas; took part in commission for boundary division with Portugal in zone of Marañon. By royal decree of 7 September 1779 appointed governor of Guayaquil; good record there for work on fortifications and public building; 1783 promoted colonel, and after ten years' active administration he underwent *residencia* without a single charge against him. In 1788 admitted to Order of Calatrava. Appointed intendant of Salta del Tucumán 30 April 1789; assumed office 19 December 1790. Here he made thorough visitation of province, and was prominent in promoting public works; in July 1794 founded town of Nuevo Oran. Promoted brigadier 1792, field marshal 1795. Through the request of viceroy Melo de Portugal and the representations of friends in Madrid he was appointed president of the *audiencia* of Charcas and

[1] Udaondo, *op. cit.*, p. 640; Mendiburu, *op. cit.*, viii, 115; Yaben, *op. cit.*, iv, 145.
[2] A.G.I., Estado 76, Joaquín del Pino to Crown, 25 July 1794.
[3] A.G.I., Aud. de Buenos Aires 64, Vértiz to Gálvez, 20 February 1782. See also Angelis, *op. cit.*, ii, 10; Udaondo, *op. cit.*, p. 714; Mendiburu, *op. cit.*, ix, 25.

intendant of La Plata by royal decree 20 October 1796; took office 16 November 1797; at the request of his brother José to the crown he was relieved of *residencia* for his administration of Salta, and no complaints were received against him. A conscientious administrator, he was well enough liked in Chuquisaca. But in his old age he lost his grasp of affairs and his relations with the *audiencia* were strained from the beginning. Received Goyeneche with deference and opposed attitude of *audiencia*; the latter deposed and imprisoned him, May 1809, holding him in custody in the university until 18 November 1809. Retired to estate near Chuquisaca. In 1815 procured title Marqués de Casa Pizarro; died Chuquisaca 1815.[1]

Josef Reseguín

Born in Spain. Army career; in expedition of Cevallos to Río de la Plata 1776–7. Lieut.-colonel of Regiment of Dragoons in Montevideo garrison. Commander of expedition sent by viceroy Vértiz for pacification of Upper Perú during Tupac Amaru rebellion. Promoted colonel and appointed commander-in-chief of Dragoons in Montevideo. Requested intendancy of Salta in November 1783. Appointed intendant of Puno by royal order 14 June 1784. Died 6 August 1788.[2]

Lázaro de Rivera y Espinosa

Native of Spain; gentry class; soldier and engineer. In 1784 in Montevideo as one of commissioners for boundary negotiations between Spain and Portugal. Appointed governor of Mojos in same year; dissatisfied with this appointment and frequently requested his relief; nevertheless he rendered zealous and efficient service there, for which viceroy Arredondo recommended him to crown. *Audiencia* of Charcas also recommended him for promotion. In 1796 was appointed intendant of Paraguay. Had a penchant for drawing up *reglamentos* (plans and constitutions); had made one for Mojos, and now made one for *pueblos de misiones* in Paraguay; his reports were intolerably prolix and he was incapable of sending a concise

[1] A.G.I., Aud. de Buenos Aires 50, Melo de Portugal to Consejo de Indias, 12 November 1795. See particularly 'Relacion de los Meritos de . . . Pizarro', in same Expediente. See also Torre Revello, 'Relación de la visita hecha a la intendencia de Salta del Tucumán por el gobernador intendente Ramón García de Léon y Pizarro', *B.I.I.H.*, xiii (1931), pp. 58–75; René-Moreno, 'Informaciones verbales sobre los sucesos de 1809 en Chuquisaca', *Revista Chilena*, ix (1877), p. 39; idem, *Ultimos días coloniales en el Alto Perú*, pp. 128–32; Udaondo, *op. cit.*, pp. 380–1.

[2] A.G.I., Aud. de Buenos Aires 66, Reseguín to Crown, 20 November 1783; Aud. de Buenos Aires 68, Loreto to Gálvez, 7 December 1784; Aud. de Buenos Aires 76, Loreto to Porlier, 20 November 1788; Udaondo, *op. cit.*, p. 747.

account of anything unencumbered with quotations from authorities ancient and modern. Frequently involved in disputes with his superiors, with the president of Charcas when governor of Mojos and now with viceroy Avilés. But a sound administrator. One of his first acts in Paraguay was to procure a census of the population (97,480 inhabitants); established primary schools with lay teachers; active in colonizing. Incurred enmity of Félix de Azara who campaigned against him in Spain on account of his opposition to the destruction of the community system of the Guaraní Indians of Paraguay; defended by his brother-in-law, viceroy Liniers, who appointed him as envoy to the Portuguese court at Rio de Janeiro, a mission which was never effected. Relieved of intendancy of Paraguay in 1806. Appointed intendant of Huancavelica in 1812.[1]

Francisco de Paula Sanz

Native of Andalucía. Long career in royal administration. Enjoyed patronage and protection of José de Gálvez, and in Buenos Aires rumour had it that he was an illegitimate son of the minister, though there is no reason to believe this. In 1777 appointed director of the tobacco revenue in the Río de la Plata, with commission to visit whole of the viceroyalty, establish *estancos* (royal monopoly tobacco stores) where none existed, and regulate the existing ones. Between 1778–81 he visited Montevideo, Paraguay, Tucumán, Cuyo, Chile, Arica, Collao, Chucuito, Puno, La Paz, Santa Cruz de la Sierra, Cochabamba, Charcas and Potosí, regulated the administration of the revenue and established new *estancos* where necessary. Appointed superintendent subdelegate of the royal exchequer in the viceroyalty of the Río de la Plata and intendant of the province of Buenos Aires 24 March 1783. An efficient administrator but involved in frequent conflicts of jurisdiction with the viceroy. On suppression of independent superintendency in 1788 he was appointed intendant of Potosí, where he took office in 1789. From the point of view of royal government he was a good official, but his very intransigence made him unpopular with Americans and even with other royal representatives; in continual conflict with the *audiencia* of Charcas. Staunch opponent of revolution of 1810; after Suipacha he was arrested and shot 15 December 1810.[2]

[1] A.G.I., Aud. de Buenos Aires 76, Loreto to Porlier, 1 March 1788; Aud. de Buenos Aires 79, Arredondo to marqués de Bajamar, 9 June 1792; Aud. de Charcas to Acuña, 25 May 1793; Udaondo, *op. cit.*, p. 762; Medina, *op. cit.*, pp. 744–5.

[2] A.G.I., Aud. de Charcas 439, Sanz to Valdés, 30 March 1789. See V. F. López, *Historia de la República Argentina* (10 vols., Buenos Aires, 1883–93), i, 482–3, whose account of Sanz's character, however, must be read with reserve.

Sebastián de Segurola
Born in Azpeitia, Guipuzcoa, 27 January 1740. Military career.
1776 took part in expedition to Río de la Plata; decorated with Cross
of Calatrava and appointed *corregidor* of Larecaja in Perú. During
rebellion of Tupac Amaru encharged by president of Charcas with
defence of city of La Paz, which he accomplished efficiently. In same
year, 1781, appointed by viceroy Vértiz governor of La Paz with
promotion to rank of colonel; 1782, brigadier. With establishment of
intendant system was maintained in La Paz as first intendant. Died
1 October 1789, in office.[1]

Marqués de Sobremonte
Third Marqués de Sobremonte. Born Seville 27 November 1745,
son of Raimundo de Sobremonte, *oidor* of *audiencia* of Seville. Entered
army September 1759 as cadet in royal guards. Promoted lieut. of
infantry battalion stationed at Cartagena de Indias February 1761,
where he spent three years, returning to Spain on account of health.
Attached to infantry regiment of Victoria at Ceuta, promoted captain, April 1769, and accompanied the regiment to Puerto Rico
where he remained for five years. In October 1776 appointed
secretary of the inspectorate-general of infantry in Spain. In January
1779 appointed secretary of the viceroyalty of Río de la Plata and
took office in January 1780. Promoted colonel. Vértiz recommended
him to Gálvez for an intendancy, and he was duly assigned to
Córdoba by royal order 24 August 1783; took office 7 November
1784. His record as intendant of Córdoba was outstanding, and he
provided a particularly creative administration, adding and improving in public works, establishing *alcaldes de barrio* in the four
wards of the city, founding guilds of artisans, creating bodies of
militia, establishing rural primary schools. His visitation and reports
were models of what they should be. At his own request he was dispensed of *residencia* on completion of term of office. In November 1797
appointed sub-inspector-general of regular troops and militia of the
viceroyalty; in this office his over-optimistic reports on the state of the
militia, implying no necessity of further regular replacements, were
partly responsible for lack of military resistance to British expedition
of 1806, and it was not until 1805 that he began to warn Godoy that
the forces at his disposal were insufficient. Appointed viceroy 1804.
His answer to the British invasion of 1806 was to collect the treasury
and make for Córdoba on pretext of going to raise troops. In 1807 he

[1] A.G.I., Aud. de Buenos Aires 64, Vértiz to Gálvez, 20 February 1782; Aud. de
Buenos Aires 37, Loreto to Valdés, 25 November 1789. See also Udaondo, *op. cit.*,
pp. 838–9; Mendiburu, *op. cit.*, x, 132–3.

was arrested by deputies of the *cabildo* of Buenos Aires near Montevideo and detained in a monastery in Buenos Aires. Replaced as viceroy by Santiago Liniers. Remained in Buenos Aires until 1809 when he returned to Spain charged with neglect of duty. Trial in Cádiz in November 1813 by a council of war; in a judgment based on inaccurate evidence he was absolved and allowed to continue his political and military career in the peninsula. Promoted field-marshal in June 1814 and in August of the same year Ferdinand VII appointed him Minister of the Council of the Indies. Resigned 31 December 1815 and later retired to Cádiz. Decorated with Grand Cross of San Hermenigildo. Died Cádiz 14 January 1827 aged 81. Sobremonte was the most outstanding of all the intendants of the viceroyalty of the Río de la Plata. The difference between his record as intendant and his conduct as viceroy is remarkable; he was, however, essentially an administrator, civil or military, and in a position demanding political initiative he was out of place. He was an extremely ambitious man and lost no opportunity of furthering his own interests at court; he was continually seeking military promotion and in 1789 he tried to procure the presidency of Chile. Nevertheless he made his mark in Córdoba: the *cabildo* appreciated his quality and even Gregorio Funes, dean of the bishopric of Córdoba, a personal enemy, had to admit that the province had experienced an unprecedented prosperity and progress under his command.[1]

Bernardo de Velazco y Huidobro
Born in Spain where he followed a military career; in 1793 took active part in Roellon campaign until peace of Basle. On 17 May 1803 appointed political and military governor of thirty *pueblos de misiones*. Promoted to rank of colonel of infantry in June 1804 and on 12 September 1805 appointed intendant of Paraguay, including jurisdiction over the *pueblos de misiones*. Promoted brigadier January 1808. In 1806–7 fought with distinction against British expeditions in Buenos Aires. On 24 July 1810 an assembly convoked by Velazco declared for separation from Buenos Aires and recognized the council of regency in Spain. Velazco organized the military defence of Paraguay, but was deposed by the creoles in June 1811.[2]

Francisco de Viedma
Born in Jaen, Andalucía, 11 January 1737, of one of principal families of the province. Administrative career. Put in charge of colonization of Patagonia, 1779–84. In 1785 promoted intendant of

---

[1] See Torre Revello, *El marqués de Sobre Monte, passim.*
[2] Udaondo, *op. cit.*, p. 926; Yaben, *op. cit.*, p. 1082.

Cochabamba, where he proved to be an administrator of integrity
and quality; submitted a lengthy and detailed description of intendancy of Cochabamba in 1793; constant concern for Indians. Died
in Cochabamba 28 June 1809, leaving all his possessions to an
institute for education of poor children.[1]

II

Financial Tables[2]

TABLE A

INCOME, CÓRDOBA[3]

Ciudades	Años	Total Grāl	Aumentos	Total
Córdoba	1784	9,994		
	1785	19,362.2¾	9,368.3¾	
	1786	31,274.8½	11,912.2¾	
		60,631.1¼	21,280.6½	21,280.6½
Mendoza	1784	10,535.1½		
	1785	18,544.1¼	8,008.7¾	
	1786	16,877		
		45,956.2¾	8,008.7¾	8,008.7¾

TABLE B

INCOME, POTOSÍ[4]

Entradas annuales en utilidad del Real Hacienda por todos los
Ramos, assi de efectos de Castilla como de la tierra, contratos Pub-
licos, viento nuebo impuesto, Pulperias, Derechos de Real Alcavala,

[1] Angelis, *Colección*, i, 443–4; Udaondo, *op. cit.*, pp. 945–6.
[2] The figures in all tables are in pesos and reales, except where otherwise indicated.
[3] A.G.I., Aud. de Buenos Aires 363, Gaspar Lozano and Rafael María Castellano,
24 March 1787.
[4] B.M., Egerton MS 1813, fols. 67–8, Cert. of Escribano del Real Hacienda,
Potosí, in 'Información producida por el Síndico Procurador General de Potosí'.

lo que a este respecto conduce, por las partidas que puestas a la lettra son las siguientes:

Entrada:	1 June −31 December 1779	45,770.7$\frac{1}{4}$
	1 January–31 December 1780	71,376.4$\frac{3}{4}$
	1 January–31 December 1781	45,062.2$\frac{1}{2}$
	1 January–31 December 1782	41,140.0
	1 January–31 December 1783	92,108.6$\frac{1}{4}$
	1 January–31 December 1784	90,023.0$\frac{3}{4}$
	1 January–31 December 1785	125,338.4$\frac{1}{4}$
		540,760.1$\frac{3}{4}$

. . . Siendo assi mismo constante y Publico que dicho ingente Cantidad se tiene con seguida en veneficio de la Real Hacienda a esfuersas del acreditado Celo y amor al Real Servicio con que tiempo del Gobierno de dicho senor Intendante se la ha reconocido, y aplaudido. . . .

TABLE C

Ramo de Tributos, Puno,[1] 1786–92

Partidos	Entero total pr. la Revista de 86 y 87	91 y 92	Aumento anual de una a otra
Chucuitu	45,647	52,828	7,181
Paucaicolla	22,312.6	26,146.3	3,833.5
Lampa	39,399.5	48,935.5	9,536
Asangaro	37,025	43,789	6,764
Caravaya	22,113.5	28,463.2	6,349.5
	166,498	200,162.2	33,664.2

[1] A.H.N., Consejos, leg 20406, pz. 8, fol. 3, Causa del Marqués de Casa Hermosa, Gob. Int. de Puno.

TABLE D

Customs, Potosí[1]

Estado General en que se manifiesta por Ramos de Real Hacienda, y particulares, las entradas, y salidas, y liquidas ganancias de Alcavalas, que ha tenido esta Real Aduana de la Villa Imperial de Potosí. 1776–87.

Años	Entradas	Salidas	Ganancias Liquidas
1776	51,926.1¾	10,730.5¾	41,195.4
1777	53,666.4	7,873.0½	45,793.3½
1778	53,732.2¼	10,378.4½	43,353.6
1779	79,359.0¼	9,100.0¼	70,259
1780	71,376.4¾	9,558	61,818.4¾
1781	45,062.2½	9,482.6	35,579.4½
	355,122.7¾	57,123.1	297,999.6¾
1782	71,140	15,818.1½	55,321.6½
1783	92,108.6¼	11,805.1¼	80,303.5
1784	90,023.0¾	12,386.2	77,636.6¾
1785	125,338.4¼	25,475.4	99,863.0¼
1786	128,406.2½	27,524.0½	100,882.2
1787	110,299.4	22,472.0¼	87,827.3¾
	617,316.1¾	115,481.1½	501,835.0¼
Diferencia	262,193.2	58,358.0½	203,835.1½

TABLE E

Alcabala Revenue, Paraguay[2]

Años	Ultimo quinquenio del Int. Alós	Años	Primer quinquenio del Int. Rivera
1791	4,669.7	1796	6,451.1
1792	7,166.3	1797	8,082.6
1793	5,221.6	1798	5,014.3
1794	6,972.2	1799	7,525.7
1795	7,897.7	1800	8,803.4
	31,928.1		35,877.5

[1] A.G.I., Aud. de Charcas 435, Rl Aduana, Potosí, 12 January 1788.
[2] A.G.I., Aud. de Buenos Aires 322, Noticia de los Valores que produjo el Real derecho de Alcabala en la Prov. del Paraguay. Asunción, 23 May 1801.

TABLE F

Alcabala Revenue, La Paz[1]

Estado que denota los acopios hechos en esta Real Aduana de la Paz
por el Ramo de Alcabalas de Castilla y Tierra en el Quinquenio de
la Revelion y en otro posterior . . .

Quinquenio antes de la Revelion		Quinquenio despues de la Revelion	
1771	35,161.4¾	1784	51,412.3
1775	60,081.7	1785	66,752.2
1776	79,116.2½	1786	93,056.4
1777	96,663.5	1787	54,203.6½
1778	120,500.3	1788	61,833.3
	391,523.6¼		327,258.2½

Diferencia: 64,265.3¾

TABLE G

Exchequer Accounts, Córdoba[2]

	Exista. en Caudal y Especies	Deudas por cobrar	Total existentes
1803	27,900.4	1,846.3¼	29,746.7¼
1805	38,095.1¼	1,786.4¼	39,881.5½
1806	63,289.¼	5,149.¾	68,438.1

[1] A.G.I., Aud. de Charcas 430.
[2] A.G.I., Aud. de Buenos Aires 467, Cuentas de Real Hacienda de Córdoba.

TABLE H

1. Production of Money by Royal Mint, Potosí[1]

Años	Marcos de Plata Rendidos	Marcos de Oro Rendidos	Años	Marcos de Plata Rendidos	Marcos de Oro Rendidos
1784	485,344	1,529.2	1794	515,211	2,190
1785	428,988	1,628.6	1795	497,511	2.034.4
1786	438,266	2,451.4	1796	518,592	2,867.4
1787	504,544	1,874.6	1797	453,300	4,069
1788	454,817	1,936.2	1798	498,505	4,021.4
1789	420,334	—	1799	470,310	2,847.2
1790	468,609	2,204.6	1800	457,537	3,353
1791	513,550	1,959.6	1801	481,268	3,501.4
1792	503,386	1,167.2	1802	266,852	2,409.2
1793	512,461	1,755	1803	276,793	2,083

2. Humboldt's Figures[2]

Años	Marcos de Plata	Marcos de Oro	Años	Marcos de Plata	Marcos de Oro
1773	231,853	—	1782	410,267	2,204
1774	377,956	—	1783	485,547	1,841
1775	396,196	—	1784	485,344	1,529
1776	480,931	—	1785	428,978	1,628
1777	485,328	—	1786	438,266	2,451
1778	577,579	—	1787	503,544	1,874
1779	544,762	—	1788	420,340	1,936
1780	581,020	3,532	1789	420,340	—
1781	447,994	1,604	1790	468,600	2,204

[1] A.G.I., Aud. de Charcas 441.   [2] Humboldt, *Ensayo político*, iii, 355.

TABLE I

REMITTANCES FROM POTOSÍ TO BUENOS AIRES[1]

Month	Year	Amount	Month	Year	Amount
May	1786	540,400	Jan.	1790	687,367.7
Sept.	1786	470,230.5⅝	Mar.	1790	117,771.6
April	1787	638,909.2½	May	1790	990,859.5
Sept.	1787	512,409.¾	Nov.	1790	603,782.6
Mar.	1788	664.709.3	April	1791	725,727.5¾
July	1788	546,109.3	Aug.	1792	713,044.6½
Feb.	1789	808,000	Feb.	1794	808,000
June	1789	606,000			

[1] A.G.I., Aud. de Charcas 704.

GLOSSARY OF SPANISH TERMS

acuerdo	a decision of a *cabildo* or other body. Also an administrative session of an *audiencia*.
aduana	customs house or revenue.
alcabala	sales tax.
alcaldes ordinarios	the two leading members of a *cabildo*, the *alcalde de primer voto*, or senior *alcalde*, and the *alcalde de segundo voto*, or junior *alcalde*.
alférez real	herald, a *cabildo* official.
almojarifazgo	export and import duties on trade between Spain and her colonies.
arroba	unit of weight, about 25 pounds.
asesor	judicial adviser who made legal decisions in the name of some official who was not ordinarily a lawyer but who was charged with judicial functions.
audiencia	superior court of justice, with administrative functions.
auto	court decision.
ayuntamiento	town council, or *cabildo*.
Banda Oriental	literally 'the East Shore', i.e. of the Río de la Plata. Roughly equivalent to modern Uruguay.
bando	proclamation, decree.
cabildo	town council. *Cabildo abierto* was a *cabildo* augmented with selected prominent citizens for extraordinary meetings.
cacique	chief.
caja real	subtreasury, or local exchequer office.
cédula	decree, issued by the crown or its minister jointly with the Council of the Indies. A decree issued without the Council of the Indies was called a *real decreto*, or royal order.
consejo	council.

contador	accountant and auditor, one of two exchequer officials in each office.
corregidor	local official with administrative and judicial authority, subordinate to viceroy and *audiencia*.
diezmos	tenths, tithes.
fiscal	prosecuting attorney in an *audiencia*.
hacienda	two senses: (1) estate or landed property; (2) exchequer, finances.
jueces reales de hacienda	exchequer officials in their capacity as judges.
junta	committee.
maravedi	Spanish coin. Thirty-four *maravedis* equalled one *real de plata*.
media anata	half year's income paid as taxation by officials in first term of office.
mita	Quechua word meaning 'turn'; conscription of Indian labour for public or private work.
oidor	judge in an *audiencia*.
ordenanza	ordinance, decree.
peso	Spanish unit of currency; equalled eight *reales*. The value varied but a rough equivalent in this period would be four shillings.
partido	subdivision within an intendancy, administered by a subdelegate.
policía	administration.
procurador	solicitor, procurator. Distinguish (1) procurator chosen by the *cabildo* to act as its spokesman and representative before higher authorities such as the viceroy or the court in Spain, (2) municipal procurator, called variously *síndico* or *procurador general*, chosen annually by the *cabildo*, whose principal function was to represent the needs and grievances of the community before the *cabildo*.
propios y arbitrios	municipal property and revenue.
pueblo	community, village.
real	Spanish silver coin; eight *reales* equalled one *peso*.
real patronato	royal patronage in ecclesiastical affairs.
real provisión	decree issued by *audiencia* having force of royal decree.
reducción	mission community.
regidor	member of *cabildo*, town councillor.

repartimiento	a division or distribution. Used in various contexts—the allotting of Indians to colonists as labourers, a grant of land, the allotment (in practice the forced sale) of commodities to Indians by the *corregidores*.
residencia	judicial review of an official's conduct at end of his term of office.
sisa	form of taxation on trade.
teniente	deputy.
tesorero	treasurer, one of two exchequer officials in each office.
tribunal de cuentas	court of appeal in fiscal cases.
visita	inspection of administration carried out by a special commissioner called a *visitador*.
vista	legal opinion.
yerba	leaf from which Paraguayan tea is made.

BIBLIOGRAPHY

I

Bibliographical Aids and Guides to Archives

Bermúdez Plata, Cristóbal, *El Archivo General de Indias de Sevilla, sede del Americanismo* (Madrid, 1951).

Catálogo de documentos del Archivo de Indias en Sevilla referentes a la historia de la República Argentina, 1514–1820, Ministerio de Relaciones Exteriores y Culto (3 vols., Buenos Aires, 1901–10).

The economic literature of Latin America. Bureau for Economic Research in Latin America, Harvard University (2 vols., Cambridge, Mass., 1935–6).

Gayangos, Pascual de, *Catalogue of the manuscripts in the Spanish language in the British Museum* (4 vols., London, The Trustees, 1875–93).

Gómez Molleda, D., *Bibliografía histórica española, 1950–1954* (Madrid, 1955).

Guia de los archivos de Madrid. Dirección General de Archivos y Bibliotecas (Madrid, 1952).

Guia de las bibliotecas de Madrid. Dirección General de Archivos y Bibliotecas (Madrid, 1953).

Handbook of Latin American studies (Harvard University Press, 1936–1950; University of Florida Press, 1951–).

Humphreys, R.A., *Latin American history. A guide to the literature in English* (Oxford, 1958).

Indice histórico español. Universidad de Barcelona. Centro de Estudios Históricos Internacionales (Barcelona, 1953–).

Jones, C. K., *A bibliography of Latin American bibliographies* (2nd edn., Washington, 1942).

Paz, Julián, *Catálogo de manuscritos de América existentes en la Biblioteca Nacional* (Madrid, 1933).

Sánchez Alonso, Benito, *Fuentes de la historia española e hispano americana* (3rd edn., 3 vols., Madrid, 1952).

Torre Revello, José, *Los archivos españoles* (Buenos Aires, 1927).

— *El Archivo General de Indias de Sevilla* (Buenos Aires, 1929).

Torres Lanzas, P., *Relación descriptiva de los mapas, planos, etc. del virreinato de Buenos Aires, existentes en el Archivo General de Indias* (2nd edn., Buenos Aires, 1921).

II

Primary Sources

1. ARCHIVES

Archivo General de Indias, Seville
  Audiencia de Buenos Aires: Legajos 13, 18, 21, 25, 37–40, 44, 45, 48–50, 63–89, 100, 140, 142, 143, 151, 153, 157, 255, 256, 264, 295, 310, 322–4, 333, 354–65, 369–72, 467, 473, 487, 606.
  Audiencia de Charcas: Legajos 423–6, 429–32, 433–42, 445–7, 454, 552–6, 560, 576, 588–90, 594, 704, 705, 710, 726–8.
  Audiencia de Lima: Legajos 802, 1118, 1119.
  Indiferente General: Legajos 843, 844, 1707, 1713, 1714.
  Estado: 76–81, 84.
Archivo Histórico Nacional, Madrid
  Consejo de Indias: Legajos 20406, 20410 n. 4, 20413 n. 3.
Biblioteca Nacional, Madrid
  MSS. 3073, 7967, 8299, 13150.
British Museum, London
  Additional MSS. 17,601, 17,604, 17,592, 32,606, 32,608, 32,609.
  Egerton MSS. 1813, 1815.
Public Record Office, London
  State Papers, Spain, 94/161–175, 94/189–201.

2. PRINTED DOCUMENTS AND CONTEMPORARY WORKS

Actas capitulares de Santiago del Estero, Introducción de Alfredo Gargaro (4 vols., Buenos Aires, 1942–6).
Actas capitulares de la villa de Concepción del Río Cuarto, años 1798–1812, Prólogo de Alfredo C. Vitulo (Buenos Aires, 1947).
Acuerdos del extinguido cabildo de Buenos Aires, Archivo General de la Nacion (Serie 3, 11 vols., Barcelona and Buenos Aires, 1925–34).
Angelis, pedro de, *Colección de obras y documentos relativos a la historia antigua y moderna de las provincias del Río de la Plata* (2nd edn., 5 vols., Buenos Aires, 1910).

Antuñez y Acevedo, R., *Memorias históricas sobre la legislación y gobierno de los Españoles con sus colonias en las Indias occidentales* (Madrid, 1797).

Azara, Félix de, *Memoria sobre el estado rural del Río de la Plata y otros informes* (Buenos Aires, 1943).

Caillet-Bois, Ricardo R., 'Un informe reservado del virrey Joaquín del Pino', *Boletín del Instituto de Investigaciones Históricas*, xi (Buenos Aires, 1930), pp. 67–90.

Campillo y Cossio, José, *Nuevo sistema de gobierno económico para la América* (Madrid, 1789).

Cañete y Domínguez, Pedro Vicente, *Guia histórica, geográfica, física, política, civil y legal del gobierno e intendencia de la provincia de Potosí, 1787* (Potosí, 1952).

—— 'La intendencia de Potosí,' 17 December 1802, in *La Revista de Buenos Aires*, xxiv (1871), pp. 161–202.

Castillo de Bobadilla, G., *Política para corregidores* (2 vols., Madrid, 1775).

Colección de documentos inéditos para la historia de España (113 vols., Madrid, 1842–95), v.

Documentos del Archivo de Belgrano (7 vols., Buenos Aires, 1913–17), ii.

Documentos para la historia argentina, Facultad de Filosofía y Letras, Universidad de Buenos Aires (Buenos Aires, 1913–)

    i. *Real Hacienda (1776–1780)*.
    ii. *Real Hacienda (1774–1780)*.
    iii. *Colonias Orientales del Rio Paraguay ó de la Plata*, Miguel Lastarria.
    iv. *Abastos de Buenos Aires (1773–1809)*.
    v. *Comercio de Indias, antecedentes legales (1713–1778)*, introducción de Ricardo Levene.
    vi. *Comercio de Indias, comercio libre (1778–1791)*.
    vii. *Comercio de Indias, consulado, comercio de negros y de extrangeros (1791–1809)*, introducción de Diego Luis Molinari.
    ix. *Administración edilicia de la ciudad de Buenos Aires (1776–1803)*, introducción de Luis María Torres.
    xviii. *Cultura. La enseñanza durante la época colonial (1771–1810)*, advertencia de Juan Probst.

Documentos para la historia del virreinato del Río de la Plata, Fac. de Filos. y Letras, Univ. de Buenos Aires (3 vols., Buenos Aires, 1912–13).

Documentos referentes a la guerra de la independencia y emancipación política de la República Argentina, Archivo General de la Nación (3 vols., Buenos Aires, 1914–26), i.

313

Ferrer del Río, A., *Obras originales del conde de Floridablanca, y escritos referentes a su persona* (*Biblioteca de autores españoles*, lix, Madrid, 1912).

Levene, Ricardo, ed., *Cedulario de la Real Audiencia de Buenos Aires* (3 vols., La Plata, 1929–38).

Moreno, Mariano, *Escritos*, ed. R. Levene (2 vols., Buenos Aires, 1943).

Novíssima recopilación de las leyes de España (Madrid, 1805).

'Nuevo método de cuenta y razón para la real hacienda en las Indias. . . . Dispuesta por la contaduría general y aprobada por el rei en 9 de mayo de 1784', printed in *Revista de la Biblioteca Nacional*, iv (Buenos Aires, 1940), pp. 267–318.

Radaelli, Sigfrido A., ed., *Memorias de los virreyes del Río de la Plata* (Buenos Aires, 1945).

Récopilación de leyes de los reinos de las Indias [Madrid, 1791]. (Reproduced in 3 vols., Consejo de la Hispanidad, Madrid, 1943.)

Representación apologética de la muy noble imperial villa de Potosí, sus tribunales, oficinas y gremios, al Exmo. S. Virrey, sobre los acaecimientos de la provincia de Chayanta, 1796, printed in G. René-Moreno, 'La mita de Potosí en 1795', *Revista Chilena*, viii (1877), pp. 407–30.

Rodríguez Casado, Vicente, and J. A. Calderón Quijano, eds., *Memoria de gobierno del virrey Abascal* (2 vols., Sevilla, 1944).

Rodríguez Casado, Vicente, and F. Pérez Embid, eds., *Memoria de gobierno del virrey Amat* (Sevilla, 1947).

Rodríguez Villa, A., ed., *Cartas político-económicas escritas por el conde de Campomanes al conde de Lerena* (Madrid, 1878). See above p. 49, n. 1.

Solórzano Pereira, Juan de, *Política indiana* [1647] (5 vols., Madrid, 1930).

'Virrey Caballero de Croix al Bailio Fray Antonio Valdes, sobre inconveniencia de aplicación de las ordenanzas de intendentes, 1790', printed in *Revista de la Biblioteca Nacional*, viii (Buenos Aires, 1943), pp. 105–41.

Zamora y Coronado, José María, *Biblioteca de legislación ultramarina* (6 vols., Madrid, 1844–6).

III

Secondary Works

Aiton, Arthur Scott, 'Spanish colonial reorganisation under the Family Compact', *Hispanic American Historical Review*, xii (1932), pp. 269–80.

Alcázar y Molina, Cayetano, *Los virreinatos en el siglo XVIII*, vol. 13 of *Historia de América y de los pueblos americanos*, edited by A. Ballesteros y Beretta (Barcelona, 1945).

Álvarez Requejo, F., *El conde de Campomanes. Su obra histórica* (Oviedo, 1954).

Arribas, Filemon, *La expedición de D. Pedro de Cevallos a Buenos Aires y la fundación del virreinato del Río de la Plata, 1776–8* (Valladolid, n.d.).

Artola, Miguel, 'Campillo y las reformas de Carlos III', *Revista de Indias*, xii (1952), pp. 685–714.

Ayarragaray, L., *La iglesia en América y la dominación española* (Buenos Aires, 1935).

Ballesteros, Pío, 'La función política de las Reales Chancillerías coloniales', *Revista de Estudios Políticos*, xv (Madrid, 1946), pp. 47–109.

Barba, Enrique M., *Don Pedro de Cevallos, gobernador de Buenos Aires y virrey del Río de la Plata* (La Plata, 1937).

Basadre, J., 'El régimen de la mita', *Letras* (Univ. of San Carlos, Lima), 1937, tercer trimestre, pp. 325–64.

Bayle, Constantino, S.J., *Los cabildos seculares en la América española* (Madrid, 1952).

Béthencourt Massieu, Antonio, *Patiño en la política de Felipe V*. Prólogo de V. Palacio Atard (Valladolid, 1954). ·

Blart, Louis, *Les rapports de la France et de l'Espagne après le Pacte de Famille, jusqu'à la fin du ministère du duc de Choiseul* (Paris, 1915).

Burgin, M., *The economic aspects of Argentine federalism, 1820–1852* (Cambridge, Mass., 1941).

Burzio, H. F., *La ceca de la villa imperial de Potosí y la moneda colonial* (Buenos Aires, 1945).

Caillet-Bois, Ricardo R., 'Apuntes para una historia económica del virreinato: gobierno intendencia de Salta del Tucumán', *Anuario de Historia Argentina*, iii (1941, published in 1942), pp. 101–23.

— 'Un ejemplo de la industria textil colonial', *Boletín del Instituto de Investigaciones Históricas*, xx (1936), pp. 19–26.

— *Ensayo sobre el Río de la Plata y la revolución francesa* (Buenos Aires, 1929).

Cárcano, M. A., *Evolución histórica del régimen de la tierra pública, 1810–1916* (2nd edn., Buenos Aires, 1925).

Cardozo, Efraím, 'La audiencia de Charcas y la facultad de gobierno', *Humanidades*, xxv (La Plata, 1936), pp. 137–56.

Castañeda, Carlos E., 'The corregidor in Spanish colonial administration', *Hispanic American Historical Review* ix (1929), pp. 446–70.

Céspedes del Castillo, Guillermo, 'Lima y Buenos Aires. Repercusiones económicas y políticas de la creación del virreinato del Plata', *Anuario de Estudios Americanos*, iii (Sevilla, 1946), pp. 669–874.

— 'La visita como institución indiana', *Anuario de Estudios Americanos*, iii (1946), pp. 984–1025.

— 'Reorganización de la hacienda virreinal peruana en el siglo xviii,' *Anuario de Historia del Derecho Español*, xxiii (1953), pp. 329–69.

Chaves, J. C., *Historia de las relaciones entre Buenos Ayres y el Paraguay, 1810–1813* (Buenos Aires, 1938).

Christelow, A., 'French interest in the Spanish Empire during the ministry of the Duc de Choiseul, 1759–1771', *Hispanic American Historical Review*, xxi (1941), pp. 515–37.

— 'Great Britain and the trades from Cadiz and Lisbon to Spanish America and Brazil, 1759–1783', *Hispanic American Historical Review*, xxvii (1947), pp. 2–29.

— 'Economic background of the Anglo-Spanish War of 1762', *Journal of Modern History*, xviii (1946), pp. 22–36.

Colmeiro, M., *Historia de la economía política en España* (2 vols., Madrid, 1863).

Coni, Emilio A., 'Contribución a la historia del gaucho', *Boletín del Instituto de Investigaciones Históricas*, xviii (1934–5), pp. 48–79.

Costa du Rels, Adolfo, 'Un precursor inesperado de la emancipación americana: el relator de la Real Audiencia de Charcas, Dr. Juan José de Segovia', *Boletín de la Academia Nacional de la Historia*, xvii (Buenos Aires, 1944), pp. 211–27.

Corona Baratech, C. E., 'Notas para un estudio de la sociedad en el Río de la Plata durante el virreinato', *Anuario de Estudios Americanos*, viii (1951), pp. 59–167.

Coxe, William, *Memoirs of the kings of Spain of the House of Bourbon* (2nd edn., London, 1815).

Danvila y Collado, Manuel, *El poder civil en España* (6 vols., Madrid, 1885–7).

— *El reinado de Carlos III* (6 vols., Madrid, 1890–6).

Desdevises du Dezert, G., *L'Espagne de l'ancien régime* (3 vols., Paris, 1897–1904).

— 'Les institutions de l'Espagne au XVIIIᵉ siècle,' *Revue Hispanique*, lxx (1927), pp. 1–556.

— 'Les missions de Mojos y des Chiquitos de 1767 a 1808,' *Revue Hispanique*, xliii (1918), 365–430.

Doucet, R., *Les institutions de la France au XVIᵉ siècle* (2 vols., Paris, 1948).

Ferres, Carlos, *Época colonial. La administración de justicia en Montevideo* (Buenos Aires, 1944).

Fisher, Lillian Estelle, *The intendant system in Spanish America* (Berkeley, Calif., 1929).

— *Viceregal administration in the Spanish American colonies* (Berkeley, Calif., 1926).

Gallardo Fernández, F., *Origen, progreso y estado de las rentas de la corona de España, su gobierno y administración* (3 vols., Madrid, 1805).

García, Juan Agustín, *La ciudad indiana* (Buenos Aires, 1900).

García Gallo, A., *Historia del derecho español* (Madrid, 1941).

Garreton, Alfredo, *La municipalidad colonial* (Buenos Aires, 1933).

Garzon, Ignacio, *Crónica de Córdoba* (Córdoba, 1898).

Gil Munilla, Octavio, *El Río de la Plata en la política internacional. Génesis del virreinato* (Sevilla, 1949).

Godard, C., *Les pouvoirs des intendants sous Louis XIV* (Paris, 1901).

González, Julio Cesar, *Don Santiago Liniers, gobernador interino de los treinta pueblos de las misiones guaraníes y tapes, 1803–1804* (Buenos Aires, 1946).

Gutiérrez, Juan María, 'El virreinato del Río de la Plata durante la administración del marqués de Loreto', *Revista del Río de la Plata*, viii (1874), pp. 212–40.

Hamilton, Earl J., 'Money and economic recovery in Spain under the first Bourbon', *Journal of Modern History*, xv (1943), pp. 192–206.

— 'Monetary problems in Spain and Spanish America, 1751–1800,' *Journal of Economic History*, iv (1944), pp. 21–48.

— *War and prices in Spain 1651–1800* (Cambridge, Mass., 1947).

Hanotaux, G., *Origine de l'institution des intendants des provinces d'après les documents inédits* (Paris, 1884).

Haring, Clarence H., *Trade and navigation between Spain and the Indies in the time of the Hapsburgs* (Cambridge, Mass., 1918).

— *The Spanish empire in America* (New York, 1947).

Helms, A. Z., *Travels from Buenos Aires by Potosí to Lima* (London, 1806).

Hernández, Pablo, S.J., *El extrañamiento de los jesuitas del Río de la Plata y de las misiones del Paraguay por decreto de Carlos III* (Madrid, 1908).

Humboldt, Alexander von, *Ensayo político sobre el Reino de la Nueva España* (6th Spanish edn., 4 vols., Mexico, 1941).

Humphreys, R. A., *Liberation in South America, 1806–1827. The career of James Paroissien* (London, 1952).

Hussey, R. D., *The Caracas Company, 1728–1784* (Cambridge, Mass., 1934).

Juan, Jorge, and Antonio de Ulloa, *Noticias secretas de América* (London, 1826).

Lafuente Machain, Ricardo de, *Buenos Aires en el siglo XVIII* (Buenos Aires, 1946).

Levene, Ricardo, *Ensayo histórico sobre la revolución de mayo y Mariano Moreno* (2 vols., Buenos Aires, 1946).

— *Historia de la nación argentina* (ed. Ricardo Levene, 10 vols., Buenos Aires, 1936–42).

— 'Historia de la segunda audiencia de Buenos Aires', *Revista de Indias*, vii (1946), pp. 239–51.

— *Historia del derecho argentino* (5 vols., Buenos Aires, 1945).

— *A history of Argentina* (Chapel Hill, N.C., 1937).

— *Investigaciones acerca de la historia económica del virreinato del Río de la Plata* (3 vols., La Plata, 1927).

— *La moneda colonial del Plata* (Buenos Aires, 1916).

— *Los orígenes de la democracia argentina* (Buenos Aires, 1911).

— *Vida y escritos de Victorián de Villava* (Buenos Aires, 1946).

López, Vicente Fidel, *Historia de la República Argentina* (10 vols., Buenos Aires, 1883–93).

Lynch, John, 'Intendants and cabildos in the viceroyalty of the Río de la Plata, 1782–1810', *Hispanic American Historical Review*, xxxv (1955), pp. 337–62.

Mariluz Urquijo, José María, *Ensayo sobre los juicios de residencia indianos* (Sevilla, 1952).

— 'Las memorias de los regentes de la Real Audiencia de Buenos Aires', *Revista del Instituto de Historia del Derecho*, i (Buenos Aires, 1949), pp. 19–26.

— 'Los guaraníes después de la expulsión de los jesuítas,' *Estudios Americanos*, vi (Sevilla, 1953), pp. 323–30.

— 'El tribunal mayor y audiencia real de cuentas de Buenos Aires', *Revista del Instituto de Historia del Derecho*, iii (1951), pp. 112–141.

Marion, M., *Dictionnaire des institutions de la France aux XVIIe et XVIIIe siècles* (Paris, 1923).

Maúrtua, Victor M., *Juicio de límites entre el Perú y Bolivia. Prueba peruana presentada al gobierno de la República Argentina* (12 vols., Barcelona, 1906), tom. iv, *Virreinato de Buenos Aires*.

Mecham, J. Lloyd, *Church and State in Latin America* (Chapel Hill, 1934).

Mendiburu, Manuel de, *Diccionario histórico-biográfico del Perú* (2nd edn., 11 vols., Lima, 1931–4; appendices, 1935).

Métraux, Alfred, 'Jesuit missions in South America', *Handbook of South American Indians* (6 vols., Washington, Smithsonian Institute, Bureau of American Ethnology, Bull. 143, 1946–50), v, 645–53.

Moore, John Preston, *The cabildo in Peru under the Hapsburgs* (Durham, N.C., 1954).

Mörner, Magnus, *The political and economic activities of the Jesuits in the La Plata region, the Hapsburg era* (Stockholm, 1953).

Muñoz Pérez, J., 'La publicación del reglamento de comercio libre de Indias de 1778', *Anuario de Estudios Americanos*, iv (1947), pp. 615–64.

Ots Capdequí, José M., *Manual de historia del derecho español en las Indias y del derecho propiamente indiano* (2 vols., Buenos Aires, 1943).

— *El siglo XVIII español en América. El gobierno político del Nuevo Reino de Granada. Aporte documental* (Mexico, 1945).

Palacio Atard, Vicente, 'Areche y Guirior, Observaciones sobre el fracaso de una visita al Perú', *Anuario de Estudios Americanos*, iii (1946), pp. 269–376.

— 'El equilibrio de América en la diplomacia del siglo XVIII', *Estudios Americanos*, i (1948–9), pp. 461–79.

— 'La incorporación a la corona del Banco de Rescates de Potosí', *Anuario de Estudios Americanos*, ii (1945), pp. 723–37.

— *El tercer Pacto de Familia* (Sevilla, 1945).

Parry, J. H., *The audiencia of New Galicia in the sixteenth century* (Cambridge, 1948).

— *The sale of public office in the Spanish Indies under the Hapsburgs* (Berkeley and Los Angeles, 1953).

Paz, Luis, *Historia general del Alto-Perú, hoy Bolivia* (2 vols., Sucre, 1919).

Pierson, William Whatley, 'The establishment and early functioning of the *intendencia* of Cuba', *The James Sprunt Historical Studies*, xix (Chapel Hill, 1927), pp. 113–33.

— 'Some reflections on the *cabildo* as an institution', *Hispanic American Historical Review*, v (1922), pp. 573–96.

Pinto, Manuel, *La revolución de la intendencia de la Paz en el virreinato del Río de la Plata, con la occurrencia de Chuquisaca (1800–1810)* (Buenos Aires, 1919).

Priestley, Herbert Ingram, *José de Gálvez, Visitor General of New Spain, 1765–1771* (Berkeley, Calif., 1916).

Quesada, Vicente G., *Virreinato del Río de la Plata, 1776–1810* (Buenos Aires, 1881).

Ravignani, Emilio, *Historia constitucional de la República Argentina* (2nd edn., 3 vols., Buenos Aires, 1930), i.

—'El virreinato del Río de la Plata (1776–1810)', in *H.N.A.*, iv, i, 27–332.

Regnault, H., *Manuel d'histoire du droit français* (Paris, 1940).

René-Moreno, Gabriel, 'El Alto-Perú en 1783', *Revista Chilena*, viii (1877), pp. 204–34.

— *Bolivia y Perú. Notas históricas y bibliográficas* (Santiago de Chile, 1907).

— 'La audiencia de Charcas 1559–1809', *Revista Chilena*, VIII (1877), pp. 93–142.

—*Ultimos días coloniales en el Alto-Perú* (Santiago de Chile, 1896–8).

Rodriguez, Mario, 'The genesis of economic attitudes in the Río de la Plata', *Hispanic American Historical Review*, xxxvi (1956), pp. 171–89.

Rodríguez Casado, Vicente, 'Causa seguida contra el marqués de Casa Hermosa, gobernador intendente del Puno', *Anuario de Estudios Americanos*, iii (1946), pp. 957–68.

Rousseau, F., *Règne de Charles III d'Espagne* (2 vols., Paris, 1907).

Ruiz Guiñazú, Enrique, *La magistratura indiana* (Buenos Aires, 1916).

Ruiz y Pablo, A., *Historia de la real junta particular de comercio de Barcelona (1758–1847)* (Barcelona, 1919).

Saenz Valiente, José María, 'Los alcaldes de Buenos Aires en 1806. Su actuación durante la primera invasión inglesa', *Boletín del Instituto de Investigaciones Históricas*, xvii (1933–4), pp. 98–141.

Sánchez Agesta, Luis, *El pensamiento político del despotismo ilustrado* (Madrid, 1953).

Sanz, Luis Santiago, 'El proyecto de extinción del régimen de las intendencias de América y la Ordenanza General de 1803', *Revista del Instituto de Historia del Derecho*, no. 5 (Buenos Aires, 1953), pp. 123–85.

Sarrailh, Jean, *L'Espagne éclairée de la seconde moitié du XVIII siècle* (Paris, 1954).

Torre Revello, José, *Juan José de Vértiz y Salcedo, gobernador y virrey de Buenos Aires* (Buenos Aires, 1932).

— *El marqués de Sobre Monte, gobernador-intendente de Córdoba y virrey del Río de la Plata* (Buenos Aires, 1946).

— 'Noticia de los vecinos mas acaudalados de Buenos Aires en la época del primer gobierno de Pedro de Cevallos,' *Boletín del Instituto de Investigaciones Históricas*, iv (1927–8), pp. 498–9.

Udaondo, Enrique, *Diccionario biográfico colonial argentino* (Buenos Aires, 1945).

Udaondo, Enrique, *Reseña histórica de la villa de Luján* (Luján, 1939).

Vieillard-Baron, Alain, 'L'établissement des intendants aux Indes par Charles III', *Revista de Indias*, xii (1952), pp. 521–46.

— 'L'intendant americain et l'intendant français,' *Revista de Indias*, xii (1951), pp. 237–50.

Vitulo, Alfredo C., 'Fundación de la villa de Río Cuarto', *Boletín del Instituto de Investigaciones Históricas*, xvii (1933–4), pp. 151–60.

Yaben, J. R., *Biográficas argentinas y sudamericanas* (Buenos Aires, 1938).

Zavala, Silvio A., *La encomienda indiana* (Madrid, 1935).

Zinny, Antonio, *Historia de los gobernadores de las provincias argentinas* (4 vols., Buenos Aires, 1920).

— *Historia de los gobernantes del Paraguay, 1535–1887* (Buenos Aires, 1887).

Zorraquín Becú, Ricardo, *La organización judicial argentina en el período hispánico* (Buenos Aires, 1952).

VICEROYALTY
San Francisco
Santa Fe
PRESIDENCY   OF
OF
GUADALAJARA
NEW
San Antonio
New
Orleans
St.Augustine
MEXICO   Vera Cruz
SPAIN
Guatemala
CAPTAINCY GENERAL
OF
GUATEMALA
HAVANA
CAPTAINCY GENERAL
OF CUBA
CARACAS
VICEROYALTY
AUDIENCIA OF
SANTA FE   BOGOTA
OF
NEW GRANADA
CAPTAINCY
GENERAL
OF
VENEZUELA GUIANAS
Quito
PRESIDENCY
OF
QUITO
VICEROYALTY OF
AUDIENCIA OF LIMA
LIMA
AUDIENCIA
OF CUZCO
AUDIENCIA
Upper
OF
Peru
Potosí
CHARCAS
VICEROYALTY OF PERU
CHILE
CAPTAINCY GENERAL OF
VICEROYALTY
OF
BRAZIL
Bahia
RIO DE JANEIRO
São Paulo
Asunción
AUDIENCIA OF
BUENOS AIRES
SANTIAGO
Montevideo
BUENOS AIRES
VICEROYALTY OF THE RÍO DE LA PLATA

SPANISH EMPIRE IN AMERICA
Late 18th. century

Spanish territory
- - - - Spanish administrative divisions

0   MILES   1000

Map 1

VICEROYALTY
OF
THE RÍO DE LA PLATA

DIVIDED ACCORDING
TO INTENDANCIES

Map 2

INDEX

Accounts, Office of, established in Buenos Aires, 37; judicial power of, 93; and superintendent Sanz, 103–4; jurisdiction of, 120; methods of, 121, 130–1; administration criticized, 136–7; negligence of, 138–9; instructions for, 142

Administration, department of, 58, 148–71, 280

Alba, duque de, 54

Alcabala, 118, 128–9, 133, 140, 165

Alcaldes de barrio, 158, 159, 160–1, 285

Alcaldes mayores, proposed abolition of, 52–3

Alcaldes ordinarios, and administration of justice, 81, 82–3, 84; and Indian tribute, 128; duties and status of, 203, 205, 206, 217, 225–7, 260; appeals from, 239, 280

Alcaldes de la Santa Hermandad, 225, 227

Alcaldes (Indian), 196, 280

Alicante, admitted to colonial trade, 19

Alós y Bru, Joaquín de, *residencia* of, 71; intendant of Paraguay, 74; dispute with *cabildo eclesiástico,* 88; reports on *misiones,* 153–4, 188, 192; biog., 291–2

Altarriba, Miguel de, intendant in Cuba, 51

Álvarez, Juan Manuel, intendant of La Paz, conflict with *audiencia* of Charcas, 249–50; biog., 292

Álvarez de Acevedo, Tomás, fiscal of *audiencia* of Charcas, 37–8

Álvarez de Arenales, Juan, subdelegate of Arque, 76

Álvarez de Soto Mayor, Antonio, intendant of La Paz, 142, 272–3; biog., 292

Alzaga, Martín de, 215, 233, 267, 271

Amat y Junient, Manuel de, viceroy of Perú, criticizes financial administration in Perú, 22, 117, 119; reports

on creation of viceroyalty of Río de la Plata, 38

Amelot, Michel, 1

Andalucía, intendant of, 49

Anson, Lord, and Falkland Islands, 34

Aragon, Bourbon reduction of, 2

Aranda, conde de, president of Council of Castile, 4; supports establishment of intendancies in New Spain, 54

Areche, José Antonio, visitor-general of Perú, 58, 117–18, 122–3

Arequipa, bishop of, denounces *repartimientos* of merchandise, 57; *cabildo* of, 230

Arizmendi, Pedro Francisco de, 182–3

Arredondo, Manuel Antonio de, regent of *audiencia* of Buenos Aires, 261

Arredondo, Nicolás de, viceroy of Río de la Plata, and ecclesiastical patronage, 88; exempt *residencia,* 92; investigates Loreto's allegations against Sanz, 107; and *cabildo* of Buenos Aires, 214–15; and *cabildo* of Santa Fe, 226; investigates intendant of Puno, 251–2

Arriaga, Julián, Minister of Indies, 56

Arroyo, Juan Andrés de, 138

Assessors, of intendancies, 81–4, 226–7, 241, 288

Asunción del Paraguay, foundation of, 25; in province of Paraguay, 62; capital of intendancy, 65; disputed academic appointment in, 88; subtreasury in, 125; public works in, 158; primary school in, 161; *encomiendas* in, 174–5; *cabildo* of, 209, 226, 229–30, 236; revolution in, 275

Atacama (Potosí), 65

Audiencias: in Spain, 2, 47, 54

— in Spanish America: appeals to, 81, 84; and viceroys, 91–2; and treasury, 136; and *cabildos,* 208; authority of, 237–8